Family Circle

CREATIVE NEEDLECRAFTS

By the Editors of Family Circle

Editorial Director/Arthur Hettich
Special Books Editor/Marie T. Walsh
Creative Director/Joseph Taveroni
Editor/Rosemary Drysdale
Art Director/Kay Susmann
Assistant Editor/Raeanne B. Hytone
Illustrations/William J. Meyerriecks
Cover Design/Sara Gutierrez

And the Editors of Family Circle Magazine
and Family Circle Great Ideas
Cover design worked in DMC Persian yarns

Published by Columbia House, A Division of CBS Inc.
Distributed to the Trade by Prentice-Hall, Inc.,
Englewood Cliffs, N.J.

CONTENTS

ISBN- 0-13-301853-9
Library of Congress Catalog Card Number: 77-9240
Printed in the United States of America

Published by Columbia House, a Division of CBS Inc., 51 West 52nd Street, New York, New York 10019
This 1979 edition distributed to the Trade by Prentice-Hall, Inc., Englewood Cliffs, N.J.

FOREWORD

As America grew from 13 tiny colonies to an entire country, all women learned the various forms of needlecrafts early in life and continued practicing these arts for the rest of their lives. Delicate samplers and intricate quilts of this period hang in museum collections throughout the country. Then millions of home knitters on the plains kept their families from freezing during the harsh winters with everything from sweaters to undies.

The Industrial Revolution made machine-produced items so popular, the fine arts of crewel, embroidery, patchwork and needlepoint were almost lost arts to succeeding generations.

Now fashion has come full cycle. Once again there is a great emphasis—both in clothing and home furnishing—on adding the personal touch that can only be achieved with creative needlecrafts. Bulky knit sweaters and lacy crochet blouses, richly embroidered shawls and needlepoint jewelry are just a few of this season's fashion stars. Indian hooked rugs, quilts for beds, walls and tables and appliquéd wall hangs are just a few of this year's decorator touches.

FAMILY CIRCLE MAGAZINE predicted this trend a decade ago and began to search out the finest designers in each of the needlecrafts and commissioned them to create exclusive designs for our readers. As this renewed interest increased with each year, more and more pages of FAMILY CIRCLE have featured trend-setting clothes, rugs, jewelry, furniture and wall hangs, plus new, time-saving methods for recreating the quilts, samplers and crewel designs from museum collections.

Our designers include Rosemary Drysdale, this book's editor and expert on embroidery and knitting; Sara Gutierrez, who designed our cover and is a needlepoint expert; Elizabeth Steidel, who specializes in crewel and wall hangs and Gail Diven, a crochet and granny square specialist.

CREDITS

Joyce Aiken: Cherry Rug; Weathervane Rug. Marianne Alee: Blouson Top. Kristina Becker: Placemats. Beattie Bodenstein: Rainbow Pillows. Jack Brodie: Checkerboard Rug. Chrisjan: Heart Pillow; Crazy Quilt Afghan; QuickPoint Bench Pad; Nine Star Design Patchwork Pillow; Christmas Stockings; Violet Pillow. Lucy Ciancia: Tree of Life. Judy Copeland: Cartridge-Ribbed Coat. Jackie Curry: Cross Stitch Signs; Rose Garden Afghan. Zelda Dana: Print Bound Baby Blanket. Chris Davenport: Easter Eggs. Kathryn Davidson: Multicolor Crocheted Coat. Laura Demme: Striped Vest. Gail Diven: Granny Square & Fabric Shawl; Quilted Jacket with Granny Squares; Bedspread and Pillows. Rosemary Drysdale: Smocked Bag; Tablecloth and Four Napkins; Mexican Cross Stitch Shawl; Cross Stitch Sampler; Rectangle Rug; Chair Seat; Placemat; Cable Bedspread; Tennis Raquet Covers; Floral Pillow & Accessories; Indian Rug; Cutwork Pillow; Blackwork Embroidered Bed Linen and Towel Set. Barbara Esposito: Gingham Pillows. Linda Giampa: Puppy Dog Quilt. Meredith Gladstone: Vest. Carol Golden: Teeny Bikini. Sara Gutierrez: Embroidered Strapless Dress or Skirt; Velvet Shawl; Picture Mats; Plastic Picture Frames. Karen Clark Hagaman: Posy Sling Chair. Anne Halliday: Daisy Rug; Braid Rug. Annie Hayum: Blouson Top. Maryann Hehir: Tablecloth. Deborah Hollingworth: Baby's Coat & Cap. Nancy Jacobsen: Wool Stitchery Bouquet Picture. Jaqueline Jewett: Short Sleeved Top. Margot Johnson: American Indian Iris Motif Belt & Neckpiece. Nancy Howell Koehler: Chair Seats. Michelle and Danielle Koenig: Ruffled Pillows. Sandra Koerlin: Chair Seat. Jean Ray Laury: Vegetable Felt Appliqués; Velvet Wall Hangings; Felt Hangings; Violet Sprigged Felt Coverlet; Pennsylvania Dutch Rug; w/ Joyce Aiken: Hex and Scalloped Flower Coverlet; Tulip Baby Quilt. Lee Lindeman: Small Car, Lady Bunny, Teddy Bear, School Bus; Footstool. Helen Maris: Evening Bag. Cathy Moore: Tunisian Crochet Pillows. William J. Meyerriecks: Line Drawings. Inge Nissen: Placemats. Ruth O'Mara: Man's Fair Isle Pullover. Stephanie Parker: Pansy Pillow; Art Deco Pillow; Orchid Pillows. Charlotte Patera: Director Chair; Felt Chest; Tailored Bridge Table Cover; Quick & Easy Pillows; Ribbon Trimmed Pillows; Needlepoint. Rosana: Hooded Sweater. Kathy Sarkin: V-Neck Sweater; Popcorn Sweater. Linda Schnadelback: Stuffed Animals. Mimi Shimmin: Bedspread; Violet Rug; Blanket Spread; Violet Beaded Mirror Frame; Bargello Pillow; Spanish Tile Rug; Oriental Runner; Rose Rug; Textured Pillow; Beaded Mirror Frame & Pillow; White Rug; Chair Cushions. Mira Silverstein: Bargello Rug. Glenora Smith: Houndstooth Bookends. Elizabeth Steidel: Scarf; Left-Handed Embroidery. Mary Lou Stribling: Bicentennial Quilt. Viola Sylbert: Crocheted Woven Hat & Scarf; Crocheted Bag & Cap. Judith Talber: Easy-To-Do Crochet Edgings. Nina Tobier: Doll Carrier. Monna Weinman: Baby Pullover; U-Neck Sweater for Men and Women; Zig-Zag Pullover; Motif Stole. Ellen Winters: Napkin Rings. Bruce Woods: Bulky Sweater.

NEEDLEPOINT AND BARGELLO

For all needlepoint stitches and blocking, refer to BASIC NEEDLEPOINT STITCHES in the HOW-TO SECTION, page 224.

PERSONALIZED PILLOWS

Give a personalized needlepoint pillow! With masking tape, bind the edges of a 6″ square of No. 10 Penelope canvas. With waterproof felt marker, draw a 4″ square in canvas center. Trace stencil initial in middle. Using your favorite stitch, work the initial and background with knitting worsted in contrasting colors. Block canvas then trim edges to ½″ of worked area. Machine-zigzag the canvas to one side of a removable pillow cover. Pin the ribbon over the canvas edges, mitering corners. Now slipstitch the ribbon in place.

TEDDY PILLOW

MATERIALS: One 8″ square of No. 12 mono (single thread) canvas; No. 20 tapestry needle; Persian wool in the following color quantities (given in 18″ strands): 12 Gold, 3 Brown, 2 Black,

brown	⊠
gold	⊡
black	⊙
blue	⧄
white	⊟
red	⧄
green	☐

5 Blue, 3 White, 2 Red and 13 Green; masking tape; two 12″ squares of fabric for pillow cover; thread to match fabric; polyester fiberfill, or one 11″ pillow form; pastel chalk.

DIRECTIONS: *Preparing the Canvas:* Bind the edges of the canvas with masking tape to prevent raveling. Draw a 5″ square in the center of the canvas to outline the area to be worked.

Needlepointing: Note: Persian wool can be divided into three strands; remove one and stitch with the remaining two. Combine the extra single strands as needed. First work the entire bear design in the Continental Stitch following the chart and counting squares carefully. Change colors when necessary. Fill in the background with Continental Stitch, starting in the upper right-hand corner. Work the entire area within the marked outline.

Blocking: Block. Allow needlepoint to dry thoroughly. Remove from board. Machine-stitch around the canvas as close as possible to the worked area.

Making the Pillow Cover: For the pillow top,

chalk a 4″ square in the center of one 12″ square of fabric. Machine stay-stitch all around, ½″ outside the chalk lines (making a 5″ square). Cut out the four-inch square on the chalk line, clipping the corners to the stay-stitching line. Press the fabric to the wrong side along the stitching, making a 5″ square opening. Pin the pillow top to the canvas right side with the needlepoint centered in the opening. Blindstitch the fabric edges to the canvas. Cut away the excess canvas ½″ from the stitching. Lightly steam-press the pillow top, easing out any fullness in the corners.

With right sides together, stitch the pillow top to the bottom around three sides and four corners, in a ½″ seam. Turn right side out; insert pillow form or fiberfill to the desired plumpness. Blindstitch the open edge.

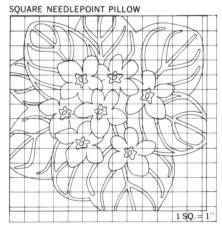

SQUARE NEEDLEPOINT PILLOW

1 SQ. = 1″

VIOLET PILLOW
(13½″ squares)

MATERIALS: No. 12 mono canvas, one 18″ square; Persian yarn in these colors and quantities: 1/5 oz. each dark purple, yellow and white; 1 oz. each medium purple and light green; 2 ozs. each dark green and light blue; lightweight green wool for backing, ½ yd.; ¼" cording, 2¾ yds.; masking tape; waterproof felt-tip marker; rustproof pins or tacks; polyester fiberfill or knife-edge pillow form.

DIRECTIONS: From green fabric cut one 15" square and enough 1½" bias strips to make a 60" length when stitched together.

Enlarging and Transfering the Pattern: Following the directions on page 224, enlarge the pillow-top pattern on white paper. Tape the pattern to a window with strong light shining through. Center the canvas over the pattern; tape in place. With a waterproof marking pen, trace the pattern onto the canvas. Remove pattern and canvas. Bind canvas edges with masking tape to prevent raveling.

Working the Canvas: Work the design with two strands of yarn in the Basketweave Stitch using medium purple yarn for the flower petals, dark purple and yellow for the flower centers, and white around the flower petal edges; work the leaves in dark green with light green veins. Fill in blue background.

Finishing: Block piece flat.

Assembling the Pillow: Make corded welting with the bias strips, pieced as necessary. Baste welting to right side of backing with raw edges even. With right sides together, stitch backing and top together in a ½" seam, leaving an 8" opening. Turn right side out; lightly press edges. Stuff pillow. Blindstitch open edges.

form; masking tape; rustproof tacks or pushpins; waterproof marking pen; yardstick. Persian yarn in the following colors and amounts: ⁴/₅ oz. Green; ⁴/₅ oz. White, ¹/₅ oz. Yellow; ¹/₅ oz. Dark Blue; ³/₅ oz. Light Blue; ³/₅ oz. Lavender.

DIRECTIONS: Cover edges of canvas with masking tape.

Draw a square to match the pillow size in the center of the canvas. With a marker lightly mark this area into 1" squares.

Use diagram to mark the geometric design on the canvas with ruler and marker, starting with shaded square at the center of the design.

Using the color key, work the pillow with the Basketweave Stitch.

Blocking: Block the canvas.

When completely dry, machine stitch as close as possible around outside of needlepoint stitching. Trim canvas to ½" seam allowance.

To Make Cording: Cut a strip of backing 1½" wide by 60" long (pieced if necessary). Fold strip over cording, edges flush. Stitch as close as possible to cording, using zipper foot.

Baste cording around edge of needlepoint, raw edges even, bringing ends together at a corner. Stitch to canvas on cording seamline.

Cut backing to match. With right sides together, stitch backing to front, leaving an 8" opening on one side. Trim corners; turn right side out. Insert pillow form. Blindstitch opening.

NINE STAR DESIGN PATCHWORK PILLOW

(Finished size 13½" × 13½")

MATERIALS: No. 10 Penelope canvas, ½ yd.; fabric for backing and cording, ½ yd. (we used suede-like fabric); ¼" cording, 1¾ yds.; #20 needlepoint needle; 14" × 14" knife edge pillow

NINE STAR DESIGN

Color photo on page 129

RIBBON-TRIMMED PILLOWS

MATERIALS: For all pillows (see individual **MATERIALS** listing for amounts of the first six items); No. 10 Penelope canvas, washable, colorfast grosgrain ribbon; fabric for backing and welting; ¼″ cotton cording for welting; Persian yarn as needed; masking tape; tapestry needle; waterproof marking pens; polyester or other pillow stuffing.

WINDOW FLOWERS

MATERIALS: Canvas, one piece 14″ × 18″; 1″-wide washable, colorfast Magenta and White dotted ribbon, 3 yds.; Bright Green fabric, one 13″ × 17″ piece, plus 1½″-wide bias strip, 60″ long; cording, 60″; Persian yarn in these colors and yardages—Turquoise, 25 yds.; Royal Blue, 21 yds.; Lime, 13 yds.; Orange, 6 yds.; Vermillion, 9 yds.; Magenta, 8 yds.

FOUR SEASONS

MATERIALS: Canvas, one piece, 11″ × 19″; 1″-wide washable, colorfast white ribbon, 1⅓ yds.; Tan fabric, one 10″ × 18″ piece, plus 1½″-wide bias strip, 56″ long; cording, 56″; Persian yarn in these colors and yardages—Magenta, 5 yds.; Vermillion, 1 yd.; Lime, Jade, Yellow, Orange and White, 3 yds. of each; Dark Green, 21 yds.; Pale Ochre, 43 yds.

BROTHERHOOD

MATERIALS: Canvas, one piece, 14″ × 18″; ⅞″-wide washable, colorfast Orange and White striped ribbon, 2¼ yds.; Magenta fabric, one 13″ × 17″ piece, plus 1½″-wide bias strip, 60″ long; cording, 60″; Persian yarn in these colors and yardages—Burnt Sienna, 38 yds.; Magenta, 23 yds.; Chartreuse, 26 yds.; Burnt Orange, 17 yds.

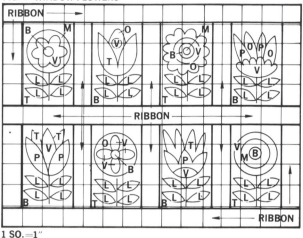

FIG. 1 WINDOW FLOWERS

1 SQ.=1″

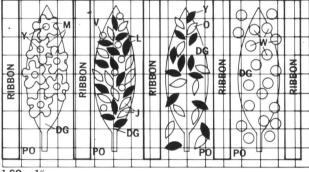

FIG. 2 FOUR SEASONS

1 SQ.=1″

ECOLOGY

MATERIALS: Canvas, 16″ square; 1½″-wide washable, colorfast Blue and White dotted ribbon, 1 yd.; Turquoise fabric, one 15″ square, plus 1½″-wide bias strip, 60″; cording, 60″; Persian yarn in these colors and yardages—Royal Blue, 31 yds.; Magenta, 63 yds.; Turquoise and Fuchsia, 15 yds. of each.

LOVE DOVE

MATERIALS: Canvas, 16″ square; 1⅝″-wide washable, colorfast Green and White dotted ribbon, 1⅔ yds; Vermillion fabric, one 15″ square, plus 1½″-wide bias strip, 60″ long; cording, 60″; Persian yarn in these colors and yardages—Hot Pink, 38 yds.; Green, 17 yds.; White, 10 yds.; Vermillion, 42 yds.

DIRECTIONS: *Enlarging the Patterns:* Following the Directions on page 224, enlarge and cut out the patterns for the needlework designs (*see* FIGS. 1 to 5).

Preparing the Canvas: Tape the enlarged pattern to a window with good light shining through. Center the canvas over the pattern; tape in place. With a waterproof marking pen, trace the pattern onto the canvas. Remove pat-

FIG. 3 BROTHERHOOD

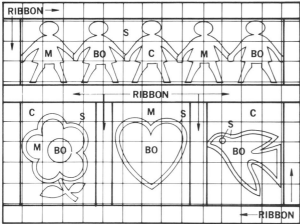

1 SQ. 1″

FIG. 4 ECOLOGY

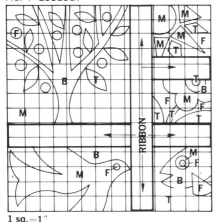

1 sq.=1″

FIG. 5 LOVE DOVE

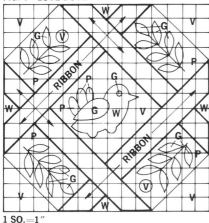

1 SQ.=1″

COLOR KEY

P—HOT PINK	M—MAGENTA
BO—BURNT ORANGE	F—FUSHIA
C—CHARTREUSE	J—JADE
S—BURNT SIENNA	W—WHITE
T—TURQUOISE	DG—DARK GREEN
B—ROYAL BLUE	G—GREEN
L—LIME	Y—YELLOW
O—ORANGE	PO—PALE OCHRE
V—VERMILLION	

tern and canvas. Bind canvas edges with masking tape to prevent raveling. Edgestitch ribbon trim in place—in areas without letters.

Working the Canvas: Work the background and design in the Half Cross Stitch, using the colors indicated by letter in the pattern (identified in the Color Key.)

Blocking the Canvas: Block. Allow needlepoint to dry thoroughly. Remove from board. Machine-stitch around the canvas as close as possible to the worked area. Trim canvas ½″ from worked area.

Making Corded Welting: Cut and stitch together as many 1½″ bias strips as needed to form a strip long enough to fit arond pillow plus 1″ seam allowance. Press seams open. Lay the cord on the wrong side of the strip; fold the strip over, matching edges. Machine-stitch close to the cord.

Assembling the Pillow: Cut the pillow *backing* to same size as trimmed, blocked canvas. With right sides together and edges even, stitch the welting to the backing, clipping welting seam allowance at corners. With right sides together, baste the pillow front to the back. Stitch in ½″ seam all around, leaving an opening in one edge. Turn right side out. Stuff pillow; slip-stitch opening.

QUICK AND EASY PILLOWS

MATERIALS: For *each* pillow: 18″ square of 5 mesh Penelope (double thread) canvas; No. 13 tapestry needle; crewel yarn (triple strand) in colors indicated below; 14″ pillow form; 16″ square backing fabric in compatible solid color; 10″ to 12″ zipper; thread.

Crewel yarn required.

Pillow A—Three Flowers

Deep Yellow (1)	2½	yards
Lemon Yellow (2)	12	yards
Orange (3)	50	yards
Magenta (4)	64	yards
Green (5)	25	yards
Turquoise (6)	32	yards
White	48	yards

Pillow B—Six Flowers

Vermillion (7)	4½	yards
Golden Yellow (8)	24	yards
Magenta (4)	30	yards
Violet (9)	47	yards
Turquoise (6)	30	yards
Navy (10)	47	yards
White	48	yards

DIRECTIONS: Both pillows are variations of the design in the pattern chart, and both are

Color photo on page 129

worked in variations of four standard needlepoint stitches (half cross, scotch, stem and brick). Leaving about 1¾″ turn-under on all edges of canvas, work design of your choice in needlepoint, following the pattern chart, color diagrams and stitch diagrams.

Note: For leaves, flowers and border, use three triple strands (nine strands) as one. For the background area use two triple strands (6 strands) as one.

Pillow A: Continue leaf motif on chart three more times to total five leaves. *Pillow measures 71 meshes* in depth (flower and five leaves = 61; one extra row at top and bottom of background = 2; four rows of white half cross stitch at top and bottom = 8). *Width is 68 meshes* (18 per motif per panel = 54; 1 vertical row background at each side of each panel = 6; four rows of white half cross stitch at each side = 8).

Pillow B: Invert motif in pattern chart for lower half. Pillow measures 72 meshes in depth (flower and two leaves = 62; ½ extra row at top and bottom of background = 2 [yarn covers only 1 horizontal pair of threads, not two]; four rows of white half cross stitch at top and bottom = 8).

Making the Pillows: Trim canvas around edges to ¾″ beyond needlepoint area. Press backing fabric 1″ under on all edges. With right sides together, pin backing to canvas, then baste around three sides and four corners, rolling the last row of needlepoint stitches so the canvas doesn't show at the seam. Machine-stitch; remove basting. Insert zipper in open side, following package directions. Trim seams; clip corners. Turn right side out and insert pillow form.

FIG. 1

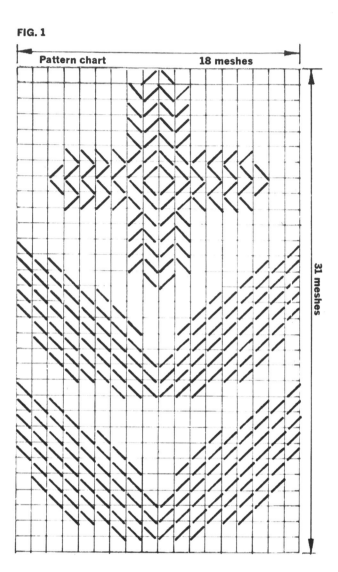

Leaves: Starting at top of right leaf, work the leaf in standard half cross stitch; for left leaf, reverse direction of same stitch.

White Border: Work in standard half cross stitch.

Flower Centers: Start Scotch stitch outside of flower center and cross three meshes diagonally, then two, then one; repeat for remaining three sides.

Flower Petals: Based on Stem Stitch, starting near completed flower centers, work four half cross stitches; reverse direction on next row. Repeat until all petals are worked.

Background: In this variation of a Brick Stitch, the stitch is worked over two horizontal double threads, with the vertical double threads split so that each thread has a vertical stitch between.

Note: For Pillow B, work over only one horizontal double thread at top and bottom of pattern panels (*see top row* of Brick Stitch).

FIG. 2   Color Diagrams   Pillow A

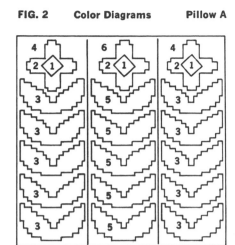

FIG. 3   Color Diagram   Pillow B

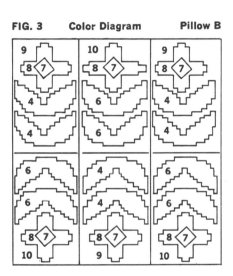

RAINBOW PILLOWS

DIAMOND RAINBOW PILLOW (16″×17″)
MATERIALS: Paternayan yarn in the following colors and quantities:
25 strands each: White; black.
13 strands each: Mauve; purple, blue, light turquoise, emerald green, dark olive green, golden yellow, orange, red, light magenta, dark magenta.

CHECKERBOARD RAINBOW
PILLOW (13″×15″)
MATERIALS: Paternayan yarn in the following colors and quantities:
25 strands each: Dark magenta, white, black; 13 strands light turquoise; 18 strands dark olive green; 13 strands light magenta; 8 strands red; 19 strands orange; 22 strands golden yellow, 11 strands light olive green, 3 strands dark turquoise; 8 strands bright yellow.
Optional Tassels: We used a coarse-textured

two-strand novelty yarn for firmer body. Any firm yarn will do. Each of the four small (4″) tassels requires ½ oz. yarn; each of the four large tassels requires 1 oz. yarn, a total of 6 oz. yarn per pillow.
GENERAL DIRECTIONS *(for both pillows):* It is important to mark off and stitch the black and white areas of the pillows first while the canvas is still perfectly square; then work the rainbow rows above and below them. Draw pillow dimensions on canvas; add a 3″ border all around. Cut out on borderline and cover edges with masking tape, then spray with clear acrylic to prevent bleeding. Using the felt-tip pen, mark off the black and white diamond and/or check areas of the pillows first as follows:
For the diamond pillow: Use the felt-tip pen to mark off a 3″ wide horizontal strip (30 meshes) 3″ down from the top borderline on the canvas. Measure 6″ down from the first strip and draw another strip 1½″ wide (15 meshes). Starting at the center, use the felt-tip marker and ruler to divide the 3″ area into eleven vertical sections, each 15 meshes wide. Divide area in half horizontally with another line from edge to edge. Now use these guidelines to draw diamond shapes, making sure top and bottom points are centered and aligned with each other. Now mark off eleven vertical sections in the 1½″ area and draw half diamond shapes, centering points as before. Using the Continental Stitch, fill in the whole 3″ diamonds in black, half-diamonds in white; alternate black and white 1½″ half-diamonds. Now work the rainbow rows as follows: 12 dark magenta; 10 light magenta; 10 red; *below diamonds*—10 rows each orange, golden yellow, dark olive green, emerald green, turquoise, blue; *below half-diamonds*—10 rows purple; 12 mauve.

For the checked pillow: Use the felt-tip pen to mark off a 2″-wide horizontal strip (20 meshes) 2″ down from the top borderline on the canvas. Measure down 5¼″ from the first strip, then draw another strip 1″ wide (10 meshes). Starting at the center of the 2″ area, use the felt-tip pen and ruler to divide it in half horizontally with a line from edge to edge. Then divide into 19 vertical sections, each 8 stitches wide and 10 stitches deep. Spray with clear acrylic. Using the Continental Stitch, work two rows of checks, alternating black and white. Repeat with only one row of checks in the 1″ area, starting with white. Now work the rainbow rows, as follows: 2 light turquoise, 3 dark olive green, 2 light magenta, 1 red, 4 orange, 2 dark magenta, 6 golden yellow; *below double checks*—4 rows light olive green, 2 light turquoise, 1 dark turquoise, 1 light olive green, 2 dark olive green, 1 light olive green, 9 dark magenta, 1 red, 2 dark magenta, 1 red, 5 light magenta, 1 orange, 6 golden yellow, 1 orange, 3 dark magenta, 1 red, 2 golden yellow, 1 dark olive green, 1 dark turquoise, 1 light turquoise, 1 red, 1 dark magenta, 1 orange, 4 bright yellow; *below single checks*—5 rows orange, 1 red, 1 golden yellow, 2 light magenta, 1 dark magenta, 5 dark olive green, 4 dark turquoise, 3 light olive green, 2 dark olive green.
Block
Finishing: Cut backing to match on straight grain for checked pillow and on the bias for diamond pillow. With right sides together, stitch backing to front, leaving a 10″ opening on one side. Trim corners; turn right side out. Insert stuffing. Blindstitch opening.
Tassels: Using coarse yarn, wind neatly over a stiff piece of cardboard (8″ for large tassel, 6″ for small tassel), 200 times. Don't pull too tightly. Wind yarn so strands lay next to each other, then wind second and third layers, etc. Tie with self-yarn at top and knot. Cut yarn at bottom of cardboard. Holding top, smooth strands of tassel so it looks neat. Tie securely 1¼″ from top, binding tassel several times with self-yarn. Smooth loose ends down, to form part of the tassel. Trim ends even.
To form a honeycomb covering for tassel head: Turn tassel upside down. Thread needle with 45″ of same yarn, knotting end. Push needle through center of tassel, coming out at a point just below binding. Work Buttonhole Stitches (*see* BASIC EMBROIDERY STITCHES, page 228) a scant ½″ apart, using the binding as the guideline. Repeat several rows of Buttonhole

Stitches, using the previous row of stitches as the anchor for your subsequent rows. Pull stitches taut.

Color photo on page 129

ART DECO PILLOW

MATERIALS: No. 12 Mono canvas, 14″ square; Persian yarn in the following amounts and colors: 1½ ozs. Dark Green (A), 1¾ ozs. Light Green (B), ¼ oz. each chartreuse (C), Dark Red (D), Light Red (E), Pink (F), and Yellow (G); white paper; masking tape; waterproof felt marker; needle; 13″ square gingham or other fabric for pillow back; polyester fiberfill; thread; pins.
DIRECTIONS: *Transferring the Design:* Following the directions on page 224, enlarge the pattern onto white paper. "Flop" 3 times to obtain full square. Tape the pattern to a window with strong light shining through. Center the canvas over the pattern; tape in place. With waterproof marking pen, trace the pattern onto the canvas. Design itself should be enlarged to a 12″ square with a 2″ border of unworked canvas on all sides. Remove pattern and canvas from window. Bind canvas edges with masking tape to prevent raveling.
Working the Canvas: Work the design, one quarter at a time with 3 strands of yarn in the stitches indicated in key. Each quarter of the canvas is worked in the reverse direction of the ones next to it, so that the stitch directions are at reverse angles in each quarter. The Gobelin is worked horizontally, slanted left and right and vertically, slanted left and right. Mosaic and Diagonal Florentine are worked slanted

FLORENTINE STITCH

FIG. 1

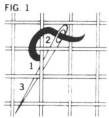

FIG. 3

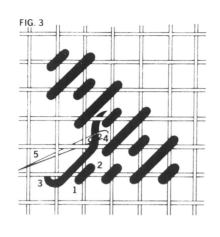

FIG. 2

SLANTED GOBELIN STITCH

COLORS:

A-DARK GREEN	D-DARK RED
B-LIGHT GREEN	E-LIGHT RED
C-CHARTREUSE	F-PINK
	G-YELLOW

STITCHES:

1-HALF CROSS (LEFT)
2-HALF CROSS REVERSE (RIGHT)
3-SLANTED GOBELIN (LEFT)
4-SLANTED GOBELIN REVERSE (RIGHT)
5-SLANTED GOBELIN VERTICAL (LEFT)

6-SLANTED GOBELIN VERTICAL REVERSE (RIGHT)
7-MOSAIC (LEFT)
8-MOSAIC REVERSE (RIGHT)
9-DIAGONAL FLORENTINE (LEFT)
10-DIAGONAL FLORENTINE REVERSE (RIGHT)

STITCH DIRECTION DETAILS

1   *0000*

2   *0000*

3

4

5   6

7

8

9

10

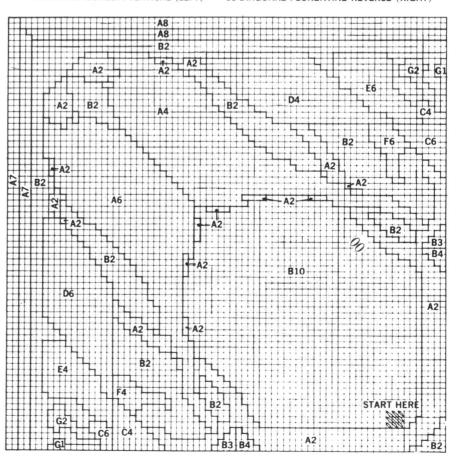

left and right. Refer to the stitch diagrams to check your direction. For example, the quarter next to section B10 would use B9 (Florentine slanted left).

Blocking: Block the pillow. Allow to dry thoroughly. Remove from board. Stitch around canvas as close as possible to worked area. Trim canvas ½″ from worked area.

Assembling: Trim canvas to allow ½″ border unworked canvas on all sides. With right sides together, stitch gingham backing and top together in a ½″ seam, leaving an 8″ opening. Turn right side out; lightly press edges. Stuff pillow. Blindstitch open edges.

⊠ LAVENDER		⊡ ORANGE	
▼ PURPLE (LIGHT)		▣ PURPLE (DARK)	
⊙ YELLOW		⊘ GREEN (DARK)	

PANSY PILLOW

MATERIALS: No. 12 Mono canvas, 14″ square; Persian yarn in the following colors and amounts: 1½ ozs. Dark Green, ½ oz. Light Green (for background), ¼ oz. each Dark Purple, Lavender, Light Purple, Yellow and Orange; white paper; masking tape; waterproof felt marker; tapestry needle; 13″ square piece of gingham or other fabric for pillow back; polyester fiberfill; thread; pins.

DIRECTIONS: Following directions on page 224, enlarge and transfer pansy design onto canvas. Design itself should be enlarged to a 12″ square, with a 2″ border of unworked canvas on all sides.

Working the Canvas: Following diagram for color key, work design as follows, using three strands of yarn: Outside Lavender border is worked in Mosaic Stitch; inside (Dark Green) border is worked with Rice Stitch. Using three strands, work Rice Stitch by crossing over four squares diagonally. Always cross in the same direction. Then, with two strands of same color yarn, box in the remaining holes in Dark Green border as shown. When all borders are complete, work the design, using 3 strands of yarn and a Half Cross Stitch.

To Complete Background: Using 3 strands of Light Green, work in this sequence: 1 vertical row Gobelin, 1 vertical row Half Cross, 1 vertical row Gobelin reversed, 1 vertical row Half Cross. Repeat until entire background is filled in. Block and complete pillow, following directions outlined in "Art Deco Pillow".

ORCHID PILLOWS

MATERIALS: *(For each pillow):* No. 12 Mono canvas, 16″ square (allows for 2″ border on each side); 3-ply Persian yarn in the following colors and amounts (one strand is approximately 33″ long): 2 oz. Dark Blue, 1 oz. Light Blue, 15 strands Dark Green, 1 strand Light Green, 1 strand Yellow, 1 oz. White, ½ oz. Palest Pink, ½ oz. Paler Pink, ¼ oz. Pale Pink, ½ oz. Pink, ½ oz. Brown; *for purple orchid:* 8 strands Palest Purple, 8 strands Paler Purple, 7 strands Purple, 6 strands Dark Purple; *for orange orchid:* 8 strands Palest Orange, 8 strands Paler Orange, 10 strands Orange, 13 strands Red; *for yellow orchid:* 12 strands Palest Yellow, 8 strands Paler Yellow, 8 strands Yellow, 10 strands Brown; 12″ foam block, 2″ wide; 13″ × 25″ fabric for pillow back (1 yd. of 54″-wide fabric is sufficient for all three pillows); white paper; masking tape; waterproof felt-tipped marker; tapestry needle; thread; straight pins.

DIRECTIONS: *Transferring the design:* Following directions on page 224, enlarge the pattern onto white paper. Tape the pattern to a window with strong light shining through. Center the canvas over the pattern; tape in place. With waterproof marker, trace the pattern onto the canvas. Design itself should be enlarged to a 12″ square with a 2″ border of unworked canvas on all sides. Remove pattern and canvas from window. Bind canvas edges with masking tape to prevent raveling.

Working the Canvas: Following diagram for color key, work design as follows, using three strands of yarn: Design is worked in Half Cross Stitch. For background, use 1 row Slanted Gobelin and 1 row Half Cross; repeat until entire background is filled.

Blocking: Block canvas. Allow to dry thoroughly. Remove from board. Stitch around canvas as close as possible to worked area. Trim canvas ½″ from worked area.

Assembling: Cut a 13″ square for back of pillow (all dimensions allow for ½″ seam allowance).

Color photo on page 130

Cut four pieces for sides, 3″ wide × 13″ long. Stitch right side of fabric side pieces to right side of canvas pillow front, leaving ½″ seam allowance. Sew corners. Sew wrong side of pillow back fabric to wrong side of 3 pillow side pieces, leaving bottom open. Turn right side out. Insert foam block. Slipstitch bottom edge closed.

ORCHID PILLOW

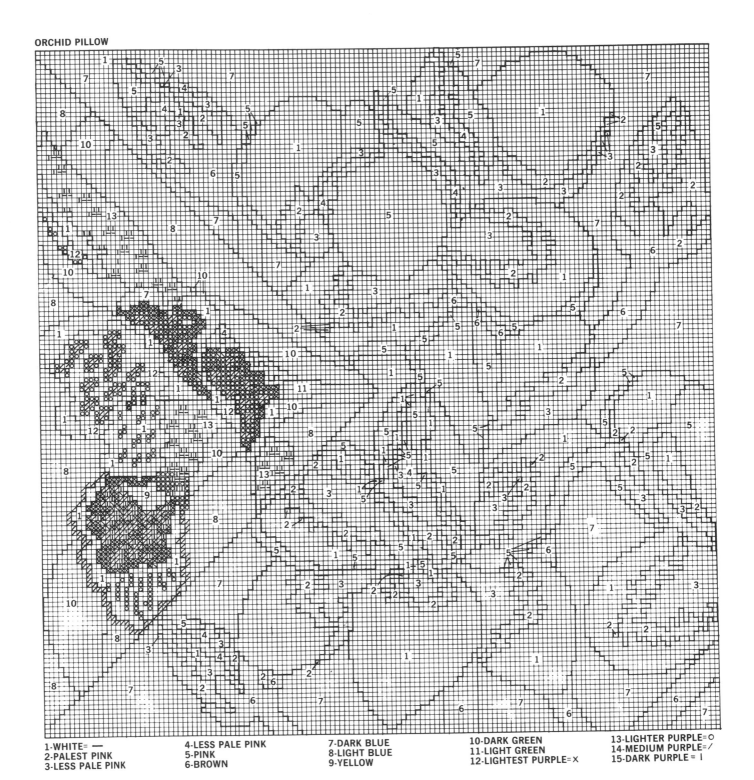

1-WHITE= —	4-LESS PALE PINK	7-DARK BLUE	10-DARK GREEN	13-LIGHTER PURPLE=O
2-PALEST PINK	5-PINK	8-LIGHT BLUE	11-LIGHT GREEN	14-MEDIUM PURPLE=/
3-LESS PALE PINK	6-BROWN	9-YELLOW	12-LIGHTEST PURPLE=X	15-DARK PURPLE = I

ORCHID PILLOW

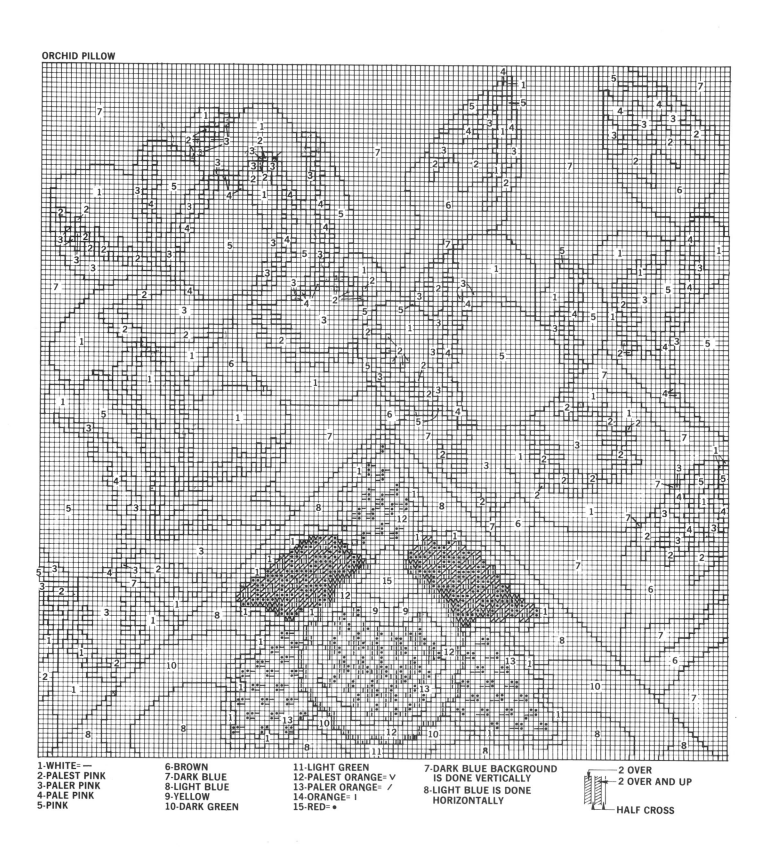

1-WHITE= —
2-PALEST PINK
3-PALER PINK
4-PALE PINK
5-PINK

6-BROWN
7-DARK BLUE
8-LIGHT BLUE
9-YELLOW
10-DARK GREEN

11-LIGHT GREEN
12-PALEST ORANGE= V
13-PALER ORANGE= /
14-ORANGE= I
15-RED= •

7-DARK BLUE BACKGROUND
   IS DONE VERTICALLY
8-LIGHT BLUE IS DONE
   HORIZONTALLY

2 OVER
2 OVER AND UP

HALF CROSS

ORCHID PILLOW

1-WHITE= —
2-PALEST PINK
3-PALER PINK

4-LESS PALE PINK
5-PINK
6-BROWN

7-DARK BLUE
8-LIGHT BLUE
9-LIGHTER YELLOW=

10-DARK GREEN
11-LIGHT GREEN
12-LIGHTEST YELLOW= ∨

13-LIGHTER YELLOW= I
14-LIGHT YELLOW= ╱
15-BROWN= •

Color photo on page 131

FLORAL PILLOW AND ACCESSORIES

MATERIALS: No. 10 needlepoint canvas (dimensions given for each project are for stitched area only—add 3″ on all sides to allow for blocking and finishing); 3-strand tapestry yarn in five colors (2 oz. of each color should be enough to complete any of the designs shown . . . allow more of the background color for larger projects); blunt-end tapestry needle; masking tape or fabric tape; light color waterproof felt-tip marker; wooden accessories and hardware for displaying needlepoint.

DIRECTIONS: The projects shown (FIG. 1) are based on using all, or part of, the flower design shown actual size on page 131.

You can use this color photograph as you would a graph, by counting the stitches for each area. To do so, divide your canvas into one-inch squares and mark with a waterproof felt-tip marker. Then copy the design, concentrating on a square at a time.

Or, you can lay your canvas directly on top of the photograph and trace the entire section of the design you wish to use onto the canvas with a waterproof felt-tip marker.

We suggest using either a Continental Stitch or Basket Weave Stitch.

Cut canvas to desired size. Seal edges of canvas with masking tape or fabric tape to prevent raveling. Transfer design to canvas in desired position, being sure to line up the center of the design with the center of the canvas.

1. *Pillow* (15″×15″): For the pillow, we used an area of the flower design for the center section (7¾″×7¾″) with a white background. We then added a 3-row-wide yellow stripe, 6 rows from the edge of the flower design, and a 2-row-wide red stripe, 8 rows from the yellow one, as shown in the photo on page 131.

2. *Dutch Shadowbox* (Stitched Area 6″×8½″): Choose an area of the design 6″×8½″ and transfer to canvas. You will have to cut into some of the flowers, so plan to measure out from the center of the page where you can include the most number of full flowers.

3. *Shadowbox Table* (Stitched Area 9¼″×14″): The full-size flower design is used in the center. We added a 2-row-wide red stripe at each end, 8 rows from the end of the flower design, and then worked another 10 rows of white on each end and another 9 rows of white on each side.

4. *Framed Needlepoint* (Stitched Area 9″ × 12″): The full sized flower design is used in the center, with an extra 5 rows of white on all sides.

5. *Tray* (Stitched Area 9″ × 12″): The addition of brass handles, ball feet and hardware transforms the frame into a tray.

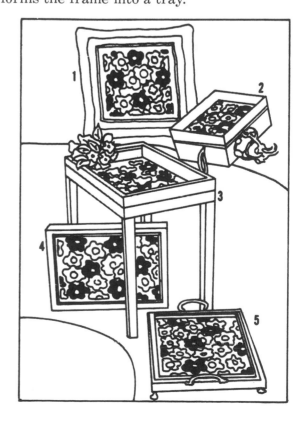

BARGELLO PILLOW

(Finished Size 14″ square.)

MATERIALS: Bucilla tapestry wool, Off White, three 100-yd. skeins; No. 14 mono (single-thread) canvas, one 18″ square; ½″-diameter ball fringe to match yarn, 4 yds.; backing fabric, ½ yd.; polyester or Dacron pillow stuffing; masking tape; permanent color, pastel felt-tip marker; tapestry needle; yardstick; brown wrapping paper; rustproof pins or tacks.

DIRECTIONS: *Preparing the Canvas:* Bind the canvas edges with masking tape to prevent raveling. Using a yardstick and pastel marker, draw a 14″ square in the center of the canvas. Then draw a diagonal line (A-A) across the square from corner to corner (*see* diag.). Draw two more diagonal lines (B-B) and two (C-C) 3¼″ apart. Repeat, drawing the lines in the opposite direction. The canvas will then be marked off into a pattern of triangle and diamond shapes numbered as shown.

Working the Design: First work the diagonal dividing lines and borders, as shown in diagram. Fill in the numbered areas, using the Bargello stitches illustrated in diagram.

Blocking: Block the pillow. Let dry thoroughly. Remove from board.

Finishing: Machine-stitch around canvas close to last worked row. Trim unworked canvas, leaving ½″ seam allowance all around. Cut the pillow-backing fabric the same size as the canvas. Baste the ball fringe to the right side of the canvas with the inner edge of the braid against the last worked row and the fringe toward the center, mitering the corners. With right sides together, pin the backing to canvas. Stitch the pieces together as close as possible to last worked row, around three sides and four corners, leaving an opening on one edge. Turn cover right side out through opening; press. Stuff the cover to the desired degree of plumpness; slipstitch opening.

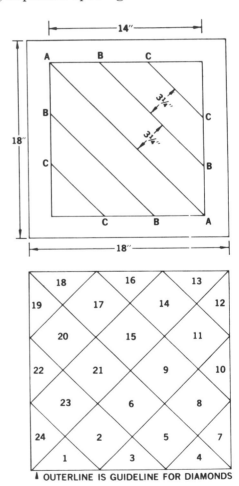

OUTERLINE IS GUIDELINE FOR DIAMONDS

TEXTURED PILLOW

MATERIALS: Bucilla tapestry wool, off white, two 100-yd. skeins; No. 10 Penelope (double-mesh) canvas, one 16″ square; ¾″-wide crochet-type lace to match wool, 1¾ yds. For *additional materials* needed see last seven items in MATERIALS for BARGELLO PILLOW, above left.

DIRECTIONS:

Preparing the Canvas: Bind the canvas edges

BARGELLO PILLOW

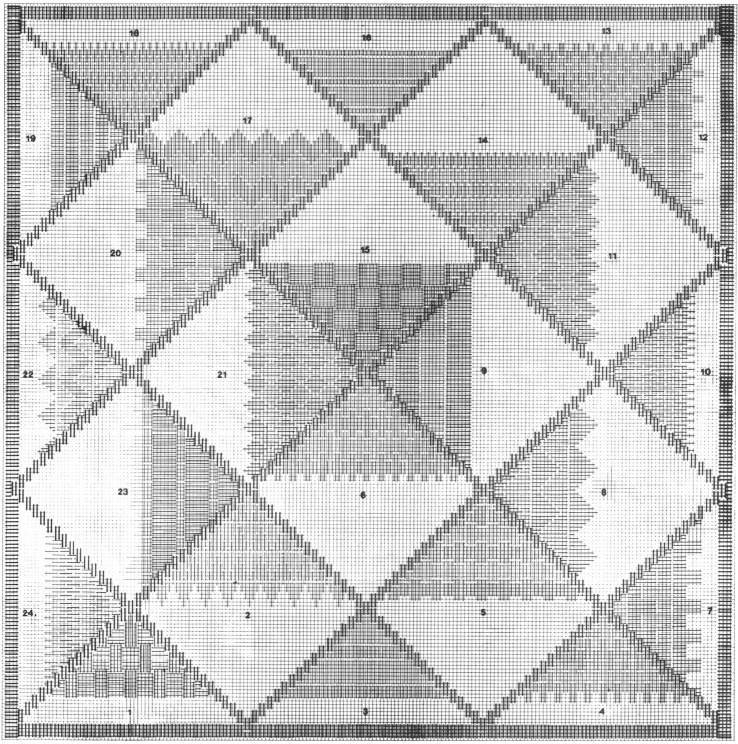

with masking tape to prevent raveling. Using a yardstick and marker, draw a 12″ square in the center of the canvas. Draw a 1″ square in the exact center of the 12″ square.
Working the Canvas: Starting with 1″ center square, work canvas from center to the edge, following the Diagram and using Stitches 1 to 8 as indicated.
Blocking and Finishing: See BARGELLO PIL-LOW DIRECTIONS.

NEEDLEPOINT PILLOW

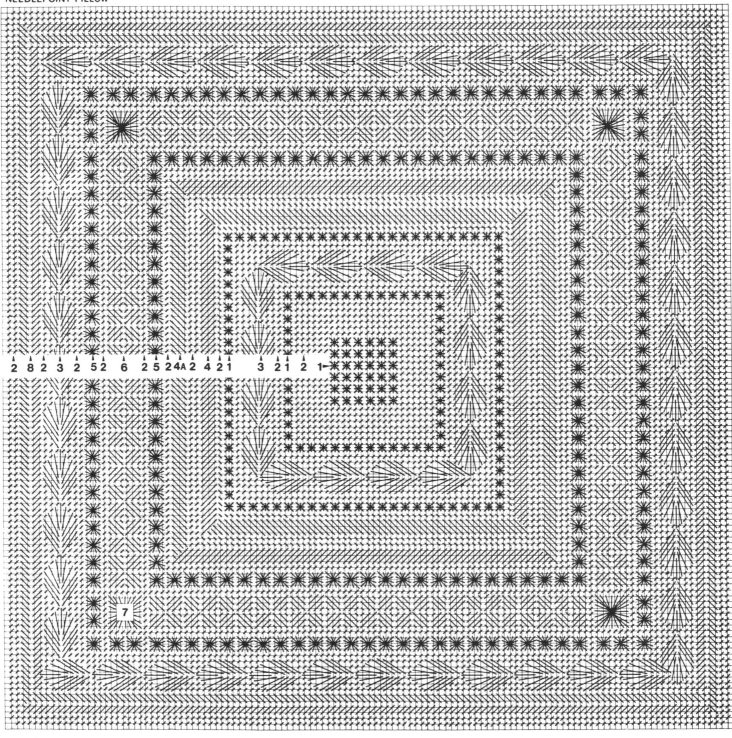

2 8 2 3 2 5 2 6 2 5 24A 2 4 2 1   3 2 1 2 1

1—SMYRNA CROSS STITCH
2—HALF CROSS
3—LEAF STITCH
4—SLANTING GOBELIN STITCH
   (WORKED VERTICALLY)
5—LEVIATHAN
   STITCH
5—LEVIATHAN STITCH
6—SCOTCH STITCH
7—ALGERIAN EYE STITCH
8—STEM STITCH

tom of brick. Place brick cover over brick, aligning corners of cover with brick. Place felt over brick bottom; secure with rubber bands. Overcast felt to edges of cover.

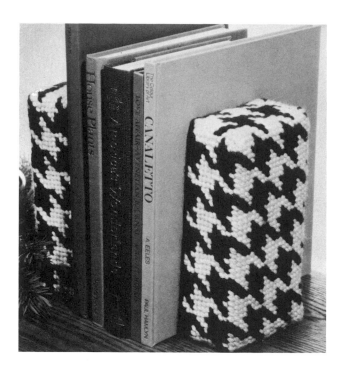

HOUNDSTOOTH BOOKENDS

MATERIALS: Two pieces No. 5 Penelope (double-thread) canvas, 12″ × 18″; masking tape; light-colored waterproof felt-tip marker; soft-lead pencil; Persian needlepoint yarn in the following colors and amounts—Cream, 2 oz.; Royal Blue, 2 oz.; tapestry needle, #13; Royal Blue felt for base of bricks; regular sewing needle; 2 bricks, ordinary size.

DIRECTIONS: Bind the raw canvas edges with masking tape to prevent raveling. With a soft pencil, mark the center of the canvas as shown in the diagram right. Count off number of stitches indicated, and draw outline of design on the canvas with felt-tip marker. Before you begin, trace the overall shape of the design onto brown paper to aid in blocking the finished project. Begin the charted pattern at top right hand corner, working from right to left in the Continental Stitch. Use two 3-ply strands of Persian yarn.

Blocking: Block the canvas. Allow to dry thoroughly. Dry flat—do not stand board on end. Remove from board.

Finishing: Machine-stitch around the canvas as close as possible to the needlepoint. Trim excess canvas ½″ from stitching line. Fold cover, wrong side out, into brick shape and sew side corners together by stitching just outside edge of needlepoint. Trim corners after joining, for a smooth fit. Turn right side out. Press corner seams open. Press side seams down toward wrong side all around. Cut felt base to fit bot-

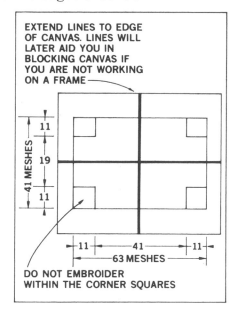

EXTEND LINES TO EDGE OF CANVAS. LINES WILL LATER AID YOU IN BLOCKING CANVAS IF YOU ARE NOT WORKING ON A FRAME

41 MESHES

11
19
11

11 41 11
63 MESHES

DO NOT EMBROIDER WITHIN THE CORNER SQUARES

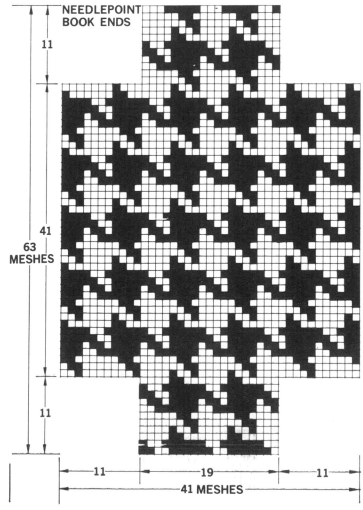

NEEDLEPOINT BOOK ENDS

11

41
63 MESHES

11

11 19 11
41 MESHES

SPANISH TILE RUG

Our rug is made of 35 squares, each measuring 10″ × 10″ finished, and approximately 50″ × 70″ overall. The number of squares you will need depends on the area you want the rug to cover. To help you approximate the amount of canvas and yarn you will need, we give the amounts required for our 35-square rug.

MATERIALS: Seven yds. No. 5 double-thread 36″ wide needlepoint canvas, cut into thirty-five 14″ squares; Fleisher's Gigantic yarn: 16 skeins white; 17 skeins blue (or any other *color-fast* rug yarn); burlap for backing rug (since burlap comes in many different widths, we cannot give the exact yardage—you will need a piece as large as your finished rug plus 1″ all around); 2 spools white carpet thread; 1 roll 1″-wide masking tape; rustproof tacks; ruler; large plywood board or other board for blocking; fabric-protector spray.

DIRECTIONS: To prevent raveling, bind all raw edges of canvas squares with masking tape. Copy the design (leave 2″ unworked canvas all around design), changing colors in each row, as indicated on design graph. The rug is worked

with a half-cross stitch. Start by coming up from back of canvas, catching the end of the yarn under the first four stitches as you work evenly from left to right. Be careful not to pull stitches too tightly. At the end of each row, turn canvas and continue working from left to right. To end stitch, take needle under four stitches on back of canvas.

Work 17 squares with a white border, a white center design and a blue background. Reverse the colors for the remaining 18 squares.

To block needlepoint squares: Any professional cleaner can block finished needlepoint for you provided your yarns are colorfast. However, if you wish to block your needlepoint yourself, follow blocking directions on page 224. Allow to dry *thoroughly* (it may take several days) before removing from board.

To join the blocked squares: With a blue-bordered square at each corner, arrange squares in seven rows of five squares each, alternating the border colors. Now return to the top left corner, place the first square from the first crosswise row face-down on top of the square next to it. With a double strand of carpet

BLUE AND WHITE NEEDLEPOINT RUG DESIGN

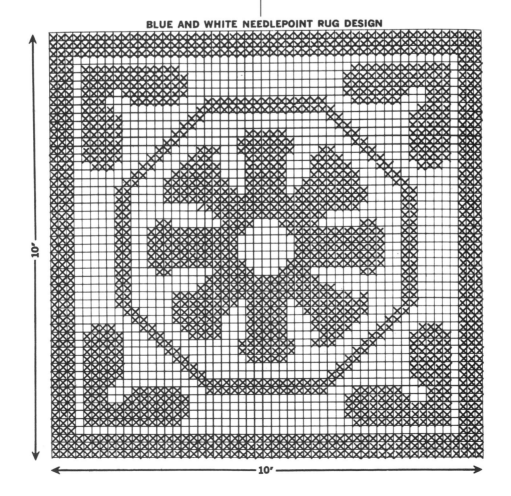

thread, use a backstitch to sew the edges together on the left side only, keeping the stitching as close as possible to the needlepoint so the canvas will not show. Cover seam with a damp cloth and lightly press open. Sew together and press the remaining squares in the row; repeat procedure for all remaining rows. Then, repeating the same sewing and pressing procedure, sew the rows themselves together. Machine-stitch the outside canvas edges of the rug two or three times to keep the seam allowance from raveling.

To back the rug: Cut a burlap backing the same size as the needlework area, plus 1″ on all edges. Turn edges under 1″ and press. Turn under canvas seam allowance and press. Pin the backing to the rug as close as possible to the last worked row. With a double strand of carpet thread, sew the backing edges to the rug, using a backstitch. In about a dozen places, catch-stitch the backing to the rug on the canvas seam allowance of the individual squares where four corners meet.

To skid-proof the rug, you may wish to sew rubber jar rings (the kind used in home canning) to the burlap backing, at the four corners, along edges and in the center.

To help retard soil: Spray rug with fabric protector.

VIOLET RUG
(Finished size approximately 42″ × 60″)
MATERIALS: No. 5 rug canvas, 40″-wide, 3¾ yds.; Bucilla Multi Craft yarn, 2 oz. skeins in these colors and quantities—Winter White, 12 skeins, Aster Purple and Emerald Green, 7 skeins each, Violet, 4 skeins, Purple and Lilac, 2 skeins each, Lime Green and Yellow, 1 skein each; 45″ wide burlap backing, 2 yds.; waterproof felt tip marker; masking tape; heavy (button and carpet) thread; rustproof pins or tacks.
DIRECTIONS: *Preparing the Canvas:* From canvas, cut fifteen 13″ squares, two 10″ × 64″ side-strips and two 10″ × 34″ end-strips. With felt tip marker, draw a 10″ (50 meshes) square in the exact center of each canvas square; on each strip, draw a 2″ border around all edges. The canvas *inside* the marked outline on all pieces is the area to be worked; the canvas *outside* the outline is the seam allowance. Bind canvas edges to prevent raveling. With felt marker, on the masking tape, label one end-strip "top" and the other "bottom"; on all squares, label one edge "top."

Enlarging and Transferring Flower Pattern: Following directions on page 224, enlarge the flower pattern; label pattern top edge. Tape the pattern to a window with strong light shining through. Center a canvas square, with "top" edge in correct position over the pattern; tape in place. With felt marker, trace the pattern onto the canvas. Remove the canvas; replace with seven other squares, tracing the pattern onto each.

Working the Design:
Note: Use the Interlocking Gobelin Stitch throughout, working the *entire area within the edges of the marked outline.* See photo for color guide, as needed.

Eight Flower Squares: With Lilac yarn, work three rows on side and bottom edges; on top edge, work two rows, leaving top mesh row *unworked* (to be filled in when squares are joined). Work background in White, leaves in Emerald Green with Lime Green veins, and flowers in various shades of Purple and Violet with Yellow centers.

Seven Checkerboard Squares: Work five rows of five 2″ squares each, alternating Purple and White as shown in the photograph.

Top End-strip: Starting at top edge, work rows as follows: five Emerald Green, two Lilac, 16 White, two Lilac, five Emerald Green.

Bottom End-strip: Leave top row unworked; work four Emerald Green rows. Complete same as for Top Strip.

Two Side-strips: Work five Emerald Green rows along the full length of the long outer edge and across the width at each end of the strip. Outline this Green area with two rows of Lilac. Work the next 16 lengthwise rows in White. At each end of the next seven rows, work 16 meshes in White. Outline the White area with two rows of Lilac. Fill in the remaining area of the side borders with five rows of Emerald Green. (*Note:* You may wish to work the corners of the borders just before you sew the strip to the completed center section, to make sure that the border rows of both sections line up perfectly.)

Blocking: On bread board, piece of plywood or other suitable surface, draw a 10″ square outline for flower and checkerboard canvases, a 6″ × 30″ rectangle for end-strips and a 6″ × 60″ rectangle for side-strips. Block.

Assembling the Rug: GENERAL DIRECTIONS: Remove masking tape from edges to be joined. When joining pieces *side-by-side*, sew by hand with heavy thread, lining up the canvas meshes at the seams and taking backstitches at frequent intervals. Trim seams to 1″; press flat. When joining pieces *top-to-bottom*, work as follows: On the top piece, fold the unworked bottom edge to the wrong side; press. (No unworked canvas should be visible on the right side.) With the Gobelin Stitch join this edge to the top row of the lower piece, changing yarns as needed to match where stitches interlock.

Color photo on page 130

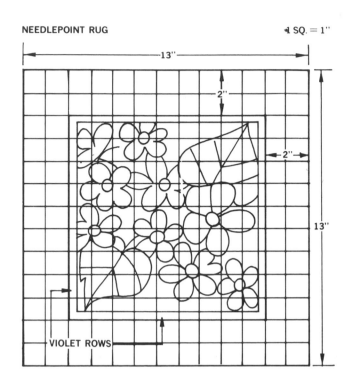

Following the GENERAL DIRECTIONS, assemble and join rug pieces in this order:

Join squares side-by-side as shown in photo to make five rows of five each.

Join the five rows, top-to-bottom, to form rug center section.

Add top and bottom strips to center section; add two side strips.

Finishing: On rug edges, press unworked canvas to wrong side, leaving one row of meshes on right side at each end for attaching fringe; catch-stitch edges in place on wrong side. Line rug with burlap. With single 9″ lengths of yarn, make 4″ fringe on both ends.

ROSE RUG

(Finished size 61″ × 92″)

MATERIALS: 9 yds. 36″-wide #5 interlock canvas; 2 sets 18″ artist's stretcher bars; large tapestry needle; carpet thread; 9 yds. rug binding; 5 yds. 36″-wide burlap OR 2½ yds. 72″-wide felt, for backing; staple gun and staples; heavy polyester rug yarn in the following colors: 32 skeins spring green, 20 skeins natural, 9 skeins grass green, 2 skeins each brick, sunset, yellow and lilac, 3 skeins each watermelon and cerise, 4 skeins each phantom red, tangerine and orchid.

DIRECTIONS:

1. Assemble the stretcher bars to make a square frame; staple corners to keep it square, and mark one edge "Top." Place frame in a corner of the piece of canvas with frame edges

parallel to threads. Trace around frame, then move it to trace 34 more blocks. Mark each top edge "Top," then cut out the 35 blocks.

2. On each block, draw two diagonal lines connecting opposite corners and mark the intersecting threads nearest the center. Starting from center, count off 23 holes to the north, south, east, and west, making a 46 × 46 mesh square. Draw lines along these meshes to make the center square.

3. Following directions on page 224, enlarge rose design. Tape enlarged rose under a canvas block, stem toward bottom edge and centers matching. With waterproof marker trace rose onto canvas. Repeat on all blocks.

4. Staple a canvas block to the frame, matching "Tops." Since the mesh may not be square, this will insure that canvas will run in the same direction throughout the rug. Working it on the frame will make it unnecessary to block the needlepoint.

5. Borders are worked first. Starting in the mesh below the bottom, draw line, and using a double strand of spring green yarn, work a row of straight vertical stitches, over three threads (two meshes) of canvas, beginning and ending six meshes to the left and right of the drawn square. Work a second row below this. Work the left and right borders, then the top border. The resultant uncovered canvas between rows will be covered later.

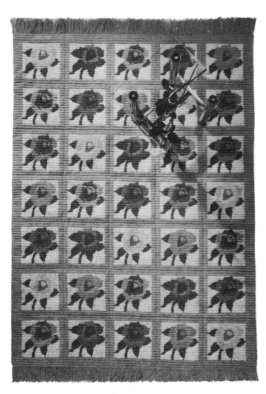

ROSE MOTIF FOR PILLOWS AND RUG

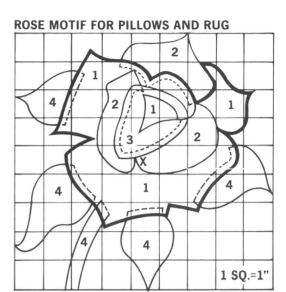

1 SQ.=1"

Note: The squares which occupy the edges of the rug have six additional stitches of border at the left or right side and two more rows of the straight vertical stitches at the top or bottom (*see photo*).

6. Work roses in colors indicated on the chart. Be sure that stitches occupy the same crosswise pair of meshes as the borders, so that the needlepoint forms a continuous rib across the whole rug. You may divide the color within these stitches where you wish, in order to follow the outlines of the roses. Fill in the stitches around the roses last.

COLOR CHART

NO. OF BLOCKS	COLORATION
4	GOLD (G)
5	RED (R)
7	VIOLET (V)
7	ORANGE (O)
6	PINK (P)
3	YELLOW (Y)
3	SHRIMP (S)

COLOR 1	COLOR 2	COLOR 3
SUNSET	YELLOW	TANGERINE
RED	WATERMELON	BRICK
ORCHID	LILAC	BRICK
TANGERINE	RED	BRICK
CERISE	ORCHID	LILAC
YELLOW	SUNSET	TANGERINE
WATERMELON	RED	BRICK

Note: Color 4 is always grass green. Borders and fringe are spring green and rose backgrounds are natural.

7. To cover the canvas: Go back and work a Backstitch (*see* BASIC EMBROIDERY STITCHES, page 228), using a single strand of matching yarn, over each vertical mesh at the bottom of each straight vertical stitch (except the bottom edge of each block).

8. Following the placement diagram, join the

worked blocks in seven rows of five blocks each as follows: With right sides together, and double strand of carpet thread, Backstitch the canvases together in and out of the meshes in the last yarn-covered row, matching mesh to mesh. Reinforce the ends and press the seams open. Repeat to complete the row. Join remaining rows the same way. Then join the rows to each other in the same way. Over the horizontal seams work Backstitch in double thread of spring green to cover canvas.

9. Turn under the side edges, pinching edge to leave one row of canvas outside last worked rows on which to work the Binding Stitch. With single thread of spring green yarn, work Binding Stitch along the sides as follows: Using a single strand of yarn, complete the first stitches, as shown in the placement diagram. Now the yarn goes back over the edge and through mesh 5, from the back to the front, then over the edge and through mesh 3 from back to front (then 6—4, 7—5, 8—6 and so on).

10. With a long double strand of yarn in needle, make loops 4″ long using the Rya stitch in the top yarn-covered row of meshes. Cut ends of loops to make fringe. Repeat at other end of rug.

11. Turn rug over. Turn under canvas at each end. Cut burlap to fit rug, piecing as necessary, and pin it to rug back. Pin rug binding along the rug edges to cover raw burlap. Stitch both edges of binding in place with carpet thread.

ROSE RUG BLOCK PLACEMENT DIAGRAM **ROW**

G	R	V	O	P	1
V	O	P	Y	S	2
S	G	R	V	O	3
P	V	O	S	G	4
O	R	Y	P	V	5
Y	P	V	R	O	6
V	R	O	P	G	7

ORIENTAL RUNNER

(Finished size: approximately 33¼″ × 76¼″)

MATERIALS: No. 5 double-thread rug canvas 36″-wide, 2⅓ yds; rug yarn in the following colors and amounts—4 lbs. blue, 3 lbs. orange and 2 lbs. white. (Be sure that all yarns are colorfast and mothproof. We used wool rug yarn which is admittedly more expensive but will give the most finished and lasting results—a wool needlepoint rug will last many generations. However, cotton or acrylics can be substituted. To estimate quantity, work one square inch in the stitch you plan to use and then rip it out and multiply by the number of square inches in each color to get the proper quantities.) Waterproof felt-tip marker; iron-on rug binding, 1½″ wide, 7 yards; masking tape; No. 13 tapestry needle; rug frame (*optional*); rustproof tacks.

Preparing the Canvas:

DIRECTIONS: Bind the raw canvas edges with masking tape to prevent raveling. With the marker, draw the outside dimensions of the rug centered in the canvas. The rug measures approximately 76¼″ × 33¼″ (394 meshes long and 169 meshes wide). If desired, attach rug to a rug frame with rustproof tacks; this will ease blocking later on by helping the rug to keep its shape while you stitch on it.

Border: With the line you have just drawn as a guide, and using the Half-Cross Stitch, stitch 3 rows of blue on all sides and then 2 rows of orange. Then stitch the four corner motifs as indicated in the pattern and color key in the diagram. Now connect the corners by filling in with the blue and white checkerboard pattern. Then outline the checkerboard design with two rows of orange.

Transferring the Pattern: Following the directions on page 224, enlarge the three patterns given onto brown wrapping paper, as directed. Place the needlepoint canvas on top of the paper pattern and pin securely in place. Trace onto the canvas the orange latticework pattern for the top half of the rug, and then reverse it and repeat for the bottom half of the rug, using a yardstick to help keep the lines straight and even. If your canvas is already on a frame, tape or pin the pattern to the back of it for transferring. Next, using the tree pattern, trace the two white trees in the orange arches at each end. Last, using the circle pattern, trace the circle of white leaves in the center of the rug. Use the photo as a guide.

Stitching: Now continue stitching with the Half-Cross Stitch. Fill in all of the orange areas first, then the two white trees and the white circle of leaves and finally finish by filling in all the remaining blue background areas.

Blocking: If you have a dry cleaner in your neighborhood that you know has had some experience with blocking needlepoint, it may be worthwhile to get an estimate from him for blocking your rug. However, if you wish to do it yourself, follow the blocking directions on page 224. Leave to set and dry overnight or preferably a few days.

Finishing: Leave rug on plywood or place rug face-down on an ironing board. Working with a small section at a time, turn unstitched canvas hems toward center, rolling stitching slightly so that no raw canvas shows. Remove masking tape and steam flat. Trim canvas edges to 1⅜". Place iron-on tape over hem edges so that it matches up with the last row of stitching. Steam-press the tape to seal canvas edges in place, squaring or mitering corners.

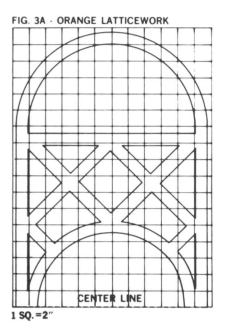

FIG. 3A - ORANGE LATTICEWORK

CENTER LINE

1 SQ.=2"

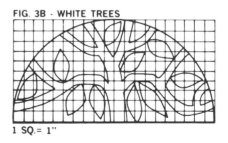

FIG. 3B - WHITE TREES

1 SQ.= 1"

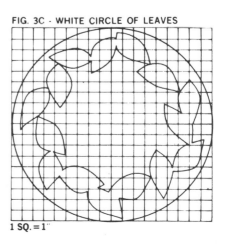

FIG. 3C - WHITE CIRCLE OF LEAVES

1 SQ.= 1"

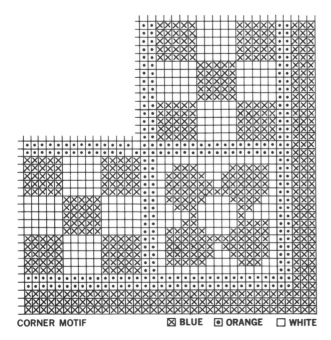

CORNER MOTIF   ⊠ BLUE   ⊡ ORANGE   ☐ WHITE

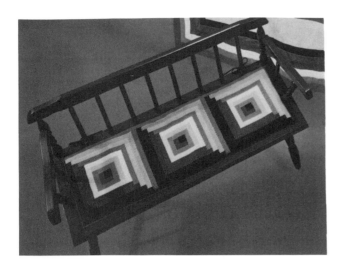

QUICKPOINT BENCH PAD

(Finished size about 12″ × 36″.)

MATERIALS: No. 5 Penelope canvas, 40″-wide, ½ yd.; firmly-woven, medium-weight lining fabric, 40″ wide, ½ yd.; matching thread; large tapestry needle; polyester batting, about 1″ thick, one piece 12″ × 36″ (*Note:* Pieces of an old mattress pad could be substituted); Bernat Quickspun yarn 8-yd. skeins, in these colors and quantities, listed in order used—4 skeins Plum (P); 1 skein each Vermillion (V), Hot Pink (HP), Orange (O), Flesh (F); 2 skeins each of Honey (H), Cream (C), Emerald (E), Fluorite Green (FG), Teal (T), Aqua (A); 3 skeins each of Gobelin Blue (GB), Horizon Blue (HB), and Rose (R); masking tape; colored chalk or felt-tip marker; rustproof tacks.

DIRECTIONS: *Preparing the Canvas:*
Bind the edges with masking tape in order to prevent it from raveling. Measure off and mark the exact center of the canvas as the starting point for the middle design. Mark the starting center point for the two end designs exactly 62

DESIGN DIAGRAM

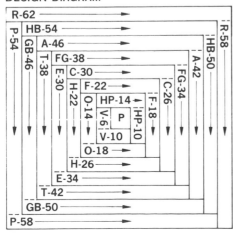

squares on either side of the center point.
Working the Canvas:
Using the Half Cross Stitch, follow the Design Diagram as a guide while you stitch. On the diagram, the colors are identified by the *letters* in parentheses in the MATERIALS listing. The *numbers* indicate how many *stitches* are worked in each stripe. The *dotted lines* across the stripes indicate that the color continues beyond the corner. First work the 6″ × 6″ center square, stitching from left to right, around the exact-center mark on the canvas. Work the stripes *4 meshes wide*, around the square, as shown. When the center design is completed, work the identical design on either side, starting at the marked center point.

Blocking the Quickpoint: Block. Let dry thoroughly.

Finishing the Pad:
Zigzag or straight-stitch around the edges of the blocked canvas, as close as possible to the last worked row. Trim canvas ½″ from the stitching. Cut backing fabric the same size as the canvas. To make ties, cut two 2″ × 24″ strips of backing fabric. Fold each strip in half lengthwise, right sides together. Stitch a ¼″ seam along the long raw edge. Turn right side out. Fold in raw edge at each end; blindstitch. Fold each tie in half crosswise. Pin the folded edge to one long edge of the backing fabric right side, 4″ from each end. Pin, then baste, the backing to the canvas, right sides together with the tie-ends in between. Stitch around edges in a ½″ seam, leaving a 24″ opening on the edge with the ties. Trim, grade and taper seams toward the corners. Turn right side out. Cut batting or pad to 11″ × 35½″. Insert through opening; smooth out. Turn in open edges; blindstitch.

BOUQUET PICTURE

Finished size measures 18″×24″.

MATERIALS: 22″×28″ piece of 13 mesh mono canvas (larger or smaller mesh canvas will mean different size piece); masking tape (to edge canvas); size 18 tapestry needle; permanent ink felt-tipped markers; pencil; white paper for pattern; 3-ply 100% wool yarns in the following colors and amounts (*Note:* Yarn amounts listed are for 13-mesh mono canvas): ½ ounce each light yellow, yellow, pale violet, light violet, medium violet, dark violet, light peach, peach, light rose, rose, pale pink, light pink, medium pink, dark pink, light turquoise, dark turquoise, light slate blue, medium slate blue,

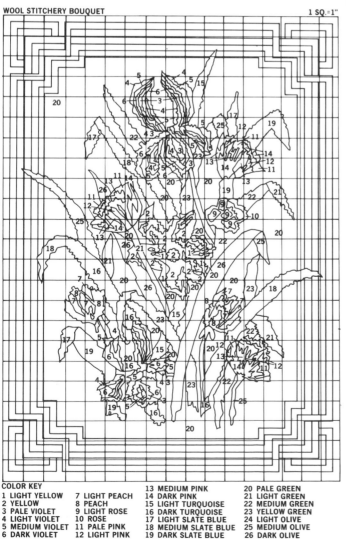

WOOL STITCHERY BOUQUET   1 SQ.=1"

COLOR KEY

1 LIGHT YELLOW	7 LIGHT PEACH	13 MEDIUM PINK	20 PALE GREEN
2 YELLOW	8 PEACH	14 DARK PINK	21 LIGHT GREEN
3 PALE VIOLET	9 LIGHT ROSE	15 LIGHT TURQUOISE	22 MEDIUM GREEN
4 LIGHT VIOLET	10 ROSE	16 DARK TURQUOISE	23 YELLOW GREEN
5 MEDIUM VIOLET	11 PALE PINK	17 LIGHT SLATE BLUE	24 LIGHT OLIVE
6 DARK VIOLET	12 LIGHT PINK	18 MEDIUM SLATE BLUE	25 MEDIUM OLIVE
		19 DARK SLATE BLUE	26 DARK OLIVE

dark state blue, light green, medium green, yellow green, light olive, medium olive, dark olive; 2 ounces pale green.

To finish: 18″×24″ wood canvas stretchers; staple gun or hammer and carpet tacks; frame, as desired.

DIRECTIONS: Following directions on page 224, enlarge pattern onto white paper. Mark outlines with heavy pencil line or felt-tipped marker. Tape edge of canvas. Mark 18″×24″ outline, leaving 2″ border on each side. Position pattern under canvas, centering it in the outline. Trace design onto canvas with felt-tipped marker. Work the design.

Flowers: The center of daffodil and rose are French knots; (see BASIC EMBROIDERY STITCHES, page 228) pink carnations are done with Long and Short Stitch; violets, tulips, rose and daffodil are all worked in the Basketweave Stitch.

Leaves: Leaves are worked in a random combination of Brick, Basketweave, Diagonal Mosaic, Mosaic and Parisian Stitches.

Stems: Stem Stitch.

Background: Basketweave with a Satin Stitch border.

To finish: If no frame is used, block canvas, either professionally or yourself. If frame is used there is no need to block canvas. Mark top and side centers on canvas and stretcher strips. Assemble stretcher corners. Use center lines on canvas to match marks on stretcher and tack or staple needlepoint in place; pull taut, alternating on all 4 sides until piece is evenly stretched.

BEADED MIRROR FRAME AND PILLOW

GENERAL MATERIALS: Waterproof marking pen; masking tape; thread to match beads; tapestry needle; sewing needle fine enough for beads to slide over; rustproof pins or tacks; steam iron; ruler. See Pillow and Frame for additional materials.

GENERAL DIRECTIONS: *Preparing the Canvas:* Bind the canvas edges with masking tape to prevent raveling. Using the Needlepoint Diagrams as a guide (FIGS. 1 and 2), count off and mark on the canvas the mesh dimensions as shown. (Because the number of meshes per inch sometimes varies, be sure to count the meshes. For example, don't automatically assume that 3″ yields 30 meshes.) Draw the outline on the canvas with a ruler and waterproof marker. Then, counting the meshes inside the outline, draw the lines that form either the beaded motifs or the needlepoint design; it is not necessary to draw both.

Stitching: Working from left to right, first fill in the needlepoint areas, using the Half Cross Stitch. Leave the beaded areas blank.

Beading: (Note: Beads are often irregular in size. Once you have determined the size beads you need, separate them from the rest and put into a saucer for convenience.)

Use a fine needle and a doubled, knotted thread. Bring the needle up through the canvas as for needlepointing. String on one bead, then work a Half Cross Stitch from right to left (*opposite to needlepointing*). Continue to work the design, incorporating one bead with each stitch, and adjusting thread tension to keep beading smooth and flat. Occasionally it may be necessary to use a larger bead to cover the canvas or to drop a bead (just work the stitch without it) to keep the canvas from buckling.

Finishing:

Block: Allow to dry thoroughly. Remove from board. Machine-stitch all around the canvas as close as possible to the worked area.

FIG. 1 PILLOW

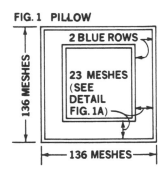

136 MESHES

2 BLUE ROWS

23 MESHES (SEE DETAIL FIG. 1A)

136 MESHES

FIG. 2 FRAME

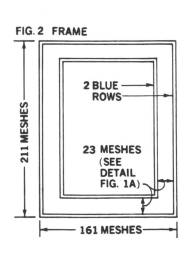

211 MESHES

2 BLUE ROWS

23 MESHES (SEE DETAIL FIG. 1A)

161 MESHES

FIG. 1A ONE QUARTER PATTERN FOR PILLOW |← DEPTH OF FRAME BORDER →|

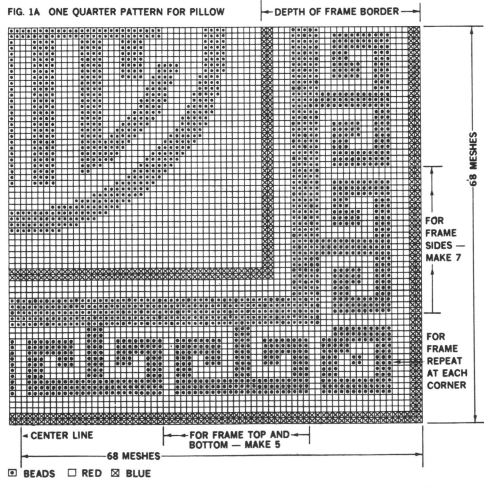

68 MESHES

FOR FRAME SIDES — MAKE 7

FOR FRAME REPEAT AT EACH CORNER

←CENTER LINE |← FOR FRAME TOP AND →| BOTTOM — MAKE 5

|← 68 MESHES →|

⊡ BEADS   ☐ RED   ⊠ BLUE

BEADED PILLOW

MATERIALS: GENERAL MATERIALS, plus #10 canvas, one 17″ square; Persian yarn, 30 yds. red, 20 yds. blue; gunmetal beads, size #8, eight clumps; blue velvet to match yarn, one 14″ square.

DIRECTIONS: Follow GENERAL DIRECTIONS for *Preparing the Canvas (using* FIG. 1), *Stitching, Beading* and *Finishing.*

Note: One-quarter of the *pillow* design is given in FIG. 1A. First mark off the meshes on the lower right quarter of the canvas; repeat for the other three quarters, turning FIG. 1A clockwise as a guide.

Finishing: Trim the unworked canvas ½″ from the line of machine-stitching. With right sides together, stitch pillow top to velvet backing in ½″ seam, around three sides and four corners, leaving an opening in the fourth side. Trim corners. Turn cover right side out; press.

For fringing, use a fine needle and a double, knotted thread. Bring needle up at seam in the center of a needlepoint stitch. String on 30 beads. Return needle to back, leaving a loop about 1″ long on the right side. Bring needle up again through the next needlepoint stitch, string on beads, return needle to back, leaving loop as before. Continue fringing all around pillow, except unseamed area.

Insert pillow stuffing through the opening; slipstitch opening. Complete fringing on this edge.

MIRROR FRAME

MATERIALS: GENERAL MATERIALS: plus No. 10 Penelope (double-thread) canvas, one piece 20″×25″; Persian yarn, 30 yds. blue and 70 yds. red; gunmetal beads, size #8, four clumps; one flat 2⅝″-wide plywood frame, ¾″ thick, with inside dimensions about 10″×15″; staple gun; ⅞″ molding, two 9 ft. strips; paint to match blue yarn; glue.
glue.

DIRECTIONS: Follow GENERAL DIRECTIONS for *Preparing the Canvas (using* FIG. 2), *Stitching, Beading and Finishing.*

Note: Borders: Use the pillow border mesh count in FIG. 1A to mark the *mirror frame* canvas, repeating the border motifs five times on the short sides of the frame and seven times on the long side, as shown on our mirror in the photo.

Finishing: Center the worked canvas, wrong side down, on the frame. With a staple gun attach the canvas to the *outer side edges* of the

frame, starting in the center of each edge and working out, and alternating from one side of frame to another until all four sides are stapled. Do not tack the corners; just tack *up to* them. Next, cut away the center of the canvas, leaving about 2″ of canvas to work with. Cut into the corners, leaving ½″ uncut. Stretch canvas and staple to the flat *inner edges* of frame, as before. At the corners, trim canvas again, leaving at least two rows in each direction; carefully staple down. There should be no unworked canvas showing on the edges. If a small amount of canvas shows at the corners, cover with a dab of thinned-down blue paint. Trim the excess canvas *slightly inside* edges.

Covering the staples: Mitering the edges, cut molding to fit the inner and outer edges of the frame. Sand and paint, taking care to cover ends, sides and a small portion of the back. Following manufacturer's directions, glue molding in place; taking care to keep glue off needlepoint. When glue is dry, paint back of frame. Insert mirror; attach hangers.

VIOLET BEADED MIRROR FRAME

MATERIALS: No. 10 Penelope canvas, 18″ × 22″; Bucilla tapestry wool (40-yd. skeins), 1 skein each Horizon Blue, Fern Green and Spring Green; Size #8 glass beads: 6 strands Light Purple G-2, 12 strands Dark Purple G-1, 1 strand Yellow; tapestry needle; sewing needle fine enough for beads to slide over; Purple sewing thread; rustproof pins or tacks; masking tape; ½″ plywood for the frame, one piece 15″ × 20″ with a 9″ × 14″ cutout in center; white fabric glue; waterproof felt-tip marking pen in a light

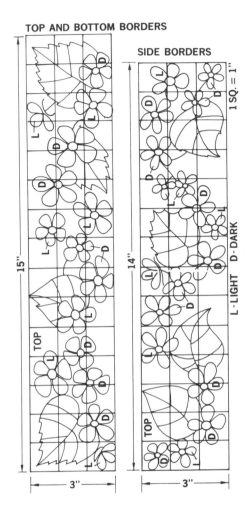

TOP AND BOTTOM BORDERS

SIDE BORDERS

1 SQ. = 1"

15"

14"

D - DARK

L - LIGHT

TOP

TOP

3"

3"

color; paint to match blue wool.

DIRECTIONS:

Center the plywood frame on the canvas; trace around the inner and outer edges to outline the canvas border area that will cover the flat part of the frame. Remove frame. In the center of the canvas border, draw free-hand flower and leaf designs, as shown in photo. *Or,* follow the directions on page 224 to enlarge the border patterns. Tape patterns to windows with strong light shining through. Center each canvas border in turn, over the correct pattern; tape in place. Trace patterns. Using the Half Cross Stitch, (*see* BASIC NEEDLEPOINT STITCHES, page 224) work the leaves, alternating light green leaves with dark veins and dark leaves with light veins. Next work the blue background area within the outlines, plus ½" beyond the outer borderline to cover the side edges of the frame. (*Note:* The canvas covering the *inner* edges of the frame need not be worked.) *Beading:* The flowers are entirely beaded. Work the yellow centers first, then the petals using light or dark purple, as indicated.

Use a fine needle and a doubled, knotted thread. Bring the needle up through the canvas as for needlepointing. String on one bead, then work a Half Cross Stitch from right to left (opposite to needlepointing). Continue to work the design, incorporating one bead with each stitch, and adjusting thread tension to keep beading smooth and flat. Occasionally it may be necessary to use a larger bead to cover the canvas or to drop a bead (just work the stitch without it) to keep the canvas from buckling. *Blocking:* Block the canvas.

Finishing:

Cut away the canvas 1½" from inner edges of worked areas; clip corners up to last row of unworked canvas (*not* to the stitching). Coat frame evenly with white glue, including inner and outer edges. Lay worked canvas over frame and press into the glue. Fold excess canvas to back of frame; glue or staple edges in place. Allow to dry thoroughly. Cover canvas on inner edges of frame completely with matching blue paint. Let dry. Install mirror or back: add screw eyes and wire.

FOOTSTOOL

Needlepoint piece measures 14" × 19", including fold allowance.

MATERIALS: Coats & Clark Red Heart® Persian-Type Needlepoint and Crewel Yarn, (pull-out skein): 18 skns Bright Green; 6 skns each Pink and Lt. Pink; 2 skns each Dark Coral, Lt. Coral and Daffodil; 1 skn White; mono canvas, 10 meshes per inch: 16" × 21" piece; 1 footstool (base measurement 9" × 14"); tapestry needle, No. 18; masking tape; paper for pattern; waterproof marker.

DIRECTIONS: Bind all edges of canvas with masking tape to prevent raveling. Following directions on page 224, enlarge design on paper. Place the design underneath the piece of canvas, centering canvas on design. With waterproof marker, trace design on canvas. Using a full strand (3 ply) yarn, cut into 24″ working lengths. Work in Half Cross Stitch throughout. Following Color Key on diagram, work extra rows with Bright Green only around each piece, so that needlepoint piece measures 14″ × 19″.
Finishing: Block to measurements. Leave pinned until completely dry. Trim excess canvas. Place needlepoint cover over padded top of footstool and staple in place underneath, pulling in corners to fit.

NOTE: WORK ALL SIMILAR PARTS ON CHART IN SAME COLORS AS INDICATED.
COLOR KEY: BACKGROUND - 064 BRIGHT GREEN   3 - 865 LT. PINK   5 - 852 LIGHT CORAL
2 - 860 PINK   4 - 044 DAFFODIL   6 - 282 DARK CORAL

POSY SLING CHAIR

MATERIALS: Samsonite Body Glove Folding Sling Chair; 3-ply tapestry wool in the following colors and amounts: ½ ounce each dark blue, light green, dark green and yellow, 1 ounce light blue; size 18 tapestry needle; thimble; Scotchgard® fabric protector; white paper for pattern.
DIRECTIONS: Following directions on page

224, enlarge pattern onto white paper. Transfer the design onto the sling (it will easily slide off

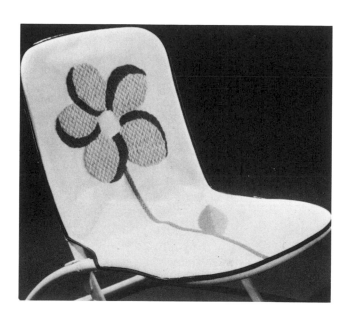

the frame.) To needlepoint, be sure to work with one hand between the layers to prevent catching the back of the sling. Using a thimble, work the design as follows: Yellow and dark blue, Basketweave Stitch.
Note: Do *not* use a Continental Stitch as it will stretch the canvas out of shape); light blue, Diamond Stitch; dark green, Brick Stitch; light green, Horizontal Brick Stitch. When design is finished, carefully clip all loose threads and spray front of chair with Scotchgard®. Replace sling on frame.

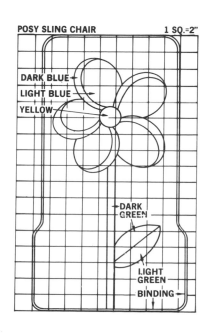

POSY SLING CHAIR   1 SQ.=2″
DARK BLUE
LIGHT BLUE
YELLOW
DARK GREEN
LIGHT GREEN
BINDING

PLASTIC PICTURE FRAMES

For a quick project we suggest 5″ × 7″ clear plastic box frames to enclose photo mats worked in Continental Stitch. Use plastic "canvas" which doesn't fray or require blocking. Create your own designs, using four-ply yarn. We added French Knot buds and Straight Stitch greens (*see* BASIC EMBROIDERY STITCHES, page 228) over the needlepoint for the cat.

PICTURE MATS

These mats are designed to be used with inexpensive plastic box frames, available in all dime stores. Our mats will accommodate standard size photographic prints; to vary them to fit other sizes, see directions following.

Blue/white lace-trimmed mat: Measures 8″ × 10″—inside opening is 4″ × 6″.

Plaid mat: Measures 8″ × 10″—inside opening is 3¾″ × 5¾″.

Rainbow mat: Measures 5″ × 7″—inside opening is 2″ × 2¾″.

MATERIALS: Columbia-Minerva Needlepoint FashionEase canvas (one sheet will be enough for one 8″ × 10″ mat and one smaller mat); Columbia-Minerva Nantuk 4-ply yarn, or any leftover 4-ply yarn in colors of your choice; single-edged razor blade; 3 yds. Wright Venice edging #181-6402, white (for blue/white lace-trimmed mat).

DIRECTIONS: Using charts as guides, mark outer and inner borders of mats on canvas with permanent marking pen (*Note:* all inside openings of mat are centered on canvas except opening in rainbow mat, which is 1½″ from top, 2¾″ from bottom.) Use canvas count, *not measurements*, for accuracy. Carefully cut on markings with razor blade. Trim inside opening to get a smooth edge. Work needlepoint as indicated in

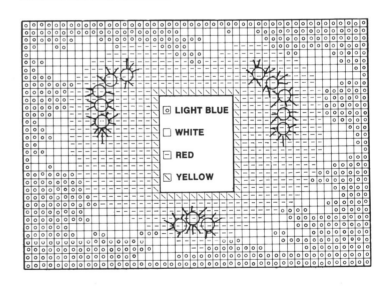

◉ LIGHT BLUE
☐ WHITE
⊟ RED
◺ YELLOW

◉ PALE GREEN
◩ PALE GREEN ◹ BEIGE ⊞ PINK ◉ LIGHT BLUE
◈ EMERALD GREEN ⊡ BEIGE ◎ PINK ☐ WHITE

¼ DESIGNS SHOWN

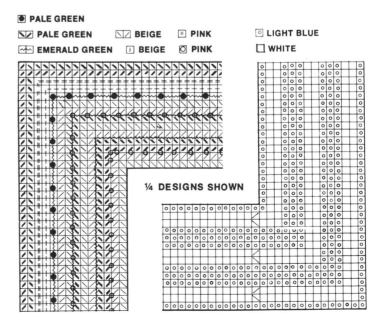

Color photo on page 130

charts in continental stitch, with details on heart mat in French knots and straight stitches (*see* BASIC EMBROIDERY STITCHES, page 228). Also, narrow lace can be glued over needlepoint strips as shown on blue and white mat. Since canvas is plastic, finished mats will not need blocking.

To adjust mats to fit other size pictures: Select the picture and mat design you plan to use. Mark outer border as before. Center your picture within outer border; trace around picture. Draw inner border two threads in from tracing marks. Cut on inner and outer borders. For large picture, eliminate as many rows of design as necessary. For smaller picture, add extra rows of needlepoint.

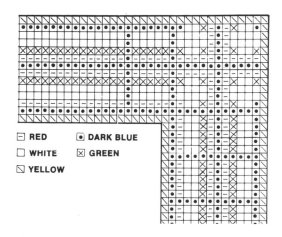

☐ RED   ⊡ DARK BLUE
☐ WHITE   ☒ GREEN
◫ YELLOW

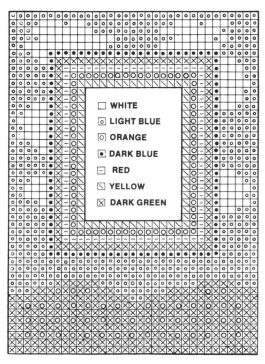

☐ WHITE
⊡ LIGHT BLUE
◎ ORANGE
⬛ DARK BLUE
⊟ RED
◫ YELLOW
☒ DARK GREEN

TENNIS RACQUET COVERS

MATERIALS: Each of these designs requires the following materials: 15″ × 20″ piece of No. 5 Penelope (double thread) canvas; masking tape; brown paper; tapestry needle; light-color waterproof felt marker; ¾ yd. white cotton fabric (for lining and backing of cover) such as duck, Indian Head, sailcloth or linen; white thread; 14″ zipper; 2 yds. of 1″-wide white cotton folded braid; wool rug yarn (in yards): *Butterfly Design:* 5 yds. Yellow, 7 Green, 4 Orange, 3 Red, 46 White; *Floral Design:* 33 yds. Blue, 2 Gold, 2 Dark Orange, 2 Light Orange, 11 Yellow, 20 White; *Zigzag Design:* 46 yds. Green, 23 White.

DIRECTIONS: Two of these attractive tennis racquet covers are worked in speedy Quickpoint, a combination of the Half Cross Stitch, which is worked from left to right, and the Continental Stitch, which is worked from right to left. This eliminates turning canvas at end of every row. *Preparing the Canvas:* Bind the canvas edges with masking tape to prevent raveling. Lay the head of your tennis racquet on a piece of brown paper. Trace the outline of the head and 2″ down throat of the handle. To allow for the thickness of the frame, draw a second line ¼″ outside the first line. Or, if you have a knife-edge cover that fits your racquet, trace around it, drawing a second line ¼″ outside the tracing line. Cut out pattern around second line. With felt marker, trace the pattern onto the canvas (marking area to be worked).

Transferring the Butterfly Design: Use the graph as a guide for size and for the number of meshes needed to make the butterfly motif. Outline the motifs on your canvas with felt marker, using the photo as a guide for placement. Quickpoint the butterflies first, then fill in the traced outline with the background color.

Transferring the Floral Design: With a felt marker, draw floral motifs freehand on the canvas, using the photo as guide for design and placement. Quickpoint the flowers first, then fill in the traced outline with background color.

Zigzag Design (work completely in Continental Stitch): Starting at the top edge of the traced outline, use the felt marker to mark *only* the green lines on the canvas, counting off the spaces as shown in the Detail Graph. Work the white (unmarked) meshes first, following the zigzag pattern the full length of canvas, then fill in remaining area with green.

Lay the needlepoint on the racket head. The worked area should extend ¼″ beyond the edge of the frame. (Work additional rows, if needed.)

Blocking the Canvas: Block. Allow needlepoint to dry thoroughly. Remove from board. Machine-stitch around the worked area. Trim away the excess canvas, leaving ½″ for seam allowance.

Sewing the Cover: Cut three pieces of white backing fabric the same size and shape as the trimmed canvas. To line the canvas, machine-baste one piece to the back of the canvas in the seam allowance. Machine-baste the other two backing pieces together. With *wrong* sides together, stitch the lined canvas to the doubled backing, with the canvas side up, leaving 17″

BUTTERFLY DESIGNS

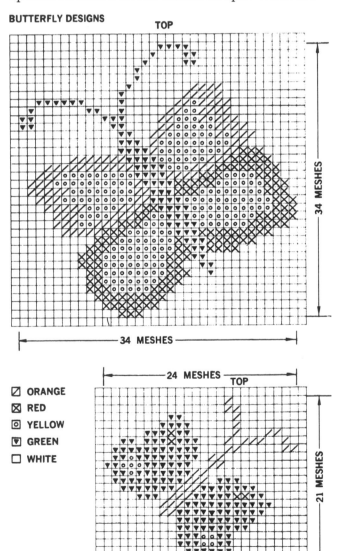

TOP

34 MESHES

34 MESHES

24 MESHES

TOP

21 MESHES

- ◩ ORANGE
- ⊠ RED
- ⊡ YELLOW
- ▽ GREEN
- ☐ WHITE

DETAIL GRAPH OF ZIGZAG DESIGN

☐ WHITE   ▲ GREEN   PARTIAL PATTERN

unstitched on one side edge. Stitch as close as possible to the outside row of needlepoint stitches so the canvas won't show at the seam. Using a zipper foot, insert and stitch the zipper at the upper end of the 17″ opening, with the edges of the zipper tapes ¼″ in from the fabric edges. Enclose *all* edges with the braid, stitching the edges of the braid along seam line. Sew a snap fastener to bottom corner of opening.

BARGELLO BELTS

MATERIALS: No. 14 mono (single thread) canvas; odds and ends of knitting worsted in three compatible colors; silk-like lining fabric; buckle.

DIRECTIONS: Both His and Her belts are made with the same Bargello pattern, (*see* Diagram), in which the vertical stitches cover two, four or six horizontal threads (the center line of each diamond shape covers eight threads—four threads in two colors). Cut a piece of canvas 3½″ wide by your waistline measurement, plus 2″ turn-under for each end. Our belt measures 2½″ wide plus ½″ turn-under on each long side (3½″ total). For this motif, it takes three full rows and two half-rows (one at top and one at bottom) to cover the 2½″ of worked canvas. To make it

easier to keep the pattern straight, fold the canvas in half lengthwise and draw a pencil line in the horizontal mesh at that point, from end to end (see center mesh in Diagram). Work a "tracking row" of the diamond motif the full length of the canvas, using the pencil line as a guide. Then work the meshes above and below this row to fill in the remaining rows, using the color key as a suggestion.

Finishing: Sew a 3½″ by belt-length piece of lining fabric to one long side with a ½″ seam, rolling the last row of needlepoint so the canvas doesn't show. Turn under canvas and lining on opposite side and whipstitch the opening. Whipstitch ends of belt; add buckles.

Color photo on page 130

AMERICAN INDIAN IRIS MOTIF BELT AND NECKPIECE

Directions are given for Belt to measure approximately 3″ × 34″ and Neckpiece to measure approximately 4½″ × 5″.

MATERIALS: Columbia-Minerva Crewel Yarn (see chart for colors and yardage); heavy cardboard; scissors; masking tape; needle; small hole puncher or manicure scissors.

Belt: 10 mesh mono-interlocking canvas, 6″ × 36″; black felt, cut 1¼″ larger in both directions than finished needlepoint for ⅝″ seam allowances.

Neckpiece: 10 mesh mono-interlocking canvas, 7¼″ × 8″; white felt, cut 1¼″ larger in both directions than finished needlepoint for ⅝″ seam allowances; 1 piece red silk cording, 36″ long.

Note: The following directions indicate sufficient yardage to complete the items using the Continental Stitch. If other stitches are used, you may not have enough yarn to complete the items.

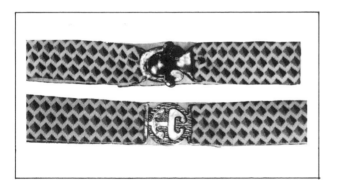

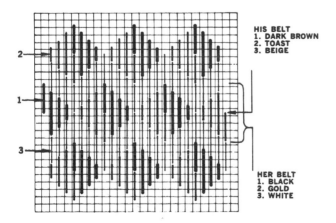

HIS BELT
1. DARK BROWN
2. TOAST
3. BEIGE

HER BELT
1. BLACK
2. GOLD
3. WHITE

GENERAL DIRECTIONS: *Color Pattern Chart:*
For many designs, the easiest and most accurate method of working is to follow a Color Pattern Chart. Keep in mind that each square on the Chart represents one stitch on the canvas. The method of counting stitches is your guarantee of a perfect copy of the design. Both designs are worked in the Continental Stitch throughout. The Color Pattern Chart shows yarn colors used in each part of the design. Each square on the Chart equals one stitch on your canvas. Colors are indicated by symbols.
Transferring the Design: Following directions on page 224, enlarge the pattern onto white paper. (The belt pattern is only half the design. "Flop" the pattern to obtain complete design.) Tape the pattern to a window with strong light shining through. Center the canvas over the pattern; tape in place. With waterproof marking pen, trace the pattern onto the canvas. Remove pattern and canvas from window. Bind canvas edges with masking tape to prevent raveling.
Sorting the Yarn: Refer to the Color Pattern Chart for the number of yards of each color. For easier selection of colors while working, cut a series of 1½″ slits across an edge of heavy cardboard for each yarn color. Draw color symbol above each slit and thread the corresponding color yarn through. This method will allow

BELT

COLOR NAME	NO. OF YARDS	REFERENCE NUMBER
▲ RED-ORANGE	13	R-50
⊡ MUSTARD	5	427
⊠ FOREST GREEN	44	528
◉ TURQUOISE	8	738
▣ BLACK	13	050
☐ GRAY	56	186

ORNAMENT

COLOR NAME	NO. OF YARDS	REFERENCE NUMBER
▲ RED	4	R10
△ ORANGE	4	424
◹ YELLOW	4	450
◼ NAVY	4	365
◱ BLUE	4	752
☐ WHITE	8	005
⊠ GOLD THREAD	14	GOLD CAMELOT

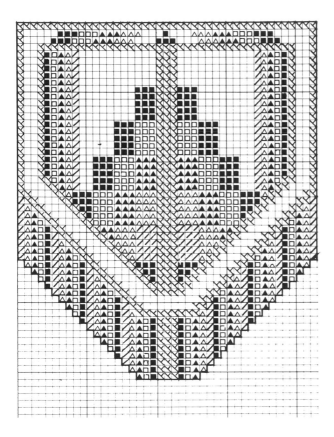

you to choose the correct color yarn as you stitch.

Cutting the Yarn: Cut lengths to about 18″, as longer pieces may fray. (*Note:* The yarn is a loosely twisted 3-ply yarn. Separate and work 2-ply throughout. Use a single strand of gold thread when working design.)

BELT:

The chart for the belt is half the design. After stitching the motifs on one half the belt, turn the chart upside down to work the second half of the pattern.

Working Motifs: Begin the first motif 2″ from the top and 3″ from the upper right corner of the canvas as indicated by the letter "A" on the Chart, using black yarn. Carefully count the stitches on the chart to work the motif. Continue in a similar manner to work all five motifs.

Hole Punching: Use hole puncher or manicure scissors to make each of the six holes for the belt ties as follows: Center holes—⅞″ from the center green bar of the first and last motifs on each end, indicated by the letter "C". Top and bottom holes—position top hole one inch above center hole and bottom hole one inch below center hole, indicated by letters "B" and "D." "D".

Working Background: Work background in

Gray yarn. Be sure there are the same number of stitches of Gray on the extreme left and right sides of the belt.

Border: Work border in Forest Green, three rows on each of the four sides of the belt.

NECKPIECE:

The chart for the neckpiece is completed as is.

Center Column: Find center row of the canvas. Working with Gold thread, stitch 3 stitches across, 1¼″ from the top of the canvas. Continue center Gold column as indicated on Chart for 34 rows.

Design: Work design on each side of center column, leaving White for last. Work inner border in Gold.

Top: Directly above Gold column, work the Navy yarn and then work outward on each side to finish top of design. Continue working center border in White.

Bottom: Work three rows again in Gold at center bottom. Work colored yarn outward to edges.

Sides and Top: Embroider last rows of Gold above stripes, on the sides and on the top to complete the neckpiece.

Blocking: Block belt and neckpiece. Leave on board until thoroughly dry. If removed while damp, canvas will revert to its original shape.

Finishing:

Belt: Pin needlepoint and fabric together with right sides facing. Baste and then machine stitch around three sides. Turn right side out, then slipstitch closed. Be sure sides are securely sewn. Stitch edges of holes to felt using green sewing thread and tiny stitches. Then thread a 3-ply, yard length of Forest Green yarn through each hole. Bring yarn through only halfway, make all ends the same length. Gather all strands together and make a knot close to the belt. Make an additional knot at the ends of each pair of 3-ply lengths of yarn. Trim excess, if any.

Neckpiece: Pin needlepoint and fabric back together with right sides facing. Baste and then machine stitch around sides and bottom. Turn right side out, then slipstitch closed. Be sure sides are securely sewn. Tie a knot at one end of the red cording. Stitch the knot to the side at the top corner, using red thread and tiny stitches to attach the cording. Measure desired length and make a second knot, trim any excess, and attach to second side in a similar manner.

(*Note:* Dry clean only.)

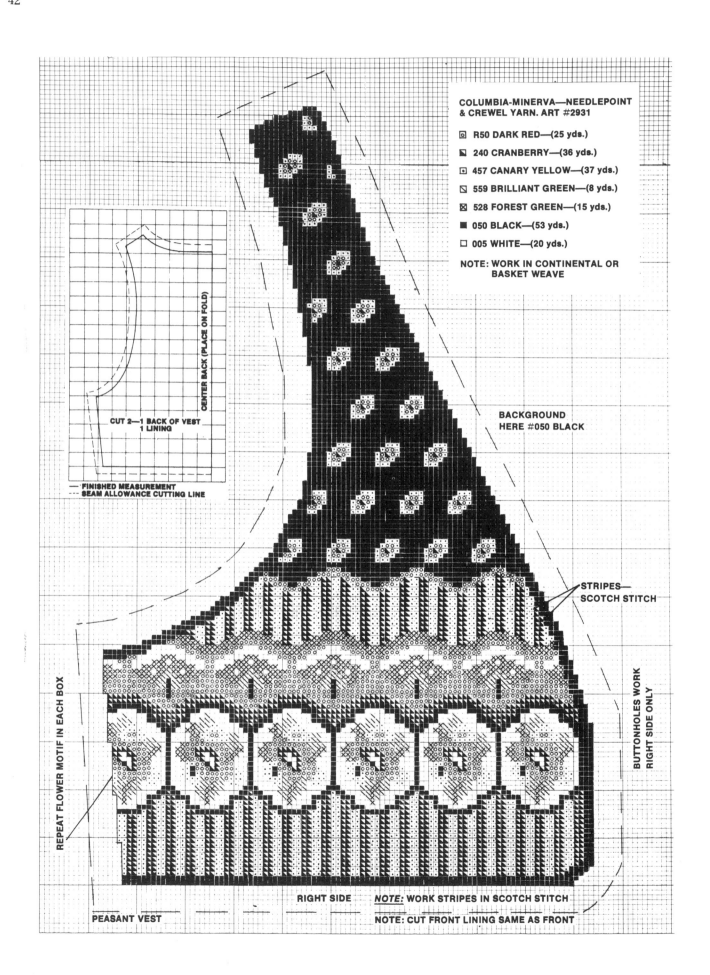

COLUMBIA-MINERVA—NEEDLEPOINT
& CREWEL YARN. ART #2931

- ⊡ R50 DARK RED—(25 yds.)
- ◪ 240 CRANBERRY—(36 yds.)
- ⊡ 457 CANARY YELLOW—(37 yds.)
- ◩ 559 BRILLIANT GREEN—(8 yds.)
- ⊠ 528 FOREST GREEN—(15 yds.)
- ■ 050 BLACK—(53 yds.)
- □ 005 WHITE—(20 yds.)

NOTE: WORK IN CONTINENTAL OR
BASKET WEAVE

CENTER BACK (PLACE ON FOLD)

CUT 2—1 BACK OF VEST
1 LINING

— FINISHED MEASUREMENT
--- SEAM ALLOWANCE CUTTING LINE

BACKGROUND
HERE #050 BLACK

STRIPES—
SCOTCH STITCH

REPEAT FLOWER MOTIF IN EACH BOX

BUTTONHOLES WORK
RIGHT SIDE ONLY

RIGHT SIDE   *NOTE:* WORK STRIPES IN SCOTCH STITCH

PEASANT VEST

NOTE: CUT FRONT LINING SAME AS FRONT

Color photo on page 132

VEST

MATERIALS: No. 10 mesh needlepoint canvas, ½ yard; 1 yard fabric for back of vest and lining; 4 buttons, ½"; Columbia-Minerva Needlepoint and Crewel Yarn (wool); 25 yards Dark Red, 36 yards Cranberry, 37 yards Canary, 8 yards Brilliant Green, 15 yards Forest Green, 53 yards Black, 20 yards White.

(*Note:* Work in continental or basketweave stitch; stripes in scotch stitch.)

DIRECTIONS: Following directions on page 224, enlarge vest pattern and transfer to canvas reversing pattern for left front. Stitch. Follow graph for stitching and details. Work right side first and do the buttonholes as marked. (*Note:* First outline the vest entirely with a row of black so you have a guideline for stitching.) Work left side to correspond to right side. Block each piece. Once pieces are blocked, cut out each one, allowing ½" seam allowance all around. In fabric, cut out fronts to correspond to needlepoint fronts, allowing ½" seam allowance. Following directions on page 224, enlarge and cut out 2 backs (one for back of vest, one for lining). Join shoulder seams of outside of vest and lining. With right sides of vest and lining facing each other, stitch around neckline and fronts and around armholes. Use needlepoint side as guide for stitching and stitch just inside of last stitched row so no canvas shows when it's turned under. Turn under, press and join side seams. Fold back hem of vest and lining; slipstitch by hand. Cut and finish buttonholes on lining. Sew on buttons.

TOYS

GENERAL MATERIALS FOR ALL TOYS (*additional materials, as well as specific quantities of canvas and yarn, are given under each toy*): Large sheet of wrapping paper; ruler; compass; black waterproof marker; masking tape; Coat's and Clark 4-strand knitting worsted, 1 large skein for the predominant colors and small skeins or leftover knitting worsted in the remaining colors; tapestry needle; No. 10 canvas, 36" wide; steam iron; rustproof pins or tacks; kapok or other stuffing material.

GENERAL DIRECTIONS

1. *To Enlarge the Pattern:* On heavy brown paper, measure off, draw and cut a square or rectangle of the canvas size specified on each pattern piece you use (*see* FIGS. 1 to 19). Draw another square or rectangle 2" inside the first; draw crisscross lines, vertically and horizontally, 1" apart in the inner shape. Then, copy our pattern, 1 square at a time, using a ruler and compass. Darken the *pattern* lines with a black waterproof marking pen. (In the unlined 2" border all around, the canvas is *not* worked, and this unworked area is not shown in Figs. 1 to 19).

2. *To Transfer the Patterns:* For each pattern piece, trace and cut 1 (or more, as needed) canvas piece in the same size as the brown paper pattern; pin to pattern right side. With pattern at the back, tape to a windowpane with a good deal of light shining through. With waterproof marking pen, trace *design lines only* onto the canvas. Set pattern aside; you will use it later when blocking the finished needlepoint. With masking tape, bind canvas edges to prevent raveling.

3. *Needlepointing:* Work the designs in the

Color photo on page 132

FIG. 1   CAR PATTERN — FIRST SIDE
        CANVAS SIZE 14½" x 22½"

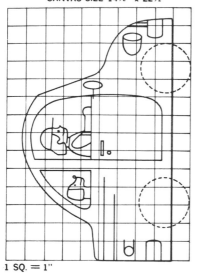

1 SQ. = 1"

FIG. 2   CAR PATTERN — SECOND SIDE
        CANVAS SIZE 14½" x 22½"

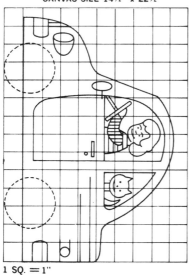

1 SQ. = 1"

FIG. 3   WHEEL FOR CAR AND SCHOOL
        BUS — CANVAS SIZE 8" x 8"

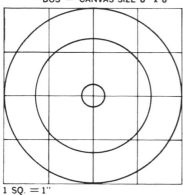

1 SQ. = 1"

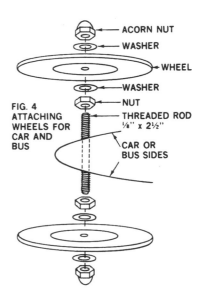

ACORN NUT
WASHER
WHEEL
WASHER
NUT
THREADED ROD
⅛" x 2½"
CAR OR
BUS SIDES

FIG. 4
ATTACHING
WHEELS FOR
CAR AND
BUS

FIG. 4A ALTERNATE WHEEL
        ATTACHMENT FOR
        CAR AND BUS

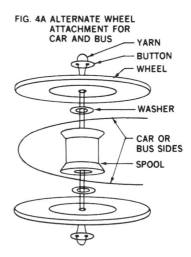

YARN
BUTTON
WHEEL
WASHER
CAR OR
BUS SIDES
SPOOL

Continental Stitch in colors shown in the photos on page 226. Work all the black outlines and black areas first, then the predominant colors, then the remaining colors.

4. *Blocking:* Block the canvas. Allow needlepoint to dry thoroughly. Remove from board. Machine-stitch around the canvas as close as possible to the needlepoint. Trim canvas 1″ from stitching line. Fold unworked canvas to back; tape down.

5. *Assembling:* Unless Directions for each toy indicate otherwise, use the Binding Stitch to join front and back pieces, leaving bottom edge open 3″ for stuffing. Stuff to desired plumpness; stitch opening. Sew limbs and ears to animal bodies with an overhand stitch.

SMALL CAR

MATERIALS (*see* GENERAL MATERIALS): Canvas, one 21″ × 36″ piece; yarn in these colors: Red, Black, Blue, Gray, White, Light Pink, Yellow, Pink, Green, Brown, Light Brown; white glue; four 4″ squares each of Black felt and cardboard; ½″-diameter Red beads, 2 for taillights; items for attaching wheels (*see* FIGS. 4 *or* 4A); ice pick or other punching tool.

DIRECTIONS: Enlarge the pattern pieces (*see* FIGS. 1-3), following GENERAL DIRECTIONS Step 1. Then follow Steps 2-5, with this exception: In Step 5, *do not* tape the unworked canvas border of wheels to the back of the canvas.
Making and Attaching Wheels (*see* FIGS. 4-4A): Cut Black felt and cardboard circles ⅛″ smaller than the worked area of the wheels. Center cardboard circle on wrong side of needlepoint wheel; fold unworked canvas border over cardboard and tape in place. Glue felt circle to wheel back. Attach wheels, using FIGS. 4 or 4A. If child is apt to unscrew rod, use thread-button method. Sew bead taillights on car back.

LADY BUNNY

MATERIALS (*see* GENERAL MATERIALS): Canvas, one 36″ × 48″ piece; yarn in these colors: Purple, Pink, Black, Orange, Tan, Yellow, Lavender, Dark Pink, White, Brown, Green and Blue; 2 small buttons; lining fabric for basket, one 6″ × 6″ piece.
DIRECTIONS: Enlarge pattern pieces (*see* FIGS. 5-11), following GENERAL DIRECTIONS, Step 1. Then follow Steps 2-5 with these exceptions: In Step 5, join ears around sides and top only; leave bottom open. Do not stuff. Leave

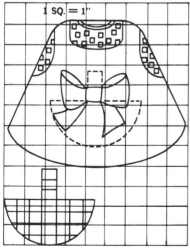

FIG. 5 BUNNY BODY FRONT AND BACK
CANVAS SIZE 11½″ x 13″

1 SQ. = 1″

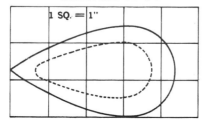

FIG. 6 BASKET FOR BUNNY FRONT
CANVAS SIZE 8″ x 8″

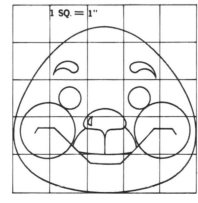

FIG. 7 BUNNY HEAD FRONT
BACK BLANK
CANVAS SIZE 8½″ x 9½″

1 SQ. = 1″

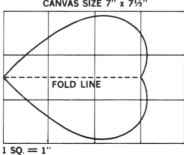

FIG. 10 BUNNY EARS FRONT
BACK BLANK
CANVAS SIZE 6½″ x 8½″

1 SQ. = 1″

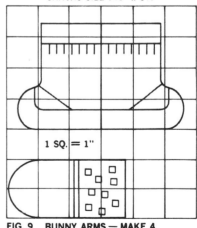

FIG. 8 BUNNY LEGS — MAKE 2
CANVAS SIZE 7½″ x 9½″

1 SQ. = 1″

FIG. 9 BUNNY ARMS — MAKE 4
CANVAS SIZE 6″ x 7″

FIG. 11 CARROTS
CANVAS SIZE 7″ x 7½″

FOLD LINE

1 SQ. = 1″

FIG. 12 TEDDY BEAR BODY
FRONT AND BACK
CANVAS SIZE 9¼" x 10½"

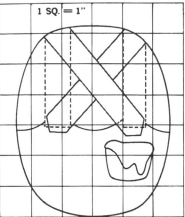

1 SQ. = 1"

FOR FRONT, OMIT POCKET, MAKE
SUSPENDERS STRAIGHT AS SHOWN
BY DOTTED LINES

FIG. 13 TEDDY BEAR HEAD FRONT
BACK BLANK
CANVAS SIZE 8¼" x 8½"

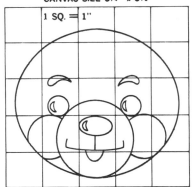

1 SQ. = 1"

FIG. 14 TEDDY BEAR EARS ACTUAL SIZE
CUT TWO FROM FELT

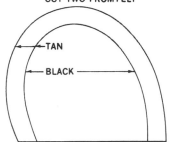

TAN

BLACK

FIG. 15 TEDDY BEAR LEG—MAKE 4
CANVAS SIZE 6½" x 6¾"

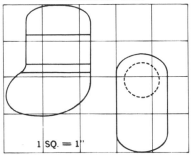

1 SQ. = 1"

FIG. 16 TEDDY BEAR ARM FRONT
BACK BLANK
CANVAS SIZE 5½" x 6½"

FIG. 17 SCHOOL BUS FIRST SIDE
CANVAS SIZE 14½" x 22½"

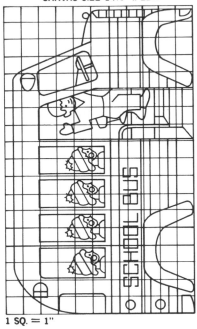

1 SQ. = 1"

FIG. 18 SCHOOL BUS DOOR
CANVAS 7" x 13"

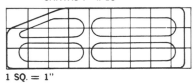

1 SQ. = 1"

FIG. 19 SCHOOL BUS SECOND SIDE
CANVAS SIZE 14½" x 22½"

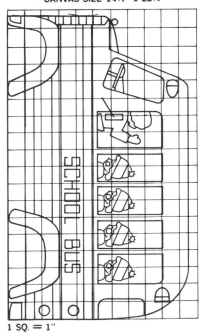

1 SQ. = 1"

openings for ears in top of head. Insert ears; sew in place.

To Make Pompon Tail: Wrap yarn about 25 times around a 2″ cardboard. Tie strands together at one end; cut through strands at other end. Trim yarns to round off the pompon; fluff up and sew in place on back.

Finishing: Basket: line with fabric. Slipstitch in place on front of doll as indicated by broken line in FIG. 5. Stuff carrots; sew on Green yarn stalks. Slip into pocket. Sew *buttons* in place on shoe straps.

TEDDY BEAR

MATERIALS (*see* GENERAL DIRECTIONS): Canvas, one 24″ × 36″ piece; yarn in these colors: Blue, Brown, Pink, White, Black and Red; 16″ of yellow string; 4 buttons, ½″ in diameter; Red and White check ribbon, 9″; Brown and Black felt scraps for the ears.

DIRECTIONS: Enlarge pattern pieces (*see figs. 12-16, following* GENERAL DIRECTIONS Step 1). Then follow Steps 2-5, with these exceptions: Cut ear pieces from felt and glue together. In Step 5, when joining front and back, leave openings for ears in top of head. Insert ears in openings; sew in place.

Finishing: Sew buttons on suspender ends. Sew yellow strings on shoes to look like laces. Attach ribbon bow at neck. Make pompon (*see* DIRECTIONS *for* LADY BUNNY). Sew in place on back.

SCHOOL BUS

MATERIALS (*see* GENERAL MATERIALS): Canvas, 1 piece, 31″ × 36″; yarn in these colors: Yellow, Gray, White, Black, Blue, Red, Pink, Green, Purple, Brown, Gold; Black felt, 1 piece 3½″ × 9″; white glue; eight ½″-diameter Red beads for taillights and warning lights; items for attaching wheels (*see* Figs. 4 *or* 4A); Gold button for radiator cap.

DIRECTIONS: Enlarge the pattern pieces (*see figs.* 17-19, *following* GENERAL DIRECTIONS Steps 1-5).

Finishing: Glue black felt, cut to fit the back of the door. Sew door in place. Sew radiator cap and red lights in place. Attach wheels, following DIRECTIONS for SMALL CAR.

CHRISTMAS STOCKINGS

MATERIALS: *For each stocking:* One piece of needlepoint canvas, 26″ × 15″; masking tape to bind canvas edges and for securing pattern; approximately 4 oz. assorted color yarn; tapes-

try needle; waterproof felt-tip marker in a neutral color (if it's too light you will have difficulty seeing it, and if it's too dark it will show through your stitching) or acrylic paints and brush (sold in needlework shops); ⅝ yd. red wool flannel for stocking back; ¾ yd. calico print for lining; rustproof tacks or pushpins; a piece of brown wrapping paper same size as pattern; 6″ square of cardboard for making tassel; about 12 yards of red or white yarn for making tassel; regular sewing needle and thread to attach tassel to stocking.

DIRECTIONS:

Transferring the Pattern: Begin by working out an arrangement of the name or initials you plan to use with a pencil in the blank section at the top. Use our lettering (see page 48) as a guide or use stencils or do your own freehand. The straighter the edges, the easier to embroider. Line up your letters with the lines of mesh on the canvas. When you are satisfied with the arrangement, draw it on the pattern in bold lines.

Then place the pattern on a flat, even surface (such as an ironing board) and place the needlepoint canvas over it, centering the stocking outline. Tape or pin corners of both to keep them from shifting. Using a waterproof, felt-tip marker, trace pattern onto canvas. If desired, fill in areas of color with acrylic paint and allow to dry thoroughly, preferably overnight.

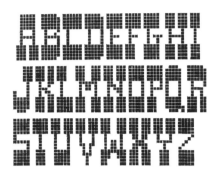

Stitching: Use either a Half Cross-Stitch (use only on Penelope canvas) or a Continental Stitch. Work in rows, filling in first the motifs and then background colors.

Note: On the Angel design, her eyelashes are embroidered in Straight Stitch (*see* **BASIC EMBROIDERY STITCHES**, page 228), after all needlepoint has been completed.

Blocking: Block the canvas. Let needlepoint dry thoroughly while flat (do not stand upright). If pressing is necessary, cover needlepoint with damp cloth and press on the wrong side with a warm iron.

Finishing: Remove the blocked needlepoint from the board. Machine or securely hand-stitch all around the needlepoint section of the canvas as close as possible to the worked area without overlapping onto it. Repeat this twice around the entire shape. Cut canvas 1″ larger than stitched stocking shape.

Cut red flannel to the same size. With right sides of fabric and needlepoint together (toes in the same direction), machine or hand-stitch together except for the opening at the top. Clip flannel seam allowance to ¼″ and canvas to ½″. Turn stocking right-side out.

Lining: From any cotton print or calico fabric, make a separate stocking ¼″ smaller all around than the outline from the original needlepoint pattern. Insert into needlepoint stocking. At top opening, turn all raw edges under and whipstitch together.

Tassel: Wrap yarn around a 6″ square of cardboard 30 times. Cut a 10″ length and slide under yarn at one edge of cardboard; pull tightly and knot yarn. Cut yarn at opposite edge and remove cardboard. Wind another 10″ length of yarn 1″ down from the top knot and tie in place, bringing ends inside the head, then down through the tassel. Trim ends to even off. Secure tassel to stocking as shown and add on a loop of yarn for hanging.

Fill with goodies and enjoy for years to come.

BARGELLO RUG

Finished size approximately 36″ × 51″.

MATERIALS: 1⅔ yds. 40″-wide #4 double mesh rug canvas; Paternayan Pat-Rug yarn: 2 lbs. Navy, ¾ lb. Red, ¾ lb. Cream, heavy tapestry needle; ruler; indelible marker. (For optional lining: 1½ yds. linen or burlap; 5 yds. 1¼″ rug

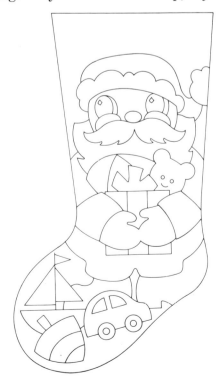

Color photo on page 132.

binding tape; strong thread.)

DIRECTIONS: Unroll canvas over a flat surface and steam it lightly. Let it dry and machine stitch or tape edges to prevent ravelling.

(*Note about counting on canvas:* Vertically, count canvas threads because the stitches are worked *over* counted threads. Horizontally, count canvas *spaces* because the stitches are *placed* in the spaces *between* the vertical canvas threads.) *All stitches are worked over four canvas threads with two strands of yarn.* Using the diagram as a guide, draw the six squares and the borders on the *threads* of the canvas. Center and stitch the patterns within the squares, following the stitch diagrams and the photo. Work stitches softly and guide the yarn so the strands lie side by side for better coverage. Work without knots and allow at least 2″ of tail end at the beginning and end of each strand of yarn, to be woven into the back later. Trim away the canvas four threads away from the large outer border. Fold back canvas on thread line of outside edge, matching canvas squares carefully; press with fingers to create a sharp edge. Clip and miter the corners and machine or hand stitch all around. After stitching, work all borders in brick stitch, through both layers of canvas where necessary. With a double strand of navy yarn, overcast the last thread around the edge, working extra stitches at corners if necessary to be sure they are covered.

Finishing: If too many canvas threads show through or if the rug is too rigid, soften it by dipping it in warm water. (Half fill a bathtub with very warm water, dissolve ½ cup salt and soak the rug for five minutes.) Drain out the water and place the rug on the bathroom floor over a thick layer of newspapers on a plastic sheet. Straighten borders, but do not pull or pin down. Change newspapers every day until the rug is completely dry. Lining is optional. An unlined rug will hang better and will be easier to repair. If you wish, line rug with linen or burlap mitered and folded to be 1″ smaller all around than rug. Pin and baste wrong sides together and slipstitch with strong thread. Add 1¼″ rug binding tape all around the edge and slipstitch; binding should not show from right side of rug. Run a few lines of large basting stitches across the lining at regular intervals, catching some of the stitches in the rug. This will prevent the lining from ballooning.

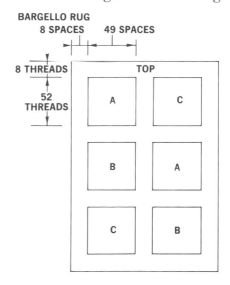

BARGELLO RUG

8 SPACES   49 SPACES

8 THREADS   TOP

52 THREADS

A	C
B	A
C	B

BARGELLO RUG - STITCH A

BARGELLO RUG - STITCH B

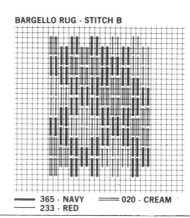

BARGELLO RUG - STITCH C

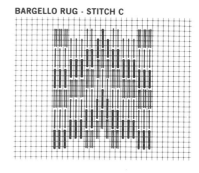

━━ 365 - NAVY   ═══ 020 - CREAM
━━ 233 - RED

COVER DESIGN

Finished size: 11″ × 14½″ (Note: directions are for front cover only.)

MATERIALS: No. 10 mono canvas, 15″ × 18½″; masking tape; size 18 tapestry needle; permanent ink felt-tipped marker; paper for pattern; 3-ply DMC Persian yarns in the following colors and amounts (1 skein= 5.4 yards): Bright Yellow, 6 skeins; Light Yellow, 4 yards; Pale Yellow, 3 yards; Yellow, 5 yards; Orange Yellow, 5 yards; White, 2 skeins; Light Grey, 4 yards; Dark Grey, 1 yard; Navy Blue, 6 skeins; Light Blue, 3 skeins; Medium Blue, 4 yards; Royal Blue, 4 yards; Blue, 4 yards; Bright Red, 2 skeins; Red Orange, 8 yards; Deep Red, 4 yards; Pink, 4 yards; Flesh, 3 yards; Bright Red Purple, 5 yards; Bright Deep Red Purple, 8 yards; Bright Lilac, 3 skeins; Deep Purple, 4 yards; Bright Green, 1 skein; Light Olive Green, 3 skeins; Deep Olive Green, 2 skeins; Brown, 3 yards.

DIRECTIONS: Following directions on page 224, enlarge pattern onto white paper. Tape edge of canvas. Mark 11″ × 14½″ outline on canvas, leaving a 2″ border on each side for finishing. Position pattern under canvas, centering it in the outline. Trace design onto canvas with felt-tipped marker. (Substitute your own saying for title, using alphabet on page 224.) Work the design with 3 strands of yarn, using stitch diagram as a guide for continental, bargello, French knots and mosaic stitches, and using cover as a color guide. Block. Finish as desired.

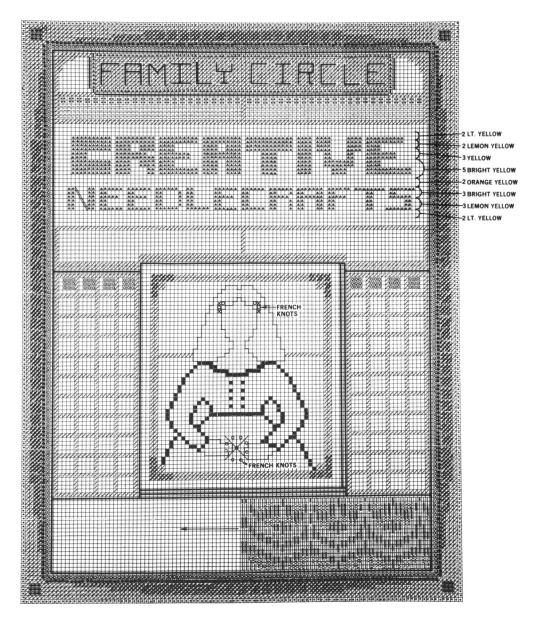

EMBROIDERY

CROSS-STITCH SIGNS

With seven-squares-to-the-inch gingham and scraps of embroidery floss you can make 5¼″ × 4¼″ CROSS-STITCH SIGNS. Tape 7″ × 11″ fabric to table and lightly mark evenly spaced border and legend, using fabric rows as guidelines. With two strands floss, stitch one cross per square; mount.

MEXICAN CROSS-STITCH SHAWL

MATERIALS: 25″-wide woven multi-purpose plain-weave white interfacing canvas, 2¼ yds.; Persian (triple strand) yarn in the following number of 36″ long strands; 20 Orange, 20 Blue, 45 Pale Pink, 3 Yellow, 6 Turquoise, 8 Magenta, and 10 Purple; tapestry needle; white buttonhole twist.

DIRECTIONS: Mark the lengthwise center of the fabric, for about 20″ at each end, with colored basting thread.

Design is worked entirely in Cross Stitch. The *larger* blue crosses are worked over six threads. All remaining *smaller* crosses are worked over three threads.

Note: In an even-weave fabric, the border motifs would work up square and would look like the chart in FIG. 1. On the fabric we have

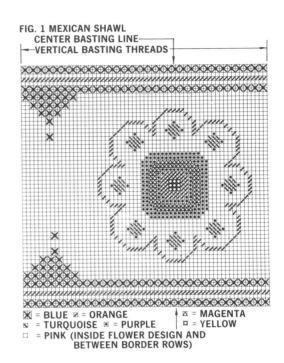

FIG. 1 MEXICAN SHAWL

⊠ = BLUE ⊡ = ORANGE ⬛ = MAGENTA
⬒ = TURQUOISE ⊞ = PURPLE ⬜ = YELLOW
⬚ = PINK (INSIDE FLOWER DESIGN AND
BETWEEN BORDER ROWS)

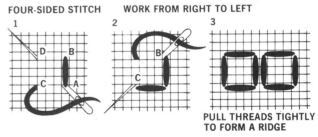

FOUR-SIDED STITCH   WORK FROM RIGHT TO LEFT

PULL THREADS TIGHTLY
TO FORM A RIDGE

used, where the threads across the width of the scarf are closer together than those along the length of the scarf, the stitched design works up elongated.

Measure 9″ up from one end on basting line and work the bottom row of the border in Fig. 1 with the larger Cross Stitches, using blue yarn. Thread a tapestry needle with one strand of yarn and knot one end. Work from right to left to the end of the row. Work back, crossing in the opposite direction, going into the same holes. To finish, run thread under a few stitches on the back of the work and trim end. Now starting at center line, count off the motif in Fig. 1 and mark with vertical basting threads where the design is to be repeated to the left and right of it. Add one more repeat of triangular border stitches at the right side. After the first row has been worked, counting the threads is a lot easier, since the previous stitches define the rows. Continue to work the whole design, making sure that the center of the chart matches the basted center line on the scarf.

Repeat the embroidery in the same way, at the opposite end of the scarf.

Six threads away from the outside of the embroidered borders use buttonhole twist to work a 4-sided stitch over 3 spaces, across the entire scarf, pulling up stitches tightly to form a ridge. *To make fringe:* Pull out all the crosswise threads up to the 4-sided stitch. Turn in and hem shawl at each side so that finished edges match the ends of the border.

CROSS-STITCH SAMPLER

(16½″ × 20½″ framed)

MATERIALS: Bleached evenweave linen, *14 threads to the inch*, one piece 20″ × 24″; size 18 tapestry needle; undivided six-strand embroidery floss in the following amounts and colors: 4 skeins Orange, 1 skein Green, 4 skeins

Brown, 4 skeins Bright Blue, 2 skeins Yellow and 3 skeins Red; yardstick; pencil; embroidery hoop; frame. *Note*: Needlework shops sell the bleached, evenweave linen, but any similarly-woven fabric will do. If your fabric has more threads to the inch, the design will be smaller. On the other hand, if your fabric has fewer threads to the inch, your design will be correspondingly larger.

DIRECTIONS: Make lines of basting stitches to mark off the border dimensions shown in photo, to center the sampler on the linen. Now lightly outline the remaining shapes on the fabric the same way, counting stitches and skipped threads (using photo as guide).

Embroidering: Insert linen in embroidery hoop, moving hoop as necessary. Using Cross-Stitch, work each stitch over two threads of your fabric. Work the borders first, then the outlined shapes, counting stitches in the photo. Work the hearts in red, orange and yellow; lettering in brown; house in blue and red; flowers in red, yellow and green; figures in red, blue, brown orange and yellow; outside border in red; inside border blue. Or arrange the colors in your own choice.

Finishing: Mount and frame the sampler.

Color photo on page 133

CROSS-STITCH SAMPLER

This adaptation of an old American sampler is done in a simple cross-stitch. It is shown here one half its original size. To enlarge, simply measure all the dimensions in the photo, then double them. Lightly outline the shapes in pencil on background fabric. Needlework shops sell the bleached, even-weave linen we used (10-12 evenly spaced threads per inch), but any similar fabric will do. Use three strands of embroidery floss (one skein of each color). To embroider the shapes, count the stitches and skipped threads in the corresponding part of the photo, then work each stitch over two threads in your fabric. Work the border first, then the inner traced areas. Mount and frame. Finished, framed size is 11″ × 15″.

EMBROIDERY PATTERNS

MATERIALS: Six-strand embroidery floss (we used DMC); embroidery needles Nos. 5, 6, 7 and 8; 5″ or 7″ embroidery hoop; tissue paper; dressmaker's carbon; embroidery scissors; J & P Coats Magic Poly-web fusible webbing; Jiffy-Sew sewing glue.

GENERAL DIRECTIONS:

1. *To transfer a design to your fabric:* Place tissue paper on the page and fold over the edges; secure all around with paper clips. Trace motif with a pencil. Remove paper and cut out tracing, leaving about 2″ of paper all around the design. Position the design and baste to the fabric, on only one long side of the paper. Slide the carbon paper under the tissue and pin *to the tracing paper* at both short ends. If you use a

medium-sharp pencil to trace the design, you'll be able to use the tissue and carbon more than once.

2. If embroidering close to the edge of a piece of fabric, enlarge the area by basting an additional piece of fabric underneath it in the seam allowance. This will enable you to fit the piece in an embroidery hoop. This technique is also recommended when embroidering a small area such as a collar, corner of a scarf and so forth.

3. When embroidering on a garment made from a pattern, cut out pieces following pattern directions. Embroider first, then sew pieces together.

4. If you wish to place motif near or on a seam,

it would be wise to baste along the seamline with contrasting thread *before* tracing the motif, to be sure embroidery won't be in seam allowance. Basting thread will also act as a guideline when garment is sewn together.

5. To "flop" a design means turning it so that it faces in the opposite direction. To do this, trace design onto tissue paper. Turn tissue over (flop) and place on a piece of white scrap paper. Retrace onto another piece of tissue paper to obtain the opposite image of the same design.

6. To keep thin fabrics from getting hoop creases, and to keep any fabric from soiling while embroidering, do the following: Lay fabric to be embroidered over inner ring of hoop.

Cover with a slightly larger piece of tissue paper and press the outer ring of the hoop over the paper-covered ring; tighten. Cut or tear away tissue to reveal only the area to be worked.

7. *Stitching and Pressing Tips:* Do not pull stitches too tightly when embroidering.

To press Satin-Stitch embroidery: Use a steam iron set at the temperature recommended by the manufacturer for the fabric you are using. Press embroidery right side down on a thick or double-folded towel.

8. Stay-Stitch curved edges and overcast any edges that tend to fray when handled—especially silk.

9. If using one motif repeatedly, retrace on fresh tissue periodically so all embroidered motifs have crisp and matching outlines.

10. When embroidering doubled fabrics (blouse collar, hat brim and so forth), slide needle between layers of fabric so stitching won't show on back of items.

BLOUSE COLLAR
Follow GENERAL DIRECTIONS, Steps 1, 2, 6, 7 and 10. Use No. 7 needle and 2 strands embroidery floss to work Satin Stitch throughout.

GIRL'S SHIFT AND BOY'S PLAYSUIT
Follow GENERAL DIRECTIONS, Steps 1, 2, 3, 4, 5 (the friendly lion is flopped on the boy's playsuit), 7 and 9. Use No. 6 or No. 7 needle and 2 strands embroidery floss. Work outlines with Backstitch and solid areas with Satin Stitch.

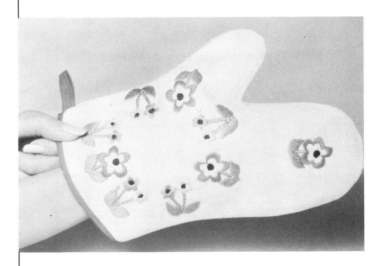

OVEN MITT *(covering)*
Follow GENERAL DIRECTIONS, Steps 1, 3, 7 and 9. Using an old oven mitt, trace to make a pattern adding ⅝″ seam allowance all around. Cut out mitt cover fabric (we used permanent-press polyester-linen). Using No. 6 needle and 3 strands embroidery floss, embroider one piece, working stems of twin flowers in Back Stitch and all remaining areas in Satin Stitch. Press (Step 9). With right sides together, stitch mitt pieces, taking ⅝″ seam. Clip curves. Press seam open. Turn right side out. Re-cover mitt cuff with new bias binding (if necessary) and add a loop for a "hanger." Slip embroidered cover onto the old mitt. Turn under seam allowance at raw edge and catchstitch to the edge of bias binding.

FINGERTIP TOWELS
Follow GENERAL DIRECTIONS, Steps 1 and 7. Use No. 8 needle and 2 strands embroidery floss to work Satin Stitch throughout. *Note*: Motif used is right half of design at upper right-hand corner on pages 54 and 55 Wash towels first. For patchwork strip, use permanent-press fabric (wash first). Join patches in ½″ seams; press open. Embroider center panel. Edgestitch onto towel. Stitch jumbo rickrack over raw edges.

HAT BRIM;
Follow GENERAL DIRECTIONS, Steps 1 and 10. *Note*: If brim is stiffened, no embroidery hoop is needed. Use No. 6 needle and 3 strands embroidery floss to work Satin Stitch throughout.

TOTE BAG PANEL
Follow GENERAL DIRECTIONS, Steps 1 and 7. Use No. 5 needle and 6 strands embroidery floss to work Satin Stitch on flowers and leaves and Backstitch on stems. Our panel was embroidered on a 3½″ strip of dress-weight linen. Press. Position panel on tote with Polyweb fusible webbing. Press, following package directions. Cover edges with rickrack, glued in place with Jiffy-Sew sewing glue.

PLACE MATS AND NAPKINS
Follow GENERAL DIRECTIONS, Steps 1, 5 and 7. Use No. 6 needle and 3 strands embroidery floss to work Satin Stitch throughout.

Color photo on page 134

PICTURE FRAME SAMPLER

To Embroider Sampler Frame: On tissue paper, draw a 7" × 9¼" rectangle, then a second one inside the first—1⅝" from the top and side lines, 2⅜" from bottom. Draw top corner boxes, nine vertical lines for side borders, then diamond shapes and top design, spaced as shown. Pin paper to a piece of linen 11" × 13¼"; baste through paper on all guidelines. Carefully tear away paper. Embroider over basting lines with 6-strand embroidery floss. Cut away inside fabric 1" from edges; slash to within ¼" of stay-stitched corners. Cover cardboard frame, overlapping fabric on back with white glue. Back with fabric-covered board.

BLANKET SPREAD

MATERIALS: Double-bed size washable blanket; Bear Brand "Go-Go" acrylic yarn, 19 skeins (2 oz. each) in White; white thread; large tapestry needle; regular sewing needle; white chalk; lightweight cardboard; yardstick.

DIRECTIONS: *Marking the Border Design:* With a yardstick and white chalk, draw straight Lines A and B on three sides of blanket, spacing A 6½" from blanket edge and B 1" from A, as indicated in FIG. 1. After couching Lines A and B, draw and couch straight Lines C (3½" from B) and D (1¼" from C). From cardboard, cut a freehand template of the leaf pattern (*see* FIG. 2). Draw straight Line E next to A, then trace the leaf pattern at intervals of 3" (from leaf base to leaf base) along Line E, except at the corners where three leaves adjoin, as shown in photo. Couch Line E and leaves simultaneously with a continuous strand of yarn. Repeat Line E procedure to make Line F inside Line D; couch F.

FIG. 1

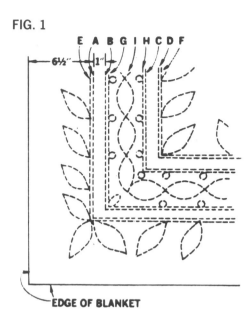

FIG. 2 LEAF MOTIF

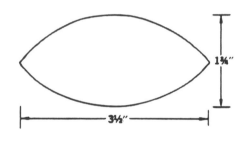

Draw and couch Lines G and H, spacing the ⅝″ loops 3½″ apart (increase the size of the loops on Line G to 1¾″ at the corners). Using the same template, draw and couch the line of leaves (Line I) in center of border, as shown.

Making Tassels: Cut a piece of cardboard 3″ × 5½″. Wrap yarn 13 times around the length of the cardboard. Tie at one end, leaving two 5″ lengths of yarn for tying tassel to the spread. Wrap a 4″ length of yarn around the tassel several times ½″ below the fold; tie and trim ends. Thread one end of the yarn at the top through a large tapestry needle and insert the needle through the spread from front to back, about ½″ from the edge. Tie both yarn's ends securely to attach the tassels, then thread the ends into the tassel to hide them. Space tassels about 2″ apart around three sides (approximately 153 tassels are needed for double-bed-size blanket). If necessary, trim the ends of the tassels evenly.

FIG. 1   **1 SQ.=1″**

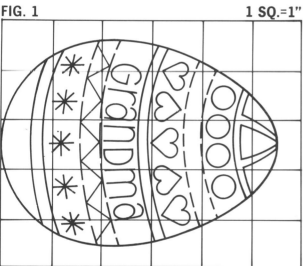

FIG. 2   **1 SQ.=1″**

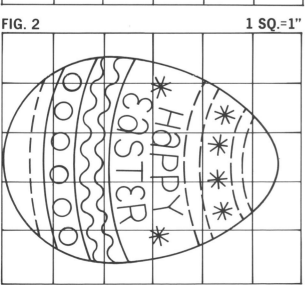

EASTER EGG PICTURES

MATERIALS: Two picture frames, about 7½″ × 8½″; two pieces of white linen, each about 12″-square; crewel yarn in assorted colors; small embroidery hoop; dressmaker's carbon; tracing wheel; masking tape.

DIRECTIONS: Following the directions on page 224, enlarge on tracing paper the egg designs in FIGS. 1 and 2. Pin tracing to linen, centering the egg. Slide dressmaker's carbon face down, under paper, and with a tracing wheel transfer design to the linen.

Embroidering: Using colors of your choice, work embroidery as follows: Back Stitch over words and solid lines; a Lazy Daisy over each star, then a French Knot in the center; Satin Stitch on the bands (between broken lines), "rickrack," circles, wedges, hearts and triangles. Work a solid row of French Knots between the two lines over "Grandma" and in the space above the lowest band on the other egg. Remove cardboard backing from frame and center it over wrong side of embroidered linen. Fold over excess linen and fasten to cardboard with masking tape. Insert picture into frame.

TABLECLOTH
AND FOUR NAPKINS

MATERIALS: Purchased tablecloth and napkins (quantities given are for size photographed, that is 70″ round cloth and 17″ square napkins); 6-strand embroidery floss as follows—5 skeins each Green, Dark Pink and Medium Pink, 4 skeins Purple and 2 skeins each Red and Light Pink; 14 yds. purchased edging; tracing paper and dressmaker's carbon paper.

DIRECTIONS: Following the directions on page 224, enlarge FIGS. 1 and 2 on transparent paper. Fold tablecloth in half, edges matching, and mark fold with basting thread. Unfold cloth and refold with the basting matching and edges even. Baste the new fold to complete quarter-mark basting. Pin FIG. 1 pattern to cloth with broken line on a quarter-mark basting and arrow 9″ from center (where basting lines cross). Trace pattern (don't trace broken line or arrow) to cloth over dressmaker's carbon. Repeat at each quarter-mark, tracing pattern face

down (to reverse the pattern) for the second and fourth tracings. Trace a trail of pairs and single flowers 15″ beyond each motif, spacing 1½″ apart. Pin FIG. 2 pattern to corner of napkin with broken lines matching napkin edges. Trace pattern (don't trace broken line). Repeat for other napkins.

Embroidery: Design is worked in Satin Stitch (3 strands in needle), Stem Stitch and Straight Stitch (2 strands in needle) and French Knots (6 strands in needle). Using green, work Stem Stitch on the thin stems and Satin Stitch on the thick stem and the leaves. Work a scattering of purple French Knots over the dots in bouquet and along floral trail. Work flowers in Satin Stitch as follows: Pale pink in center circle, dark pink in three petals and medium pink in two petals. Take two long red straight stitches across each petal over the Satin Stitches. On the wrong side, press the embroidery through a damp turkish towel. Stitch decorative edging around cloth and napkin edges.

FIG. 1 TABLECLOTH MOTIF   1 SQ. = ½"

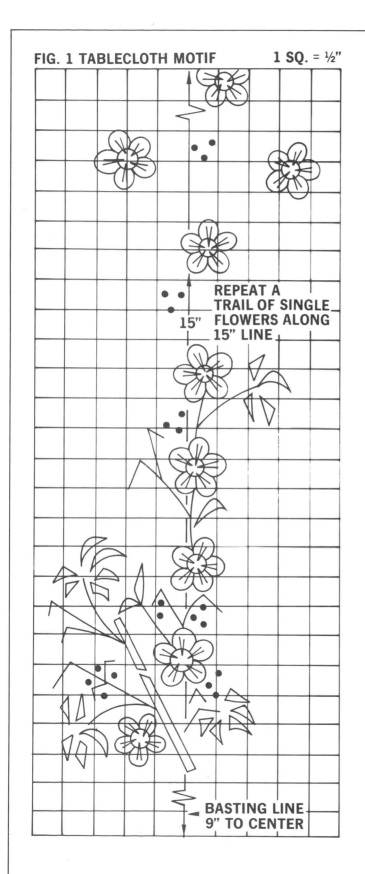

15"

REPEAT A TRAIL OF SINGLE FLOWERS ALONG 15" LINE

BASTING LINE 9" TO CENTER

FIG. 2 NAPKIN CORNER MOTIF   1 SQ. = ½"

EDGE OF NAPKIN

HEART PILLOW

MATERIALS: 1¼ yards 45″-wide Burgundy linen; matching thread; 2¼ yds. 2″-wide pre-ruffled lace trim; polyester fiberfill; transfer pencil; DMC embroidery floss in the following colors and amounts: 1 skein each Orange, Red, Pink, Salmon, Turquoise, Olive Green, Light Green, Yellow, Black, 2 skeins White; PeriLusta embroidery floss, 1 skein each Cerise, Light Blue.

DIRECTIONS: Following the directions on page 224, enlarge the pattern for the heart shape and embroidered design onto tissue paper. Turn paper over; on the reverse side, redraw all lines with the transfer pencil. With this side down, center the pattern on a square of linen roughly 2″ larger all around than the heart. Pin securely; pin in place around edges. Press paper with hot iron in a circular motion to transfer the design to the fabric; remove pattern.

To Embroider: Center the fabric in the embroidery hoop. With two strands of floss and the Outline Stitch, embroider lettering, heart outline, stems and antennae. Embroider flowers, berries etc. in the colors they might be in nature (red strawberries, orange lady bugs, etc.). Use French Knots for strawberries, flower centers, lady bugs, bees' and butterflies' eyes, dots around heart and scattered dots. Everything else is Satin Stitch.

Finishing: When embroidery is completed, carefully wash in cold water; block to shape. Cut out on line indicated. Cut pillow back to same size, using pattern. For ruffle, cut bias strip of linen 4″ wide and 74″ long, piecing if necessary. Fold in half lengthwise and press lightly. Gather open edges (treat as single layer), using two rows of stitching, and pin in place around the embroidered heart to make sure gathering fits the heart edge. Now remove ruffle, and beginning at bottom point of the heart, baste lace on top of ruffling, then baste entire piece to heart shape on seam line, with lace ruffling between right side of heart and linen ruffling. Machine stitch. At bottom point, seam ruffling ends together by hand, turning both front and back seams to the inside, to make a heart point. Seam back to front, right sides together, making sure ruffling is laying flat between front and back. Leave 6″ opening on side for stuffing. Trim seams, clip curves, turn right side out. Press sewn edges lightly. Stuff. Hand stitch closed.

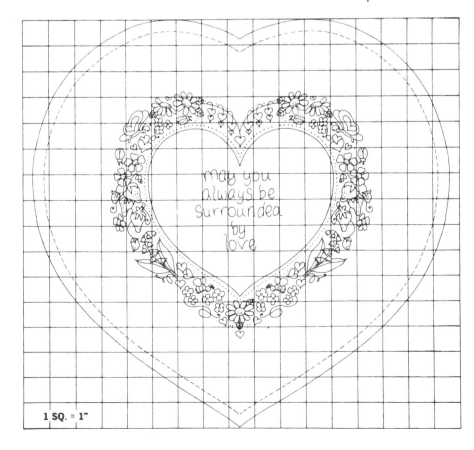

1 SQ. = 1"

EMBROIDERED STRAPLESS DRESS OR SKIRT

MATERIALS: Butterick shirt pattern 6140; 45" wide, 100% cotton fabric; eight round lace doilies—four 2½", three 4" and one 5"; 1¼" wide lace trim, 2 yds.; 1½"-wide crochet-type lace edging with one scalloped edge, 2 yds.; 6-strand embroidery floss in nine colors, plus three shades of green; dressmaker's tracing paper; white thread.

DIRECTIONS: Cut out skirt; do not sew together. Following the directions on page 224, enlarge the embroidery pattern. Using dressmaker's carbon trace onto right side of skirt front piece, centering 5" above bottom edge. Using photo as a guide, and satin stitch throughout, work multi-colored flowers and buds, then work stems and leaves changing green floss at random. Edgestitch doilies in place by hand or machine. Complete skirt, using pattern directions. Add laces at the hem, as shown in the photo.

EMBROIDERY DIAGRAM FOR DRESS/SKIRT   1 SQ. = 1"

Color photo on page 134

CREWEL EMBROIDERED HANDBAGS

MATERIALS: *White bag:* ½ yd. White felt; Persian yarn, 24" lengths of each: 2 Yellow, 5 Orange, 5 Hot Pink, 5 Green and 5 Turquoise; 6-strand embroidery floss, 1 skein each: Dark Green, Blue, Red and Violet.

Brown bag: ½ yd. brown felt; Persian yarn, 24" lengths of each: 2 Yellow, 6 Orange, 5 Hot Pink, 3 Green and 2 Turquoise; 6-strand embroidery floss, 1 skein each: Dark Green, Blue, Red and Caramel.

Both bags, each: Buckram, 1½ yds.; buttons with chain (one set); 2 buttons to match each set; crewel needles (one for yarn, one for floss); 10" embroidery hoop; tracing wheel and dressmaker's carbon.

Note: If edge of bag is whipstitched with yarn *(see photo),* five 24" lengths should be allowed in desired color.

DIRECTIONS: Enlarge the design in FIG. 1 (white bag) or FIG. 2 (brown bag) by drawing crisscross lines vertically and horizontally on brown wrapping paper, spacing the lines ½" apart. Then copy the embroidery design and outline of bag pattern around it, drawing freehand, one square at a time, plus center guidelines. Cut out bag pattern. Repeat for bag back pattern (FIG. 3), spacing lines 1" apart. Cut two pieces of felt 3" larger all around than the bag patterns; draw a 3" line at the exact

FIG. 1 WHITE BAG PATTERN 1 SQ. = ½" ⊢ CENTER LINE

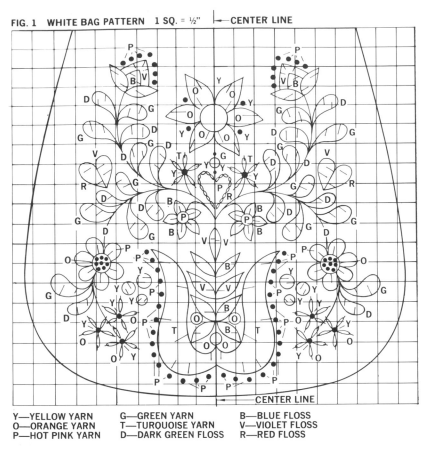

Y—YELLOW YARN   G—GREEN YARN   B—BLUE FLOSS
O—ORANGE YARN   T—TURQUOISE YARN   V—VIOLET FLOSS
P—HOT PINK YARN D—DARK GREEN FLOSS R—RED FLOSS

FIG. 2 BROWN BAG PATTERN 1 SQ. = ½" ⊢ CENTER LINE

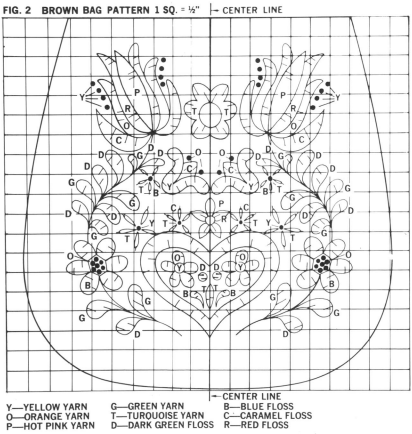

Y—YELLOW YARN   G—GREEN YARN   B—BLUE FLOSS
O—ORANGE YARN   T—TURQUOISE YARN   C—CARAMEL FLOSS
P—HOT PINK YARN D—DARK GREEN FLOSS R—RED FLOSS

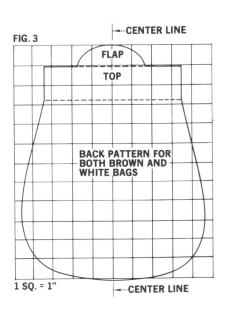

FIG. 3

⊢ CENTER LINE

FLAP

TOP

BACK PATTERN FOR BOTH BROWN AND WHITE BAGS

1 SQ. = 1"   ⊢ CENTER LINE

center at top and bottom of each. Draw a light lengthwise pencil line to mark the center on two pieces of dressmaker's carbon, cut the same size as the enlarged patterns for bag front and back. Tape the carbon to the felt, matching center lines. Place the enlarged pattern over the carbon, again lining up center lines and tape to the felt. *For front*, trace pattern outline and design with wheel, using the tip of a hard pencil for fine detail. *For back*, trace outline *only*. Remove patterns and carbon. Place felt front in embroidery hoop. Embroider the design—using 3 strands of the embroidery floss, and 2 strands of the Persian yarn (following the stitch code, and color key letters with FIG. 1 or 2). Remove from hoop. Cut out bag on pattern outline. Steam-press to remove creases made by hoop. Cut out bag back on pattern outline.

Lining: Using the same enlarged patterns, cut one more felt, front and back.

Strap-Gusset: Cut two strips of felt, each 1¾″ × 53″.

Interlining: From buckram, cut one strap-gusset strip 1¾″ × 53″; one bag back and one front. Cut buckram back into three pieces on the pattern's broken lines (this makes flap "bendable").

Assembling the pieces: For the front, sandwich the buckram between the two felt pieces. Sew together on the machine, close to the edge, using zigzag stitch. Repeat for back, inserting the three buckram pieces in their original order. Assemble the strap-gusset pieces. Stitch edges as for bag front, using a zigzag stitch close to the edge.

Sewing bag: Using matching thread, overcast the strap-gusset to the bag front with one end of the strap even with the top edge of the bag at the right front. Overcast all around, up to the other top edge. Let the rest of the strap hang loose. Then attach bag back the same way. Whipstitch the edges of the bag and strap with yarn in a contrasting color, if desired. Sew one button to the top of the gusset, one to the gusset center-bottom and another to the bag front in the middle of the upper center embroidered flower. Sew the button-with-chain to the center of the flap. Make a buttonhole in the end of the strap; slip it over the bottom button. Make a second buttonhole where the strap covers the top-gusset button. To use as a handbag, button the strap to the bottom button; for a shoulder length strap, button strap to the top button. If the chain on the chain-button is too long, loop it around the flap-button.

Color photo on page 134

TABLECLOTH

Finished embroidered center measures 26″ in diameter.

MATERIALS: #18 tapestry needle; 21-threads-to-the-inch evenweave linen or homespun fabric, or purchased tablecloth (size depends on table size).

Note: Use embroidery needle for homespun or purchased tablecloth. DMC #3 coton perlé in the following amounts and colors: 6 skeins Brown, 3 skeins Dark Green, 5 skeins Medium Green, 5 skeins Light Green, 2 skeins Light Pink, 2 skeins Medium Pink, 2 skeins Dark Pink, 2 skeins Dark Purple, 1 skein Red, 1 skein

EMBROIDERED TABLECLOTH   1 SQ.=1″

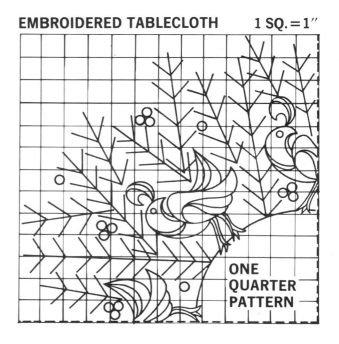

ONE
QUARTER
PATTERN

Dark Red, 1 skein Gold; transfer pencil; large embroidery hoop; basting needle and thread; tracing paper for pattern.

DIRECTIONS: *Enlarging and Transferring the Pattern*: Fold fabric in half lengthwise; press. Baste along fold; press out fold. Repeat for width. (These will be guidelines for centering design on fabric.) Following directions on page 224, enlarge pattern; transfer onto tracing paper (design given repeats in quarters). Retrace this enlarged design on large sheet of tracing paper which has been folded in quarters; repeat original tracing in each of the quarters until circular design is complete, making sure front half of bird matches back half where sections meet, and pine branches also match. Turn tissue over; on reverse side, redraw all lines with transfer pencil. With this side down, center the pattern on the basting lines on tablecloth. Pin securely to the right side of the tablecloth. Pin in place around edges, smoothing paper out from center to remove any wrinkles or pleats. Press paper with hot iron in a circular motion to transfer the design to the fabric. Unpin and remove pattern.

To embroider: Using hoop, embroider as follows, using photo and diagram as guides: Chain and Lazy Daisy Stitches (or Single Chain) are used throughout. Place fabric in embroidery hoop (since the design is large, you will have to work it a section at a time). With Chain Stitch, embroider the birds. Use the photo as a guide. (Positions of dark purple and dark pink are switched on every other bird.) Birds' eyes and red berries are pairs of Chain Stitches worked in opposite directions. Work pine branches in brown Chain Stitch; work pine needles in Lazy Daisy or Single Chain Stitches, working dark green closest to center, then medium green, then lightest green. Work each section of stitches from the center (near branch) outward. *Note:* To conserve floss, do not carry it across back of large sections of cloth; instead, start and end floss frequently.)

To finish: Remove basting stitches; fold edges of cloth over once and over again; press and hemstitch. For optional edging: Cut all leftover thread into equal lengths (approximately 21″ each). Count out how many of each there are and separate into equal piles. Separate colors as to how you would like to see them alternate. Work Blanket or Buttonhole Edging Stitch over 2 threads wide and 6 threads (¼″) high, tying one color to the next as you get to the end of each color. Press entire cloth on wrong side over towel or padding to finish.

CREW NECK SAMPLER SWEATER

MATERIALS: Heavy plain-knit sweater; DMC crewel yarns in various colors; crewel needle; stiff cardboard, 15″ × 20″; white tissue paper.

DIRECTIONS:

1. On tissue paper, draw a freehand design of clouds, house, flowers, monogram, etc., as shown (*see photo on page 67*), *or* be creative and draw your own design.

2. Insert cardboard between sweater front and back to provide a firm, flat work surface. Pin paper designs to sweater front.

3. Embroider designs through the paper, using colors and stitches of your choice, *or* copy the original design which was worked as follows:

Clouds—light blue Stem Stitch

Bird—brown Stem Stitch

Sun—yellow Stem Stitch, Straight Stitch and French Knot

Rows, *starting at top (work over a line of basting to keep rows even):*

Blue flowers—Lazy Daisy Stitch with French Knots; green leaves—Lazy Daisy Stitch

Purple row—Open Cretan Stitch; maroon—French Knots

Pink row—Buttonhole Stitch

Green row—Herringbone Stitch

Brown row—Chain Stitch

Aqua row—Cretan Stitch

Yellow row—Blanket Stitch

Tree—Green Lazy Daisy Stitch; pink French Knots; brown Stem Stitch

Flower—Purple French Knots; green Lazy Daisy Stitch

House roof—Red Buttonhole Stitch and Stem Stitch; remainder, coral Stem Stitch

Monogram—Blue Stem Stitch

Bottom row—Green Stem Stitch

Trim on sleeves—Green Blanket Stitch

EMBROIDERED RIBBED TURTLENECK SWEATER

MATERIALS: Turtleneck sweater with thin, vertical-knit ribs; crewel yarns left over from other projects—we used DMC in 10 different colors; crewel needle; stiff cardboard, 15″ × 20″.

DIRECTIONS:

1. Insert a cardboard between the sweater front and back to provide a flat, firm work surface.

2. Select the embroidery stitches you want to use from those illustrated in the BASIC EMBROIDERY STITCH section. Use yarn colors of your choice.

3. Separate each crewel strand and work with

Color photo on page 134

SWEATER WITH EMBROIDERED YOKE AND SLEEVES

MATERIALS: Sweater with yoke of horizontal-knit ribs; leftover crewel yarns, Knit-Cro-Sheen, 6-strand embroidery floss (DMC) and pearl cotton, in a variety of colors; crewel needle; stiff cardboard, 15″ × 20″.

DIRECTIONS: Follow the directions for the Turtleneck sweater, noting the following exceptions:

1. We worked the horizontal ribs of the yoke, and occasionally the space between the ribs. Since these ribs are comparatively wide, heavier threads and/or more of them can be used and the stitches can be larger and closer together than on the narrow-ribbed turtleneck.

2. Use narrow cardboard or a thin book inside the sleeves.

3. Repeat the stitch, but not the color, on two consecutive rows to make an interesting pattern. Skip fewer ribs than in the turtleneck sweater.

only a single thread. Work the stitches in vertical rows, starting at the bottom and using the sweater ribs as guidelines. Keep stitches rather short and measure by eye the distance between them. Maintain an even moderate tension; tight stitches will cause puckering and loose stitches may get caught and pulled during wear. (For greatest eye appeal, change colors and stitches every row, skipping one or two ribs between embroidery rows.)

4. On the turtleneck area, embroider a small bouquet using Lazy Daisy stitches and French Knots. Finish the sweater bottom edge with Blanket Stitches, using two threads instead of one.

Note: All sweaters should be hand-washed in cool water with a product recommended for woolens.

TREE OF LIFE

MATERIALS: 22½″ × 22½″ square of flat-faced linen; Bucilla 3-ply Persian yarns in the following colors: Baby Blue (137), Bright Blue (32), Prussian Blue (138), Coppertone (17), Russet (41), Sun Yellow (98), Gold (77), Purple (31), Violet (30), Light Violet (53), Medium Fern (7), Dark Green (132), Dark Peacock (84), Light Pink (13), Medium Pink (14), Dark Pink (15), approximately ½ skn. each; dressmaker's carbon; pencil; tracing paper; ruler; scissors; large-eye crewel needles (sizes 3 or 4); 5″ round or 8″ oval wooden embroidery hoop; cardboard; straight pins.

DIRECTIONS: Following directions on page 224, enlarge pattern onto tracing paper. Transfer design onto center of linen fabric using dressmaker's carbon. Do not trace outside lines. On wrong side of fabric, mark outside lines with dressmaker's carbon; baste.

To embroider: Use 1-ply yarn in needle throughout, following letters and stitch details on diagram. Where Satin Stitch is indicated,

inside lines denote direction of stitch. Peacock's body, all stems and tendrils are worked in Stem Stitch, unless otherwise indicated. Tree trunk and lower branches are worked in Chain Stitch; all small solid circles are French Knots wrapped twice; peacock's head is worked in Satin Stitch.

To finish: With terry towel between, place embroidery wrong side up on cardboard slightly larger than design area. Stretch and pin fabric outside basted lines of picture until straight. Press gently with dry iron and wet cloth.

TREE OF LIFE
1 SQ. = 1″

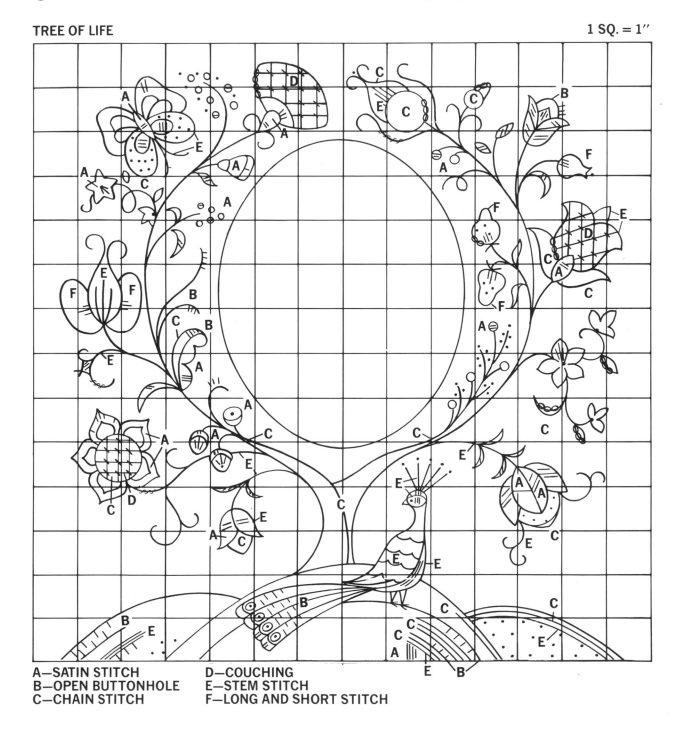

A—SATIN STITCH
B—OPEN BUTTONHOLE
C—CHAIN STITCH
D—COUCHING
E—STEM STITCH
F—LONG AND SHORT STITCH

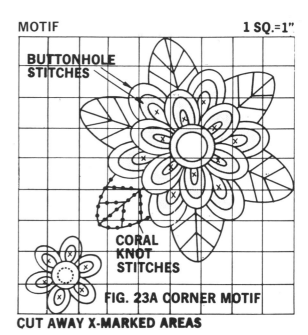

MOTIF   1 SQ.=1"

BUTTONHOLE STITCHES

CORAL KNOT STITCHES

FIG. 23A CORNER MOTIF

CUT AWAY X-MARKED AREAS

CUT-WORK PILLOW
(13" × 13")

MATERIALS: Yellow fabric, 1 yd.; tightly woven White linen, 18" × 18"; White Perle cotton, one spool; dressmaker's carbon; polyester fiber filling.

DIRECTIONS: Following the directions on page 224, enlarge the designs. Baste a 14" square on the white linen. Using dressmaker's carbon, trace center motif onto center of white linen, then trace corner motifs equidistant from it. To fill in the petals, work very close buttonhole stitches, with the knot edge against the edges which will be cut out (see x-marks in illustration). All petals of the center motif are worked with a double row of Buttonhole Stitches, as differentiated by the shaded areas. For the outer portion reverse the stitching direction so that the knotted edge is at the outer edge of the petal. Work the center circle with Buttonhole Stitches; then fill in with a mass of French Knots. Corner flower petals are a single row of Buttonhole Stitches, surrounding French Knots. Work large leaves with Coral Stitch, using two strands cotton. Using very sharp scissors with pointed blades, cut away x-marked areas, being careful not to cut embroidery. Press pillow top face down on several layers of terry toweling. From yellow yardage, cut two 14" squares. Baste one square to back of pillow top as liner. From remainder, cut four 5" strips from straight grain of fabric.

Making and Applying Ruffle: Stitch short ends of ruffle strip in ½" seam; press seam open. Fold in half lengthwise, wrong sides together. Stitch gathering rows ¼" and ⅜" from raw edges. Pull up a bobbin thread to pillow dimensions and distribute gathering evenly.

To Apply: With right sides together, baste ruffle around completed pillow top, raw edges even.

To Assemble Pillow: Pin *completed* pillow top to backing with right sides together and raw edges even (ruffle or welting if any, will already be stitched to top). Take ½" seam, unless otherwise directed for individual pillows, leaving an opening large enough to insert pillow or stuffing material. Trim corners or clip curves. Turn right side out; stuff. Slipstitch opening.

RED AND WHITE PRINT BAG WITH SMOCKING

MATERIALS: ½-yd. 36"-wide challis with small print, for cover, ½-yd. 36"-wide White duck, for lining; Red perle cotton, 1 skein; needle; gripper-snap tape, two 11" lengths; one pair of wooden handles, approximately 4" × 12" with ⅜" × 11" slot for fabric ends to go through; tailor's chalk.

GENERAL DIRECTIONS: *Cutting and Assembling Bag:* Following the directions on page 224, enlarge bag pattern (*see* FIG. 1) and cut out on fold of paper. Cut out the shaded area (for snap tape placement). Using the opened enlarged pattern, cut two pieces from the cover fabric and two from lining fabric. Trace the cutout area on right sides of lining pieces with tailor's chalk. Stitch 11" strip of socket side of

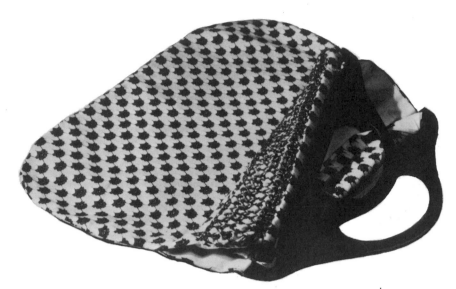

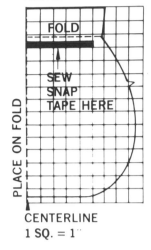

FIG. 1 BAG AND
LINING
PATTERN

PLACE ON FOLD

FOLD

SEW
SNAP
TAPE HERE

CENTERLINE
1 SQ. = 1"

FIG. 2 GATHERING ROW GUIDE
FOR SMOCKING

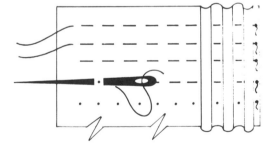

FIG. 3 SMOCKING CABLE STITCH

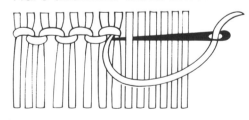

FIG. 4 SMOCKING
CHEVRON STITCH

snap tape in the traced areas. With right sides together, stitch two cover pieces together from notch to notch around sides and bottom, taking ½" seam. Secure thread ends. Trim seams; clip curves. Press seams open. Turn right side out. Repeat previous step using the lining pieces, but don't turn right side out. Slip lining inside of bag. Turning seam allowances inside along side edges and across each end, pin lining to cover; slipstitch. Stitch one 11" section of ball portion of tape to each top edge on lining side. (You may want to pin tape in place before sewing so that sockets and balls match up evenly.)

Smocking Instructions: Cut a strip of challis 3" × 40". Leaving ⅜" seam allowance all around, use the fabric's evenly-spaced flower pattern as a guide to stitch eight rows of gathering threads (see FIG. 2), spacing the stitches ¼" apart the complete length of the strip.

(*Note:* If your fabric does not have an evenly-spaced pattern, use tailor's chalk and a yardstick to mark rows of dots ¼" apart, leaving ¼" between the rows.) Draw up the gathering threads until the smocking is 13" long, plus seam allowance at each end. Tie thread-ends securely. Smooth gathers evenly into folds. Embroider only through the tops of folds on right side of the strip with red perle cotton, using a long enough strand to complete each row. Begin each row with a knot at the lefthand side of strip, and end with a double stitch on the last fold on wrong side. From top down, work:

Three rows of Cable Stitch
Three rows of Chevron Stitch
Three rows of Cable Stitch

Remove gathering threads. Turn under seam allowance all around and slipstitch smocked strip to top of bag.

SHADOW-STITCH EMBROIDERED SCARF

MATERIALS: Light pastel-colored scarf, chiffon or imitation; 6-strand embroidery floss (we used 1 skein each of Turquoise, Blue-Green, Lime and Purple); dressmaker's carbon; pencil; scissors; generous supply of tissue paper; #7 embroidery needle; transparent tape; embroidery hoop, 7″ or 8″ (large enough to enclose entire design).

DIRECTIONS: Following directions on page 224, trace, or reduce design from diagram onto tissue paper. Spread scarf out carefully, pressing lightly with a cool iron if necessary. Tape scarf lightly to flat surface, wrong-side up. Place and center tissue design on wrong side of scarf and *tape* into position (pins could mar the

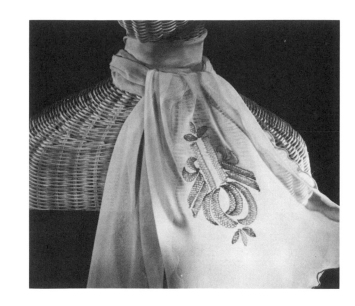

SHADOW STITCH SCARF DESIGN

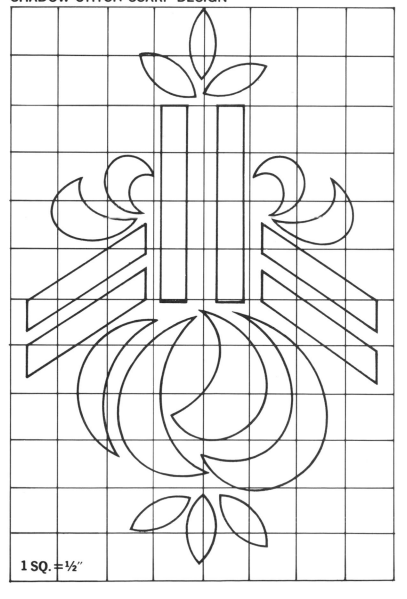

1 SQ. = ½″

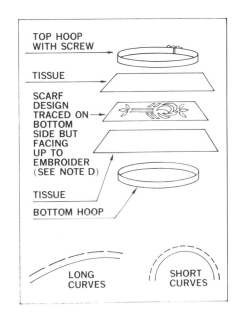

TOP HOOP WITH SCREW

TISSUE

SCARF DESIGN TRACED ON BOTTOM SIDE BUT FACING UP TO EMBROIDER (SEE NOTE D)

TISSUE

BOTTOM HOOP

LONG CURVES

SHORT CURVES

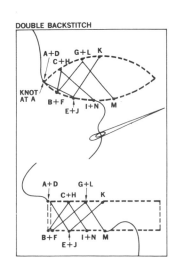

DOUBLE BACKSTITCH

fabric). Slide dressmaker's carbon underneath tissue and trace design onto scarf. Place bottom ring of embroidery hoop on flat surface. Place tissue paper over hoop, leaving enough to overlap edges generously. Place scarf over tissue paper, with design centered on hoop. Place another piece of tissue over scarf. Place top ring of embroidery hoop on top and tighten. Tear away tissue above and below hoop to work. (These steps are important, for the chiffon will show damage marks if these precautions are not taken.) Embroider design using #7 needle and 3 strands separated from the 6-strand floss. Follow diagrams for Double Backstitch. Double Backstitch is also known as Herringbone Stitch or Shadow Stitch. Practice the stitch on a scrap of fabric first, so that the chiffon is not damaged. Work stitches wider on long curves, shorter on narrow curves. When beginning, leave a 3-inch strand which can be threaded underneath sides of completed stitches, and tie a single knot 3 inches above the end. For squared-off areas, stitch small backstitches on end before starting double backstitch. Right side of scarf will show only backstitches. Through the sheerness of the scarf you will see crossed threads of herringbone stitches which are worked on wrong side of scarf, therefore called shadow-stitch embroidery.

VELVET SHAWL

MATERIALS: 54″-wide Black velvet, 1½ yds.; same amount of 54″-wide lining fabric; 5½″-wide Black fringe, 3 yds.; 18″-wide iron-on woven White interfacing, ½ yd.; fine-point permanent color grey needlework marker; two 10-yd. skeins of Brown 6-strand embroidery floss; Persian yarn in the following number of 10-yd. skeins, 3 White, 2 Medium Red, 2 Apricot Brandy, and 1 each Apricot, Bright Yellow, Dark Red, Medium Shocking Pink, Spearmint and Chartreuse; 14″ and 6″ diameter embroidery hoops.

DIRECTIONS: Fold the 54″ square of shawl fabric in half diagonally, edges matching. Pin 2″ from the fold to keep fabric from shifting. Then slash along fold. Cut lining the same way. Remove pins. Following directions on page 224, enlarge bouquet design with pencil directly onto the uncoated side of the interfacing. Then trace over the pencilled design with permanent needlework marker. Cut out about ⅛″ outside the drawn lines. Trace as many small motifs (a through e) as you need. (We used 5 daisies (a), 6 poppies (b, c), and 6 leaves (d, e).) Place the

interfacing bouquet, coated side down, in desired position on the shawl and iron it on as follows: With just the tip of a dry iron fuse the center of the interfacing without touching the velvet with the iron. Then place a piece of cotton cloth on top and iron well, through the cloth. Place and fuse the small traced motifs in the same way. Use the large hoop when working the bouquet and the small hoop for the small motifs. *Always remove the hoop when you put down the work* to avoid the hoop's marking the fabric. Placing a strip of tissue paper between the hoop and the nap also helps to avoid marks. (Marks usually disappear when they are ironed from the back of the velvet with a dry iron.) With one strand of yarn in needle, work the whole design in Satin Stitch. With full 6 strands of floss in needle, work brown French Knots around yellow centers. With small scissors trim away the interfacing close to the embroidery. Baste the embroidered shawl to the lining, wrong sides together and edges matching. Stitch ⅝″ from edges leaving 10″ opening on longest side of shawl. Turn shawl right side out and slipstich opening. Turning under raw ends of fringe ½″; lap it over the two shorter shawl edges. Pin, mitering at the corner, and stitch in place.

VELVET SHAWL

1 SQ. = 1"

W—WHITE
Y—LIGHT YELLOW
A—APRICOT

AB—APRICOT BRANDY
P—MED. SHOCKING PINK
R—MED. RED

DR—DARK RED
C—CHARTREUSE
S—SPEARMINT

EMBROIDERED BED LINEN AND TOWEL SET

MATERIALS: Sheets, pillowcases and towel set; tracing paper; dressmaker's carbon; tissue paper (towels only); J. & P. Coat's 6-strand embroidery floss in these colors: White, Pink, Canary Yellow, Nile Green, Dark Orange, Dark Yellow, Beauty Pink, Crimson, Indian Pink, Light Aquatone, Avocado, Coral Pink, Coral Glow, Dark Aquatone. *For towels*, use 1 skein of each color. *For bed linen*, use 2 skeins of Crimson, Indian Pink and Coral Glow; 3 skeins of White, Nile Green and Avocado; 1 skein of all other colors.

DIRECTIONS: Trace the rose design from the page onto tracing paper. Use dressmaker's carbon and a well-sharpened hard-lead pencil to transfer the design to the bed linen in the de-sired positions. Draw freehand end flowers (4½″ long) to complete design, using photo as a guide.

For use on the *towel set*—trace the pattern for the rose plus two freehand end flowers *separately* on pieces of tissue paper. Baste the tissues securely in place in positions shown.

Note: Embroidery is worked right through the paper; tear away when design is completed. Embroider the design, using the photo and the colors indicated by number on the pattern as guides. Work flowers and leaves in Satin Stitch and flower stems in Stem Stitch using three strands of floss on bed linen and six strands on the towel set. Also use six strands for the French Knots on all items; on the towel set, work the knots as shown on pattern, *after* tearing away the tissue.

1 White
4-A Pink
10-A Canary Yellow
26 Nile Green
38 Dark Orange
43 Dark Yellow
65 Beauty Pink
120 Crimson
124 Indian Pink
201-A Light Aquatone
216 Avocado
217 Coral Pink
218 Coral Glow
222 Dark Aquatone

MOTIF FOR BLANKET WITH COLOR KEY

• DARK PINK
○ LIGHT PINK
✕ GREEN
▨ TURQUOISE
◻ WHITE

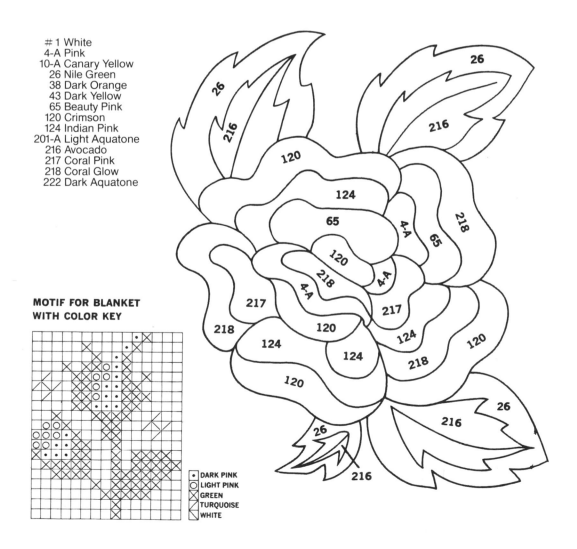

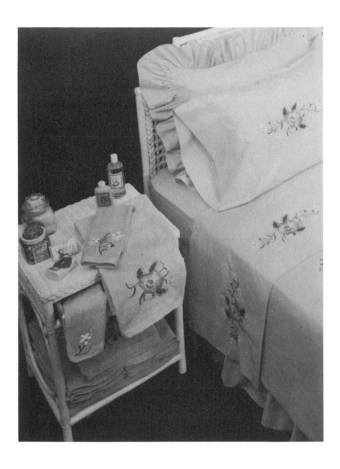

by weaving a 6″ tail of floss behind previously worked stitches. To make it easy for you, all our designs are worked on 22 threads to the inch even-weave linen.

GENERAL MATERIALS: Even-weave linen in the size required; black 6-strand embroidery floss; size 22 tapestry needle; colored basting thread; scissors; square embroidery frame (*optional*—even-weave linen can be worked without a frame); masking tape.

How to find the center of any shape fabric: On back of fabric draw diagonal lines from corner to corner. The center point occurs where lines cross. Draw vertical and horizontal lines from center point to divide fabric into quarters. Baste these guidelines so that the basting thread runs between the threads of the fabric.

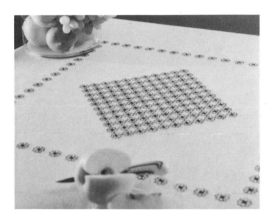

EMBROIDERED BLANKET

MATERIALS: Thermal blanket with honeycomb weave, 3-strand Persian yarn in these colors and quantities: turquoise, 6 yds.; white, 5 yds.; green, 35 yds.; light and dark pink, 7 yds. of each.

DIRECTIONS: Decide how many motifs you want and where you want them. For each motif, mark off a 10″ square with rows of basting stitches. In the center of the basted square, start the embroidery with the center row of the motif working one Cross Stitch in each *woven* square of the blanket. Use three strands of yarn in the colors indicated in the Color Key with the diagram. On one half of the blanket work all the designs facing in one direction; reverse the direction on the other half.

BLACKWORK EMBROIDERY

GENERAL INFORMATION: All the designs given here are worked by counting threads and outlining them with simple straight stitches of black thread to form a geometric pattern which is repeated to form a design or fill an area. A close pattern produces a dark design; an open pattern—a light design. In all the pattern graphs each square equals two threads. End off

BRIDGE TABLE CLOTH

(46″ square)

MATERIALS: General Materials, plus 5 skeins of black embroidery floss; even-weave linen, 52″ × 52″.

DIRECTIONS: Cover fabric edges with masking tape. Find center of fabric; baste guidelines. On wrong side of fabric, measure 9¾″ from center point along each guideline and mark with a pin. At these marks, draw vertical and horizontal lines which cross each other at corners. Baste on these lines to form border guideline. Using three strands of floss, make Single Cross Stitch at center point of fabric. Using the pattern and the Back Stitch, enclose the Cross Stitch in a box and add boxes at the four corners. Repeat motifs (connecting them with Cross Stitches) until you have a diamond-shaped pattern measuring approximately 9⅝″ square. Using the border guideline corners as center points, work one motif at each corner. These motifs measure ⅞″ square. Fill guide-

TABLE CLOTH EACH SQ. = 2 THREADS

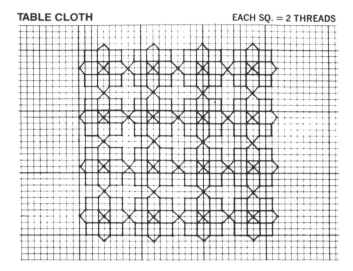

lines between corners with motifs, spacing evenly (ours are about ⅜″ apart) to complete the border. Remove basting and masking tape. Place embroidery face down on a terry towel and iron with a wet-pressing cloth and hot iron; allow to dry. Turn edges under 1″ then 2″ to form a double-turned hem. Press in place, overlapping at corners. Hem by hand with small invisible stitches.

BOLSTER PILLOW
(about 18″ long)

MATERIALS: General Materials plus 6 skeins black embroidery floss; even-weave linen: One piece 19″ × 26″; two pieces 9″ in diameter for ends; one 18″ bolster 8″ in diameter, or polyester fiberfill pillow stuffing, about 1¼ pounds; 2″-wide lace with scalloped edge, 3 yds.

DIRECTIONS: Cover fabric edges with masking tape. Find center of fabric; baste guidelines. Using three strands of floss, make Eye Stitch

at center point of fabric. Using the pattern, work around the Eye Stitch to form the motif as in Steps a, b and c. When center row of design is completed, work two more rows and connecting square on both sides of it. Add end rows, spacing them 37 threads from the edge of the center panel of embroidery. Remove basting and masking tape. Press. Cut four 26″ lengths of lace. Turn ends under ½″. Pin straight edge to 26″ sides of embroidery, 1½″ in from raw edge on right side. Add a second row of lace ½″ in from the first. With right sides together, stitch 19″ edges in ½″ seam to make bolster cover, leaving 10″ open at seam center. Press seam open. Pin lace inward to keep it out of the way. With right sides together, stitch end pieces to ends of bolster. Turn cover right side out. Remove pins from lace. Insert bolster; blindstitch open edges.

BOLSTER PILLOW EACH SQ. = 2 THREADS

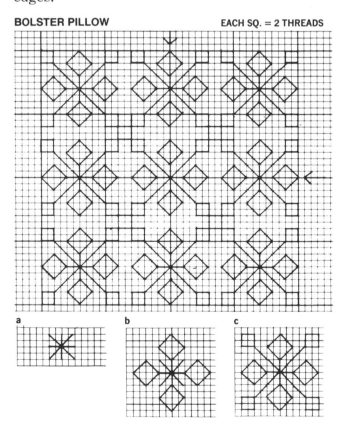

EYE STITCH

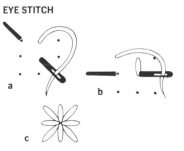

APPLIQUÉ

VEGETABLE FELT-APPLIQUÉ
MATERIALS: Felt yardage or squares in various colors; white fabric glue.
DIRECTIONS: Following the directions on page 224, enlarge the patterns and cut out.

PICTURE PANELS: Cut out felt vegetables, leaves and stems in colors and number you wish and apply to felt background, then frame.

HOT MITT: Slipstitch felt appliqués to purchased hot mitt.

APRON:
MATERIALS: ½ yd. each of solid and gingham fabric.
Cutting: *Apron* 18″ × 36″ and *waistband* 4″ × 18″ from solid color; *two pockets*, each 9½″ × 10″ and *two ties*, each 4″ × 36″ from gingham.
DIRECTIONS: Make narrow hems at all side edges and 2″ hem at the bottom of the apron. Stitch pocket pieces right sides together, leaving opening. Turn and press. Slipstitch opening. Iron felt appliqué to pocket over fusible webbing. Edgestitch pocket to apron about 3″

from one side, at top of hem. Turn under ½" at ends and one long edge of waistband. Sew gathering row at top of apron. Stitch it to raw edge of waistband, right sides together, pulling apron up to fit. Make narrow hems on long edges and one end of ties. Pleat other end to 1½". Lap one at each end of waistband over wrong side near raw edge. Baste. Fold waistband to wrong side. Pin ends together to enclose ties and place long folded edge over apron raw edges. Stitch ⅛" from all waistband edges.

HOT PADS: Buy an asbestos disc from dime or hardware store. Trace around it on felt, twice. Cut out on outer side of tracing line. Slipstitch appliqué to one circle. Whipstitch edges of the two circles together over asbestos.

SHOPPING TOTE:
MATERIALS: One yd. 39" fabric; felt appliqués.
DIRECTIONS: Cut bag 32" × 21"; cut two straps, each 32" × 9".
Sewing: Fold a bag piece in half matching 21" sides. Seam side and bottom. *To square corners:* At seamed corner, pull back away from front, bringing seams together. Pin. Draw 3" line across corner, perpendicular to the seams. Stitch on line. Repeat at other corner. Turn. Fold bag vertically from each corner and edge-stitch fold to top of bag to give appearance of boxing strip. Turn under and stitch 3" hem at top. Turn in one long edge of strap ½" and press. Fold strap twice lengthwise, matching second fold to pressed edge for 3" wide straps. Stitch large X from corner to corner through bag and strap. Appliqué felt pieces with fusible webbing.

1 SQ.=1"

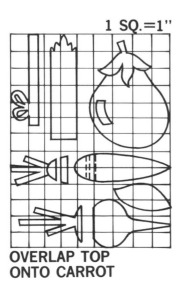

**OVERLAP TOP
ONTO CARROT**

GINGHAM PILLOWS

MATERIALS For one pillow, 14" square, plus 3½" ruffle: 44"-wide gingham, 1 yd.; 16" square of batting and of muslin; scraps of fabric for borders and appliqués; pillowform or stuffing.
DIRECTIONS: *Cutting:* From gingham cut 15" square back, 11" square center front panel and 3 yds. x 8" ruffle. From contrasting fabric cut borders—two pieces each 11½" × 3" and two pieces each 15" × 3".
Assembly (Seam allowance ½".):
1. Seam short borders to top and bottom of center front panel. Seam long borders to remaining sides.
2. Piece ruffle if necessary. Seam short ends. Fold lengthwise, right sides out, and gather raw edges.
3. Edgestitch appliqués to front panel *(directions for each pillow appliqué follow).*
4. Place front panel over batting over muslin. Baste layers across centers. Zigzag stitch over appliqué edges through all layers. Straight stitch along borders and 1" inside edge of plate in Artichoke pillow.
5. With right sides together and raw edges even, stitch ruffle to pillow top.
6. With right sides together, stitch back to front

(with ruffle in between) around three sides and four corners, leaving 10″ open on one side. Turn right side out. Insert pillow form. Whipstitch open edges.

APPLIQUÉ DIRECTIONS: Following the directions on page 224, enlarge the patterns in FIGS. 1–16 on brown paper and cut out. Half patterns are given for most appliqués, so pin them to folded fabric for cutting.

Apple Appliqué: Cut four calico apples (FIG. 1). From muslin: cut one underbasket (FIG. 2); cut five strips each 6½″ × 4″ and 1 band, 9″ × 2″.

1. Overlap three apples, starting 1″ from top border of front panel. Edgestitch.

2. Stitch underbasket over apples, 3½″ from top border.

3. Fold strips in half lengthwise and stitch ¼″ from long edges. Center the seam and press. To simulate staves, stitch strips over underbasket, seams down, lower edges turned under and matching underbasket bottom.

4. Cover raw upper ends of strips with band, turning in its edges ½″.

5. Trace underbasket on strips; stitch on drawn line. Trim away excess muslin.

6. Stitch single fruit over basket, as shown.

Strawberry Appliqué: Cut eight calico strawberries (FIG. 3) and eight green leaves (FIG. 4). From muslin: Cut one underbasket (FIG. 5); five strips each 6½″ × 3½″ and four strips each 8″ × 3½″.

1. Overlap seven strawberries, then leaves, starting 1″ from top border. Edgestitch over all raw edges.

2. Stitch underbasket over berries, 4½″ from top border.

3. With the shorter strips, turning under both ends, follow Step 3 of Apple Pillow. Prepare longer strips the same way and weave them in and out of the vertical strips.

4. Work Steps 5 and 6 of Apple Pillow.

Egg Appliqué: Cut six muslin eggs (FIG. 6). Cut one basket (FIG. 7).

1. Overlap five eggs, starting 2½″ from top border. Edgestitch over all raw edges.

2. Stitch basket over eggs, then one egg over basket.

Lemon Appliqué: Cut seven calico lemons (FIG. 8) and one green leaf (FIG. 9). Cut one bowl (FIG. 10).

1. Overlap six lemons, starting 2″ from top border. Edgestitch over all raw edges.

2. Stitch bowl over lemons, then one lemon and leaf over bowl.

Mushroom Appliqué: Cut 12 brown mushroom

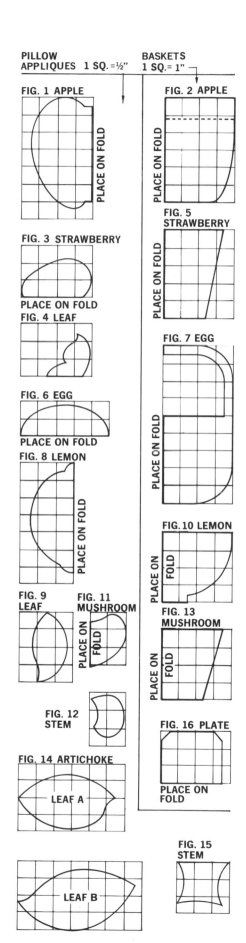

caps (FIG. 11) and 10 tan stems (FIG. 12). Cut one basket (FIG. 13).

1. Overlap nine caps and seven stems, starting 1½" from top border. Edgestitch over all raw edges.
2. Stitch basket over mushrooms 5½" from top border.
3. Stitch three mushrooms over basket.

Artichoke Appliqué: Cut two light green (FIG. 14A), four medium green (FIGS. 14A and B) and four dark green (FIG. 14B) leaves, and one dark green stem (FIG. 15). Cut one white plate (FIG. 16).

1. Center and edgestitch plate, starting 3" from top border.
2. Stitch light green leaves, starting 2" from border. Overlap with three medium green leaves 2½" from border. Overlap with four dark green leaves 3½" from border over a centered stem.
3. Stitch medium green leaf over plate.

RUFFLED PILLOWS

MATERIALS: *For Rooster, Hen, Wreath, and Bowl and Pitcher pillows:* Solid fabric, 16½" square and a strip (can be pieced) 5⅝" × 123"; thread to match; printed fabric, 16½" square and a strip 3⅝" × 123"; thread to match; fabric scraps for appliqué; thread to match; one bag of polyester fiberfill for each pillow; pencil; paper for patterns; white glue; Stitch Witchery® fusible webbing; scissors; pins.

For Strawberry pillow: Solid fabric, two 16½" squares and a strip 7" × 123"; thread to match; fabric scraps for appliqué; thread to match; green thread for vines; one bag of polyester fiberfill; pencil; paper for patterns; white glue; Stitch Witchery® fusible webbing; scissors; pins.

DIRECTIONS: *For Rooster, Hen, Wreath, and Bowl and Pitcher pillows:* Following directions on page 224 enlarge appliqué pattern and trace onto paper. Cut out pattern pieces and trace onto fabrics. Cut out. Using photo and pattern as guides, form design on solid square of fabric, keeping pieces in place with a dab of white glue. Working one piece at a time, attach pieces together and to solid fabric square, following Stitch Witchery® directions. For stitching down appliqués with a zigzag sewing machine, set the length of the stitches very close to give the effect of satin stitching, using photo and pattern as guides. Stitch over all raw edges; press appliqué smooth. If necessary, piece long strips of solid and print fabrics with ½" seams; press seams to one side. With right sides together, stitch solid strip to print strip with a ½" seam along one long edge. Trim seam to ¼"; press toward solid strip. Fold wrong sides together with raw edges even; press along fold to leave 1" border of solid fabric as shown. With right sides together, stitch ½" seams in short ends of strip; turn; press. Baste raw edges together with long machine stitches, ⅜" from edge; stitch again ¼" from previous stitching. Gather ruffle carefully to a 64" long strip. Pin ruffle to appliquéd square, right sides together, overlapping 2" of ruffle at bottom of square. Stitch ruffle to square, just inside second row of gathering stitches. With ruffle still toward appliquéd square, pin right side of print fabric to right side of appliquéd square, keeping ruffle free. Stitch a ½" seam through all thicknesses on three sides; turn and press, pressing ruffle away from squares. Stuff with polyester fiberfill until firm; fold ½" under on free edge of back square and whipstitch opening closed, tucking in seam allowance of ruffle and front square.

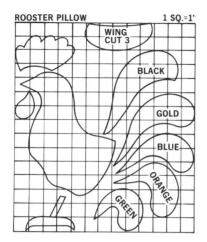

ROOSTER PILLOW   1 SQ.=1"

WING CUT 3

BLACK

GOLD

BLUE

ORANGE

GREEN

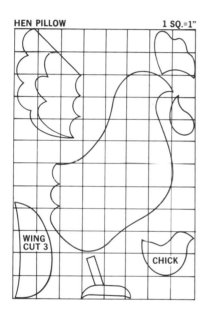

HEN PILLOW   1 SQ.=1"

WING CUT 3

CHICK

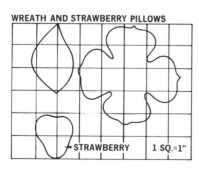

WREATH AND STRAWBERRY PILLOWS

STRAWBERRY   1 SQ.=1"

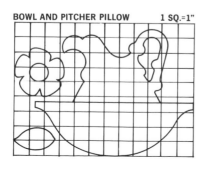

BOWL AND PITCHER PILLOW   1 SQ.=1"

For Strawberry pillow: Follow directions for other pillows, with the following changes: Do not use Stitch Witchery® to attach appliqué to solid fabric square. Instead, stitch partially around each strawberry, leaving a small opening at the top. With a pencil point or other narrow object, stuff a small amount of polyester fiberfill into each strawberry to pad it, then finish stitching around. Do not press appliquéd design. To make ruffle, fold solid fabric strip in half lengthwise; stitch ½" seams in both short ends and continue following directions for other pillows.

FELT CHEST

MATERIALS: Fiberboard storage chest (ours is 24" wide × 28" high × 12" deep); White spray paint and White spray primer; background fabric (we used ¾ yds. 42" wide fabric); scraps or one 9" × 12" piece each of Orange, Yellow, White and Magenta felt (or colors of your choice); fabric glue; dressmaker's carbon; tracing paper.
Note: This design fits large drawers 22½" × 5½" and a pair of small drawers, each 11¼" × 5½", all with center knobs.
DIRECTIONS: Enlarge diagrams on tracing paper. Trace bird wing and flower centers separately, for cutting patterns. Remove drawers and knobs. With primer, spray drawer fronts, knobs, and chest front, top and sides. Allow to dry. Spray with paint, drying between coats, until woodgrain is covered (spraying the drawer fronts white will keep the color of the

fabric true). Measure drawer fronts, adding at least 1″ to each edge. Cut fabric for each drawer. Mark position of drawer knob on fabric.

For small drawers: Bird diagram should be positioned on drawer fabric so that center of heart meets inside edge of drawers (1″ from fabric edge) with flower and bird traced on either side of knob *(see photo).* Through dressmaker's carbon trace stems and enough of design to indicate placement of appliqués. For other small drawer turn pattern over and repeat, matching heart sections.

For large drawers: Broken lines indicate lengthwise and crosswise centers of drawers. Fold fabric in half both ways and press fold to mark centers. Place flower diagram on fabric, matching broken lines to pressed foldlines and trace placement marks same as for small drawers. Turn pattern over and repeat for other side of drawers. With couching stitch, sew yarn to fabric over stem line. Cut felt appliqués in colors indicated. Paper-punch two bird's eyes. Sew wing and eye to each bird and center to flowers using small running stitch. Then sew appliqués to drawer fabric. Press out foldlines. Center fabric over drawer front and replace knobs, cutting tiny slits for screws. With design straight and centered on drawer, turn excess fabric over the edges and glue as follows: Brush strip of glue to each side of drawer. Stretching fabric taut, fold fabric edge over glue. Repeat for bottom, then top, folding or mitering corners neatly.

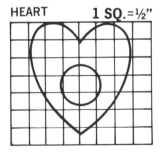

HEART   1 SQ. = ½″

DIRECTOR'S CHAIR

MATERIALS: 9″ × 12″ felt pieces: one Orange, one Yellow, one Green, one Magenta (or felt scraps in four colors); Green yarn, 1 yd.; tracing paper; dressmaker's carbon; fabric glue; white quilting thread.

DIRECTIONS: Following directions on page 224, enlarge the designs on tracing paper. Trace off bird wing and centers for flowers and hearts separately, for cutting patterns. With pencil, lightly mark center of chair back at top and bottom edges. Position bird pattern on chair back, aligning heart with center marks. With dressmaker's carbon, trace stem lines and just enough of design to show position of appliqués. Turn pattern over and repeat for other side of chair to complete the design. On chair seat, mark midpoint. To locate, place yardstick diagonally corner to corner and mark light line at approximate center. Repeat with opposite corners to make an X at center. Position flower pattern on seat so that dot on pattern is over X on canvas and long broken line extends diagonally to seat corner. Trace as for chair back. Turn pattern over and repeat for opposite corner. For remaining two corners, repeat except for yellow circles near center. Cut motifs from tracing paper to use as patterns. With couching stitch and quilting thread sew yarn to canvas seat and back over stem lines. From patterns, cut felt appliqués and ⅝″ circles in colors indicated (bird's eyes can be cut with paper punch, if available). Sew wing and eye to each bird, centers to flowers and circles to

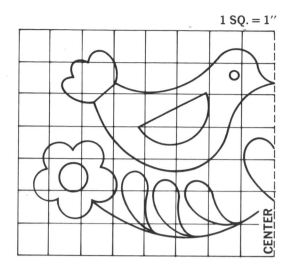

1 SQ. = 1"

CENTER

1 SQ. = 1"

CENTER

hearts, using small running stitch. Affix appliqués in place temporarily with dab of glue, then sew to canvas. Replace canvas on chair frame.

FIG. 1 LEAF FOR QUILT

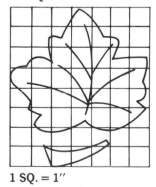

1 SQ. = 1"

FIG. 2 RIPPLE QUILTING PATTERN FOR BANDS AND BORDER

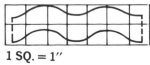

1 SQ. = 1"

MAPLE-LEAF QUILT FROM SCRAPS

Approximately 80" × 100"

MATERIALS: *White Fabric:* a used but unworn double or queen size bed sheet for the backing, and a twin-size sheet for the blocks; 44"-wide Green polyester-cotton, 2⅞ yards; 90" × 108" quilt batting; scraps of washable print fabric for leaves (altogether about 2 yds., 45" wide); cardboard; white quilting thread; masking tape.

DIRECTIONS: *Pattern:* Following the directions on page 224, enlarge the leaf and stem patterns in FIG. 1 and the ripple quilting pattern in FIG. 2 on cardboard; cut out.

Cutting: Cut 20 white blocks, each 17" square. From the full length of green fabric, cut 10 green strips, each 3¼" wide. Cut three of these strips into sixteen 17" bands. Cut 80 leaves and 80 stems as follows: Trace around pattern on right side of fabric. Cut out a scant ¼" outside the traced lines.

Sewing (¼" seam allowance): Appliqué each block as follows: Clip inside corners of leaves. Turn under edges of leaves and stems on drawn lines, except top of stem. Pin four of each to a block, alternating colors, slipping top of stem under leaf. Slip-stitch turned edges. Alternate five blocks with four short bands; pin right sides together and seam. Repeat, to make four

Color photo on page 135

rows. Alternate the four joined rows with three of the longer bands. Pin and stitch. Trim end of bands flush with blocks. Seam two borders to quilt short edges, matching centers (ends will extend equally). Seam borders to long edges the same way. Press borders outward. At corners, turn under overlapping border on the diagonal and slipstitch, to mitre. Trim diagonal seam allowance to ½". On the floor, lay out backing sheet wrong side up and tape at corners. Over this, center the batting and then the top, right sides up. Smooth out wrinkles and pin through all layers. Remove tape. Baste from center outwards to each side and corner. Quilt (work ⅛" running stitch through all layers) around each leaf and on leaf to simulate veins. Quilt white background surrounding leaves with diagonal lines about 1" apart. Trace FIG. 2 (ripple quilting pattern) along the block bands and borders, then quilt on these lines, placing the pattern at dotted lines to retrace. Remove basting. Trim away excess batting and backing, to match top quilt. Pin binding to right side of quilt along two opposite sides, row edges even. Machine stitch ¼" seam through all layers. Turn binding to wrong side, turn under ¼" and slipstitch to the back. Repeat at the remaining sides of the quilt.

VELVET WALL HANGING

MATERIALS: *Velvet (or velveteen)*, ¼ yd. each Dark Green, Light Green and Gray-Olive, and ⅜ yd. Olive-Gold; *⅛"-wide velvet ribbon:* 2½ yds. Bright Green, 1 yd. Olive; *⅝"-wide velvet ribbon:* 2 yds. Olive and ¼ yd. Coral; *2"-wide velvet ribbon:* ⅔ yd. Coral; lining fabric, one 27" × 31" piece; 3"-wide buckram tape, 1½ yds; two 1½" drapery rings; several shades of green and olive thread; dressmaker's carbon and tracing wheel; transparent tape; felt scraps (or 9" × 12" squares) in Pink, Coral, Brick, Pale Apricot, Gold, Chartreuse, Lime, Light Olive, Dark Olive, Green and Aqua.

DIRECTIONS:

1. Following the directions on page 224, enlarge the A to J patterns in the chart, including the outlines. Cut out each section separately; label each and *number* the inner sections, as shown. These sections will be the basic background area.

2. Tape each pattern (except D; see *Note* below) to velvet of the background color indicated in the chart. With carbon and tracing wheel, trace the four corners of the outlines and portions of each design, enough to mark its placement for

Color photo on page 136

future use.

(*Note:* For D, use two pieces of 2"-wide coral ribbon.)

3. Cut velvet 1" larger than the enlarged patterns all around. Remove patterns. Label the velvet sections A, B, and so forth.

4. Tape or pin Section A pattern to felt color No. 2 (Color No. 1 is not used in A). See legend for felt color numbers. Trace and cut out all areas marked "2"; pin in marked position on velvet background. Using various colors of thread and different length stitches, zigzag edges of each piece. (You may wish to experiment first with scraps.)

5. Continue to cut and appliqué A Section areas in other colors until completed.

6. Now pin or tape paper pattern on the worked velvet to check its size; sometimes the appliqué stitching causes the fabric to pucker. Trim velvet ½" from pattern edges.

7. Repeat steps 4, 5 and 6 for Section Patterns B to J.

8. With right sides together, pin the sections together as shown in the Assembly Chart. Stitch in ½" seams. Lightly press seams, using a needleboard, if available; if not, use a piece of velvet, right side up, on the ironing board.

9. Using a narrow zigzag stitch, or other decorative machine stitch, topstitch the ribbon trim in place, as shown in photo.

10. On wrong side of appliqué baste a strip of 3"-wide buckram tape ½" from top and bottom edges. With right sides together, pin appliqué and lining fabric together. Stitch ½" seam on top and side edges, catching buckram ends in the side seams. Remove basting from top edge.

11. Trim corners and seams. Turn hanging right side out. Turn in bottom edges ½"; zigzag across, catching in lower edge of buckram. Remove basting. Press, if necessary.

12. Sew drapery rings to top corners.

FIG. 1 WALL HANGING PATTERN DIAGRAM AND ASSEMBLY CHART

1 SQ. = 1″

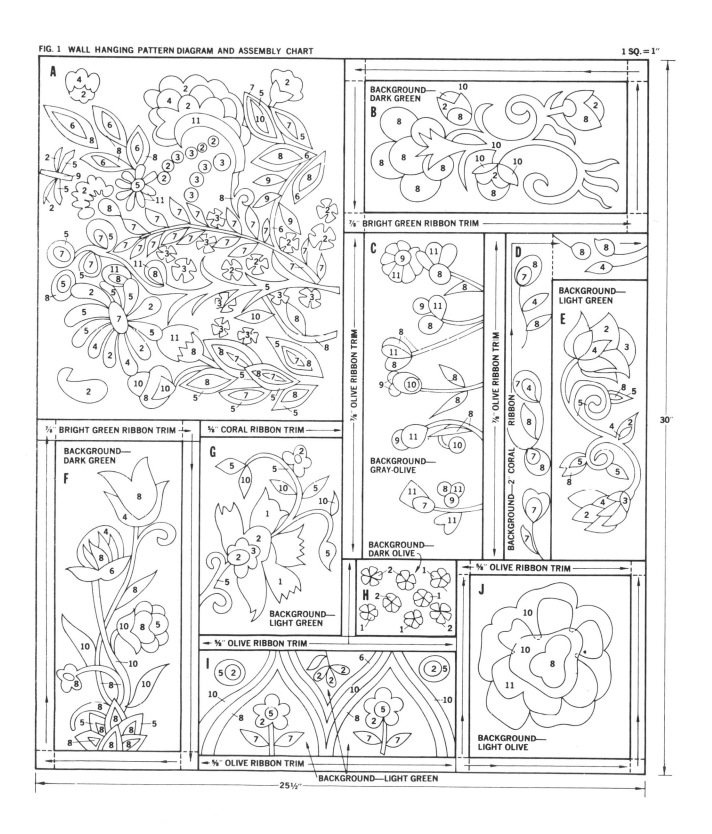

LEGEND FOR FELT COLORS

1—PINK	5—GOLD	9—DARK OLIVE
2—CORAL	6—CHARTREUSE	10—GREEN
3—BRICK	7—LIME	11—AQUA
4—PALE APRICOT	8—LIGHT OLIVE	

TAILORED BRIDGE TABLE COVER

Designed to fit a standard-size 34″ × 34″ card table. Completed size, 44″ × 44″, including the 5″ fitted drop all around

MATERIALS: 45″-wide Beige linen, 1⅜ yds. or any similar washable fabric of the same width (pre-shrink, if necessary); Kettle Cloth®, or firmly-woven cotton, in the following colors and amounts: ¼ yd. each Orange and Green, and ⅛ yd. each Turquoise and Magenta; polyester-core thread in colors to match all fabrics; embroidery needle; 4 regular large snaps, or gripper snaps with attachment; iron-on mending tape, 1 package; double-fold bias tape, 1 package in Turquoise; Beige broadcloth, 1⅜ yds., or any lightweight 45″-wide cotton suitable for lining; light color dressmaker's carbon and tracing wheel; tracing paper; transparent tape; white tailor's chalk; yardstick.

DIRECTIONS: Following the directions on page 224, enlarge the corner and center patterns in FIG. 1 on separate pieces of tracing paper.

Cutting the tablecloth:

Trim both linen and lining fabrics so that they measure 45″ × 45″; set lining aside.

Transferring the patterns:

Using a yardstick and white tailor's chalk, draw 18″ and 6″-long guidelines on the linen fabric right side, as shown in FIG. 1A. Place the enlarged corner motif on the corner of the fabric, aligning the pattern center line with the chalk line on the fabric. Tape pattern at top and bottom. Slip dressmaker's carbon under the tracing paper and trace only enough marks along

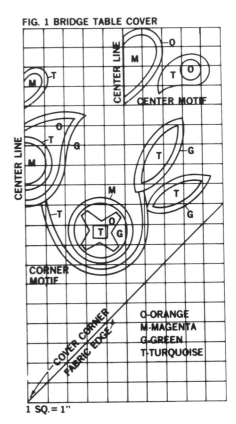

FIG. 1 BRIDGE TABLE COVER

CENTER LINE

CENTER MOTIF

CORNER MOTIF

COVER CORNER
FABRIC EDGE

O-ORANGE
M-MAGENTA
G-GREEN
T-TURQUOISE

1 SQ. = 1″

FIG. 1A CHALK GUIDE LINES

6″   18″   6″   18″

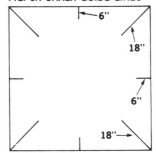

FIG. 2 WHIPSTITCHING APPLIQUE EDGES

¼″

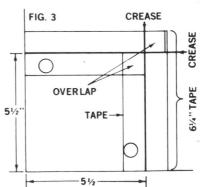

FIG. 3   CREASE   CREASE

OVERLAP

5½″   TAPE

6¼″ TAPE

5½

the outside lines of the motifs to indicate placement. Be very sure that the tracing is accurately placed because some dressmaker's carbon leaves a virtually indelible mark on the fabric. Now turn the paper over and trace the other side of the motif to make the complete pattern. Repeat for remaining three corners. Trace the center motifs at the edges of the crop 1″ from edge and halfway between the corners, again turning the pattern over to complete it. Repeat for remaining three sides.

Cutting the appliqué pieces:

Because the motifs are appliquéd to each other in layers, they are shown layered in FIG. 1. Therefore, using your enlarged tracing paper pattern, tape it to Kettle Cloth or cotton *of the colors indicated* in FIG. 1, and, with dressmaker's carbon and wheel, trace the outlines of each layer of the motifs. Be sure to trace enough for all four corners and sides. Now cut out the traced fabric, adding ¼″ all around (this will be turned under when the pieces are whipstitched in place).

Stitching the Layered appliqués:

Using the large tulip in the corner motif as an example, the pieces are appliquéd to each other as follows: Turn under and pin ¼″ a little of the way around the magenta circle. Pin this at the center to the middle of the turquoise circle. Using a single strand of magenta thread, whipstitch the folded edge to the turquoise fabric (*see* FIG. 2), spacing the stitches ⅛″ apart. (As you stitch around it is easier to tuck the raw edge under with the tip of the needle, than to try to form a perfectly round circle with straight pins.) Now appliqué the turned-under edges of the turquoise circle to the orange tulip shape, using turquoise thread, then the orange shape to the green bottom layer. Pin the layered appliqué over the traced outline on the table cover and whipstitch in place. Repeat for remaining pieces. Last, pin the turquoise curves of the bias tape in place, tucking the cut ends of each under the appliqué pieces they link.

Pressing the cloth into shape:

When the appliqués are completed, press creases into the fabric to outline the size of the table top. To do this, turn one edge of the cover under 5½″ and firmly press the fold line the full length of the fabric; repeat for other three sides. Now, press into each squared-off corner a diagonal crease from the outer to the inner corner. These pressed creases are a part of the cover's design.

Reinforcing the corners:

Turn the cover appliquéd side down on your work surface. Cut 8 pieces of mending tape 5″ long and 8 pieces 6¼″ long. Press them on either side of the corner creases, overlapping the ends as shown in FIG. 3. This will stiffen the corners to insure a crisp, tailored look.

Fitting:

Add snaps or gripper snaps, ½″ from crease and edge, as shown in FIG. 3.

Lining:

With right sides together stitch lining to cover, taking ½″ seams and leaving 20″ open on one side. Clip corners. Turn right side out. Press the open edges to the inside and whipstitch the opening. Press the cover, ironing the creases again to set them firmly.

Note: Whenever the cloth is laundered be sure to press the creases again to retain the crisp, neat effect.

HEX AND SCALLOPED FLOWER COVERLET

MATERIALS: Half wool/half rayon felt in three colors 72″-wide in amount required for your bed size (*see* DIRECTIONS); thread to match felt colors; soft cotton/blend fabric for lining (*optional*); yardstick; chalk; cardboard.

DIRECTIONS: Following the directions on page 224, enlarge 6¾″-diameter hex and scalloped flower motifs, spacing the lines 1″ apart. Cut out pattern. On separate pieces of paper or cardboard trace each section of the design that is to be cut from each color felt; cut out. The separate patterns are used to make the hex and flower motif layers.

Note: For the hex design, cut the shaded background circle (we used yellow) ¼″ smaller than the circumference of the spoke layer that covers it (we used red).

Determining Coverlet Size: The easiest way to make this coverlet is to start with the backing—one large piece of felt pieced to the desired size of the finished coverlet. It should equal the top of the bed measurement, plus 20″ at each side and at the foot of the bed (if the coverlet is to touch the floor). Add another 2″ for hem. The squares are appliquéd to this large piece.

Standard Bed Sizes are:

Twin: 39″ × 75″

Double: 54″ × 75″

Queen: 60″ × 80″

King: 76″ × 80″

Once you have the correct bed top measurements you can determine the width of the border (top or hem) in relationship to the size of the appliqué squares.

Determining Hem Border: A double bed for example, measures 54″×75″. If you add a 20″ drop, plus 2″ for hem you need a backing piece measuring 98″ wide by 97″ long. If the appliqué squares are 8″×8″, you can use eleven across. That uses up 88″ of the width and leaves 10″-5″ at each edge, of which 2″ is the hem allowance. That would leave 3″ at each edge for a band or border of color at the hem edge. *A queen size bed* measures 60″ wide by 80″ long. If you wish the coverlet to go to the floor, add 22″ (20″ to reach the floor and 2″ for hem). Therefore, a floor-length queen-size coverlet measures 104″×102″. You would need two 102″ lengths of 72″-wide felt, or 5²/₃ yds. Because felt selvages aren't always even, count on a usable 70″.

Determining Top of Bed Border (as the yellow band is added in the photo): If you wish the border band to outline the top of the bed *instead of the bottom*, do this: Measure the top of the bed and see how many squares fit into it. For instance, a queen-size bed is 60″ wide. If you used seven squares, each 8″×8″, that would use

56″ of the width leaving you with 4″ to spare. A 2″ wide band could be sewn at that point, and the next square would start on the drop of the coverlet. The length is figured the same way (with any leftover or uneven inches used at the top for the edge binding). Always measure your bed. There are variations in size and thickness of mattresses, as well as variations in bed height. Generally, the figures we have used will serve as a guide for standard-size beds. But remember, casters on a bed may change the height, and so will the type of frame. Also, if you want your coverlet to cover the pillow, add another 8″ or more across the top and sides of the quilt. For a *water bed*, make a quilt the size of the bed top, measuring inside the wood frame, plus about 6″ at each edge to tuck in.

Determining Felt Yardage: Use graph paper to draw the dimensions of the required pieces, in an area equalling 70″ wide (the usable width of the felt).

1. Mark off the dimensions for the coverlet backing pieces to determine the yardage.

2. To determine the amount needed for the squares that cover the backing, jot down the figure obtained in Step 1 (one of those colors

FLOWER

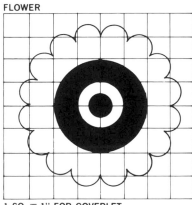

1 SQ. = 1″ FOR COVERLET

HEX SIGN

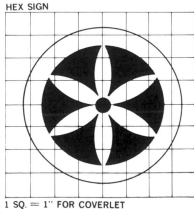

1 SQ. = 1″ FOR COVERLET

should also be the backing color). Half of the backing will be covered with one color, and half with another, as the squares alternate. If you needed 5²/₃ yards of backing color, you would then need an additional 2²/₃ yards each of the backing color and one other color.

3. To determine the amounts needed for the layered appliqué pieces, cut the pieces needed to appliqué four of the squares, layer by layer, using colored paper. Place these on yardage and you can determine very closely how much you will need of each color to do four squares. Multiply that to get a total.

Making the Coverlet:

4. Using the figures for your size bed, cut bed top, side drop and foot-drop pieces.

5. Stitch side and foot-drop pieces to bed top, taking ½″ seams.

6. Mark a lengthwise chalk line down the center of the bed-top piece as a guide for placement of squares. (If your backing color is repeated on the top of the quilt you can use the leftover backing felt for appliqué pieces.)

7. Next, mark the square dimensions on the felt (half of backing color, half of another) and cut out.

Stitching Appliqués to the Squares:

8. *Hex*—First sew the background circle (we used yellow) in place on the felt square (using the photo on page 88 as a guide). Tack it at the outside edges. A few stitches will hold it secure enough for you to proceed. Then the spoke design is sewn over the circle. Sew the outside edge of the hex sign first, then sew the cut-out areas. Last, add the center dot.

9. *Scalloped Flower*—First sew the scalloped flower to square. Then add the three remaining circles, one at a time. On the last circles, it is not necessary that the stitches go all the way through all layers. Just be sure each circle is sewn to the layer beneath it. The stacked circles build up thickness in the center, adding to the weight and luxuriousness of the coverlet. Also, it is much simpler to sew this way.

Stitching the Squares to the Backing:

Finished appliquéd squares are now sewn to the previously marked backing piece, starting at the center chalkline and working out to the edges.

Lining (optional): The quilt may be lined with any lightweight material, though lining is not essential. The lining can be whipstitched in place to the bottom side of the quilt. When the 2″ hem is turned back, it will cover the edge of the lining.

FELT WALL HANGINGS

MATERIALS: White or Ecru doilies in any size or shape; wool-rayon felt in six to nine colors; 6-strand embroidery floss in colors that match or coordinate with the felt; thread to match doily.

GENERAL DIRECTIONS: Stacked felt projects are cut and appliquéd one layer at a time, and generally stitched together from the top down, using the layer with the doily as the starting point. For *sewing down layers,* and the *larger shapes* appliquéd to them, use tiny running stitches with a single strand of embroidery floss, working about ⅛″ from the edge of the felt. Pull the floss so there is no slack. The tightened thread makes an interesting edge pattern. The *smaller felt appliqués* are attached in the same way, or with one or more French Knots, using two or three strands of embroidery floss (*see* BASIC EMBROIDERY STITCHES page 228). To attach the *lining* to the bottom felt layer, use the tiny running stitch, or overcast the flush edges, working the stitches ⅛″ apart with a single strand of embroidery floss.

Starting the stack: Choose your doily (or doilies) and blindstitch it all around to a piece of felt cut about ¼″ larger all around than the doily itself. Now that the doily is firmly anchored to its felt background layer, the remaining felt can be stacked in either of two ways. Three of the hangings have felt shapes appliquéd to the top of the doily. For Hangings 2 and 3, the felt pieces should be stacked and stitched to each other, then stitched to the top of the doily as a unit. In Hanging 6, the yellow felt circles are attached with a single French Knot. When an unadorned doily forms the top layer, tack it to its background layer at several places in the middle, in addition to blindstitching it around the edge.

Stacking the layers: Our wall hangings are composed of three to seven layers under the felt-backed doily. The outlines of these layers are suggested by the shape of the doily, with each layer enlarged and exaggerated in shape until the hanging's bottom layer is the desired size. Each of these layers is appliquéd with felt cutouts: We used round, oval and teardrop shapes, letters, and occasionally flower and/or petal shapes.

Note: Always be sure to finish sewing and appliquéing each layer before cutting the succeeding one. To achieve continuity of color when adding appliqués, it is a good idea to "bring down" some color; that is, using felt pieces in the same color as the previous layer, as you work from the top to the bottom. Remember, the joy of doing stacked felt work is in allowing your imagination to be your guide as you cut and appliqué the layers. When you start you never know just what shape the final piece will take, and it is a challenge to form different outlines for each of the layers.

The bottom layer: Allow one or two inches extra felt at the top of the final layer as the casing for the dowel from which the hanging is suspended. After this layer had been appliquéd, make the *lining* by tracing the outline on another piece of felt and cutting out the shape. Using a single strand of embroidery floss, work tiny running stitches, or an overcasting stitch, all around the hanging to join the bottom layer to the lining, leaving the casing ends open for the dowel. Insert the dowel and attach a length of decorative cord at the dowel ends as a hanger.

Hanging 1: Two 2½" diameter doilies on seven layers of felt in six colors. *Dimensions:* 14½" × 18½". *Casing Length:* 5".

Hanging 2: One 6" × 12" doily with three stacked felt layers on top and three beneath; six colors in all. *Dimensions:* 17½" × 18½". *Casing Length:* 11".

Hanging 3: One 6½" diameter doily with three stacked felt layers on top and four beneath; six colors in all. *Dimensions:* 11" × 18". *Casing Length:* 11".

Hanging 4: One 4¾" diameter doily on eight layers of felt in six colors. *Dimensions:* 14" × 22". *Casing Length:* 10".

Hanging 5: One 5½" diameter doily on five layers of felt in six colors. *Dimensions:* 12½" × 19". *Casing Length:* 6½".

Hanging 6: One 5" diameter doily with one layer of felt circles on top and eight layers of stacked felt beneath; six colors in all. *Dimensions:* 17" × 18". *Casing Length:* 11".

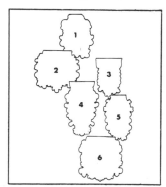

KEY TO STACKED FELT WALL HANGINGS

VIOLET SPRIGGED FELT COVERLET
(58" × 79")

MATERIALS: 72"-wide felt in the following colors and quantities: 3 yds. Violet; 2½ yds. Pale Blue; 1 yd. White; ⅓ yd. Emerald green; 1 ball soft cotton cord and soft chalk in a light color; thread to match felt colors; tailor's chalk and yardstick; lining *(optional)* 6 yds. 45"-wide polyester cotton; lightweight cardboard.

DIRECTIONS: The backing, borders and blocks of our easy-to-make coverlet are cut out first. Using the yardstick and tailor's chalk, mark the dimensions of the coverlet pieces on the felt and cut out as follows:

Violet Felt: 78" × 59" backing; two side border strips, 2½" × 68"; top and bottom border strips one each 2½" × 42"; 13 blocks, 7" × 7".

White Felt: Two side border strips 1½" × 71" each; top and bottom border strips, one each 1½" × 47"; 27 blocks, 7" × 7".

Pale Blue Felt: Two side border strips, 5" × 81" each; top and bottom border strips, one each 5" × 50" (the extra 1" on the width of these pieces becomes the hem); 14 blocks, 7" × 7".

The Appliqués: This coverlet has a random arrangement of 27 long- and 27 short-stemmed violet designs *(see violet blocks diagram)*. The blocks are appliquéd as shown, or reversed (flowers facing up instead of down) or turned

COVERLET DIMENSION AND PLACEMENT DIAGRAM

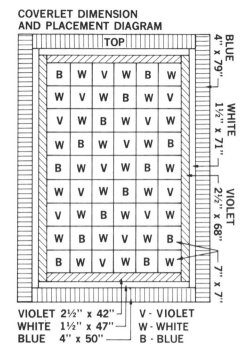

	TOP				
B	W	V	W	B	W
W	V	W	B	W	V
V	W	B	W	V	W
W	B	W	V	W	B
B	W	V	W	B	W
W	V	W	B	W	V
V	W	B	W	V	W
W	B	W	V	W	B
B	W	V	W	B	W

BLUE 4" x 79"
WHITE 1½" x 71"
VIOLET 2½" x 68"
7" x 7"

VIOLET 2½" x 42" ┐ V - VIOLET
WHITE 1½" x 47" ─┤ W - WHITE
BLUE 4" x 50" ──┘ B - BLUE

VIOLET BLOCKS

LONG-STEMMED BLOCK   **SHORT-STEMMED BLOCK**

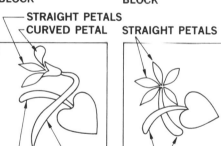

STRAIGHT PETALS
CURVED PETAL
STRAIGHT PETALS

SHORT STEM
LONG STEM
SHORT STEMS

VIOLET APPLIQUE PIECES

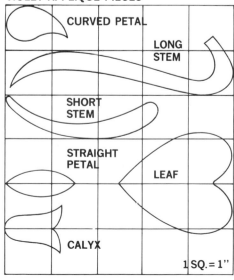

CURVED PETAL
LONG STEM
SHORT STEM
STRAIGHT PETAL
LEAF
CALYX

1 SQ. = 1"

over left to right. First, following the directions on page 224, enlarge the appliqué pieces on cardboard and cut out; cut appliqué pieces as follows:

Green Felt: 81 short stems, 27 long stems, 54 leaves, 27 calyxes. Then the small appliqué pieces are cut from the leftover felt and stitched to the blocks. All the pieces are then placed on top of the backing and whipstitched in place around the edges. Hem all around and the coverlet is finished.

Preparing Felt: Remove creases and wrinkles from felt by pressing lightly on the wrong side with a *dry* iron. If the cut edges are crooked, draw a straight line with yardstick and tailor's chalk and cut off the crooked part.

Cutting:

White Blocks (27) with Violet Flowers: Cut 65 straight petals (5 per flower) for the 13 short-stemmed blocks; cut 14 curved and 28 straight petals for the 14 long-stemmed blocks.

Violet Blocks (13) with White Flowers: Cut 35 straight petals (5 per flower) for the 7 short-stemmed blocks; cut 6 curved petals and 12 straight petals for the 6 long-stemmed blocks.

Blue Blocks (14) with White and Violet Flowers: Cut 20 white and 15 violet straight petals for seven of the blocks (5 per flower) for the short-stemmed blocks; cut 6 white and 8 violet straight petals and 3 white and 4 violet curved petals for the long-stemmed blocks.

Appliquéing the Blocks: Pin pieces to blocks as shown on Violet Block diagram, or turned or reversed. Using thread of a matching color, whipstitch appliqués around edges. Petals should be sewn so that they puff slightly, meaning that the outside edges of the pieces are nudged in just a touch with the tip of the needle as they are sewn.

Marking the Backing: When you have finished appliquéing all the blocks, the next step is marking the positions of the blocks and borders on the 58" × 79" backing as shown in the placement diagram. There are two ways to do this. Use a yardstick and tailor's chalk. Or, use a carpenter's plumb line with cord and chalk. Pull a sufficient length of cord over soft chalk and tape taut at edges on a blue side border measurement line. Snap the cord and it will hit the felt to establish the line. Add remaining borderlines, following chart for placement and length; then fill in the grid of 7" squares.

Sewing Block and Borders to Backing (See Optional Lining): Following the horizontal rows in the placement diagram, place a blue block in the top left corner. Whipstitch the top edge in place; stitch remaining top row blocks on their top edges. Place the blocks for the second row, letting the stitches catch the bottom edge of row one as well as backing and the top edge of row two. Continue until all horizontal rows of blocks are in place. Repeat to connect vertical edges of blocks, making sure to catch backing fabric as you sew. Add the violet and white borders in the same way, catching two edges with one stitch. *Add Optional Lining*, if desired. Add blue border turning 1″ excess blue felt to quilt back and whipstitching edge to backing (through lining, if used) to form a hem and cover the basting.

Optional Lining: Cut fabric yardage in half, crosswise. Stitch together to form one large piece; press seam open. Cut to measure 58″ x 79″. Place right side up over coverlet back, edges flush and even; baste around edges.

TULIP BABY QUILT

(finished size without the optional scalloped border, 36″×48″)

MATERIALS: Washable cotton or cotton-blend fabric. Choose a firmly-woven fabric (not a stretch material): broadcloth, lightweight sailcloth or sports cotton are all practical and come 44″-45″ wide. You will need 3 yds. light blue (1½ yds. for quilt, 1½ yds. for scalloped edge), 3 yds. dark blue (1½ yds. for quilt, 1½ yds. for scalloped edge), 2⅓ yds. dark green and ½ yd. white; 4 yds. 44″-45″ neutral color thin cotton-blend fabric for lining the quilt and scalloped border (2 yds. for quilt and 2 yds. for scalloped edge); Dacron polyester quilt batting; seven 5-yd. packages of blue bias binding (for scalloped edge); heavy-duty thread in blue, white and dark green for machine appliquéing; quilting thread in blue; cardboard; ruler; pins or pinless pattern holder spray.

DIRECTIONS: Following the directions on page 224, enlarge the tulip with stem motif on page 93 onto paper or cardboard, spacing the lines 1″ apart, including the shaded stem portion and a pair of leaves. For optional scalloped border, enlarge the basic scallop/flap pattern, as well as a heart shape which will be used at each of the four corners. Cut out patterns and use as directed.

Cutting: Cut all required pieces from the straight grain of the fabric. Our quilt top is made of 36 blocks: 18 light blue and 18 dark blue (finished size of each block is 6″×8″; cut size of each is 7″×9″). Each block is machine-appliquéd with the tulip and leaf design, then joined to-

gether in horizontal rows, lined, backed and quilted.

Blocks:

Light Blue: Cut 18, each 7″ × 9″.

Dark Blue: Cut 18, each 7″ × 9″.

Appliqués:

Tulip Heads: Cut 18 white; cut 18 light blue.

Tulip Stems: Cut 36 dark green.

Tulip Leaves: Cut 72 dark green.

Lining: Cut one piece, 2″ larger all around than finished size of joined blocks for quilt top (*see* Sewing, Step 7).

Border—Dark Green:

Quilt Front: Cut two strips 3½″ wide by 42″.
   Cut two strips 3½″ wide by 54″.

Quilt Back: Cut two strips 4½″ wide by 42″.
   Cut two strips 4½″ wide by 54″.

Scalloped Edge (optional, see FIG. 2) *The flap pieces are cut into rectangles first, then cut into oval shapes after stitching.* For the layered scalloped edge, our quilt required 11 light blue flaps for each short side and 13 for each long side. We used 10 dark blue flaps for each short side and 12 for each long side, plus a dark blue heart at each corner of the dark blue layer.

Light Blue: Cut 48 rectangles, each 5″×6″.

Dark Blue: Cut 44 rectangles, each 5″×6″.

Cut four hearts (one for each corner of scalloped edge).

TULIP WITH STEM

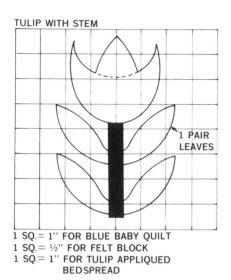

1 SQ.= 1" FOR BLUE BABY QUILT
1 SQ.= ½" FOR FELT BLOCK
1 SQ.= 1" FOR TULIP APPLIQUED
BEDSPREAD

1 PAIR LEAVES

FIG. 2 FLAP PATTERN

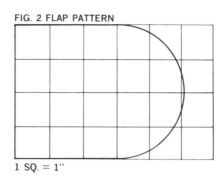

1 SQ. = 1"

FIG. 2A CORNER HEART

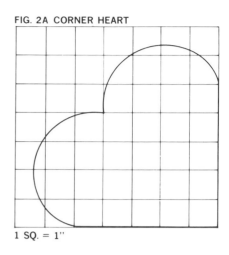

1 SQ. = 1"

FIG. 3 CUTTING AND STITCHING FLAP

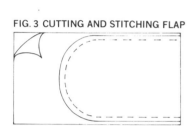

FIG. 4 LAYERING SCALLOPED EDGE FOR STITCHING

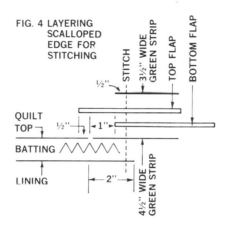

FIG. 5 FINISHING GREEN BORDER

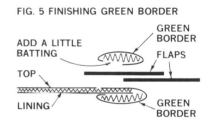

Lining for Scalloped Edge—Cut same amount as needed for flaps and hearts.

Sewing:

1. For a two-piece look, make a row of zigzag stitching on the tulip head as indicated by dotted line, using matching thread.

2. Pin appliqués to blocks, or hold pieces in place with a spray of pinless pattern holder, following label directions.

3. Using heavy-duty matching thread and a narrow and open zigzag stitch, machine-baste (or hand baste) pieces in position. All thread should lie on top of the appliqué pieces, with the outer edge of the stitch on the cut edge of the appliqué. Baste all 36 blocks.

4. Adjust zigzag indicator to obtain a wide closed zigzag (also called Satin Stitch). Stitch over all the previously stitched lines.

Joining the Blocks: When all blocks have been appliquéd, you are ready to join them.

5. Place all blocks on table to determine arrangement. Ours is done in rows of alternating pairs (*see photo*). Taking ½" seams, join blocks on long edges to make six horizontal bands of six blocks each.

6. Stitch bands together with ½" seams, making sure to match all vertical seams. This is now called the quilt top.

7. Measure top. Cut lining fabric 2" larger than quilt top all around.

8. Cut a thin layer of batting the same size as the lining (separating layers if they seem too thick).

9. Place batting over lining, edges even.

10. Center quilt top over batting and pin through all three thicknesses (the batting and lining will extend 2" all around top).

11. Baste diagonal lines from corner to corner, then at center across length and width, making sure the lining side is not puckered or wrinkled; redo, if necessary. Remove pins.

Quilting the Layers: Start quilting stitches at one edge and continue stitching across all six blocks to the opposite edge, instead of outlining individual blocks one at a time.

12. Using a single strand of quilting thread, take small running stitches straight up and down through all layers, working ¼" inside the seams.

13. At this point the quilt can be finished by covering the edges with green strips as shown in FIGS. 4 and 5 and simply eliminating the scallops. A scalloped edge made with lined flaps and hearts (96 pieces in all) may be added as follows.

Scalloped Edge:

14. Place each flap piece on top of lining piece, edges even. Pin together.

15. Trace the flap pattern piece on the top fabric. *Do not cut out yet.*

16. Open bias tape and place on flap with right sides together, so that the raw edge of the tape is flush with the pencil line (the bias tape lies on the inside of pencil line). Stitch tape on first fold.

17. Cut away excess fabric on the pencil line. Pull the bias tape over the raw edges and slipstitch on the lining side. When all flaps are completed you are ready to attach them to the quilt with the green border.

18. The scalloped edge is made up of four layers: The 3½″-wide front green border, the two layers of flaps and the 4½″-wide back green border. All pieces are stitched to the quilt edges in one stitching operation, as shown in FIG. 4. Take the time to study the position of the layers, as described in Step 19. It's easier than it looks.

19. The lining extends 2″ beyond the quilt all around. Layering of the following pieces is done from the bottom up.

   Place 4½″-wide green strip over backing so it butts the quilt top edge.

   Place bottom layer of flaps 1″ out on green border with their side edges flush (placing hearts at corners so their curved edges extend beyond the dark blue border).

   Place top layer of flaps ½″ inside quilt top edge, as shown.

   Place 3½″-wide green strip as shown, even with the *curved* ends of the top row of flaps.

   Stitch as shown in FIG. 4.

20. Place some scraps of batting on the green borders before pulling them over the quilt edges. Turn green edges under ½″ and slipstitch to quilt on front, then on back (FIG. 5), trimming and mitering corners.

21. Finish quilting the perimeter of the quilt. Remove lines of basting.

APPLIQUÉD CRIB BUMPER

Note: Measurements are given below for both portable (24½″ × 38½″) and standard-size (27½″ × 51½″) cribs, with appropriate yardage variations.

MATERIALS: *For portable crib:* 1 yard 45″-wide yellow cotton/dacron fabric; 1 yard quilting Pellon®. *For standard crib:* 2½ yards 45″-wide Yellow fabric; 2½ yards quilting Pellon®. For both sizes: Scraps, or ¼ yard each White,

CRIB BUMPER APPLIQUÉS　　　1 SQ. = 1″

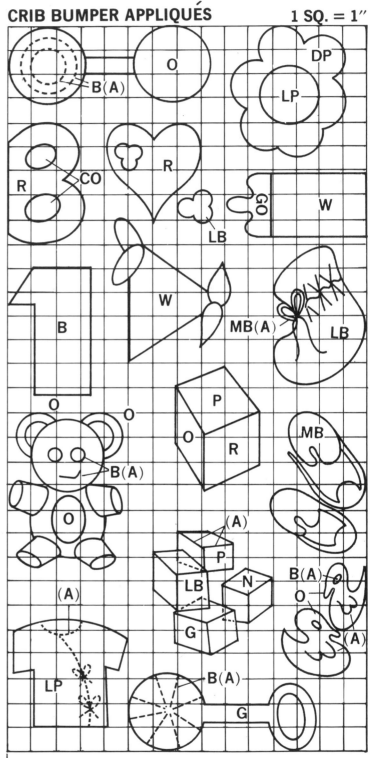

(A)-APPLIQUÉ	GO-GOLD
B-BLUE	W-WHITE
O-ORANGE	MB-MEDIUM BLUE
LP-LIGHT PINK	Y-YELLOW
DP-DARK PINK	G-GREEN
R-RED	N-NAVY
CO-CUT OUT	P-PURPLE
LB-LIGHT BLUE	

Light Blue, Medium Blue, Green, Orange, Red, 2 Pinks, Gold, Purple, Navy fabrics; threads to match; dressmaker's carbon; tailor's chalk; tracing paper.

DIRECTIONS: Cut yellow fabric as specified below:

Porta-Crib

2 double pieces 7½″ × 40″—sides
2 double pieces 7½″ × 25½″ — ends
2 single pieces 7¼″ × 40″—sides (pockets)
2 single pieces 7¼″ × 25½″—ends (pockets)
4 single pieces ¾″ × 20″ for ties, or use narrow bias tape.

Standard Crib

2 double pieces 7½″ × 53½″—sides
2 double pieces 7½″ × 29″—ends
2 single pieces 7¼″ × 53½″—sides (pockets)
22 single pieces 7¼″ × 29″—ends (pockets) 4 ties, same as above

Porta-Crib: Trace and cut out all appliqué designs. Cut out complete blocks for the small block design. For the large block, cut the top and right side of the orange portion ¼″ larger and the top of the red portion ¼″ larger. (This is to be overlayed by the purple on top and the red over the orange on the side.) Place all pocket pieces right side up. Measure and mark with chalk intervals of 5½″ to form 7 pockets for each side section. Mark one 7¾″ pocket on each side of a 10″ center pocket on each end section. Center the designs on the pocket areas; pin and appliqué, using close machine zigzag. Add the detail appliqué designs; trim all appliqués; press. To make ties, fold under each long edge to form ¼″-wide tie; stitch along both sides of each tie. Or, you may use narrow bias tape. Join the pocket sections together at the ends with ¼″ seams, leaving one end open. Make a ½″ hem along the top edge. Join the back inside sections together at the ends; join the back outside sections together at the ends, with ¼″ seams. To join the Pellon, cut ¼″ off each end, butt two ends together and seam with a wide zigzag.

Standard Crib: Follow directions for Porta-Crib, but mark 9½″ pockets on each side of a 10″ center pocket on the two end pocket sections. On side sections, mark 7½″ pockets. *To Assemble:* Place the band of Pellon on the floor. Place the two backs, right sides together on top, and place the pocket band on top of that, with appliqués down. Even all pieces at the bottom; pin and sew ¼″ seam along the bottom, on one end. At the top edge, sew together *only* the backs and Pellon. Trim Pellon close to seam. Turn right side out through the open end, and

slipstitch closed. "Quilt" the back by holding up the top and sewing 2 lines down the length of the bumper. (They should evenly divide the width.) Through all layers, stitch along the pocket marks to form the pockets. In the same way, stitch along divisions of side and end sections to form corners. Attach the center of 1 long tie at each corner. Slipstitch the ends together forming the complete bumper. Wash in warm water and dry on warm gentle cycle.

Color photo on page 136

PUPPY DOG QUILT

MATERIALS: (*About 34″ × 44″ plus 3″-ruffle around quilt.*) Polyester quilt batting, one piece 33¼″ × 44″; thread, two large spools of White, one small spool of Brown (or colors to match your fabric); cardboard; brown wrapping paper; dressmaker's carbon and tracing wheel; fabric remnants for appliqué quilt pieces and two larger pieces for lining and ruffles—see Fabric Cutting Chart for fabrics and quantities used.

DIRECTIONS: Following directions on page 224, enlarge and cut out patterns for puppy appliqués (*see* FIG. 1). Number each appliqué. Also enlarge the design for the assembled puppy (*see* FIG. 2) on a 10½″ square of paper, centering the dog on the square, as shown. You will use this later as a guide for placing appliqué pieces. Number sections as indicated. Using the enlarged appliqué patterns, cut Nos. 1-13, in the quantity and fabric indicated in the Chart. Also cut quilt pieces Nos. 14-16 (backing squares and ruffle strips) for which *dimensions* are given in the Chart (no patterns required). Keep fabric pieces in piles, separated by number, until ready to use. With dressmaker's carbon and tracing wheel, mark the location of eyes on No. 1 pieces and nose on No. 8 pieces. With edges even, pin the puppy pattern (*see* FIG. 2) to each No. 14 backing square and trace the entire design to use as a placement guide for the appliqués.

Stitching the Dog Patches:

Note: If you want your stitching to show, use white thread and a simple in-and-out stitch that overlaps the appliqué edges ⅛″ (*see dog's ear and eye in* Fig. 2), *or* use machine zigzagging. If you want invisible stitching, use slipstitch with matching thread. In all cases, turn the raw edges under ¼″ as you work, making sure the tracing lines don't show.

Order of Appliquéing: Stitch the eyes to No. 1 pieces and the nose to No. 8 pieces. Pin dog sections to the backing squares No. 14, within the traced outlines. Stitch all sections in place. Stitch a triangle, piece No. 15, to each corner of backing square.

Assembling the Quilt Top: Taking ⅜″ seams, sew strips, No. 16, to the *side* edges of each completed patch (*see photo*), making four horizontal rows of three squares and four strips each. Sew remaining No. 16 strips together with the little No. 17 squares between and at each end, to make the five long horizontal strips that join the rows of patches and frame the top and bottom edges (*see photo*).

Making the Ruffle: Stitch ends of five ruffle pieces together to make one big circle. Press seams open. With *wrong* sides together, fold the circle in half lengthwise; press the folded edge. Pin raw edges together. Starting and stopping at each seam, stitch a row of machine gathering stitches ½″ from pinned edges; add another row ⅜″ from edge. Pull up the bobbin thread to gather each stitched section to a length of *about* 35″. Secure the thread-ends by wrapping them in figure-8 fashion around a pin in the fabric. Pin the ruffle in place around the quilt-top, right side, with raw edges even. If necessary, unwind thread-ends and release or tighten the gathering until the ruffle fits the quilt edge exactly. Tie thread-ends securely. Stitch ruffle in place. Turn quilt-top to wrong side; press ruffle seam toward center.

Assembling the Quilt: Lay batting piece on quilt back, tucking the edges under the ruffle seam; trim edges to fit. Hold batting in place by pinning through all layers from the quilt top side. Pin fabric lining piece in place on top of batting, turning under the edges as needed to fit. Slipstitch lining in place, *or* use the in-and-out stitch used for the puppy appliqués. Turn quilt over to right side. With matching thread, quilt around outside edge of dog, the edge of backing square and triangles, where indicated by broken lines in FIG. 2.

FIG. 1 APPLIQUÉ PATTERNS

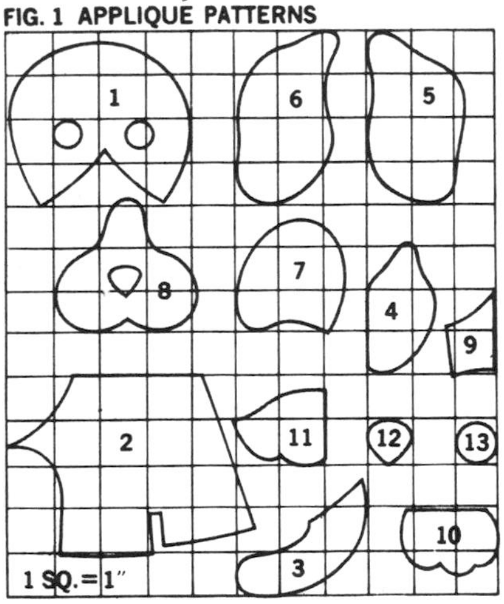

FIG. 2 COMPLETE PUPPY DESIGN

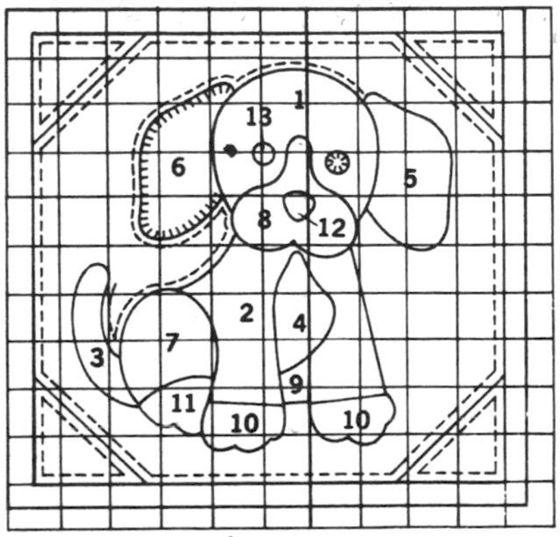

IIIIII APPLIQUÉ STITCHES 1 SQ.=1″
---- QUILTING STITCHES

FABRIC 36″ Wide	DESCRIPTION	AMOUNT	CUTTING DIRECTIONS QUANTITY	PATTERN PIECES
A	Brown with small white dots	⅔ yd.	12 *each*	Nos. 1, 2 and 3
			8	No. 16 Strip: 1¾″x10½″
B	Brown and white gingham	½ yd.	12 *each*	Nos. 4, 5, 6, 7
			20	No. 17 Square: 1¾″x1¾″
C	White background with small brown print	⅙ yd.	12	No. 8
D	Brown background with small white print	⅔ yd.	12 *each*	Nos. 9, 11 and 12
			24	No. 10
			23	No. 16 Strip: 1¾″x10½″
E	White background with small blue print	¼ yd.	24	No. 13
			48	No. 15 Triangle: 3⅝″x3⅝″x5⅛″
F	Solid-color light blue	1¼ yds.	12	No. 14 Backing Square: 10½″x10½″
G	Medium-blue with fine pin stripe	1⅓ yds.	5	Ruffle Strips: 7″x54″
H	Blue and white with small overall print	1¼ yds. (or 1 yd. of 45″ fabric)	1	Lining Piece: 45″x34″

PATCHWORK

Color photo on page 136

THREE ALL-PURPOSE TOTES

To Make Crazywork Patch Fabric: Loosely arrange patches, right side up, over muslin foundation, recutting and overlapping as desired for "crazy" shapes. Overlapped edges are left raw. Uppermost edges must be turned in. Pin from center outwards. Slipstitch through all layers. At outside edges, trim patches to match size and shape of foundation piece required below and baste along seamline. Embroidery stitches may be worked over the crazywork seams, if desired.

PATCHWORK FRINGED TOTE

MATERIALS: Ecru cotton fringe, 1⅛ yds.; one set wooden handles; 44"-wide Brown print for patches, ¼ yd.; 44"-wide muslin for patches and lining, ⅜ yd.; striped fabric, ⅜ yd.

DIRECTIONS: *Pattern:* Draw a 3" square on thin cardboard. Draw diagonal line connecting two opposite corners. Cut on line for triangle pattern.

Cutting: Cut 48 brown and 48 muslin triangles; from striped fabric, cut five strips 4" × 12½" and one handle 3" x 50", piecing if necessary.

Sewing: ¼" *seam allowance*. Seam triangles on long edges to make squares. Seam six squares to make a row. Make eight rows in all. Seam two rows together at the long edges, to make four double rows. Alternate the single strips with the four double patchwork rows. Pin and stitch. Lay this piece over muslin, right sides together. Stitch ¼" from edges around three sides and four corners. Turn right side out. Slipstitch opening. Turn under each end and stitch, to make 1¾" casings. Fold bag in half crosswise, wrong sides together and, starting at bottom, edgestitch each side to middle of top patched row. Topstitch fringe at sides and bottom of bag. Fold fabric handle in half lengthwise, right sides together. Stitch long sides. Turn. Slipstitch ends. Slide wooden handles through casing. Slip fabric through slots and tie in a bow.

PATCHWORK TOTE WITH BRAIDED HANDLE

MATERIALS: One calico back and two pieces of ticking, each 11″ square; two 4″ × 44″ strips each of Blue, Yellow and Lavender calico; scraps of Blue, Yellow, Lavender and Aqua calico to cut patches and borders.

DIRECTIONS: *Cutting:* Cut four lavender and one blue patch, each 2¼″ square. Make a triangle pattern of the dimensions illustrated. Trace four aqua triangles. Cut them ¼″ *outside* the drawn lines. Fold triangle pattern in half to get pattern for corner patches. Trace four times on aqua and cut ¼″ *outside* drawn lines. Cut two yellow borders 5½″ × 1¾″ and two 8″ ×1¾″. Cut two lavender borders 8″ × 2″ and two 11″ × 2″.
Sewing: ¼″ seam allowance.
Patch Panel: Seam two large aqua triangles to opposite sides of two lavender squares. Seam two lavender squares to opposite sides of the blue square. Seam 3 rows of square together, with blue square at center. Seam small triangle to each lavender patch, making a 5½″ square.
Borders: Seam short yellow border to opposite sides of patch panel. Seam long yellow border to remaining sides, to make 8″ square. Seam short lavender borders, then long ones, in the same way, to make 11″ square. Press. Seam front to back, right sides together, at side and bottom edges. Seam two pieces of ticking the same way. Turn bag right side out. Drop ticking inside. Turn under ¼″ at top edges, pin together and edgestitch.
Handles: Sew each two 44″ strips of matching color together at short ends to make one strip. Fold in half lengthwise, turn in raw edges and edgestitch. Braid the three strips and sew together securely 3″ from ends. Cut two 1″ × 2″ strips of lavender. Turn in long edges and wrap around handle at ends of braiding. Whipstitch to top of bag at side seams, over handle with braid "tassel" extending.

BORDER PRINT TOTE (with wooden handles)

MATERIALS: Thirty assorted patches, each 2¼″ square; 3¼″-wide border, 1¼ yds.; ½ yd.

muslin for lining; 15″ × 14″ calico for bag back; wooden handles.
DIRECTIONS: ¼″ *seam allowance.* Sew six rows of five patches each. Seam rows to each other to make bag front panel. To make bag front, sew border to one short and two long sides of panel, mitering corners. Seam front to back at lower edge. Cut muslin lining to match. Lay bag over muslin, right sides together. Stitch ¼″ from edges around three sides and four corners. Turn right side out. Slipstitch opening. Fold bag in half crosswise, right sides together. Stitch sides for 9″ from the bottom. Turn bag right side out. Fold under top edges about 1½″, through slot in handles. Turn in raw edges and slipstitch.

PILLOW TOP

DIRECTIONS: Stitch twenty-five 3½″ squares together into a 13½″ square with ½″ seams. Cut solid color backing to fit; stitch to top with right sides together, leaving 6″ open on one edge. Turn right side out and stuff. Slipstitch open edges together.

DOLL CARRIER

This carrier is designed to carry from small to medium-sized dolls. Neck and waist straps may be lengthened or shortened depending upon size of child.
MATERIALS: ½ yard each 45″-wide of 2 identical print fabrics in contrasting colors (we used Red and Green); dacron batting; scissors; matching threads; paper for pattern.

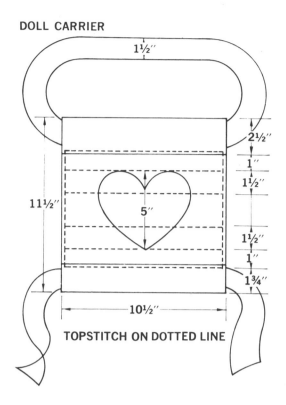

DOLL CARRIER

1½″

2½″

1″

1½″

11½″   5″

1½″

1″

1¾″

10½″

TOPSTITCH ON DOTTED LINE

DIRECTIONS: Cut one 12″ × 17″ piece of each print fabric. Following directions on page 224, enlarge and trace heart shape onto paper; cut out pattern. Using pattern, cut a heart shape from green print. Appliqué heart shape to center of red 12″ × 17″ piece by hand, or use close machine zigzag. Right sides facing, sew the two 12″ × 17″ pieces together, leaving one short side (bottom) open; turn. Cut out four 8½″ × 10½″ pieces of batting. Place all batting layers between sewn together fabric pieces, 5″ down from top and 5″ from bottom. Topstitch along dotted lines through all layers. Fold 5″ top piece over (towards heart) and stitch it down to make a casing for neck strap. Fold 5″ piece at bottom up (towards heart) and stitch down, making casing for waist strap.

Neck Strap: Cut out two 28″ strips red calico, 4″ wide. Sew together, right sides facing, leaving one short end open; turn. Slide through top casing. Slipstitch ends together to make circular strap.

Waist Strap: Cut out two 42″ strips red calico, 4″ wide. Sew together, right sides facing, leaving one short end open; turn. Slipstitch open end closed. Slide through waist casing; tack in place, with equal lengths on either side.

Pouch: Cut 10″ × 12″ piece red calico; hem ¼″ all around. Wrong side facing green calico, sew this piece onto carrier along side and bottom edges, making pouch for doll.

PLACEMATS

DIRECTIONS: Line 14″ × 17″ print placemats with blue fabric; stitch edges with 1″ wide seam binding. Use ½″ binding on 14″-square napkins. Make a red, lined 7″ ring ¾″ wide; press flat. Sew bottom layer to mat in two rows, 1″ apart. On top layer, sew 5″ lined heart made from a freehand pattern. Fold napkins and insert in rings.

TOTE BAG

Finished size: 16½″ × 17″ approximately.
Note: Measurements for individual strips are given before sewing. See specific sewing instructions for seam measurements.

MATERIALS: Fabric remnants (cotton or cotton blend) in the following colors and amounts: *Color A* (dark print): 2 strips, each 1¾″ × 36″; 2 strips, each 2″ × 36″; 1 strip, 2¾″ × 45″ (for tote handles); 1 strip, 1¾″ × 17″ (for seamline facing). *Color B* (solid color): 1 strip, 1¾″ × 36″. *Color B and C* (assorted colors and prints): 32 strips, each about 2¾″ long in the following widths—4 strips, ¾″ wide; 6 strips, 1″; 8 strips, 1¼″; 10 strips, 1½″; 4 strips, 2″. *Color D* (calico print): 1 strip, 2″ × 36″. *Color E* (green and white print): 1 strip, 2″ × 36″. *Horizontal and Vertical Band of Stripes* (not lettered on diagram): 24 multicolor strips, each about 1½″ × 4½″. *Bottom Band* (solid color): 1 strip, 3″ × 36″. In addition to the cotton strips, you will need cotton or dacron quilt batting, 18″ × 36″, ¾ yard of 36″ white cotton or cotton blend fabric for lining; white thread.

DIRECTIONS: First, sew the 32 strips *(Color C Band)* together, following diagram here and the photograph shown below as a guide. Alternate the widths and colors according to which prints and solids look best side by side. Start by sewing 1 strip to another, along the 2¾″ side, allowing ⅛″ seam. Repeat this procedure until all 32 strips are sewn together, creating 1 long strip measuring about 2¾″ × 33½″. Next, construct the *Horizontal and Vertical Band of* Stripes.

PATCHWORK TOTE BAG

```
┌─────────────────────────────────┐
│ A                               │
├─────────────────────────────────┤
│ B                               │
├──┬──┬──┬──┬──┬──┬──┬──┬──┬──┬───┤
│  │  │  │  │  │  │  │  │  │  │   │
│ C│  │  │  │  │  │  │  │  │  │   │
│  │  │  │  │  │  │  │  │  │  │   │
├──┴──┴──┴──┴──┴──┴──┴──┴──┴──┴───┤
│ D                               │
├─────────────────────────────────┤
│ A                               │
├─────────────────────────────────┤
│ E                               │
├───────┬──────┬────┬─────────────┤
│       │      │    │             │
│       ├──────┤    ├─────────────┤
│       │      │    │             │
├───────┴──────┴────┴─────────────┤
│ A                               │
└─────────────────────────────────┘
```

This is done by sewing together 3 of the multicolor strips, along the 4½″ sides, allowing ⅛″ seams between each. Then sew another 3 strips together in the same way. Repeat this procedure 6 more times, until you have 8 bands of 3 strips each. Then, following the diagram shown here, sew 1 band, held vertically, to another band, held horizontally. Continue alternating until all 8 bands are connected. Note: Allow ⅛″ seams. Now you are ready to sew together all the strips for tote. Start by sewing *Strip B* to one of the 1¾″ × 36″ *Strip As*. Next, add *Color Band C*, then *Strip D*, another *Strip A* (2″ × 36″), *Strip E*, *Horizontal and Vertical Band of Stripes*, another *Strip A* (2″ × 36″) and, finally, *Bottom Band*. Your pieced fabric should now measure about 17¼″ × 36″. Mark it at the center (18″ in from edge) with tailor's chalk or by pinning. This will become your center fold line. *Add the Handles:* Take the *2¾″ × 45″ Color A strip* and fold it in half lengthwise, right sides facing. Stitch down the length of strip, allowing ¼″ seam, to form a long tube. Turn tube right side out. Next, cut the tube in half to create 2 tubes, each measuring 2½″ × 22½″. Each tube will form 1 handle on either side of tote. Pin 1 end of 1 tube to top of pieced fabric (on Strip A), about 7½″ in from *left side of pieced fabric* and even with top of fabric. Pin other end of this tube to Strip A also, 4″ away from first end (or 6½″ in from center fold line). Stitch both ends in place, allowing ½″ seam. Repeat this procedure for other handle, pinning both ends of second tube the same distance from *right side edge of pieced fabric* and center fold line. You will now have 2 handles sewn to pieced fabric.

Lining: Take the ¾ yard of 36″ white cotton and stitch (along 36″ side) to the remaining 1¾″ × 36″ *Strip A* (see MATERIALS list), allowing ¼ seam. Next, place this lining on top of pieced fabric, with *Strip A of lining* matching up with *Strip A of pieced fabric*, right sides facing. Stitch the 2 *Strip As* together, along 36″ length, allowing ¼″ seam. As you do so, you'll be attaching the lining to the pieced fabric and you'll be sewing the 2 handles into the seam allowance. *Note:* You'll be leaving 2 sides and bottom unstitched at this point.

Quilting: Now, open up lining and pieced fabric and place on flat surface so that pieced fabric is wrong side up. Lay the quilt batting on the lining half of the fabric. Then fold the pieced fabric over the batting. Pin the fold precisely along the seam into which the handles are sewn. Top-stitch around the bag (through all 3 layers—pieced fabric, batting and lining), beginning at the bottom left of pieced fabric, going up along side of fabric, ¼″ in from edge. When you've sewn up the side as far as the seam-line between *Strip A* and *Strip B*, then turn your fabric and continue top-stitching following seam line between A and B, from left to right across the pieced fabric. Stop when you reach the end of fabric at top righthand corner. This top-stitching will keep the 3 layers from slipping out of alignment. Continue to top-stitch over each straight seam between strips, ending with the *Horizontal and Vertical Bands.*

Sewing Side and Bottom Seams: Fold the bag along the center fold line, so right sides of pieced fabric are facing and handles are at top. Sew side seam, allowing ½″ seam. Then to give side seam a finished look, lay *Strip A* (the 1¾″ × 17″ one) along seam line, face down. Stitch one 17″ side of strip into seamline; press seam to left, then fold strip A over the seam line, turn under raw edge and hand-stitch in place. Next, stitch bag along bottom, allowing ½″ seam. Clip threads, turn bag and press.

TOTE

Lined, 12½″ wide × 14″ × 3½″

MATERIALS: 44″ wide quilted fabric, one yard; 44″ wide lining, ⅝ yd.; 12″ zipper; batting, 12″ × 24″; scraps of four fabrics for patchwork; two hammer-on snaps.

DIRECTIONS:

Cutting:

From quilted fabric: Front and back, each 13½″ wide × 15½″; boxing 4½″ × 42½″; shoulder strap 7″ × 37″; two pocket strips, each 5″ × 13½″ wide;

two zipper panels, each 8″ × 12½″; inside pocket 7″ square.

From lining fabric: Front and back, each 13½″ wide × 15½″; two pocket linings, each 5½″ × 13½″ wide; backing for patchwork, 12″ square.

From scraps: 3⅛″ squares as follows: five each of orange and yellow and four each of green and brown (or colors of your choice).

Assembly: Draw a diagonal line connecting opposite corners of each patch; cut on drawn line. Seam (¼″) patches in pairs, then join pairs to make squares *(see photo)*. Seam three squares to make a row and three rows to make a block. Quilt the patchwork pocket, stitching on the seamlines. Trim batting to match top. Trim backing ½″ larger than top. Turn in edges of backing ½″ and fold them over the top to make ¼″ binding. Edgestitch. Center the pocket on bag front 3″ below top edge. Stitch side and

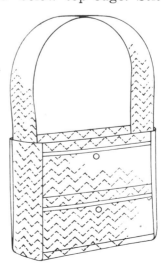

bottom edges. Place pocket linings over pocket strips, right sides together, top and side edges even. Stitch ¼″ from top edge to make binding. Turn right side out and press, raw edges even. Pin lower pocket to bag back *(see backview)*, right sides together and top edge downward with seamline 2″ from lower bag edge. Stitch bottom seam of pocket and turn it upwards; baste side edges to bag. Pin upper pocket in the same way with seamline 7½″ from lower bag edge. Apply a snap to center of each pocket and to bag underneath. Center and stitch inside patch pocket to lining 4″ from top edge. Assemble tote and line it. Apply zippered panels. Make and apply shoulder strap like turned handles.

AMERICANA QUILT
(95″ × 111″)

MATERIALS: 44″-wide fabric for patches as follows: 3 yds. solid Blue (we used cotton velveteen), 2 yds. of Red print and 1½ yds. of solid White; 44″-wide Blue print fabric for patches and borders, 3 yds.; 44″-wide fabric for quilt back, 9 yds.; polyester batting, 95″ × 111″ (piece two batts if necessary); quilting thread and needle; thimble; tailor's chalk; yardstick.

DIRECTIONS: *Cutting (¼″ seams allowed):* Fold backing crosswise into three equal parts; cut along folds. Seam at long edges. Press seams open. Across the 44″ width of the blue print fabric cut ten 4″-wide strips. Piece to make two borders 102″ long and two borders 118″ long. Use tailor's chalk and yardstick to mark the yardage into patches, each 4½″ square; 229 solid blue, 130 blue print, 152 red print and 110 white; cut out patches. Piece batting, if necessary, by butting two edges together. Sew from one piece to the other in long diagonal stitches.

Sewing: (¼″ seam allowance):
Lay out the blocks row by row, following the diagram. Turn the first block over the second, right sides together, and pin the adjoining edges. Continue across the row, pinning the patches together, then stitch pinned edges. Place one Row 11 over the center row, right sides together. Pin with raw edges even, carefully matching each seam. Stitch. Continue adding Rows 10 to 1 in the same direction, as shown in diagram. Add the other 10 rows to the opposite side of the center row. Spread out the backing wrong side up on the floor. Tape the corners down to keep it from moving. Center and place the batting over the backing. Center and place

LAYOUT FOR PATCHWORK QUILT

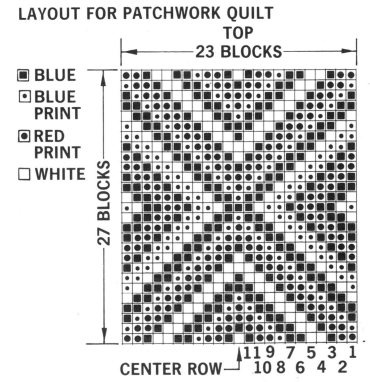

the quilt top over the batting. There should be a 1½″ border of batting outside the quilt top. Pin sparsely from the center outwards through all layers. Then baste with long stitches from the center to each corner and from the center to the middle of each edge. Add a few more basting rows from the center outwards so the layers are securely together. Untape. Starting at the center, sew runnng stitches along each crosswise seam through all layers. Repeat in the lengthwise seams. Pin a shorter border over a shorter quilt edge, right sides together and edges matching. Stitch ¼″ from long edges and trim short edges flush with quilt. Repeat at opposite quilt edge. Turn quilt over and trim backing, if necessary, even with batting. To bind quilt edges, turn border edge under ¼″ and slipstitch the fold to the back of the quilt over the previous line of stitching. Pin remaining borders over unbound quilt edges, leaving 1″ of border extending at each end. Stitch ¼″ seam. Trim backing if necessary and turn under binding edge. Slipstitch to previous stitching. Turn in ends of binding and slipstitch them together.

JUMPER
Skirt length 38″
MATERIALS: 44″-wide muslin, 2¾ yds.; 44″-wide pink calico, 1 yd.; 44″-wide dark and light calico for blocks, ⅞ yd. each; 2″-wide ecru lace ruffling, 2 yds.; waist fastener; two ½″ buttons.
DIRECTIONS: *Cutting:* 2¼″ squares, 264 each of light and dark calico.
Pink strips as follows:
34, each 7½″ × 2½″ for vertical strips.
 4, each 71½″ × 2½″ for horizontal strips.
 2, each 28″ × 2½″ for shoulder straps.
one 11½″ × 2½″ for bib top border.
one 3″ × 7½″ and one 1½″ × 7½″ to finish closing at center back.
one 2½″ × waistlength plus ½″ for waistband.
Sewing: (¼″ seam allowance):
Patchwork Blocks:
Seam four rows of four squares each, alternating dark and light calico. Seam rows together so colors alternate in both directions. Repeat to make 33 blocks in all.
Skirt: Make four rows as follows: Alternate eight blocks with eight vertical strips; pin and seam. Press seams open. Sew horizontal strip to bottom of one of these rows. Add three more rows and strips in same way. Lay resulting skirt over muslin, right sides together. Stitch along a pink strip, for lower edge. Trim sides and top of muslin to match skirt. Turn right side

out. Stitch center back seam up to top of top horizontal row.
Back closing: Bind underlap with strip 3″ wide. Face overlap with strip 1½″ wide. Run gathering row ¼″ from top edge of skirt.
Waistband: With right sides together and ¼″ extending at each end, pin waistband over gathering row, distributing fullness evenly. Stitch. Turn upwards. Face waistband with similar strip of muslin, leaving open for 5½″ each side of center front.
Bib: Seam a 7½″ strip each side of a patchwork block, then seam 11½″ strip across top. Lay bib over muslin, right sides together. Stitch along top and side edges. Trim bottom of muslin to match bib. Turn right side out. Slide bib into opening in waistband, matching center fronts. Slipstitch waistband facing over bib.
Straps: Seam each pink strip to a muslin one at the long sides. Turn right side out. Turn in and slipstitch ends. Stitch a strap under each corner of the bib.
Finishing: Sew fastener at ends of waistband. Sew buttons to inside of waistband and make buttonholes in straps to match. Press bib, straps, waist and hem edges, then edgestitch. Slipstitch ruffling to inside of skirt at lower edge, allowing about 1″ of lace to show.

STUFFED ANIMALS
MATERIALS: Cotton calicos, ginghams, patterns, prints, solids, corduroys (wide-wale corduroy is nice for fronts of elephant ears and saddle blanket); washable yarn (for rabbit's tail); trimming fringe (for lion's mane and tail);

shredded Dacron polyester for stuffing; buttons for eyes and elephant's saddle blanket (for small children, eyes should be embroidered); scissors; chalk; thread.

BASIC DIRECTIONS: *Lion, Rabbit, and Cat:*

1. Using 4″ squares of fabric, lay out for animal desired: 3 rows of 4 squares across for fronts of lion and rabbit (back of lion and rabbit are made with a single piece of fabric 1′ × 1½′); 5 rows of 3 squares across for front and back of cat. Sew squares together with ¼″ seam, one row at a time. Press, then sew all the rows together, matching seams. Press.

2. Following directions on page 224 enlarge patterns. Cut out patterns and pin on patchwork piece. *For cat,* fold material in half, pin the top of the pattern on the fold in the material. Cut cat body back and front from patchwork piece, leaving fold of material intact. *For lion and rabbit,* pin respective pattern on patchwork piece and cut out front. Pin pattern to fabric for back and cut out. (If you wish to make the back out of patchwork, double the number of rows of squares—6 rows of 4 squares each; fold the fabric in half, and pin the top of the pattern on the fold of the material as for cat.)

3. Cut front of head and tail from one piece of material. Cut back of head and tail from a different material, contrasting pattern and/or color.

4. Pin backs and fronts of body, head, and tail fabrics, right side together, and sew separately with ⅜″ seam, leaving space open between ears on head, top of tail, and 3″ opening on back end of body for turning and stuffing. Reinforce at beginning and end of seams. Clip seam allowance to seam line on curves of tail, head, and body. Turn each unit right side out (use a pin to carefully pull out the points of the ears on the head). Iron tail and head.

5. Stuff head loosely but evenly (don't pack stuffing in). Fold under ⅜″ seam allowance between ears and pin or baste. Stuff tail tightly, leaving about ⅜″ unstuffed at base. Stuff body so it is full but soft. Insert tail into opening of body and stitch opening closed, making sure to catch tail with stitch.

6. Sew the face through the entire thickness of head, as in quilting. Enlarge the face pattern and transfer the pattern onto the head. If the material of the head is light in color with little pattern, you can use a straight machine stitch with dark thread to create the face.

(Sewing on the reverse side of the head will create puffy cheeks which are very attractive.) If the material of the head is a dark color or a heavy pattern, use a machine satin stitch (a medium or wide, closely-spaced zigzag) in a very bright thread. Experiment with the width and length of the stitch, and practice turning curves evenly before you sew the face. Back stitch or tie the threads securely at beginning and ends.

7. *Trimmings:* For the rabbit, straight-stitch triangles onto his ears. For the eyes of all animals, sew buttons securely onto head through all thicknesses (or embroider eyes if animal is for a baby). For lion's mane, sew fringe around head on the back by hand or machine, starting and finishing behind an ear. Sew fringe to the end of his tail. For rabbit's yarn tail, wrap yarn around a 3½″ strip of cardboard about 20 times (more if the yarn is thin), tying it at one end with a short strip of yarn. Then slip yarn off cardboard (don't cut loops yet) and insert tied end into body opening. Pin seam allowance, and stitch securely. Cut loops of yarn and trim to round shape.

8. Sew completed head to body with ¼″ seam, stitching between ears.

Elephant: Patchwork for elephant consists of 2 pieces of 3 rows of 4 squares across (see patchwork directions for lion, rabbit, and cat) or from one piece of material using highly contrasting material for ears, tail, and saddle blanket.

1. Following directions on page 224 enlarge pattern. Pin patterns to material and cut out 2 sides for body, 2 fronts of ears, and two backs of ears in contrasting fabric. For the tail, cut 3 strips of different materials (coordinating colors with body and ears) 1¼″ wide × 8″ long.

2. With right sides of fabrics together, pin and sew ear fronts and backs together, leaving open the side that will be attached to body. Turn, clip seam allowance on curves, and press. Stuff ears. Turn ⅜″ seam allowance of opening under and baste or pin.

3. Pin ears in position one on each side of body (sides are not yet sewn together). Stitch securely with as small a seam as possible. (A novice might find it easier to sew ears on by hand with overcasting stitch after body is completed.)

4. For eyes, sew buttons securely (fancy metal buttons or wooden beads are nice). (For tiny children, eyes should be embroidered.) Or, sew eyes on after body is completed.

5. For the tail, fold each strip of material in half lengthwise, press, and pin the three strips together at one end. Baste. Pin to one side of body in position at rear.

6. Pin both sides of body together, right sides facing, making sure the tail is on the outside and matching the edges in the trunk area. Sew the body together with ⅜″ seam, leaving an opening for stuffing under the tail. Reinforce the beginning and end of the seams. Clip the seam allowance to the seam line so curves turn smoothly, paying special attention to the curves between the legs and the trunk and legs.

7. Turn the body right side out and stuff. Turn under the seam allowance at opening and overcast it closed. Braid the tail, stitching across the end and trimming, leaving 1″ "fringe."

8. Cut out saddle blanket pattern from two different materials. With right sides together, pin and sew with a ⅜″ seam, leaving a 2½″ opening along one of the long ends for turning and stuffing. Turn, press, and stuff very thinly but evenly. Turn under seam allowance of opening, pin and sew closed. Quilt,

sewing through entire thickness, in rows or following pattern of material. Make a buttonhole diagonally in each corner, and pin blanket on elephant, marking position of buttons. Sew buttons onto body securely and button on saddle blanket.

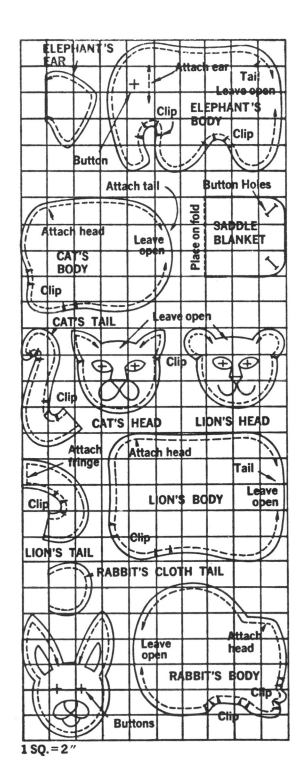

1 SQ. = 2″

DIAGONAL STRIPED QUILT

(Finished size: Approximately 98″ × 114″)

MATERIALS: 44″-wide cotton or cotton and polyester blend fabric in these solids and prints (we used eagle- and star-printed seersucker, ½ yd. each blue, blue-on-white print, white-on-red print, red-on-white print, 1 yd. white, 4 yds. red, 5 yds. white-on-blue print); 10 yds. lining fabric; ½″ Dacron batting; quilting thread; well-sharpened chalk pencil; straight-edge.

GENERAL INFORMATION: This striking diagonal-stripe quilt may win you more salutes than the flag itself, and possibly more than you deserve because it is much easier than it looks to put together. The diagonal stripes emerge automatically as you follow our diagram to stitch colored squares together into horizontal rows and the rows into the center block (FIG. 1). To this you add red border strips and drop panels, then baste the whole quilt-top to batting and lining. After quilting, the red hem border is added.

Note: This quilt will fit a double bed. For other sizes, add or subtract rows of squares or adjust the dimensions of the squares, borders and drop panels, as needed.

GENERAL DIRECTIONS: Preshrink fabrics; press. Cut off selvages; trim fabric ends even with grain. Stitch all pieces with right sides together. Seam allowance is ¼″ unless otherwise indicated. Press seams flat, to side or down, before stitching a crossing seam.

DIRECTIONS: *Cutting Fabric Pieces:*

Note: When cutting 6″ squares, first cut 6″ strips across full fabric width; use a 6″ square cardboard pattern to mark strips into squares. From white fabric, cut 37 six-inch squares. From blue, white-on-red print and red-on-white print, cut 18 six-inch squares. From blue-on-white print, cut 17 six-inch squares. From white-on-blue print, cut 18 six-inch squares and eight 20″ strips across full fabric width (for foot and side drop panels). Divide the red fabric into equal squares by drawing chalk lines across, spaced at a distance equal to the fabric width (with selvages removed). In each square, mark off three 6″-wide bias strips, *alternating the direction in which the diagonal lines are drawn.* Cut out bias strips. From the *long edges* of the fabric remaining, cut 3″ strips on the straight grain of the fabric which, when pieced, will form a border for the bottom and sides of the completed center block of squares. Also cut 18 six-inch squares. Cut *lining* fabric

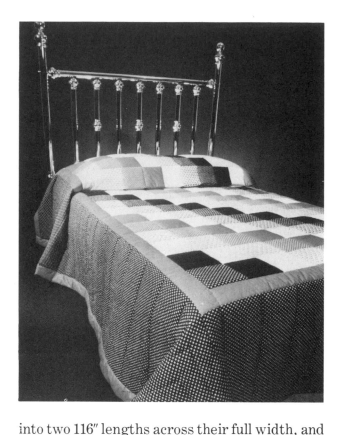

into two 116″ lengths across their full width, and two more 116″ lengths, each only 7″ wide.

Stitching: To make the center block, stitch the 6″ squares together into 16 rows of nine each using the Color Key with the Diagram in FIG. 1 as a guide. (Note that rows 11 and 12 are the same to allow for a fold under the pillows without distorting the diagonal pattern.) Stitch the 16 rows together, *taking care to match the corners of the squares. For bottom border,* measure the width of the completed bed-top block. Cut a length of the 3″ border strip as long as this measurement. Pin and stitch the border across the bottom of the bed-top block. *For side borders,* measure entire length (including bottom border); pin and stitch. When you piece one whole 20″ strip to two pieces from a second strip to make the foot drop panel, you will have two piecing seams. Adjust the fabric so that these seams align with those in the quilt top (FIG. 1). Stitch to quilt-top bottom edge. Now trim panel to quilt-top measurement (including size borders). Repeat the same piecing procedure for the side drop panels, using FIG. 1 as a guide. Stitch panels to side borders. Press all side and foot seams to center of red border. Curve the bottom corners of the spread, using an old bedspread as a guide. Or, use a string-and-pin compass to draw the curved line with the chalk pencil. Cut off on chalkline. Place batting long

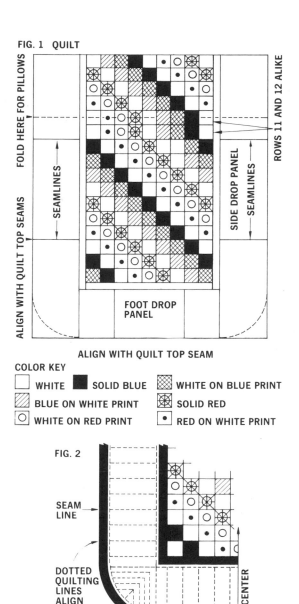

FIG. 1 QUILT

FOLD HERE FOR PILLOWS

ALIGN WITH QUILT TOP SEAMS

SEAMLINES

SIDE DROP PANEL

SEAMLINES

ROWS 11 AND 12 ALIKE

FOOT DROP PANEL

ALIGN WITH QUILT TOP SEAM

COLOR KEY

☐ WHITE ■ SOLID BLUE ▨ WHITE ON BLUE PRINT

▨ BLUE ON WHITE PRINT ⊕ SOLID RED

⊡ WHITE ON RED PRINT • RED ON WHITE PRINT

FIG. 2

SEAM LINE

DOTTED QUILTING LINES ALIGN WITH QUILT TOP SEAMLINES

CENTER

apart. Check frequently to make sure that lining fabric remains smooth and unpuckered. Starting at the top, roll quilt into a cylinder, leaving about three rows of squares exposed at the bottom. Lay cylinder on table. With small running stitches, straight up and down through all layers, quilt along all horizontal and vertical seamlines. When entire top is quilted, smooth out drop panels and work parallel rows of quilting over chalklines aligned with the quilted seams on the spread top (FIG. 2). When panels are finished, draw a diagonal chalkline from border corner to curved edge and use it as a guideline to work corner quilting, as shown in FIG. 2. (If you use a hoop to quilt corners, keep the tension loose.) Trim lining to batting size, when necessary.

Finishing: Press a ½″ hem on one long edge of the 6″ bottom border strip. Stitch other edge across top (head) of quilt in a ½″ seam; trim ends even with quilt side edges. On the remaining border strip, turn in ½″ on one end. Pin and baste flush with quilt corner edges, continuing around remaining three quilt sides (easing fullness around corners so border will lie flat when it is turned under). Trim strip at top end, allowing ½″ to turn in. Stitch; remove basting. Turn border over the batting to wrong side and pin folded edge to lining on stitching line; slipstitch.

CRAZY QUILT AFGHAN

Approximately 43″ × 70″.

GENERAL DIRECTIONS: Our crazy quilt afghan is easily made up of pieced patchwork blocks backed with muslin and embroidered. These blocks are stitched into diagonal rows to form a rectangle, then overlaid with ribbon to emphasize the diamond-like pattern. After the border strips are added and ribbon trimmed, the afghan top is laid over batting and backing and quilted. The top edges are turned to the back ½″ beyond the ribbon to form a pretty border and, at the same time, bind the edges.

MATERIALS: 2⅜ yds. of 60″-wide Magenta wool for back and borders; *for patches:* ⅜ yd. 60″-wide Magenta wool flannel *(patches only),* ¼ yd. 60″-wide Pumpkin flannel; ⅝ yd. each of 48″-wide Rose and Pink moire; ⅝ yd. 44″-wide Green velveteen; ½ yd. 44″-wide Red velveteen; 24 yds. 1¼″-wide ribbon; about 48 skeins 6-strand embroidery floss in fabric colors, including Yellow; 9 yds. 36″-wide muslin; cardboard for pattern about 10″ square; quilt batting 54″ × 84″; 14″ diameter embroidery hoop.

edges side by side on floor so they butt (do not overlap). Use long back and forth stitches on batting surfaces to join edges. Turn and repeat stitching on other side. Trim finished batt to measure 98″×114¾″. Taking ½″ seams, stitch the two side (44″) lining panels together on the long edges; add a narrow (7″) panel to each side edge to make one piece 99″×116″. Stitch 6″ bias strips together until you have about a 12 yd. length. Lay lining on floor, wrong side up. Secure corners with masking tape on bare floor (or with T pins on carpeting). Center joined batting on top of lining. Center quilt-top on batting, right side up; smooth out wrinkles. Pin all layers together; baste through all layers, starting at center and stitching to ½″ from edges and spacing the basting lines about 4″

DIRECTIONS: *Pattern (no seams allowed):* Draw an 8½″ square on cardboard and fill in with 1″ squares to form a grid, copying FIG. 1; include patch numbers and arrows. Cut out the six patches.

Cutting: Trace around patch patterns on wrong side of fabric, leaving ½″ between lines. You will cut about ¼″ *outside* the drawn lines. Continue, without wasting fabric, until required number of patches (*see legend with* FIG. 2) are drawn. Cut out. From large magenta yardage (*see* FIG. 3) cut two 3″ strips from the length, then two 3″ strips from the width. The remaining piece will be the quilt back.

From muslin, cut thirty-five 18″ squares.

Assembling Blocks: Patchwork: Following FIG. 2 for color, assemble fifteen A blocks and twenty B blocks, as follows. Match, pin and stitch the *seam lines* in this order: patches 1 to 2 to 3; patch 4 to 5, then these to patch 6; press seams open. Seam the two sections to make block; press seam open. Center, pin and edge-stitch each patch block (9″ square) over an 18″ muslin square (when embroidering, the square is held in place in the hoop by the surrounding muslin).

On twelve B blocks, chalk a broken diagonal seamline between opposite corners; ⅜″ away draw a cutting line (*see* FIG. 4). Cut along cutting line. The 12 larger parts are the ends and sides of the afghan top. Discard all but four of the cut-away pieces. Save these four to make the corner patches. Fold them, matching the short sides, to mark the center of the long side.

Embroidering: Draw freehand heart designs on patches (*see* FIG. 2). Engage embroidery hoop in the muslin to prevent crushing velvet. Embroider, (*see* **BASIC EMBROIDERY STITCHES** page 228) using three strands of divided 6-strand floss in needle (*see* FIG. 2 *stitches*). Cut away excess muslin ¾″ outside patchwork edges to make 10½″ square blocks. Arrange blocks on floor (*see* FIG. 5). Rotate some for design variety, where you wish. Sew blocks into diagonal strips, matching center of corner patch to center of side of Block A. Press seams open. Then sew strips together, matching seams; press seams open. Carefully draw new edges on corner patches even with sides and ends. Cut along drawn lines. Starting at one corner, center ribbon over parallel seams covering muslin and raw edges. Pin and edge-stitch. Repeat, in opposite direction, to form diamond-like pattern. Sew border to each end, trimming border flush with sides. Press seams open. Seam border to sides, in same way. Pin inside edge of ribbon ¼″ inside border seam, mitering corners. Edgestitch ribbon.

Quilting: Center batting over *wrong* side of backing; center afghan top, *right side up,* over batting. Baste layers, from center to edges. Quilt (⅛″ running stitches up and down through all layers) near each side of ribbons. Turn wrong side up. Trim batting and backing 1″ inside top border edges. Turn in ½″ at edges of top; turn again ½″ and pin to afghan back to form border binding; slipstitch.

CRAZY QUILT PILLOW:

MATERIALS: *one 14″ × 14″ pillow:* Scraps of fabric and 6-strand embroidery floss left from afghan; two 18″ squares of muslin; two 14″ squares Magenta flannel; 1¼ yds. each of 1¼″-wide ribbon and lace edging; 12″ square quilt batting; stuffing.

DIRECTIONS: Piece patchwork block, apply to a muslin square and embroider as you did for the quilt. Pin ribbon over raw edges of patchwork, mitering corners. Stitch inside edge. Center patchwork over quilt batting, over a muslin square. Baste. Quilt along stitched edge of ribbon. Trim away excess batting and muslin near quilting. Lap and pin outside edge of ribbon over lace edging, easing lace around corners. Center pieced squares over a magenta square. Pin and stitch along outer ribbon edge. With right sides together, seam magenta squares around three sides and four corners. Trim corners. Turn; stuff; slipstitch opening.

FIG. 1
PATCHWORK
PATTERN

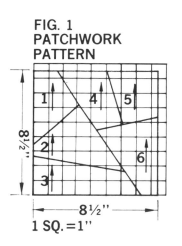

8½"

8½"

1 SQ. = 1"

FIG. 3 BACK AND
BORDER CUTTING
DIAGRAM

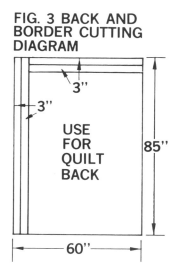

3"

3"

USE
FOR
QUILT
BACK

85"

60"

FIG. 2 COLOR AND EMBROIDERY DIAGRAM FOR A AND B BLOCKS

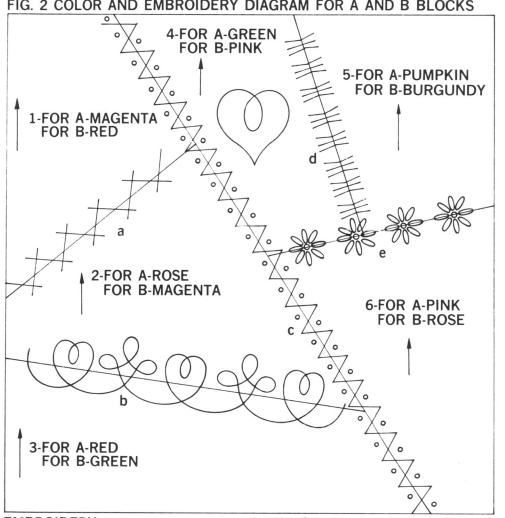

4-FOR A-GREEN
FOR B-PINK

5-FOR A-PUMPKIN
FOR B-BURGUNDY

1-FOR A-MAGENTA
FOR B-RED

d

a

2-FOR A-ROSE
FOR B-MAGENTA

e

6-FOR A-PINK
FOR B-ROSE

c

b

3-FOR A-RED
FOR B-GREEN

FIG. 4

DISCARD EXCEPT 4,
FOR CORNERS

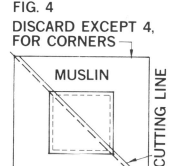

MUSLIN

CUTTING LINE

⅜"

USE FOR ENDS
AND SIDES

FIG. 5
SEAMING DIAGRAM

EMBROIDERY:

a-HERRINGBONE STITCH
b-STEM OR OUTLINE STITCH
c-STRAIGHT STITCHES WITH
  FRENCH KNOTS
d-STRAIGHT STITCHES IN
  GROUPS OF THREE
e-LAZY DAISY STITCH

CUTTING:

PATCH 1-15 MAGENTA, 20 RED
PATCH 2-15 ROSE, 20 MAGENTA
PATCH 3-15 RED, 20 GREEN
PATCH 4-15 GREEN, 20 PINK
PATCH 5-15 PUMPKIN,
         20 BURGUNDY
PATCH 6-15 PINK, 20 ROSE

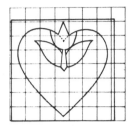

Fig. 1

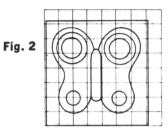

Fig. 2

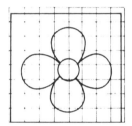

Fig. 3

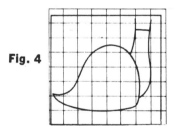

Fig. 4

Color photo on page 137

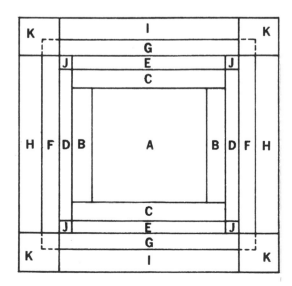

PATCHWORK APPLIQUÉ PILLOWS

MATERIALS *(for each pillow)*: One 16″ knife-edge pillow form, or kapok, or shredded foam for stuffing; one piece of gingham, calico or percale, approximately 18″ square for pillow backing, plus scraps of the same fabrics (choose fabrics of the same weight and resiliency to ensure even work).

DIRECTIONS: To enlarge the patterns for the decorative center motifs (*see* FIGS. 1-4), draw crisscross lines, vertically and horizontally, on brown paper with a ruler, spacing the lines 1″ apart. Then copy our design, one square at a time, using a ruler and/or a compass, as needed. Cut out pattern. Cut out the center motifs; then cut squares and strips of the dimensions specified in FIG. 5.

Assembling Pillow Top: By hand or machine, appliqué the motif to the center A square, using zigzag satin stitch. Use straight stitch for remaining construction; make all seams ½″ wide. With right sides of fabric together, stitch B strips to side edges of the center A square; stitch C strips to top and bottom edges of the square. Following the same procedure, add on strips D, E, F, G, H and I. The pillow top should now measure 17″. Turn under ½″ on all edges of square J and K. Press folded edges. Pin squares in place, as shown in FIG. 5. Topstitch with either straight or zigzag stitch.

For pillow back: Cut the square of backing the same size as the pillow top. With right sides together, stitch backing to top around three sides and four corners, leaving a 12″ opening on one side. Turn right-side out. Insert stuffing. Slipstitch open side, turning edges in. *Or*, insert a zipper in the fourth side, following package directions.

Fig. 5

Cut Size (½″ seam allowance included)

A—8″ square	F—2″ x 12″
B—2¼″ x 8″	G—2″ x 14″
C—2¼″ x 10½″	H—2½″ x 14″
D—1¾″ x 10½″	I—2½″ x 17″
E—1¾″ x 12″	J—¾″ x ¾″
	K—1½″ x 1½″

TABLECLOTH

The following directions are for making a cloth to fit a 48″ round table, 28″ high. In order to make it smaller, measure the diameter of your table and add the height twice. This is the total length your cloth must cover, plus a 2″ hem allowance on each side. Divide this length by 5¼″ to find out how many rows of patches you must make. For a 36″ diameter table, 28″ high, the cloth must be 96″ long, including hems. Divided by 5¼″, you get 18.29 rows which is rounded to 19 rows. Using graph paper and a compass, draw a circle that is 19 squares in diameter. By counting the squares in the circle, including those which are only part of a square, you get the total number of patches needed for the cloth, and the number needed for each row.

MATERIALS: 1⅓ yds. each of seven different cotton/cotton blend fabrics in Red coordinating prints; one 81″ × 96″ quilt batt; one 25″ × 60″ quilt batt (both polyester); Red washable yarn; large-eyed tapestry needle; straight pins; scissors; pencil; cardboard; ruler; yardstick; tape measure; pinking shears (for napkins).

DIRECTIONS: Preshrink all fabrics by soaking in a basin of hot water for half an hour. Press when dry. On a piece of cardboard, carefully mark a 6″ square. Cut out, rechecking measurement. This 6″ square will be your master pattern for the cloth patches. On the *wrong* side of one piece of red fabric, measure a 6″ strip across the width of the fabric, using a yardstick and the master pattern as a guide. Draw a pencil line across the fabric on the 6″ measurement. Repeat seven more times until you have measured a total of eight 6″-wide strips on the fabric. Carefully cut across the width of the fabric on the pencil lines. Using the cardboard square as a guide, mark off the strip in 6″ squares (there will be a small unusable piece left over). Cut on pencil lines into seven patches 6″ square. When the eight strips have been cut into patches, there will be a total of 56 square pieces, each 6″. Repeat this marking and cutting procedure with each one of the six other red fabrics, making a total of 392 patches. The cloth is made of 22 rows of patches; the eight longest rows contain 22 patches each. Working on a large, flat surface, lay out the first row of 22 patches, placing the fabrics randomly. Place the second row of patches next to the first row, taking care that the same two fabrics are not next to each other. Pin the patches in each row and stitch. Press the seams to one side. Pin the two rows together, matching at seamlines, and

stitch. Press seam to one side. These two rows are the center of the cloth and should be long enough to extend from the floor to the table top, across the center of the table and down to the floor again on the other side, plus at least a 2″ hem allowance. Before stitching the remaining rows, check this measurement with the first two sewn rows by placing across the middle of the table. Following the procedure for the first two rows, lay out six more rows of 22 patches, three each on the sides of the two sewn rows. Pin, stitch and press. Sew each row together. Press. There are now eight rows completed. Lay out two rows on each side of sewn piece of 20 patches. Pin, stitch, press. The remaining rows are one each of 18, 16, 14, 12 and 8 patches on each side of center piece. Pin, stitch, press as above. There are 22 rows of patches in all. Press entire tablecloth.

Assembly: Place the cloth right side down on a large flat surface. Carefully center the larger quilt batt in the center of the cloth on the wrong side. Pin; baste in place. From the smaller batt, cut pieces to fill in the sides, overlapping the batt pieces at least 1″. Pin together carefully. If necessary, piece together small pieces of batting to fill in. Join the pieces of batting by carefully overcasting the lapped pieces together. The batting should extend to the cloth edges. Place cloth on table. Check that the cloth is the right length all around, allowing at least 2″ for the hem. Pin hem. Thread a large-eyed tapestry needle with a long piece of red yarn. Starting with the first patch intersection off the table top, place the needle in one patch and bring it up in the patch diagonally opposite. Make a bow and cut yarn. Repeat this step all around the sides of the cloth, spacing the bows two patches apart.

(*Note:* When inserting needle in patch, be sure to do so about ⅜″ from the seam line to avoid trying to pull the needle through the seam allowance.)

Remove cloth from table and place on flat surface, right side down. Even the hemline by cutting away the excess fabric from the hem allowance. Turn under the raw edges and pin, making certain that the hem allowance contains a double layer of batting. Blindstitch hem, being careful not to catch the cloth top in needle. The stitches should go through the hem allowance and the batting only. If the finished cloth needs pressing, carefully steam, holding iron above the surface of the cloth. Never place it directly on the cloth. This avoids flattening the batting.

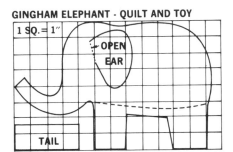

GINGHAM ELEPHANT - QUILT AND TOY

1 SQ. = 1″

OPEN EAR

TAIL

CHILD'S GINGHAM ELEPHANT QUILT

Finished quilt size: approximately 39″ × 52″.

MATERIALS: 2 yards 45″-wide gingham for back; pastel ginghams for patchwork front and appliqués (we used ¼ yard of five 45″-wide ginghams); 39″ × 50″ piece glazed polyester quilt batting and 6 pieces each 10″ × 14″; 3-strand embroidery floss in Pink, Blue and Black; scraps of yarn (for tails); white thread; needle; scissors; pins; ruler; paper for pattern.

DIRECTIONS:

Cut 2½″-wide strips of varied lengths from different colors of gingham checks. (We used strips between 6″ and 10″ long; a total of 26 strips were used.) Arrange them in long strips that measure 40″ long when joined with ¼″ seams. Sew strips together to make the top of the quilt measuring 40″ × 52″, using a ¼″ seam; press seams all one way. When top is complete, cut batting to fit; place on back fabric, allowing the back to stick out around edges. Cut back, but do not cut off selvage, and allow at least 2″ excess all around batting. Place top of quilt over batting; smooth out; pin 3 layers together (back on bottom, batting, then top, right side up),

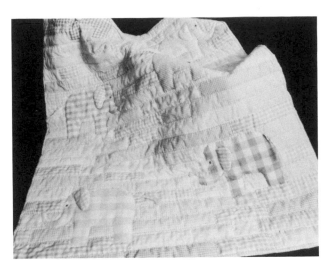

first on the diagonals, then up sides to hold all three layers securely. Place on a large table; quilt by hand or machine with running stitch along each patchwork seam. Trim batting and quilt top edges evenly; cut back edges to same width all around, about 1½″ larger all around than top and batting. Turn the raw edges under ¼″, then fold to front; sew back overlap to top of quilt, mitering corners.

To make elephant appliqués: Following directions on page 224, enlarge and trace patterns for body, 2 ears and tail onto paper; cut out only one body for each of the 6 appliqués, making sure to allow for ¼″ seams. Clip edges; press raw edges under all around. Cut batting on seam line; place under elephant. Pin to quilt, placing three one way, three the opposite, as desired. Cut out tails on lines. Press long edges in to center; press one short edge under. Cut strands of yarn; place on short edge that has been pressed under. Press tail in half the long way; pin; sew; press so seam is on center bottom. Sew tail under elephant, positioning as shown in diagram. Sew elephant to quilt, using running stitch close to edge, going through all layers and backing of quilt. Catch base of tail in as you go (rest of tail hangs free). Embroider eyes and mouths.

Ears: Transfer to gingham; cut out, allowing for ¼″ seams. Cut out batting ears on seam line. Place ears, right sides together; place batting under them. Sew around edge on line, leaving open as shown in diagram; trim and clip curves. Turn. Fold opening edges under; slipstitch closed. Sew to head with running stitch, going through all layers. Tack back of ear to head with thread through bottom layer of ear and elephant top. Stitch around eye and along one side of mouth.

MACRAMÉ

WHITE SLING

MATERIALS: White jute, 24 strands, 2 yds. long; plastic beads $5/16''$ in diameter, 120 Green and 120 Blue; $3/4''$ in diameter, 12 faceted Blue. *Note:* Be sure the holes of your beads are large enough for the jute strands to go through.

DIRECTIONS: Align strands; tie overhand knot at one end, leaving 5″ long tassel. Thread each tassel strand with three small beads, alternating blue-green-blue and green-blue-green. Secure beads with overhand knot 1½″ from tassel end.

Section 1: Holding two strands together in each hand, tie a double knot 1″ above tassel; repeat five times. Repeat 1″ above the first six knots, using one cord from one knot and one cord from the adjacent knot.

Section 2: Straighten out each group of four strands and tie 1½″ of square knots (*see* FIGS. 1A to 1F).

Section 3: String a pair of small beads (1 blue, 1 green) on each *outer* strand, then make an overhand knot (anchor strands hang free until Section 2 is repeated). With a double knot, tie two adjacent outer strands 2¼″ from beads. Make an overhand knot 1¾″ further along these

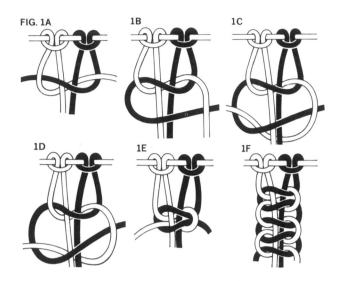

FIG. 1A 1B 1C

1D 1E 1F

outer strands and string another pair of beads.
Sections 4 and 5: Repeat Sections 2 and 3.
Section 6: Repeat Section 2.
Top Beads: On each outer cord, string one small blue and green bead, then an overhand knot to keep beads in place. Make another overhand knot 1½″ above previous one. String four more beads, alternating colors and secure with overhand knot.
Adding Big Bead Drops: Thread needle with long double strand of white sewing thread. At all the intersections of the outer strands in Sections 3 and 5, push the needle through the double knot leaving a 3″ tail. Thread a large blue bead and one small green and bring needle back through blue; make a double knot, drawing thread up tight. Tie; cut off excess thread.
Finishing: Smooth out strands and tie an overhand knot at proper place for desired height of planter. Trim off excess 1½″ above knot.

CHAIR SEATS

GENERAL DIRECTIONS: Macrame patterns may appear extremely complex, but the art of macrame depends heavily on a few basic knots, one of which is that old sailor's favorite, the *half-hitch.* Each of the chair seats employs a variation of the *double half-hitch* (logic would suggest that a double half-hitch is a whole hitch, but it is not so designated). Before attempting any of the seats, make sure that you understand this knot. Basically, it is used to tie a rope or cord to a pole, ring or another cord. One end of the tying cord is passed around the other object, brought over and under itself and through the loop that is formed. Repeat the process, then tighten to complete the knot (*see* FIG. 1). The term *horizontal* is used to denote that part of

the pattern that runs from side to side of the seat; *vertical* that from front to back. All knotting is done with a *knot-bearing* cord. This is usually a horizontal cord, and is generally quite a bit longer than the other cords. The knot-bearing cord is worked across the pattern and tied to each vertical cord it intersects. Sometimes a very long knot-bearing cord will be used to work the entire seat pattern. At other times a new knotting cord is started every few rows. Occasionally each row will have a separate knotting cord. We used three variations of the basic knot.
Basic Knot Variations:
Horizontal double half-hitch (HDHH) Tie the crossing cords to the knotting cord (*see* FIG. 2).
Vertical double half-hitch (VDHH) Loop the knotting cord around the crossing cords (*see* FIG. 3). The same knot-bearing cord can be tied in alternate ways, if the pattern calls for it.
Lark's head or *reversed double half-hitch* (RDHH) (*see* FIG. 4). Double the cord to form a loop over the other object (spindle, crossing cord and so on) and bring the two ends back through the loop.

SEAT FOR SPINDLE-POST CHAIR

MATERIALS: 20-ply polished white cotton cord; white glue.
DIRECTIONS: This is a relatively easy beginner's project. The cord is tied directly to the chair frame with RDHH. Within the pattern, the knots are all HDHH. Our chair, with a 14″ × 12½″ seat, required 30 cords, 29 of which measure 9 feet long. The knot-bearing cord is 62 feet long. Double all the shorter cords, and double over one end of the knotting cord to the same length as the shorter cords. Using the RDHH, attach the doubled end of the knotting cord to the left side of the front spindle. Attach all the other cords to the front spindle, spacing them evenly and leaving at least ⅛″ between each (*see* FIG. 5). Begin knotting by picking up only the *end* knot-bearing cord and laying it horizontally over the other cords. Tie HDHH (double loops) over the knot-bearing cord (*see* FIG. 6). At the end of the first row, attach the knotting cord to the right side spindle, using an RDHH, then begin the second row of knotting. Each succeeding row will be tied in the same manner, although the knotting must be pulled tighter as the chair narrows toward the back. When you have completed all the rows, loop each set of double cords over the rear spindle and tie an RDHH in each set of doubled cords, pulling the

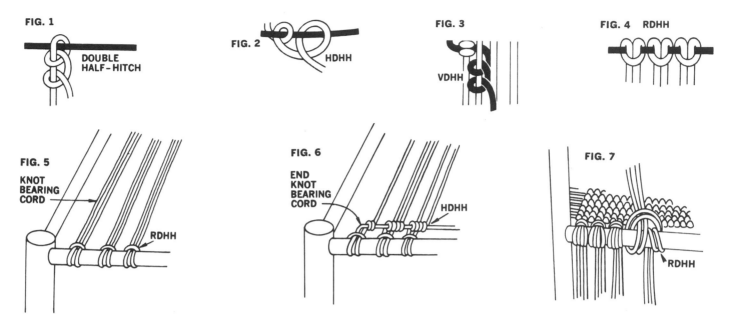

FIG. 1 DOUBLE HALF-HITCH

FIG. 2 HDHH

FIG. 3 VDHH

FIG. 4 RDHH

FIG. 5 KNOT BEARING CORD RDHH

FIG. 6 END KNOT BEARING CORD HDHH

FIG. 7 RDHH

knot firm and pushing the loose ends through to the underside of the seat (see FIG. 7). With the knotting cord, tie at least one row of HDHH along the underside of the seat. Trim all loose ends to 1½″, then glue and conceal the ends under the bottom row of knots. The final step is to fill the ⅛″ space between cords on front and side spindles. With a single cord, start at the back of one side spindle and work the cord around the side, front and other side, tying RDHH between each cord set.

SEAT FOR PERFORATED FRAME CHAIR

MATERIALS: Thick polished linen cord (60/6); tacks.

DIRECTIONS: Chairs of this type were originally caned, and the holes in the frame may be spaced quite erratically. The macrame pattern is very open to accommodate such variations. There are four rows of HDHH, followed by two rows of VDHH. This design is repeated until the seat is finished. You can work out modifications to fit your particular chair. First count the holes in the front edge of the chair frame; ours has 25. Twelve vertical cords will be needed, each doubled (the 25th hole will accommodate the knot-bearing cord). To determine length, measure the front-to-back frame opening and multiply by 12. For the chair shown with a 12″ x 14″ seat, 11 cords 14 feet long were cut; the twelfth, knot-bearing cord, was 37 feet. Start by doubling over 7 feet of the 37-foot long cord. Thread the remaining 30-foot length of this cord *up* through the first hole at the left front of the chair fame, and the 7-foot end *up* through the second hole (see FIG. 8). Thread a doubled 14-

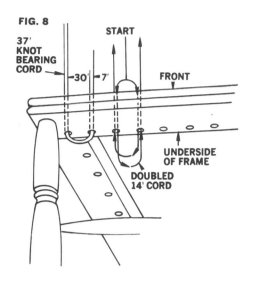

FIG. 8

37' KNOT BEARING CORD

30' — 7'

START

FRONT

UNDERSIDE OF FRAME

DOUBLED 14' CORD

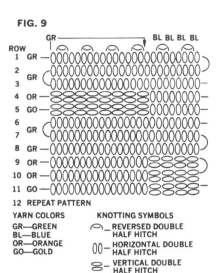

FIG. 9

GR ——— BL BL BL BL

ROW
1 GR
2 GR
3
4 OR
5 GO
6 GR
7
8 GR
9 OR
10 OR
11 GO
12 REPEAT PATTERN

YARN COLORS
GR—GREEN
BL—BLUE
OR—ORANGE
GO—GOLD

KNOTTING SYMBOLS
⌒ — REVERSED DOUBLE HALF HITCH
OO — HORIZONTAL DOUBLE HALF HITCH
8 — VERTICAL DOUBLE HALF HITCH

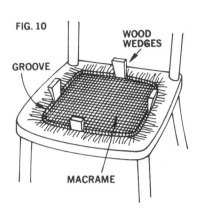

FIG. 10

WOOD WEDGES

GROOVE

MACRAME

Color photo on page 137

foot section *down* through the next pair of holes, cross it underneath and bring the ends back up through the opposite holes (*see* FIG. 8). Repeat with the remaining cords, and lay all the ends over the back of the frame. Lay the knot-bearing cord over the vertical cords and tie HDHH at each intersection. To allow for the open pattern, skip a little space between each knot. Pull each knot tight to avoid stretching. End the first row by threading the knotting cord down through the open hole at the right side of the frame front. To start the second row, bring the knotting cord up through the second hole on the right side and repeat knotting, as in the first row. The third and fourth rows are the same, then the knot pattern is changed to VDHH for the fifth and sixth rows, then back to HDHH for four more rows, and so on. Since our chair has only 23 holes in the back frame, the knot-bearing cord is left temporarily hanging underneath after the final row of knotting. Pull the vertical cords down through the holes in the back of the frame. Each cord is then brought up through the hole on its right, then returned through the original hole (the cord on the far right is simply left hanging). With all cords now hanging from the bottom of the chair, turn it upside down and secure the cord ends to the knot-bearing cord with a row of HDHH tight up against the bottom of the frame. Knot a final row of HDHH, then tie each individual cord with a simple overhand knot. Cut off excess and tack the ends to the underside of the frame. Finally, weave a single cord in and out of alternating holes on each side of the frame to give the seat a finished, unform appearance.

SEAT FOR SOLID-FRAME CHAIR

MATERIALS: Swedish rya rug yarn, 4 colors (Green, Blue, Orange, Gold); batting; ⅜" plywood and ⅛" hardboard (both large enough for seat); 4 flat-head wood screws, 1½" long, with washers; epoxy cement.

DIRECTIONS: For this seat, the macrame work is done on a "knotting board," a work surface to which you can pin the cords. The completed design is then fastened over padding to a plywood seat. The knotting board may be any work surface; perhaps best is a piece of insulation board or similar material. First, make a pattern for the seat. Tape a sheet of paper under the chair seat and draw around the inside of the frame opening. Remove the pattern and expand the outline to overlap the frame opening—normally about 1" all around. Use this pattern to cut a seat base of ⅜" plywood, with a matching piece of ⅛" hardboard. Drill four holes through *both* plywood and harboard so that the aligned holes fall within the chair frame opening. Set aside hardboard. Counter-sink the holes in the plywood, then insert the bolts through the plywood and bond in place with epoxy cement, or any other adhesive that will bond metal to wood. Set aside the plywood. The finished macrame material will be applied over a layer of batting, so the pattern must be made larger than the plywood—in this case, 1½" larger all around. Make a pattern to this size and pin it to the knotting board. The design for this seat uses a repeating combination of HDHH and VDHH in four different colors. For the 12" × 13½" seat shown, 42 cords were cut, each 24 feet long (28 green, 14 blue). See FIG. 9 for color placement, then tie cords as indicated in the drawing. Cut and tie orange and gold cords as shown in FIG. 9. The pattern is repeated across the seat from one side to the other—seven times in this instance. Work from the back of the seat to the front, enlarging the pattern on both sides as you progress by adding new vertical cords to the knotting cords with RDHH. Pin cord ends to the board to hold them in place.

Note: This design calls for many knot-bearing cords rather than just one long one. Each time the horizontal color is changed, start a new knotting cord; vertical cords will also have to be added as colors change. As work progresses, unpin and check occasionally to make sure that the design will cover both plywood and padding. When the pattern is complete, place batting over the plywood seat and stretch the macrame over the batting. Staple or tack the macrame to

the bottom of the plywood. Place the seat on top of the frame with the bolts through the frame opening. Place the hardboard over the bolts beneath the frame and attach with washers and nuts. Align the seat on the frame and tighten the nuts.

SEAT FOR CHAIR WITH SPLINE CONSTRUCTION

MATERIALS: Polished India twine; reed spline; white glue.

DIRECTIONS: The spline is a narrow piece of flexible wood that has been forced into a groove in the chair frame to hold the seat in place. You will almost surely have to replace the spline in an old chair. First remove the old spline carefully with a wood chisel and examine the size of the groove. If it is very shallow or narrow, the relatively thick macrame will not be properly held by a spline, and some other type of chair seat will be needed. The seat for the rocker uses only one knot—HDHH. The finished seat is then turned over with the reverse side up. The knotting pattern complements the woven design of the back of our rocker. Lay paper over the chair seat and trace around the empty groove to make a pattern. Pin the pattern to a knotting board (*see* SOLID-FRAME SEAT). For this chair, with a 17" × 15½" seat, 132 eight-foot cords were cut; these cords are *not* doubled. Start knotting at the back, or narrow end, of the pattern. Allow 4" of free cord at the end of each row, pinning to the knotting board, then work in the first cord using the HDHH. Attach the second horizontal cord in the same manner, and work downward until the pattern is completed. Make sure that the knotted area extends partially beyond the groove in the chair. Dampen the reed spline until it becomes very pliable, then fit it into the empty groove and cut off excess with a sharp knife, leaving a ¼" overlap. Put the spline aside—but keep it damp. Apply an even layer of glue inside the groove. Dampen the loose ends of the macrame seat material, then place over the chair frame. Make sure that the cords are straight and that the pattern corresponds to the groove. Drive the cord ends into the groove with a mallet and scrap of hardwood wedge, beginning at the back of the seat. Leave the wedge in place at the center back, then drive the sides into the groove, again leaving wedges in place. Finally, drive the front of the seat macrame into the groove. Use additional wedges, if needed, to hold the macrame seat in place tightly (*see* FIG. 10). Cut off excess cord ends; cords should not be visible above the outer edge of the groove. When the glue has dried, remove the wedges. Spread another thin layer of glue in the groove, then place the shaped spline and press it into the groove. Cut off any overlap with a sharp knife. Drive the spline firmly into the groove with the mallet and an upturned wedge, moving the wedge all around the seat and striking light but firm blows. When the spline is in place, allow glue to dry and the job is done.

BEADED MACRAMÉ NECKLACES

Note: Macramé jewelry has become a very popular homecraft, and a wide assortment of beads is available at many craft and hobby stores. Our necklaces offer suggestions as to the shapes and types of beads; you may wish to vary your own designs with different beads. Cutting apart old jewelry you may have on hand is another source.

GENERAL DIRECTIONS: Both necklaces are made using the Square Knot (SQ) or variations

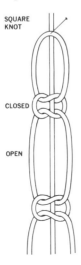

on it. As shown in the diagram, there are two outer cords and one center (holding) cord. The closely worked sections are a series of tightly made SQ's called Closed Square Knots (CSQ); variations are simply loose SQ's called Open Square Knots (OSQ). Both necklaces are worked one side at a time, from the center of the holding cord out. When working, it is best to tack or pin the strands down to a piece of wood or heavy cardboard surface to keep them straight and even.

DISC CHOKER

MATERIALS: One 23″ piece (holding cord) and two 62″ pieces (outer cords) waxed linen cord; five ½″-diameter discs and five ¼″-diameter beads.

DIRECTIONS: Locate the center of the holding cord; pin the center to the top of work surface, allowing one half to dangle behind work surface. Fold one of the 62″ cords in half and make one CSQ directly onto the holding cord, as shown in Figure. String 1 bead and all 5 discs onto holding cord. Continue as follows: * 2 CSQ, 1 OSQ, 1 bead, 1 CSQ. Repeat from * three more times. Make 7 CSQ's; then work in a 3-strand braid until end; finish off by tying all strands into a firm knot. Unpin. Turn necklace so that finished side now dangles beneath work surface; with the other 62″ piece of cord, folded as for first half, begin with one CSQ beneath the one already formed, then work the other half of the necklace in the same order as the first.

COFFEE BEAN CHOKER

MATERIALS: One 23″ piece (holding cord) and two 62″ pieces (outer cords) waxed linen cord; one coffee bean (or large central bead) with hole for stringing; ten ¼″-diameter beads.

DIRECTIONS: Locate the center of the holding cord; pin center to work surface, allowing one half of cord to dangle behind work surface. String the coffee bean on the holding cord. Fold one of the 62″ cords in half and make one CSQ directly onto holding cord. Then work as follows: 1 bead (all beads strung on holding cord), 1 CSQ, 1 OSQ, 2 CSQ, 1 bead, 2 CSQ, 1 OSQ, 1 CSQ, 1 bead, 5 CSQ, 1 bead, 1 CSQ, 1 OSQ, 5 CSQ, 1 OSQ, 4 CSQ, 1 bead, 3 CSQ. Make a 3-strand braid to the end; end off in a knot. Unpin. Turn necklace so the finished side now dangles beneath work surface. With the other 62″ piece of cord, folded as for the first half, make 1 CSQ directly beneath coffee bean, and continue to work in same order as the first side.

RUG HOOKING

HOOKED CHAIR CUSHIONS

MATERIALS: *(for two cushions):* Burlap, 2 yds.; craft and rug yarn, 1 skein each Eggshell, Village Blue and Midorange; punch needle; hooked rug adhesive backing; cardboard; adjustable hooking frame or canvas stretchers (available at crafts and hobby shops); cord or twine; waterproof felt-tip markers.

DIRECTIONS: Using the directions on page 224, enlarge the 12″ diameter hex motif on same page on paper or cardboard, spacing the lines 1¾″ apart. Cut out pattern, then cut out inner shaded areas.

Transferring the Design: Measure seat of chair. Cut the burlap backing to the dimensions of the chair seat, adding 6″ all around. Draw the outline of the chair dimensions on the back of the burlap backing, centering it on the fabric. Center the motif inside the outline and trace. Now machine-stitch a 2″ hem all around the backing to reinforce the edges. This leaves a 2″ area between hem and marked outline.

Putting the Backing on the Frame: Following manufacturer's directions, attach the backing wrong-side up inside the frame through the reinforced hemmed area.

Note: It is important that the grain of the fabric be straight after all the sides have been tightened. For smaller projects you may find it adequate to thumbtack the fabric to stretcher bars.

Hooking: One strand of yarn is used throughout. Set needle adjustor to make long loops, following the directions on page 121. Begin hooking at the center of the backing wrong side. Work the small areas first, outlining with a row of loops and then filling in the areas. When you come to the end of a skein of yarn or change colors, push all yarn ends through to the front side and cut off even with the loops. In large areas (like the background) all hooking should be done in the same direction (that is, either up and down or sideways). Keep the rows close to insure a thick and solid pile on the right side. Do not hook the 2″ area between the outline and the hem.

Adding Latex Backing: Before the fabric is removed from the frame, the back should be coated with latex rug backing. This serves two purposes. It anchors the stitches and prevents sliding and skidding. Apply the latex with a piece of cardboard, thoroughly saturating the lines of stitching. Allow to dry overnight.

Finishing the Edges: Remove fabric from frame and cut off the hem. Turn under the raw edge of the unhooked area ½″ and machine-stitch all around. Now turn the entire unhooked area to the back and whipstitch with heavy-duty thread to backing (not to yarn stitches).

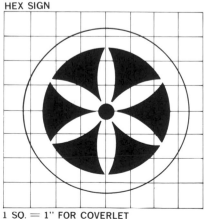

HEX SIGN

1 SQ. = 1″ FOR COVERLET
1 SQ. = 1¾″ FOR CHAIR CUSHIONS

GENERAL DIRECTIONS FOR LATCH HOOKING

TO MAKE KNOTS WITH LATCH HOOK: Fold a piece of yarn in half and slip hook through loop so that latch is above and open. Then, starting at extreme lower left corner of design and with desired color, insert hook in one mesh and out the mesh directly above, so that threads of canvas are over hook and latch is open. Now move the hand holding the yarn up and to the right, so that yarn is caught in hook. Pull hook slightly, closing latch over yarn. *Do not let go of the ends of yarn* in fingers. Pull hook down so that it is pulled back through mesh, until ends of yarn over hook are visible, then let go of yarn ends and pull hook completely through canvas, pulling ends of yarn through, forming the knot.

Note: If ends of yarn are even, pull them to tighten knot; if they are not even, pull the shorter end, so that they are even. This will tighten knot at the same time.

HOW TO LATCH HOOK: The hooking is *always* done in one direction, starting at one end and working each subsequent row above the one just finished. The best way to hold the canvas is the most comfortable way. Most experienced latch-hook craftpersons prefer to sit at a table (one that is not too high) with the article spread out across the table, one end or bottom edge towards them. A firm pillow under article, placed in lap and over edge of table at area being worked, may be helpful too. Another satisfactory method is to use a bridge table; place article in same manner as above and stretch it across table, leaving 4 or 5 rows of unhooked canvas extended beyond edge of table. Then with blocks of felt-covered wood or heavy cardboard (to protect your table), use vises to anchor the article securely on each side. Work each row completely across article, beginning at extreme lower left and working to right, hooking proper colors in correct number of knots in any given section. Then, if anchored, when exposed rows are finished, remove and expose 4 or 5 more rows, reset vises and continue your hooking. After you have completed 10″ or 12″ of the project it is helpful to start rolling the finished end so that it is not so cumbersome—fasten roll at ends with large safety pins.

GENERAL DIRECTIONS FOR USING PUNCH NEEDLE

To Thread Punch Needle: Thread yarn through eye (A) from outside, drawing through tube and out eye (B), leaving 1-inch of yarn extending.

from point.

Note: For short loops, use wire gage; for long loops, remove wire gage.

HOW TO MAKE PUNCH NEEDLE PROJECT: Attach rug foundation to frame, stamped-side up—*always work from this side*. Hold needle, grooved-side toward direction you are working. Push point through backing fabric, as far as it will go. Being sure that the 1-inch end of yarn remains on under side, withdraw needle carefully to surface, *but do not raise* above surface. Make stitches close, 5 stitches to the inch and follow design outline on foundation first, then fill in balance.

Note: When ending a skein of yarn, or when changing colors, push needle through foundation and then cut yarn at eye (B). Trim these ends to length of loops.

RUG PUNCH NEEDLE

TECHNIQUE FOR MAKING KNOTS

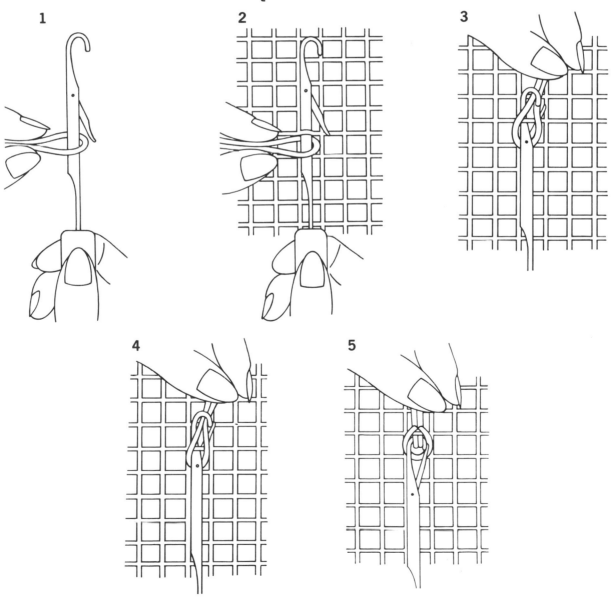

Color photo on page 138

PENNSYLVANIA DUTCH RUG

MATERIALS (for a 32″ × 48″ rug): Three 2 oz. skeins Yellow, four 2 oz. skeins White, one 4 oz. skein Rust, one 4 oz. skein Paddy Green, five 4 oz. skeins Coffee Brown; 40″-wide monk's cloth, 1⅔ yds.; punch needle; cord or twine; adjustable hooking frame (available at craft and hobby shops); hooked rug adhesive backing; cardboard; felt-tip markers.

DIRECTIONS: Using the directions on page 224, enlarge the star and heart motifs on paper or cardboard, spacing the lines 2″ apart. Cut out the shaded areas.

Note: From here on, the technique for making the rug is the same as for the chair cushion, including the 6″ fabric requirement outside the outline marking the rug dimensions. Use long loops for rug.

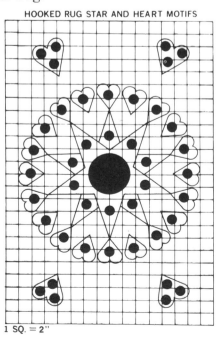

HOOKED RUG STAR AND HEART MOTIFS

1 SQ. = 2″

CHERRY WREATH RUG

(Approximately 30″ × 68″)

MATERIALS: Natural undyed burlap, 45″ × 82″; adjustable hooking frame or canvas stretchers (available at craft shops); Bucilla Multi-craft acrylic yarn, 2 oz. skeins in the following colors and quantities: Red, 3 skeins; Pink, 5 skeins; Green, 6 skeins; White, 13 skeins; permanent waterproof felt-tip marking pen; punch hook; size F rug hook or a large crochet hook; one quart latex adhesive rug backing; pushpins; string; carbon paper and pencil.

DIRECTIONS:

1. Following the directions on page 224, enlarge the cherry wreath design on a 20″ square of paper, using a grid with the lines spaced 2″ apart. Be sure to mark the X in the exact center.

2. Lay burlap out flat on work surface, making sure fabric grain is straight; secure at corners with pushpins. Draw a 30″ × 68″ rectangle centered on fabric to mark rug outline.

3. Using felt-tip markers, draw two more rectangles inside the outline, the first one ¾″ from the outline *(for the red border)* and the second 1¾″ from previous one *(for the pink border)*.

4. To find the exact center of the rug (so you can trace the wreath motifs in the right places), cut two long pieces of string and pin them on the diagonal at the precise corners of the inner rectangle. Mark an X in the center where the strings cross each other.

5. Using a plate as a guide, round the corners of all the rectangles.

6. Place enlarged patterns on burlap, with carbon paper between. Align the X-marks with a straight pin and edges of pattern with borderlines. Tape pattern in place across corners. Trace wreath design.

7. Repeat at each side of center motif, leaving 1″ between tracings.

8. Center burlap over frame with marked side up (this will be the wrong side when the rug is finished). Stretch and tack to outside edges with pushpins every 2″ to 3″, making sure to keep fabric grain straight.

9. Set punch hook to make short loops, following directions on page 121. Work all green shapes first, then continue with pink and red cherries. Fill in borders, then white background.

10. Remove rug from frame and place right-side up on table. Using rug hook (or crochet hook), pull all yarn ends through rug and cut off even with hooked surface.

11. Turn rug over again and coat back with

latex adhesive to keep yarn loops from pulling out; allow to dry overnight.

12. Trim burlap, leaving 2″ all around to form hem. Turn hem to back of rug and stitch to backing (clipping hem at corners and overlapping to prevent bulk).

CHERRY WREATH DESIGN FOR HOOKED RUG

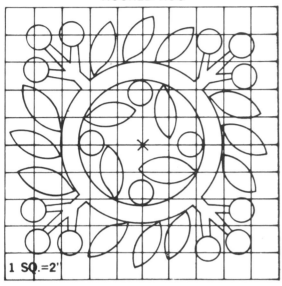

1 SQ.=2'

WEATHER VANE RUG

MATERIALS: Natural undyed burlap, 48″ × 72″; adjustable hooking frame or canvas stretchers (available at craft stores); Bucilla Multi-craft acrylic yarn (2 oz. skeins), 9 each of the following colors: red, white and black; punch hook; size F rug hook or large crochet hook; latex rug backing, one quart; masking tape; waterproof felt-tip marker in a light color.

DIRECTIONS:

1. Lay burlap backing out flat on work surface, making sure fabric grain is straight; secure at corners with tape.

2. Draw a 36″ × 60″ rectangle centered on backing to mark rug outline (*see* rug dimension diagram).

3. Using marker, draw inner dimension lines. Trace weather vane designs in center of 12″ × 15″ areas (*see photo for positioning*).

4. Stretch backing over frame with marked side up (*this will be the wrong side when the rug is finished*).

5. Set punch hook to make short loops, following directions on page 121. Work all weather vane designs first, then the white background around them. Next work the borders around the

FIG. 6 RUG DIMENSION DIAGRAM

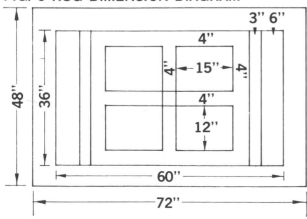

blocks, then the end strips.

6. Remove rug from frame and place right-side up on table. Using rug or crochet hook, pull all yarn ends through rug and cut off even with hooked surface.

7. Turn rug over and coat back with latex adhesive; dry overnight.

8. Trim burlap, leaving 2″ all around to form hem. Turn hem to back of rug and stitch to backing, clipping hem at corners and overlapping to prevent bulk.

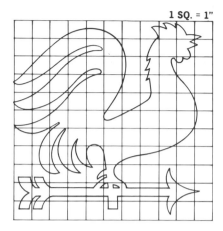

1 SQ. = 1"

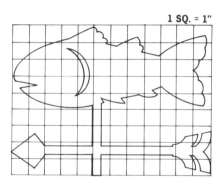

1 SQ. = 1"

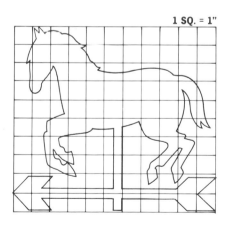

1 SQ. = 1"

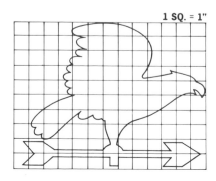

1 SQ. = 1"

WHITE RUG

MATERIALS: Thirty-two 100 yd. skeins of Bucilla Multi-Craft acrylic yarn, off-white; jute or canvas backing, one 40″ × 62″ piece; light-colored, fine-point permanent marking pen; light-colored permanent wide marker or acrylic paint; yardstick; adjustable Punch Needle tool; rug frame or stretcher bars; rug adhesive; polyester core thread.

DIRECTIONS:

1. Using a fine-point marking pen, draw the outline of the finished rug size (36″ × 58″) on the backing fabric, leaving 2″ all around the outline.

2. Starting at one end of the outline, draw lines across, spaced as shown (see FIG. 1), dividing the outline into rows A–H. Reverse the canvas and draw lines on the other half, starting again at the end and working toward the center. The two lines in the center will form Row I.

3. Draw the design in each row as follows:

A Rows: Draw sixteen 1″-wide bars alternating with 1¼″-wide bars (see FIG. 2). Fill in the 1¼″ bars with light-colored marker or paint, spacing them as shown (see FIG. 3). Color in the triangles and diamonds formed by the diagonal lines.

C Rows: No design.

D Rows: Drawing the design in this row will be easier if you first make a pattern. From cardboard, cut a rectangle 5″ × 9″. In the center of this, draw another rectangle, 2½″ × 5½″, as shown (see FIG. 4). Using the dimensions given, draw a dotted line across each corner, as shown. Cut away the corners on the dotted lines. Also draw a dotted line across each corner of the *inner rectangle,* using the dimensions given. Cut away the *inner area* of this rectangle on the dotted lines and on the two long *solid* lines, as shown. Trace the finished pattern (the shaded area of FIG. 4) four times across the row, centering it between the top and bottom border lines. Color the areas inside and around the designs, not the pattern shape itself.

E Rows: No design.

F Rows: Starting and stopping 2″ from each side edge, draw 15 evenly-spaced circles, 1½″ in diameter across the row. Color all areas *except* inside the circles.

G Rows: No design.

H Rows: Draw eight evenly-spaced diagonal stripes (see FIG. 5). Color remaining areas.

I Row: No design.

Working the Design: (*Note:* In this type of tufting or punchwork, the usual hooking method is reversed and you work from the back of the rug,

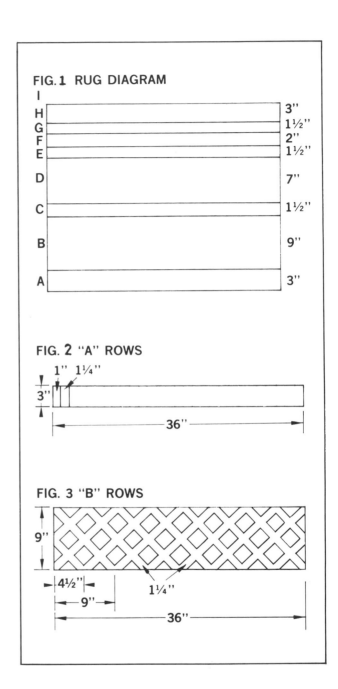

FIG. 1 RUG DIAGRAM

I
H   3"
G   1½"
F   2"
E   1½"
D   7"
C   1½"
B   9"
A   3"

FIG. 2 "A" ROWS

1"   1¼"
3"
36"

FIG. 3 "B" ROWS

9"
4½"
9"
1¼"
36"

where the design has been drawn, through to the front.)

1. Tack canvas, with design up, to rug frame or stretcher bars.

2. *Following directions on page* 121, thread the rug punch needle, set it to make short loops and work a sample. Turn the sample over and check the right side to make sure that no bare canvas is showing. If there are bare spots, space your loops more closely.

3. Work one row at a time, using short loops on the *colored* areas and long loops on the *uncolored* areas, including the *circles* in Rows F.

4. When one or two rows are completed, apply latex backing, following manufacturer's directions. Let latex dry. Move rug down in frame. Continue tufting and applying latex until rug is completed.

Finishing:

1. When latex on the last section is completely dry, turn rug over. Cut long yarn-ends even with loops. Check to make sure that the canvas is completely covered. If there are any blank spots, simply fill them in with loops of the correct height.

2. Remove rug from frame. Turn canvas raw edges under 1", then 1" again. Handstitch edges in place, using a doubled polyester thread; if the needle becomes sticky, clean it by rubbing off the accumulated latex.

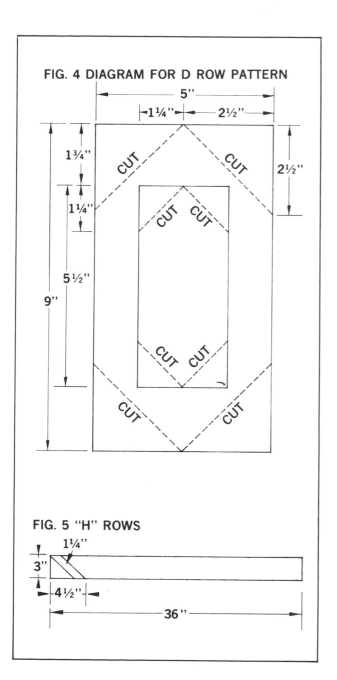

FIG. 4 DIAGRAM FOR D ROW PATTERN

FIG. 5 "H" ROWS

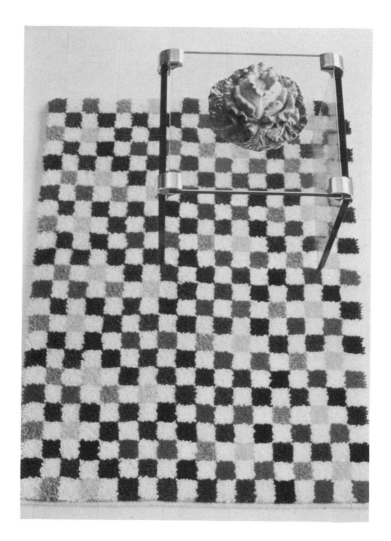

CHECKED LATCH-HOOK RUG
SHORT SIDE

ONE QUARTER OF RUG · REPEAT 3 MORE TIMES

□-105 WHITE	T-155 TURQUOISE
R-110 RED	P-157 PURPLE
A-134 ROYAL	K-158 KELLY
H-151 HOT PINK	Y-161 YELLOW
O-152 ORANGE	M-162 MAGENTA

CHECKED RUG
Finished size approximately 33″ × 44½″.
MATERIALS: Reynolds' Pre-cut "Tapis Pengouin" (40 g. bundles): 25 bundles white, 3 bundles each red, royal, hot pink, orange, turquoise, purple, kelly, yellow, magenta; Reynolds' Uncut "Tapis Pengouin": 2 (50g) balls white; latchet hook; large-eyed tapestry (blunt) needle; 1⅜ yds. 40″-wide (3.3 hole) rug canvas.
DIRECTIONS: Following color placement diagram, latch-hook squares six knots across and six knots deep. (Work in center of canvas, so 2″-3″ border remains all around hooked section of canvas.) To make knots, *see* HOW TO LATCH-HOOK page 121. *Work in one direction only.* This is so all knots on rug will lie in the same direction. After finishing knots, cut away excess canvas, leaving a border 4 squares wide all around. Fold the border in half, and with a double strand of (uncut) white, overcast all around the rug, going into the second square of canvas and working over corners twice to be sure they are completely covered.

INDIAN RUG *(36" × 68")*

MATERIALS: Penelope rug canvas (3½ meshes per inch), 40" × 75"; Bucilla pre-cut wool or acrylic rug yarn (1 oz. packs): 40 White, 28 Redwood, 45 Chinese Blue; latch hook; waterproof light and dark felt-tip markers; brush-on anti-skid backing; rug hemming tape; masking tape; button thread.

DIRECTIONS: Tape corners of rug canvas to floor or work surface. With dark marker draw a line 2" from edge all around; this is the hem. Draw line 4" (15 meshes) in from first all around; this is the border. Draw rows of 4" squares (or count 15 × 15 meshes) to fill the area inside the border, using the chart as a guide. Remove masking tape. Starting at top left corner of rug and using one strand of yarn, hook all horizontal meshes, changing color as required, following directions on page 121. When rug is completed, edgestitch hem tape around edges; turn to back, overlapping corners, and sew to rug back, using button thread. Coat rug with brush-on anti-skid backing.

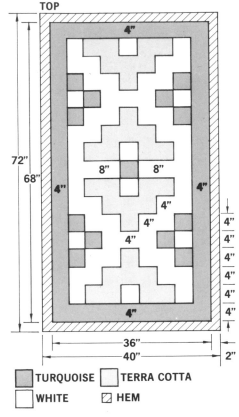

FIG. 2 LATCH HOOK INDIAN RUG

TURQUOISE · TERRA COTTA · WHITE · HEM

(see page 8)

(see page 12)

(see page 10)

130

(see page 15)

(see page 36)

(see page 26)

(see page 39)

(see page 19)

132

(see page 43)

(see page 43)

(see page 49)

(see page 53)

134

(see page 67)

(see page 58)

(see page 63)

(see page 65)

(see page 83)

(see page 95)

(see page 84)

(see page 97)

(see page 110)

(see page 116)

(see page 118)

138

(see page 122)

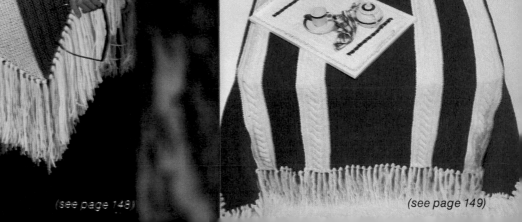

(see page 148)

(see page 149)

(see page 155)

140

(see page 172)

(see page
170)

(see page 173)

(see page 175)

141

(see page 177)

(see page 184)

(see page 187)

142

(see page 191)

(see page 188)

(see page 197)

(see page 195)

(see page 201)

(see page 199)

(see page 206)

(see page 209)

144

(see page 220)

(see page 211)

(see page 216)

(see page 212)

KNITTING

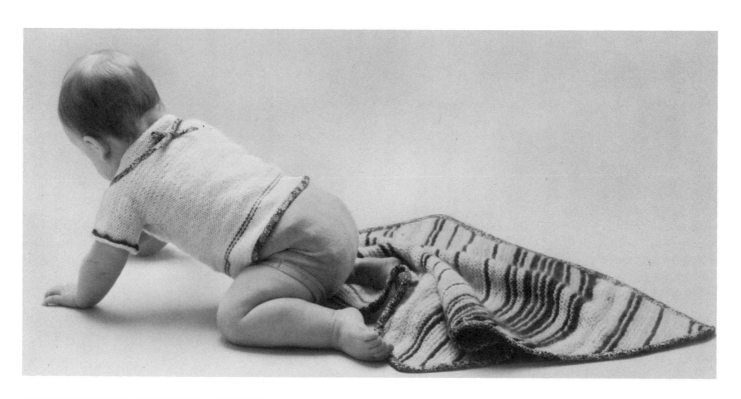

PRINT-BOUND BABY BLANKET

Blanket measures approximately 29″ square.

MATERIALS: Unger Fluffy (50 gram balls): 1 ball each Aqua, Salmon Pink, Beige small amounts of Yellow, Red, Green and Blue, small amounts of about 1 oz. each of other assorted sport weight yarns in White, Light Peach, Teal or any desired color and yarns at hand in the appropriate weight; circular needle No. 6 for sport weight yarn or No. 8 if knitting worsted weight yarn is used, *or any size needle which will obtain the stitch gauge below*; leftover print fabric for binding (or ½ yd. purchased fabric).

GAUGE: Sport Weight Yarn on No. 6 needles, 11 sts = 2″; 10 rows (5 ridges) = 1″. Knitting Worsted Weight Yarn on No. 8 needles, 4 sts = 1″; 7 rows (3 ridges) = 1″.

Note: Blanket is worked in garter st (k every row) on the diagonal, using either sport weight yarn or 4 ply worsted yarn. Any combination of textures can be used as long as resulting gauges are uniform. Two strands of sport yarn will equal one strand of knitting worsted; two strands of fingering yarn equals one strand of sport yarn. Work back and forth on circular needle.

Stripe Pattern: Stripe pat is worked in random stripes of 2, 4 or 6 garter st rows with desired color changes made on right side of work. If wider bands of color are desired increase number of rows for each desired color accordingly. Always join new color at beg of right side row. When changing colors carry last color used loosely along right edge for 4 rows, then cut off.

Blanket: First Half: Starting at bottom left corner, cast on 4 sts. *Row 1 (right side):* K 1, inc 1 st in thread lying between sts by inserting tip of left needle under horizontal thread and knit thru back of lp formed, k 2, inc 1 st in thread lying between sts, k 1. *Row 2:* K. *Row 3:* K 1, inc 1 st in thread between sts, k to last st, inc 1 st in thread between sts, k 1. *Row 4:* K. Rpt Rows 3 and 4 until there are 166 sts (about 82 garter st ridges) for sport yarn or 116 sts (about 57 garter st ridges) for knitting worsted, end Row 4. *Next Row:* K 1, inc 1 st in thread between sts, k to last 3 sts, k 2 tog, k 1. *Next Row:* K. Rpt last 2 rows 3 times forming corner.

Second Half: Next Row: K 1, k 2 tog, k to last 3 sts, k 2 tog, k 1. *Next Row:* K. Rpt last 2 rows until 4 sts rem. Bind off loosely.

Finishing: Press blanket into an even 29″ square.

Fabric Trimming: Cut a bias strip of material 1½″ wide and 116″ long, piecing as necessary. With right side of fabric trim facing right side of blanket, machine stitch fabric to blanket. Fold trim over edge of blanket, mitering corners. Turn under raw edges ¼″ and slipstitch to back of blanket. Slipstitch mitered corners tog.

JIFFY-KNIT TRIANGULAR SHAWL

MATERIALS: Knitting Worsted, 8 oz. each Coral, Orange, Hot Pink, Watermelon, 4 oz. Yellow; Susan Bates knitting needles Size 50 (1″). Use 4 strands of a color held tog for each stripe. With 4 strands of a color cast on 72 sts. * Decreasing one st at both ends of each row, k 2 rows. Change to next color. Rpt from * until no sts remain. End off.

Fringe: Matching stripes along decreased edges, use four 18″ strands for each fringe. Then make 2nd row of knots 1″ below first knots.

PILLOW TOP

MATERIALS: Bear Brand, Fleisher's or Botony Twin-Pak Knitting Worsted or Machine-Washable Win-Knit (4 oz. pak); or Bucilla Machine-Washable Softex (4 oz. ball): 6 oz. of any color; knitting needles, 1 pair No. 10, *or any size needles which will obtain the stitch gauge below;* a 14″ fabric-covered, knife-edge pillow.

GAUGE: 3½ sts = 1″.

Note: Use 2 strands of yarn held together throughout.

DIRECTIONS: Starting at a corner with 2 strands of yarn held together, cast on 3 sts. Work in garter stitch as follows: *Row 1:* K each st across. *Row 2:* Inc in first st; inc in next st, k last st. There are 5 sts on needle. *Row 3:* K each st across. *Row 4:* Inc as before in first st, k 2, inc in next st, k 1—7 sts on needle. *Row 5:* K each st across. *Row 6:* Inc in first st, k each st across until 2 sts rem on left-hand needle, inc in next st, k last st—9 sts on needle. *Rows 7 through 38:* Rpt Rows 5 and 6 alternately 16 times more—at end of 38th row there are 41 sts on needle. Keeping 2 sts at each end in garter st, work rem sts in stockinette stitch as follows: *Row 39 (wrong side of work):* K 2, p in each st across until 2 sts rem on left-hand needle, k 2. *Row 40:* Inc in first st, k each st across until 2 sts rem on left-hand needle, inc in next st, k last st—2 sts increased. *Rows 41 through 54:* Rpt Rows 39 and 40 alternately 7 times more—at end of 54th row there are 57 sts on needle. Work in garter st as follows: *Row 55:* K across. *Row 56:* Rpt Row 40. *Rows 57 and 58:* Rpt Rows 55 and 40—61 sts on needle. *Rows 59 and 60:* K each st on each row—61 sts. This is center of pillow top, diagonally from corner to corner. *Row 61:* K across. *Row 62:* K 1, decrease by k 2 tog; k each st across until 3 sts rem on left-hand needle, k 2 tog, k 1—2 sts decreased. *Rows 63 and 64:* Rpt Rows 61 and 62—57 sts rem on needle. Work in stockinette stitch as follows: *Row 65 (wrong*

side): K 2, p in each st across until 2 sts rem on left-hand needle, k 2. *Row 66:* K 1, k 2 tog, k each st across until 3 sts rem on left-hand needle, k 2 tog, k 1—2 sts decreased. *Rows 67 through 78:* Rpt Rows 65 and 66 alternately 7 times more—43 sts rem on needle. Work in garter stitch as follows: *Rows 79 through 116:* Rpt Rows 61 and 62 alternately 19 times—5 sts rem. *Last Row:* K 1, sl 1 st; k 2 tog, psso; k 1. Bind off rem 3 sts.

Finishing: Block to measure 14″ × 14″. Matching knitted edges to seams on pillow, sew pillow top in place, catching each st along edges.

SQUARE MOHAIR SHAWL

MATERIALS: Columbia-Minerva Amy II, 1-oz. balls: 4 balls Rich Green (A), 3 balls Bright Green (B), 2 balls Bright Clear Gold (C), 1 ball White (D); an alternate color scheme: Bristol Blue (A), Violet (B), Bright Green (C), White (D); 1 pair knitting needles No. 11, 14″ long, *or any size needles which will result in the gauge below.*

GAUGE: 3 sts = 1″; 9 rows = 2″.

MEASUREMENT: Finished shawl measures about 40″ square.

DIRECTIONS: With color A, cast on 120 sts. Marking *Row 1* as right side of shawl, work in garter st (k each row) for 22 rows—there are 11 ridges on right side. *Next row (right side):* K 15 A; attach color B and k 90 B; attach another ball of color A and k 15 A. *Note:* When changing color, always twist one color around the other to prevent making holes. Always drop unused color to the *wrong* side of work. *Following row:*

K 15 A, k 90 B, k 15 A. Rpt last row until there are 11 ridges of color B on right side. *Next row (right side):* K 15 A, k 15 B; attach color C and k 60 C; attach another ball of color B and k 15 B, k 15 A. *Following row:* K 15 A, k 15 B, k 60 C, k 15 B, k 15 A. Rpt last row until there are 11 ridges of color C on right side. *Next row (right side):* K 15 A, k 15 B, k 15 C; attach color D and k 30 D; attach another ball of color C and k 15 C, k 15 B, k 15 A. *Following row:* K 15 A, k 15 B, k 15 C, k 30 D, k 15 C, k 15 B, k 15 A. Rpt last row until there are 23 ridges of color D on right side. Break off color D and 1 ball of C. *Next row (right side):* K 15 A, k 15 B, k 60 C, k 15 B, k 15 A. Rpt last row until there are 11 ridges of color C on right side counting from last ridge of color D. Break off color C and 1 ball of color B. *Next row (right side):* K 15 A, k 90 B, k 15 A. Rpt last row until there are 11 ridges of color B on right side counting from last ridge of color C. Break off color B and 1 ball of color A. *Next row (right side):* With color A, k across all sts. Rpt last row until there are 11 ridges on right side counting from last ridge of color B. Bind off loosely. Weave in ends and steam very lightly.

PONCHO

MATERIALS: Bear Brand or Fleisher's "Wool and Shetland Wool" or Botany Scottie (2 oz. ball): 4 balls White (W), 2 balls each Tangerine (T), Rust (R) and Green (G); knitting needles, 1 pair No. 10½, *or any size needles which will obtain the stich gauge below:* crochet hook, Size H; tapestry needle.

GAUGE: 3 sts = 1″. Each square measures 11½″ x 11½″. *Note:* Always mark the right side of work.

Front Triangle: Starting at corner with W, cast on 3 sts. Work in garter stitch as follows: *Row 1 (right side):* K 1; inc in next st; k last st. There are 4 sts on needle. *Row 2:* K 1, inc in next st, k 2—5 sts on needle. *Row 3:* K 1, inc in next st, k rem sts—one st increased. *Rows 4 through 52:* Rpt last row 49 times more—55 sts on needle. Bind off—this is neck edge.

Back Triangle: Starting at neck edge with G, cast on 55 sts. *Row 1 (right side):* With G, k 1, decrease by k 2 tog; k rem sts—one st decreased. *Rows 2, 3 and 4:* Rpt Row 1 three times—51 sts rem at end of Row 4. Drop G, pick up T and continue as follows: *Rows 5 through 8:* With T rpt Row 1 four times—47 sts rem at end of Row 8. Drop T, pick up G. *Note:* Carry picked up colors loosely along edge. *Rows 9 through 48:* Rpt Rows 1 through 8 five times more—7 sts rem. Break off T. With G, rpt Row 1 three times—4 sts rem. *Last row:* Sl 1 st, k 3 tog., psso. Fasten off by cutting yarn and passing cut end through rem loop on right-hand needle; pull up snugly.

First Square: Same as Front Triangle until Row 52 has been completed—55 sts on needle. Break off W, attach R. *Row 53:* With R, k 1, k 2 tog, k rem sts—one st decreased. *Rows 54, 55 and 56:* Rpt Row 53 three times—51 sts rem at end of Row 56. Drop R, pick up G and continue as follows: *Rows 57 through 60:* With G rpt Row 53 four times—47 sts rem at end of Row 60. *Rows 61 through 100:* Rpt Rows 53 through 60 five times more—7 sts rem. Break off G. With R rpt Row 53 three times—4 sts rem. *Last Row:* Sl 1 st, k 3 tog, psso and fasten off. *Second Square:* Work as for First Square only making alternate stripes of R and T. *Third Square:* Starting with R (instead of W), work as for First Square only making alternate stripes of G and W. *Fourth Square:* Starting with T (instead of W), work as for Front Triangle until Row 52 has been completed—55 sts. Break off T, attach R. *Row 53:* With R, k 1, k 2 tog, k rem sts—one st decreased. Rpt Row 53 until 4 sts rem. *Last*

Color photo on page 138

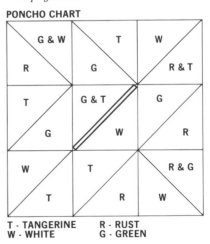

PONCHO CHART

G & W	T	W
R	G	R & T
T	G & T	G
G	W	R
W	T	R & G
T	R	W

T - TANGERINE R - RUST
W - WHITE G - GREEN

Row: Sl 1 st, k 3 tog, psso and fasten off. *Fifth Square:* Work as for Fourth Square making first half with T and second half with W. *Sixth and Seventh Squares:* Work as for Fourth Square making first half with T and second half with G. *Eighth Square:* Work as for Fourth Square making first half with R and second half with G.

Finishing: Baste neck edge of Front Triangle to neck edge of Back Triangle to form a square. Block all squares to measure 11½″ × 11½″. Arrange squares as shown on chart. With matching yarn, sew squares together, catching nobs at ends of matching rows and being careful to keep seams elastic.

Fringe: Wind W 50 times around a 10″ square of cardboard. Cut strands at one edge thus making 20″ strands. Cut more strands as needed. Using 5 strands for each fringe, knot 14 fringes along the edge of each square around entire outer edge of poncho. Trim evenly. For neck opening, rip out the basting joining the front and back triangles.

CABLE BEDSPREAD

Directions are given for a twin bed. To make a larger spread, increase the width of the narrow blue seed stitch panels between the rows of cable by casting on more stitches. (*Note:* Always work with an odd number of stitches for the seed stitch pattern.)

MATERIALS: Malina yarn (100% Acrilan wear-dated) 4 oz. skeins in the following quantities and colors: 10 skeins Snow White, 21 skeins Sapphire Blue; knitting needles: 1 cable needle and 1 pair No. 7 needles *or any size which will obtain the stitch gauge below;* size F crochet hook for securing fringe in place.

GAUGE: Sapphire Blue seed stitch 4 sts = 1″; 8 rows = 1″.

White cable 22 sts = 5″; 8 rows = 1″.

Color photo on page 138

FINISHED BLOCKED MEASUREMENTS:		
WHITE CABLE PANEL	(MAKE 4)	4″ WIDE
NARROW TOP SAPPHIRE		
STITCH PANEL	(MAKE 1)	5″ WIDE
CENTER SAPPHIRE SEED		
STITCH PANEL	(MAKE 1)	12″ WIDE
SIDE SAPPHIRE SEED		
STITCH PANEL	(MAKE 2)	16″ WIDE
LENGTH FOR ALL		98″ LONG

DIRECTIONS: *White Cable Panels* (make 4): With No. 7 needles and White cast on 22 sts. *Row 1:* (rs) k 1, p 2, k 1, p 3, slip next 4 sts onto a cable needle and hold in front of the work, k next 4 sts, k the 4 sts from the cable needle, p 3, k 1, p 2, k 1. *Row 2:* K 3, p 1, k 3, p 8, k 3, p 1, k 3. *Row 3:* K 1, p 2, k 1, p 3, k 8, p 3, k 1, p 2, k 1. *Row 4:* Repeat Row 2. *Rows 5, 7, 9:* Repeat Row 3. *Rows 6, 8, 10:* Repeat Row 2.

Repeat these last 10 rows for cable pattern. Work in pattern until panel measures 98″ long. Bind off.

Narrow Top Panels (make 2): With No. 7 needles and with Sapphire Blue cast on 21 sts. *Row 1:* * K 1, p 1; repeat from * across ending with k 1. Repeat row 1 for seed stitch pattern. Work until panel measures 98″. Bind off.

Center Panel (make 1): With No. 7 needles and Sapphire Blue cast on 51 sts. Work in seed stitch pattern until panel measures 98″. Bind off.

Side Panels (make 2): With No. 7 needles and Sapphire Blue cast on 65 sts. Work in seed stitch pattern until panel measures 98″. Bind off.

Finishing: Block each panel to measurements. Stitch panels together using White or Sapphire Blue yarn as follows:

To Assemble: Sew one white cable strip to each side of 12″ blue center panel. Add 5″ blue panels, then remaining white cable strips. Finish by joining 16″ sections (one on each side), as shown in the photograph.

Fringe: Cut White yarn into strips 14″ long, or as long as needed on your bed. Following the diagram, (*see* HOW TO KNIT page 232), using crochet hook and *five* strands of yarn, attach fringe around three sides of the spread at ¾″ intervals.

PLACE MAT

Directions are given for a 12″ × 18″ place mat.

MATERIALS: Coats & Clark (Speed-Cro-Sheen mercerized cotton) 100 yd. balls; 2 balls White, 1 ball Blue Sparkle; knitting needles, 1 pair No. 4, *or any size which will obtain the stitch gauge below.*

GAUGE: 4 sts = 1″; 11 rows = 1″.
FINISHED BLOCKED MEASUREMENTS: 12″ ×
18″
DIRECTIONS: Cast on 50 white stitches.
Row 1: K across. *Rows 2 & 3:* K across. Continue
in pattern as follows: *Row 4:* (rs) K 3 * k 2 tog
(yo) twice, k 2 tog. Repeat from * to last 3 sts k
3. *Row 5:* K 3 * k 1 (k 1, p 1) into 2 yo's of previous
row, k 1. Repeat from * to last 3 sts k 3. (Rows 4
and 5 form the lacy pattern.) *Rows 6 & 8:* Repeat Row 4. *Rows 7 & 9:* Repeat Row 5. *Row 10:*
K 3 White. Attach Blue, * k 2 tog (yo) twice, k 2
tog. Repeat from * to last 3 sts. Using second
ball of White, attach White and k 3. (*Note:*
Twist the Blue yarn around White yarn to prevent a space forming.) *Row 11:* K 3 White.
Change to Blue * k 1 (k 1, p 1) into 2 yo's of
previous row, k 1. Repeat from * to last 3 sts.
Change to White, k 3. *Row 12:* K 3 White.
Change to Blue * k 2 tog. (yo) twice, k 2 tog.
Repeat from * to last 3 sts. Change to White. k 3
White. *Row 13:* Repeat Row 11. Break off Blue
yarn. Continue working Rows 4 and 5 (pattern
rows), using White, until work measures 16″
from cast-on edge, ending with row 5 (57 pattern holes will be made).
For second blue stripe: Next rows: Repeat rows
10, 11, 12, 13. Break off Blue yarn. *Next rows:*
Work 6 more pattern rows with White. Then k 3
rows. Bind off.
Finishing: Sew off ends of yarn on wrong side.
Dampen finished piece and block by pinning to
padded surface of ironing board on clean cloth
with rust-proof thumbtacks; stretch piece to
measure 12″ × 18″. Allow to dry. If desired,
piece can be sprayed with a spray starch after
blocking and ironed dry on the wrong side,
using a pressing cloth.

RECTANGLE RUG

(Directions are given for a rug approximately
89″ × 53″).
MATERIALS: Bucilla Yarn (Multi-Craft, 100%
Bulky Acrylic) 2 oz. skeins in the following
amounts: 14 skeins Light Gold, 13 skeins Antique Gold, 12 skeins Winter White; knitting
needles No. 10½, *or any size which will obtain
the stitch gauge below;* large-eye tapestry needle.
GAUGE: 3 sts = 1″; 5 rows = 1″.
FINISHED BLOCKED MEASUREMENTS:
Each rectangle measures 10″ × 5″.
DIRECTIONS: Cast on 30 Light Gold stitches.
Row 1: k across. Repeat Row 1 until rectangle
measures 5″. Bind off loosely. Work a total of 28

Light Gold rectangles, 25 Antique Gold rectangles, and 24 White rectangles each 10″ × 5″
following the directions for Light Gold rectangle.
Finishing: Block each rectangle to measurements and sew off ends of yarn. Sew the rectangles together in the order shown in the diagram, using an overcast stitch and matching
color yarns.
GENERAL INFORMATION: There are a
number of commercial rug backings available to
protect the life of your rug and make it skid-
proof. Sponge rubber and cushioning, as well as
vinyl runners, are sold by the yard. This rug is
washable, therefore choose a washable backing.
As another solution, you can sew rubber jar
rings—the kind used in home canning—to the
back of the rug, at the four corners and along
the edges.
Sew-on rug binding and iron-on tape binding
will help to preserve the rug and keep edges in
shape. Some are available by the yard in approximately 1¼″ to 1½″ widths.. Sew-on bind-
ings come in neutral colors. The iron-ons come
in a wide range of attractive colors.

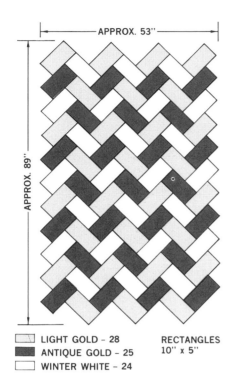

APPROX. 53"

APPROX. 89"

LIGHT GOLD – 28   RECTANGLES
ANTIQUE GOLD – 25   10" x 5"
WINTER WHITE – 24

CHAIR SEAT

MATERIALS: Coats & Clark yarn (Red Heart Hand knitting Worsted) 4-oz. skeins in the following colors and quantities: 2 skeins White (W), 2 skeins Apple Green (G); knitting needles, 1 pair No. 7, *or any size that will obtain the stitch gauge below.*

GAUGE: 5 sts = 1"; 6 rows = 1"

FINISHED BLOCKED MEASUREMENTS: 24" × 24".

DIRECTIONS:

Cast on 120 sts with Apple Green. Work in st st (k 1 row, p 1 row) as follows:

Row 1: K 2 G * k 3 W, k 3 G. Repeat from * to last st, k 1 G. *Row 2:* * P 2 W, p 1 G. Repeat from * to end. *Row 3:* K 2 W, * k 3 G, k 3 W. Repeat from * to last st k 1 W. *Row 4:* * P 2 G, p 1 W. Repeat from * to end. *Row 5:* K 2 W * k 3 G, k 3 W.

CHAIR SEAT CHART

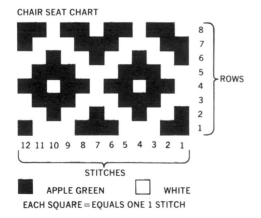

8
7
6
5   } ROWS
4
3
2
1

12 11 10 9 8 7 6 5 4 3 2 1

STITCHES

APPLE GREEN   WHITE
EACH SQUARE = EQUALS ONE 1 STITCH

Repeat from * to last st, k 1 W. *Row 6:* * P 2 W, p 1 G. Repeat from * to end. *Row 7:* K 2 G, * k 3 W, k 3 G. Repeat from * to last st, k 1 G. *Row 8:* * P 2 G, p 1 W. Repeat from * to end. *Row 9:* Repeat Row 1. *Row 10:* Repeat Row 2.

Continue working pattern Rows 1—8 until piece measures 24" or desired size. Bind off loosely with green yarn.

Finishing: Block the piece to measurements. Sew off loose ends.

Note: The pattern can also be worked by following the chart. The chart is for 12 sts and 8 rows. Repeat the pattern 10 times (120 sts) and work Rows 1—8 until the piece measures 24".

CREW-NECK PULLOVER

Directions are given for Size Small (8-10). Changes for Medium (12-14) and Large (16) are in parentheses.

MATERIALS: Coats & Clark "Red Heart" Hand Knitting Worsted, 4-ply (4 oz. skns); 4 (4-5) Lt. Oxford; 1 skn Oxford; or Coats & Clark "Red Heart" Wintuk † 4-ply (3½ oz. skns); 4 (4-5) Lt. Oxford; 1 skn Oxford; knitting needles Nos. 6 and 9, *or any size needles which will obtain the stitch gauge below.*

GAUGE: No. 9 needles: 9 sts = 2"; 6 rows = 1".

FINISHED MEASUREMENTS:

SIZES:	SMALL (8-10)	MEDIUM (12-14)	LARGE (16)
BUSTLINE:	33½"	37"	39"
WIDTH ACROSS BACK OR FRONT AT UNDERARM:	16¾"	18½"	19½"
LENGTH FROM SHOULDER TO LOWER EDGE:	24½"	26"	26½"
LENGTH OF SIDE SEAM:	18"	18½"	18½"
LENGTH OF SLEEVE SEAM:	17½"	18"	18½"
WIDTH ACROSS SLEEVE AT UPPER ARM:	12"	13"	13½"

Back: Starting at lower edge with Oxford and No. 6 needles, cast on 76 (84, 88) sts. *Row 1 (right side):* K 1, * p 2, k 2, Rpt from * across, end with p 2, k 1. *Row 2:* P 1, * k 2, p 2. Rpt from * across end with k 2, p 1. Rpt Rows 1 and 2 alternately for ribbing until total length is 4½", end with a wrong-side row. Break off Oxford; attach Lt. Oxford. Change to No. 9 needles. With Lt. Oxford, work in st st (k 1 row, p 1 row) until total length is 18 (18½, 18½)", end with a p row.

Armhole Shaping: Continuing in st st throughout, bind off 5 (6, 6) sts at beg of next 2 rows. Dec one st at each end every other row 5 (6, 6) times—56 (60, 64) sts. Work even (no more decs) until length is 6½ (7½, 8)" from first row of armhole shaping, end with a p row.

Shoulder Shaping: Continuing in st st bind off 6 (6, 7) sts at beg of next 4 rows; bind off 6 (7, 6) sts at beg of following 2 rows. Place rem 20 (22, 24) sts on a stitch holder for neckband.

Front: Work same as for Back until length is 4½ (5½, 6)" from first row of armhole shaping, end with a p row.

Neck Shaping: Row 1: K 23 (24, 25); place rem 33 (36, 39) sts on a stitch holder. *Row 2:* Working in st st over set of sts on needle only, dec one st at beg of row—neck edge. Dec one st at neck edge every other row until 18 (19, 20) sts rem. Work even, if necessary, over rem sts until length of armhole is same as on Back, end at armhole edge.

Shoulder Shaping: Row 1: Bind off 6 (6, 7) sts at beg of row; complete row. *Row 2:* Work across. Rpt Rows 1 and 2 once more. Bind off rem 6 (7, 6) sts. Leaving center 10 (12, 14) sts on front holder, slip rem 23 (24, 25) sts onto a No. 9 needle; attach Lt. Oxford at neck edge and work to correspond with opposite side, reversing shaping.

Sleeves: Starting at lower edge with Oxford and No. 6 needles, cast on 40 (44, 44) sts. Work in ribbing same as for Back for 4½", inc 14 (14, 16)

sts evenly spaced across last wrong-side row—54 (58, 60) sts. Break off Oxford; attach Lt. Oxford, and change to No. 9 needles. With Lt. Oxford, starting with a k row, work in st st until total length is 17½ (18, 18½)", end with a p row.

Top Shaping: Continuing in st st, bind off 5 (6, 6) sts at beg of next 2 rows. Dec one st at each end every other row until 20 (18, 18) sts rem. Bind off 2 sts at beg of next 4 rows. Bind off rem sts. If Knitting Worsted is being used, block pieces to measurements. If Wintuk is being used, pin pieces to measurements on a padded surface; cover with a damp cloth and allow to dry; *do not press.* Sew shoulder seam.

Neckband: With right side facing, using Oxford and No. 6 needles, k sts on back stitch holder, pick up and k 19 sts along left front neck edge to front holder, k sts on front holder, pick up and k 19 sts along right front neck edge—68 (72, 76) sts. Work in k 2, p 2 ribbing for 7 rows. Bind off loosely in ribbing. Sew right shoulder seam, including neckband. Sew side and sleeve seams. Sew in sleeves.

TURTLENECK SWEATER

Directions are given for size Small (8–10). Changes for sizes Medium (12–14) and Large (16) are in parentheses.

MATERIALS: Knitting Worsted, 4-ply: 8 (10,

13) ozs. Tan; Spinnerin Frostlon Petite (1 oz. balls): 6 (7, 9) balls White; Knit-Cro-Sheen (250 yd. balls): 2 (2, 3) balls Ecru; knitting needles No. 10½, *or any size needles which will obtain the stitch gauge below.*

GAUGE: 3 sts=1"; 4 rows=1".

Note: Use one strand each of knitting worsted, Petite and Knit-Cro-Sheen held tog throughout.

MEASUREMENTS:

SIZES:	SMALL (8-10)	MEDIUM (12-14)	LARGE (16)
BODY BUST SIZE:	30"-32"	33"-35"	37"

Back: Starting at lower edge with one strand of each yarn held tog, cast on 46 (50, 56) sts. Work in k 1, p 1 ribbing for 16".

Raglan Armhole Shaping: Keeping continuity of ribbed pat throughout, bind off 3 sts at beg of next 2 rows. Dec one st at both ends of every other row 9 (11, 13) times—22 (22, 24) sts rem. Slip these sts onto a stitch holder.

Front: Same as Back. *Sleeves:* Starting at lower edge, cast on 22 sts. Work in k 1, p 1 ribbing for 2". Keeping continuity of ribbed pat, inc one st at both ends of next row and every 8th (6th, 6th) row thereafter 6 (8, 10) times. Work even on these 34 (38, 42) sts until total length is 17" (17½", 17½").

Raglan Top Shaping: Work same as Raglan Armhole Shaping of Back—10 sts rem. Slip these sts onto a stitch holder.

Finishing: Matching Raglan Shapings, sew left sleeve bet front and back. Sew right sleeve to front only.

Turtleneck Collar: With right side facing, sl the sts onto needle in this order: Back, left sleeve, front, right sleeve. Keeping continuity of ribbed pat, work in ribbing until collar measures 20". Bind off very loosely in ribbing. Sew collar and rem raglan seam. Sew side and sleeve seams.

DICKEY

Directions are for one size to fit all, for either a man or woman.

MATERIALS: Bucilla Multi-Craft Yarn (2 oz. ball) or Bear Brand Twin-Pak Knitting Worsted (4 oz. ball) or Bear Brand Twin-Pak Machine-Washable Win-Knit (4 oz. ball): 7 oz. White; knitting needles, 1 pair No. 9, *or any size needles which will obtain the stitch gauge below;* 3 stitch holders; tapestry needle.

GAUGE: 9 sts = 2"; 5 rows = 1".

Note: When using Knitting Worsted, use 2 strands held tog throughout.

Back: Starting at lower edge, cast on 57 sts. *Row 1:* P 1, * k 1, p 1. Rpt from * to end of row. *Row 2 (right side):* K 1, * p 1, k 1. Rpt from * to end of row. Mark the right side of work. These 2 rows establish ribbing. Rpt Rows 1 and 2 alternately until length is 6" from beg ending with Row 2 (when measuring length be sure to stretch width to 12½").

Shoulders: Purling the p sts and knitting the k sts, bind off the first 17 sts for shoulder, continue in ribbing as established until there are 23 sts on right-hand needle; slip these 23 sts just worked onto a stitch holder for back of neck; bind off rem 17 sts.

Front: Work same as Back until length is 9" from beg ending with Row 2.

Neck Shaping: Row 1: Work in ribbing across the first 21 sts, slip these 21 sts just worked onto a stitch holder for right side; work across next 15 sts, slip these 15 sts just worked onto another stitch holder for front of neck; work across rem 21 sts for left side.

Left Side: Row 1: Work in ribbing to within 2 sts before front-of-neck stitch holder, decrease by k 2 tog. *Row 2:* Work in ribbing as established across. Rpt Rows 1 and 2 alternately 3 times more—17 sts rem. Work 5 rows in ribbing. Starting at neck edge, bind off same as back shoulders.

Right Side: Starting at side edge, slip sts from right side holder onto knitting needle having point at neck edge. Attach yarn at neck edge.

Row 1: Decrease as follows: Sl 1, k 1, psso, complete row in ribbing. *Row 2:* Work in ribbing as established across. Rpt Rows 1 and 2 alternately 3 times more—17 sts rem. Work 5 rows in ribbing. Starting at side edge, bind off same as back shoulders. Sew right shoulder seam.

Turtleneck Collar: With right side facing, starting at left shoulder, pick up and knit 13 sts along left front neck edge—this is right-hand needle; slip the 15 sts on front stitch holder onto left-hand needle, then work in ribbing as established across these 15 sts; with right-hand needle pick up and k 13 sts along right front neck edge to shoulder seam; slip the 23 sts on back stitch holder onto left-hand needle, then work in ribbing as established across these 23 sts—64 sts in all. Work in k 1, p 1 ribbing until collar measures 5" from back of neck. Bind off loosely in ribbing.

Finishing: Sew left shoulder seam. Sew collar seam having seam on wrong side when collar is turned to right side. Pin back and front sections to measure 12½" wide. Steam lightly through damp cloth.

KNEE SOCKS

MATERIALS: Columbia-Minerva Nantuk Sweater & Afghan Yarn (2 oz. skein): 1 skein each Green (G), Red (R), Blue (B), Black (Bk), Yellow (Y); "Boye" double-pointed knitting needles, 1 set each No. 3 and No. 4 *or any size needles which will obtain the stitch gauge below;* tubular elastic.

GAUGE: No. 4 needles: 6 sts = 1"; 8 rows = 1".

DIRECTIONS: *Stripe Pattern:* 1 rnd R, 1 rnd G, 1 rnd R, 3 rnds G, 2 rnds Bk, 1 rnd R, 2 rnds B, 2 rnds R, 1 rnd Bk, 2 rnds Y, 1 rnd Bk, 1 rnd R, 2 rnds B. Rep these 20 rnds for stripe pat.

With No. 3 needles and G, cast on 60 sts. Divide sts on 3 needles. Join with care not to twist sts on needles. Work around in k 1, p 1 rib for 2". Mark end of rnds. Change to No. 4 needles. Work in stripe pat for 20 rnds. * On next rnd, dec 1 st in center of each needle * (57 sts). Continue stripe pat for 19 rnds more. Rep between *'s (54 sts). Continue in stripe pat until there are 5 complete stripe repeats (100 rnds) or to desired length to beg of heel. Cut all colors.

Heel and Foot: Sl 4 sts from first needle to 2nd needle, sl 9 sts from 2nd needle to 3rd needle, sl 14 sts from 3rd needle to first needle (28 sts on first needle for heel, 13 sts on each of 2nd and 3rd needles for instep).

Heel: Join G to first heel st and work back and forth in st st 28 sts for 2½", end with k row.

Turn heel—Row 1: P 16, p 2 tog, p 1, turn. *Row 2:* Sl 1, k 5, sl 1, k 1, psso, k 1, turn. *Row 3:* Sl 1, p 6, p 2 tog, p 1, turn. *Row 4:* Sl 1, k 7, sl 1, k 1, psso, k 1, turn. Continue in this way to work 1 st more every row until all sts have been worked—16 sts on needle. With same needle, pick up 16 sts on side of heel, with 2nd needle k across 26 sts of instep, with 3rd needle pick up 16 sts on other side of heel, with same needle k 8 sts from first needle. There are now 24 sts on each of first and 3rd needles (heel) and 26 sts on instep needle. Cut G.

Gusset: Work in stripe pat. *Rnd 1:* First needle—k to last 3 sts, k 2 tog, k 1; 2nd needle—k across instep sts; 3rd needle—k 1, sl 1, k 1, psso, k to end. *Rnd 2:* Knit. Rep these 2 rnds until there are 13 sts on each of first and 3rd needle.

Foot: Continue in stripe pat on 52 sts until there are 40 rows in stripe pat. With G only, work until foot measures 2" less than desired length from back of heel to tip of toe.

Shape Toe: Rnd 1: First needle—k to last 3 sts, k 2 tog, k 1; 2nd needle—k 1, sl 1, k 1, psso, k to last 3 sts, k 2 tog, k 1; 3rd needle—k 1, sl 1, k 1, psso, k to end.

Rnd 2: Knit. Rep these 2 rnds until there are 5 sts on each heel needle, ending with first needle. Place all heel sts on 1 needle. Cut yarn leaving 12" end. Weave heel and instep sts tog. Weave elastic thru wrong side of sts of first 3 rnds of cuff. Secure end.

RAGLAN CARDIGANS
FOR MEN AND WOMEN

Directions are given for Women's small size (10-12) and Men's small size (42-44). Changes for Women's medium (14-16) and large (18) sizes and for Men's medium (46-48) and large (50) sizes are in parentheses.

Note 1: Changes between Women's and Men's sizes are indicated by a slanted line 00/00. The figures before the line are for Women; the figures after the line are for Men. When instructions are the same for both, they appear only once.

MATERIALS: Caron Dazzle-Aire, Knitting Worsted Size, 4 Ply (4 oz. skns): 4 (5, 5)/6 (6, 7) skns White or any color. *For embroidery:* Use odds and ends of knitting worsted in appropriate colors of your choice; knitting needles, 1 pair each No. 5 and No. 8, *or any size needles which will obtain the stitch gauge below:* crochet hook, Size F; 5 bone rings ¾″ in diameter for Women's cardigan, 5 buttons ¾″ in diameter for Men's cardigan.

GAUGE: 5 sts = 1″; 13 rows = 2″.

FINISHED MEASUREMENTS:

SIZES:					
WOMEN			MEN		
SMALL	MEDIUM	LARGE	SMALL	MEDIUM	LARGE
(10-12)	(14-16)	(18)	(42-44)	(46-48)	(50)
BUST OR CHEST:					
35″	39″	42″	45″	48″	51″
BACK WIDTH AT UNDERARM:					
17″	19″	21″	22″	23″	25″
FRONT WIDTH AT UNDERARM: (excluding band)					
9″	10″	10¾″	11½″	12½″	13″
SLEEVE WIDTH AT UPPER ARM:					
13″	14″	15½″	16½″	17″	18″

DIRECTIONS: *Back:* Start at lower edge with No. 5 needles, cast on 84 (94, 104) / 110 (116, 124) sts. Work in k 1, p 1 ribbing for 1½″. Change to No. 8 needles and work in st st (k 1 row, p 1 row) until total length is 14″ for Women's sizes or 15″ for Men's sizes (or desired length to underarm) ending with a p row.

Raglan Armholes: Continuing in st st throughout, bind off 3 sts for Women's sizes, 4 sts for Men's sizes at beg of next 2 rows. Dec one st at each end every other row until 24 (28, 30)/32 (34, 36) sts rem. Bind off rem sts for back of neck.

Note 2: Make Left Front first for Women and Right Front first for Men. Motif on Left Front will be embroidered in duplicate stitch after knitting has been completed.

For Women's Sizes Only: Left Front: With No. 5 needles, cast on 48 (54, 58) sts. *Row 1 (wrong side):* P 5 for front band, k 1—*fold ridge;* work in p 1, k 1 ribbing across rem sts. *Row 2:* Work in p 1, k 1 ribbing across to within last 6 sts, p 1, k 5 for front band. Front band will be folded to right side when front has been completed. Rpt Rows 1 and 2 alternately for 1½″, ending with a wrong-side row.

For Men's Sizes Only: Right Front: With No. 5 needles, cast on 62 (66, 70) sts. *Row 1 (wrong side):* Work in k 1, p 1 ribbing across to within last 6 sts, *k 1—fold ridge;* p 5 for front band. *Row 2:* K 5, p 1, work in k 1, p 1 ribbing as established over rem sts. Rpt Rows 1 and 2 alternately for 1½″, end with a wrong-side row. Front band will be folded to right side when front is completed.

For All Sizes: Change to No. 8 needles and keeping the 6 border sts as established, work in st st (k on right side, p on wrong side) over other sts until same length as Back to underarm, end at side edge.

Raglan Armholes: Row 1: At side edge, bind off 3 sts for Women's sizes; bind off 4 sts for Men's sizes; complete row. *Row 2:* Work over 6 sts of

Color photo on page 139

band as before, *work next 2 sts tog—dec made at neck edge inside band;* complete row. Now, dec one st at armhole edge every other row and *at the same time*, dec one st at neck edge inside band every 4th row 11 (14, 14)/16 (18, 19) times. If necessary, keeping neck edge straight, continue to dec one st at armhole edge every other row until the 6 sts of band rem. Place rem 6 sts on a safety pin. With pins mark the position of 5 buttons evenly spaced along front band, having first pin ¾" from lower edge and last pin ½" below beg of neck shaping.

To make a buttonhole—starting at front edge, work first st, bind off next 2 sts, work next 3 sts as before, bind off following 2 sts; complete row. On next row, cast on 2 sts over each group of bound-off sts. Make buttonholes on Right Front for Women; on Left Front for Men.

Right Front for Women's Sizes/Left Front for Men's Sizes: Making buttonholes in line with pins, work to correspond with other Front, reversing position of front band and shaping.

Sleeves: With No. 5 needles, cast on 38 (40, 44)/ 44 (46, 48) sts. Work in k 1, p 1 ribbing for 1½". Change to No. 8 needles and work in st st,

increasing 4 sts evenly spaced on Row 1. Then, inc one st each end every 1" for Women's Sizes; every ¾" for Men's Sizes until there are 66 (70, 78) / 84 (88, 92) sts. Work even until total length is 16 (16½", 17)" / 17½ (17½, 18)", ending with a p row.

Raglan Shaping: Continuing in st st, bind off 3 sts for Women's Sizes, 4 sts for Men's Sizes at beg of next 2 rows. Dec one st at each end every other row until 6 sts rem for all sizes. Bind off.

Finishing: Block pieces to measurements. Sew side, sleeve and raglan seams. Sl front band sts from safety pin onto a No. 8 needle, attach yarn and continue to work 6 sts of band as before until long enough to fit along neck edge to center back. Bind off. Finish other front band in same way; sew ends of bands tog, then sew to neck edge. Fold front bands to right side at fold ridge and stitch in place, stretching outer edge along neck so that it lies flat. Overcast along edges of buttonholes, through both thicknesses.

Buttons for Women's Cardigan (Make 5): With crochet hook, ch 4. Join with sl st to form ring. *Rnd 1:* 6 sc in ring. *Rnd 2:* Hold a bone ring over top edge of last rnd, working over ring, make 2

FIG. 1
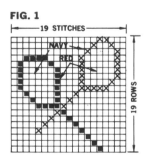

FIG. 3
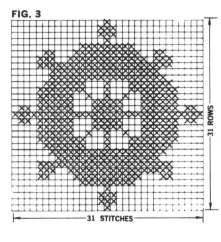

FIG. 5
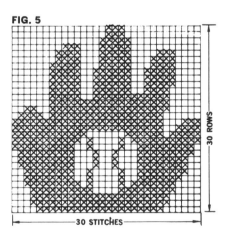

FIG. 2
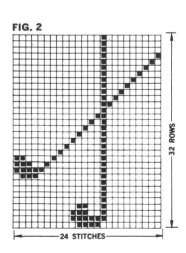

FIG. 4
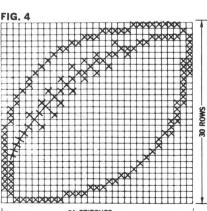

FIG. 6
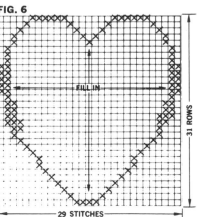

sc in each sc around. Join to first sc. Break off and fasten. Wrong side of crochet is right side of button.

Sew on buttons.

Embroidery: With basting lines, mark off a section of stitches and rows (see chart) on the upper section of the left front for motifs *(see* FIGS. 1 to 6).

MOTIF	WIDTH	DEPTH
TENNIS RACKETS	19 sts	19 rows
GOLF CLUBS	25 sts	32 rows
SKIING (SNOWFLAKE)	31 sts	31 rows
FOOTBALL	31 sts	30 rows
BASEBALL	30 sts	30 rows
FENCING (HEART)	29 sts	31 rows

Following the chart, embroider motifs in duplicate stitch (*See* HOW TO KNIT page   ) inside the basting-outlined section. For the tennis racket motif and football work the outlines in duplicate stitch. Then divide a length of yarn in half and, use 1 strand, work crisscross diagonal lines inside racket (*see* FIG. 1) in long straight stitches, fastening at intersections with tiny single stitches, and plain straight stitches for football lacing.

BABY HAT AND MITTENS

MATERIALS: Bear Brand Twin-Pak Knitting Worsted or Machine-Washable Win-Knit (4 oz. pak): 1 pak; knitting needles, 1 pair each No. 6 and No. 10 for hat; 1 pair each No. 2 and No. 4 for mittens, *or any size needles which will obtain the stitch gauge below;* crochet hook, Size H; tapestry needle.

GAUGE: No. 10 needles: 7 sts = 2″ ″; 5 rows = 1″; No. 4 needles: 6 sts = 1″; 8 rows = 1″.

HAT:

Starting at face edge with 2 strands of yarn held tog and Size 6 needles, cast on 48 sts. Work ribbing as follows: *Row 1:* * K 1, p 1. Rpt from * to end of row. *Row 2 through 8:* Rpt Row 1 seven times. *Next Row:* P each st across. Change to No. 10 needles and work in stockinette stitch until 4½″ from last row of ribbing.

Back Shaping: Bind off 2 sts at beg of each of the next 8 rows—32 sts rem. Bind off rem sts. Fold in half and sew back seam.

Ties and Neck Band: With No. 6 needles and one strand of yarn, cast on 8 sts. Work in k 1, p 1 ribbing for 10″. Join another strand of yarn and, with 2 strands held tog, continue for another 10″. Break off one strand and continue for 10″ more. Knitting the k sts and purling the p sts, bind off.

Finishing: Steam pieces through damp cloth.

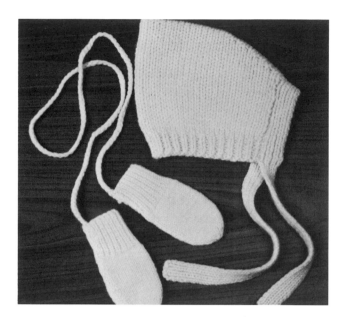

Gather neck edge of hat to fit center 10″ of band and sew in place.

MITTENS:

Starting at wrist edge with No. 2 needles and one strand of yarn, cast on 32 sts. Work in ribbing same as Hat for 2″. Change to No. 4 needles and work in stockinette stitch until total length is 4½″ ending with a p row.

Tip Shaping: Row 1: * K 6, decrease by k 2 tog. Rpt from * across—28 sts rem. *Row 2 and all even numbered rows:* P across. *Row 3:* * K 5, k 2 tog. Rpt from * across—24 sts rem. *Row 5:* * K 4, k 2 tog. Rpt from * across—20 sts rem. *Row 7:* * K 2 tog. Rpt from * across—10 sts rem. *Row 9:* Rpt Row 7—5 sts rem. Break yarn leaving a 12″ end. Thread this end into a tapestry needle, slip rem 5 sts onto it and draw tog, fasten securely. With same end, sew seam.

Cord: With 2 strands held tog, and crochet hook, make a 30″ chain. Fasten off. Sew a mitten to each end of cord.

SCARF AND BERET SET

MATERIALS: Bucilla Melody (40 gram ball): *Scarf:* 5 balls; *Beret:* 2 balls; knitting needles, 1 pair No. 9 for Scarf, 1 pair No. 4 for Beret, *or any size needles which will obtain the stitch gauge below;* crochet hook, Size H; 21″ round elastic; tapestry needle.

GAUGE: No. 9 needles: 4 sts = 1″; 6 rows = 1″; No. 4 needles: 6 sts = 1″; 8 rows = 1″.

SCARF:

Starting at a narrow edge with No. 9 needles, cast on 39 sts. *Row 1:* K 1, p 2, * k 2, p 2. Rpt from * across. *Row 2 (right side):* P 1, k 2, * p 2, k 2. Rpt from * across. Rpt Rows 1 and 2 alter-

nately until total length is 66″ ending with Row 2. Purling the p sts and knitting the k sts, bind off loosely.

Fringe: Wind yarn 50 times around a 6″ square of cardboard. Cut strands at one edge thus making 12″ strands. Cut more strands as needed. Using 7 strands for each fringe, knot 10 fringes along each narrow edge of scarf. Trim evenly.

BERET:

Starting at center top with No. 4 needles, cast on 6 sts. *Row 1:* Inc in first st; inc in each rem st—12 sts on needle. *Row 2 and all even numbered rows:* P in each st across. *Row 3:* Rpt Row 1—24 sts on needle. *Row 5:* * K 1, inc in next st. Rpt from * across—36 sts. *Row 7:* * K 2, inc in next st. Rpt from * across—48 sts. *Row 9:* * K 3, inc in next st. Rpt from * across—12 sts increased. Continue to inc 12 sts, evenly spaced on every knit row until there are 96 sts on needle ending with a p row. *Next Row:* K each st increasing 6 sts (instead of 12 sts), evenly spaced across. *Following Row:* P across. Rpt last 2 rows alternately until there are 144 sts on needle ending with a p row. Work 10 rows even in stockinette st, ending with a p row. *Next Row:* * Dec by k 2 tog, k 22. Rpt from * across—138 sts. *Following 3 Rows:* P 1 row, k 1 row, p 1 row. Rpt last 4 rows 2 times more until 108 sts rem, ending with a p row.

Facing: Row 1: With right side facing, p across to form a ridge on right side. Starting with a p row, work in st st for ⅞″. Bind off loosely.

Finishing: Weave seam. Overlap ends of elastic for 1″ and sew securely. Fold facing to wrong side over elastic circle and sew in place.

T-SHAPE SWEATERS

Knit-to-measure T-shape sweaters are constructed from three separately knitted pieces: two interchangeable pieces for front and back (these form the stem of the "T") and a third yoke/sleeve piece (the top of the "T"). We also give you instructions for establishing a gauge and altering size so you can create a garment that fits you perfectly. Following our general instructions are directions for making two interpretations of the basic T-sweater. You can be your own designer by varying the colors and stitches used.

GENERAL DIRECTIONS:

1. *To establish a stitch gauge:* Choose in the vicinity of a No. 10 knitting needle and cast on 20 sts with knitting worsted or using in the vicinity of a No. 11 knitting needle, cast on 12 to 16 sts with bulky yarn. Work for 10 to 12 rows in stitch pattern (stockinette stitch or garter stitch). Place swatch on a flat surface and measure in center of piece, counting the number of stitches and rows in 1″ or 2″. If the gauge is too small, try larger needles; if the gauge is too large, try smaller needles until you obtain the gauge specified in the design.

2. *To substitute yarn:* Make a sample with yarn and obtain a gauge as given above, then calculate the number of stitches to be worked in the instructions by multiplying the number of stitches per inch by the number of inches to be made.

3. *To alter the size measurements:* Make a swatch as specified, measure to gauge, multiply the number of stitches per inch by the number of inches to be made and change the instructions accordingly.

4. *To measure piece lengths:* Place knitted pieces on flat surface, measure across to insure proper width in all pieces and then measure length.

5. *To alter sleeve length on the striped T-Sweater (Style 1):* Add or subtract the number of stitches per inch to or from the total width of the piece (*see* FIG. 1).

6. *To alter sleeve length on the White T-Sweater (Style 2):* Work the white/blue stripe and/or cuff longer or shorter than specified in instructions (*see* FIG. 2).

7. *To assemble:* With yoke placed lengthwise, find center front and center back; mark with pins. Measure 8 (9, 10)″, or half the total width of the front or back piece, to the left and to the right of marked center, to indicate placement of body pieces. Pin body pieces to yoke within

these measurements and seam across chest. Fold sweater back to sweater front and sew sleeve and side seams.

8. Materials are given for small size (6–8) for the two sweaters which follow. Changes in size may be made to measure according to instructions, above.

FIG. 1 STYLE 1
FRONT AND BACK YOKE AND SLEEVES

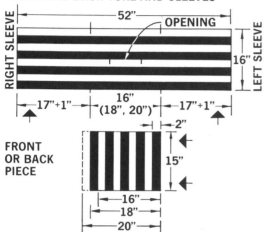

STRIPED T-SWEATER WITH DRAWSTRINGS

MATERIALS: Reynold's Poemes, approximately 14 ozs. each Red (A) and Green (B) yarn for a small size (6–8) and 2 ozs. more of each color for every 2″ increase in width; knitting needles, *any size needles which will give stitch gauge below;* crochet hook size F.

GAUGE: 7 sts=2″; 12 rows (6 ridges)=2″.

Front Body Piece: 16″ (small) or desired width across back or front x 15″ or desired length. (*Note:* Body is worked from side to side.) With A, cast on number of sts to measure 15″ or

desired length. Work in garter st (k each row) for 12 rows, including cast-on row. Piece should measure 2″. * With B, k 12 rows (2″). With A, k 12 rows (2″). Rpt from * for necessary amount of stripes to equal desired width across front. Bind off.

Back Body Piece: Work same as Front Body Piece.

Front and Back Yoke and Sleeves: 50″ (small) or desired width of yoke x 16″. *Note:* Drawstring loops will add 1″ to end of each sleeve. With A, cast on number of sts to measure 50″ or desired width of yoke. Work in garter st for 12 rows including cast-on row. Piece should measure 2″. Change to B and work in alternating stripes of 12 rows B, 12 rows A as on body. Work until 11th row of 4th stripe from beg has been completed.

Front Neck: Next Row: With B work row 12 of 4th stripe and k to center 28 sts, bind off center 28 sts (8″), k rem sts. *Next Row:* With A, k left front sts; cut yarn. Join A after the 28 bound-off sts and k right front sts.

Back Neck: With the one ball of A, k right front (now called right back) sts, cast on 28 sts, k left

front (now called left back) sts. Complete A stripe, then continue for back, alternating colors every 12 rows (2″) as before, ending with a B stripe after 8 stripes have been completed (16″). Bind off.

To Assemble: See GENERAL DIRECTIONS.

Loops for Drawstrings: Insert crochet hook into edge st at seam, ch 3, sk 3 knitted rows along edge, dc in the 4th knit row, ch 1. Rpt from * around edge, end ch 1 into first ch of ch-3 loop.

Drawstrings: Make a ch desired length, turn. Skip first ch, sl st back into each ch. Thread drawstring thru crocheted loops. Work loops and drawstrings around lower edge of sweater and around lower edge of each sleeve.

WHITE T-SWEATER WITH STRIPES AND DIAMOND PATTERN

MATERIALS: Columbia-Minerva Nantuk Bulky, approximately 20 ozs. Winter White (A), 4 ozs. Sapphire (B), 2 ozs. each Scarlet (C), Kelly (D) and Bright Yellow (E) for a small size (6–8), and 2 ozs. more of each color for each 2″ increase in width; knitting needles, *any size needle which will give stitch gauge below.*

GAUGE: 3 sts = 1″; 4 rows = 1″.

Pattern Notes: Do not use bobbins for color changes; wind pattern colors into small balls. Change colors on wrong side, lock strands by picking up new color from under dropped color. Cut and join colors as needed. Run in ends on wrong side.

Front Body Piece: 16″ (small) or desired width across back or front × 20″. With A, cast on number of sts to measure 16″ or desired width across back or front. *Border:* Work in garter st (k each row) for 1″. *Next Row (right side):* K. *Next Row:* K 4, p to within last 4 sts, k 4. Rpt last 2 rows until piece measures 8″ from beg, end wrong side. Then continue in st st (k on right side, p on wrong side) on all sts until piece measures 20″ from beg. Bind off.

Back Body Piece: Work same as Front Body Piece.

Left Sleeve: With A, cast on number of sts to measure 17″ or desired width of sleeve. *Cuff:* Work in garter st for 4″ (or as desired if the sleeve length was altered).

Striped Section: Note: Work with 5 balls of A and 5 balls of B, one for each stripe. Tie each ball with a rubber band. *Next Row (right side):* K 5 B, * 5 A, 5 B. Rpt from * across, end 6 A. *Next Row:* P 6 A, * 5 B, 5 A, Rpt from * across, end 5 B. Rpt these 2 rows until stripe section measures 9″ (or as desired if the sleeve length was

altered). Cut off A and B.

Diamond Motif Band: Following chart (*See* FIG. 3.) from row 1 thru row 27, work in st st, ending on right side *(see pat notes)*. This section should measure about 6″. With A continue in st st for 2 rows (½″). *Next Row (wrong side):* P 6 A, * 5 B, 5 A. Rpt from * across, end 5 B. *Next Row:* K 5 B, * 5 A, 5 B. Rpt from * across, end 6 A. Continue in st st with A only for 2″ more, end wrong side.

Neck Borders and Opening: Next Row (right side): With A, k across row. *Next Row:* With A, p to center 8 sts for front, k 8, p rem sts for back. Rpt last 2 rows once more.

Neck Opening: Back: Next Row (right side): With A, k half the sts, turn. Put rem sts on a holder for front. *Next Row (wrong side):* With

A, k 4; p rem sts. Rpt last 2 rows for 8″, end right side. Sl sts on a holder.

Front: Next Row (right side): From front holder, with A, k all sts. *Next Row:* With A, p to within last 4 sts, k 4. Rpt last 2 rows for 8″, end right side.

Front and Back: Next Row (wrong side): Working in one piece again with A, p to 4 garter sts, k 4 sts on front; then with same ball of yarn, k 4, p rem sts from back holder. *Next Row:* With A, k all sts. *Next Row:* With A, p to 8 garter sts, k 8, p rem sts. Rpt last 2 rows once more.

Right Shoulder and Sleeve: Continue in st st with A for 2″, end wrong side. *Next Row:* K 5 B, * 5 A, 5 B. Rpt from * across, end 6 A. *Next Row:* P 6 A, * 5 B, 5 A. Rpt from * across, end 5 B. With A continue in st st for 2 rows (½″).

FIG. 3

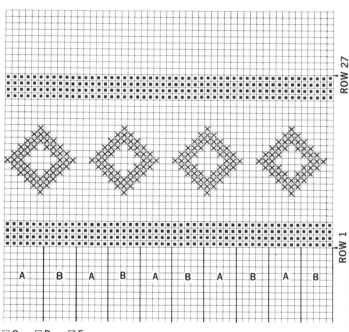

ROW 27

ROW 1

□ C   ▣ D   ☒ E

Diamond Motif Band: Follow chart (FIG. 3.) from row 1 thru row 27 working in st st, ending on right side. This section should measure 6″.

Stripe Section: Work same as stripe section on left sleeve starting and ending with wrong side pat rows. Break off B.

Cuff: With A only, work in garter st for 4″ or same amount of inches as on left sleeve. Bind off.

To Assemble: See GENERAL DIRECTIONS; however, sew side seams for 13″ or necessary amount from underarm at yoke in order to leave 7″ of seam open at lower edge for slit. Sew sleeve seams weaving garter st cuff seam.

BROTHER/SISTER FAIR ISLE SWEATER/HAT

Directions are given for Size 2. Changes for Sizes 4 and 6 are in parentheses.

MATERIALS: Bucilla Spice (1¾ oz. Balls): *Girls:* 2 (3, 3) balls Winter White (A), 2 (3, 3) balls Misty Blue (B); *Boys:* 2 (3, 3) balls Misty Blue (A), 2 (3, 3) balls Winter White (B); knitting needles, 1 pair each No. 9 and No. 10½, *or any size needles which will obtain the stitch gauge below.*

GAUGE: 3 sts = 1″; 4 rows = 1″.

Note: Directions are given to match our photograph. In our photo the bottom edge of the boy's sweater is worked in white and the bottom edge of the boy's hat is worked in blue.

MEASUREMENTS:			
SIZE:	2	4	6
CHEST:	22″	24″	26″
WIDTH ACROSS BACK OR FRONT AT UNDERARMS:	11″	12″	13″
WIDTH ACROSS SLEEVE AT UPPER ARM:	9″	10″	11″

SWEATER

Back: Starting at lower edge with B and No. 9 needles, cast on 31 (35, 37) sts. *Row 1 (wrong* side): P 1, * k 1, p 1; rpt from * across. *Row 2:* K 1, * p 1, k 1; rpt from * across. Rpt these two rows until 5 (7, 9) rows in all have been made, inc one st at end of last row—32 (36, 38) sts. Change to No. 10½ needles and work in st st (k 1 row, p 1 row) for 2 (2, 4) rows, ending with a p row. (*Note:* When working color pat, always twist color not in use around the other once to prevent making holes in work. Carry color not in use loosely along wrong side of work, twisting strands tog every 3rd st when carrying across 4 or more sts. When necessary, cut yarn and attach where needed.) Work all k rows from right to left of chart, all p rows from left to right, working in between lines indicating size being made. Pat is worked in st st (k 1 row, p 1 row). Starting with Row 1 on chart, work as directed to end of Row 20, mark each end of last row for underarms. Continue to follow chart to end of Row 25. Cut B. Continuing with A only, work even in st st until length from underarm markers is 3 (4, 4½)″, ending with a p row.

Neck Shaping: Row 1: K 11 (13, 14); place these sts just worked on a st holder for right back; k 10, place these 10 sts on a separate st holder for neckband, k rem 11 (13, 14) sts. *Row 2:* P across sts on needle only to within last 2 sts, p 2 tog. *Row 3:* K 2 tog, k to end of row. Work even in st st over 9 (11, 12) sts until length from underarm marker is 4½ (5, 5½)″, ending with a p row. Bind off rem sts for shoulder. Slip right back sts from first holder onto a No. 10½ needle, attach yarn at neck edge and work to correspond with opposite side, reversing shaping.

Front: Work same as Back until length above underarm markers is 2½ (3½, 4)″, ending with a p row.

Neck Shaping: Row 1: K 13 (15, 16), place these sts just worked on a st holder for left front; k 6, place these 6 sts on a separate st holder for neckband, k rem 13 (15, 16) sts. Continuing in st st, dec one st at neck edge every row 4 times. Work even over 9 (11, 12) sts until length from underarm marker is same as on Back; end with a p row. Bind off. Slip left front sts from holder onto a No. 10½ needle and work to correspond with opposite side, reversing shaping.

Sleeves: Starting at lower edge with B and No. 9 needles, cast on 19 (23, 25) sts. Work ribbing same as for Back for 7 (7, 9) rows. Change to No. 10½ needles and k 1 row, increasing 5 sts evenly spaced across row—24 (28, 30) sts. P next row. Work first 6 rows for pat (*see* Chart) over these sts. Cut B. With A, continuing in st st throughout, inc one st at each end of next row. Work 7

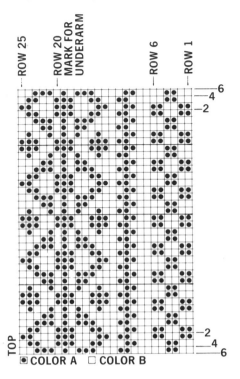

COLOR A   COLOR B

rows even. Inc 1 (0, 1) st in next row—27 (30, 33) sts. Work even until total length from beg is 8½ (9½, 10½)″ or desired length to underarm, ending with a p row. Bind off. Sew right shoulder seam.

Neckband: With right side facing, using No. 9 needles and A, pick up and k 56 (60, 62) sts evenly spaced along entire neck edge, including sts on holders. Work in k 1, p 1 ribbing for 1 (1, 1½)″. Bind off loosely in ribbing.

Finishing: Pin sweater to measurements on a padded surface; cover with a damp cloth and allow to dry; do not press. Sew left shoulder seam, including neckband. Sew side seams up to markers; sew sleeve seams, sew in sleeves, matching underarm seams.

HAT

Starting at outer edge of cuff with No. 10½ needles and A, cast on 47 (51, 55) sts. Work in ribbing same as for Back of Sweater for 4″, ending with a row on wrong side. *Next Row:* Inc in first st, k across—48 (52, 56) sts. Starting with a p row, work 3 rows in st st (p on wrong side, k on right side). Attach B. Work pat as follows: *Row 1:* * K 2 A, k 2 B; rpt from * across. *Row 2:* Working colors as established on last row, p across. *Row 3:* * K 2 B, k 2 A; rpt from * across. *Row 4:* Working colors as established on last row, p across. *Rows 5 and 6:* Rpt Rows 1 and

2 of pat. Break off A. With B only, work in st st until length from beg is 8½ (9, 9½)", ending with a k row.

Top Shaping: Row 1: * P 2, p 2 tog; rpt from * across—36 (39, 42) sts. *Rows 2 through 5:* Work 4 rows even in st st. *Row 6:* * K 1, k 2 tog; rpt from * across—24 (26, 28) sts. *Row 7:* P across. *Row 8:* * K 2 tog; rpt from * across—12 (13, 14) sts. Leaving a 20" length, cut yarn. Thread this end in a tapestry needle and slip through rem sts; pull sts tightly tog and secure on wrong side; sew back seam. Turn 2" cuff to right side.

WESTERN-STYLE CARDIGAN

Directions are given for size 6 Months. Changes for Sizes 12 Months, 18 Months and 2 Years are in parentheses.

MATERIALS: Bernat Berella Sportspun (2 oz. skeins): 2 (2, 3, 3) skeins White (A), 1 skein Pink (B); knitting needles, 1 pair each No. 2 and No. 5, *or any size needle which will obtain the stitch gauge below;* set of dp needles No. 5; 5 small buttons for sweater; 16 (17, 18, 19)" white grosgrain ribbon ⅝"-wide; crochet hook Size B for working fringe on yoke.

GAUGE: 6½ sts = 1"; 8½ rows = 1".

MEASUREMENTS:

SIZES:	6 MOS.	12 MOS.	18 MOS.	2 YRS.
CHEST (closed):	19¼"	21¼"	23¼"	25"
WIDTH ACROSS BACK AT UNDERARMS:	9¼"	10¼"	11¼"	12"
WIDTH ACROSS EACH FRONT AT UNDERARM:	5½"	6"	6½"	7"
WIDTH ACROSS SLEEVE AT UPPER ARM:	7¼"	7½"	7¾"	8"

Back: With No. 2 needles and A, cast on 61 (67, 73, 79) sts. *Row 1 (right side):* K 1 * p 1, k 1; rpt from * across row. *Row 2:* P 1, * k 1, p 1; rpt from * across row. Rpt these 2 rows for ribbing for 1", ending on the wrong side. Change to No. 5 needles and st st (k on right side, p on wrong side). Work 6 rows. Follow chart for 3 rows. Continue to work in st st with A until piece measures 6½ (7, 7½, 8)" from beg or desired length to underarm, ending on the wrong side. *Armhole Shaping:* Bind off 4 sts at beg of next 2 rows. Work until armholes measure 1", ending on the right side. Break off A. Join B. P 3 rows. Continue in st st until armholes measure 3¾ (4, 4¼, 4½)".

Shoulder Shaping: Bind off 5 (6, 7, 7) sts at beg of next 4 rows, then 5 (5, 5, 7) sts at beg of next 2 rows. Bind off rem 23 (25, 27, 29) sts.

Left Front: With No. 2 needles and A, cast on 36 (40, 42, 46) sts. *Row 1 (right side):* P 1, * k 1, p 1; rpt from * across to last 5 sts; k 1, p 1, k 1, p 1, k 1 (seed st border). *Row 2:* K 1, p 1, k 1, p 1, k 1, (seed st border); k 1, * p 1, k 1; rpt from * across row. Rpt last 2 rows until ribbing measures 1", ending on the wrong side. Change to No. 5 needles. *Row 1 (right side):* K to last 5 sts, work 5 border sts in seed st. *Row 2:* Work 5 border sts in seed st, p to end of row. Rpt last 2 rows until 6 rows have been completed. Follow chart for 3

WESTERN STYLE CARDIGAN

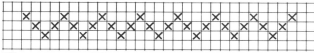

| | COLOR A | ☒ | COLOR B |

rows keeping border sts in A in seed st. Continue in established pat with A until piece measures same as back to underarm, ending on the wrong side.

Armhole Shaping: Next Row (right side): Bind off first 4 sts, finish row. Continue in established pat until armhole measures 1", ending on the right side. Break off A. Join B. P all sts for next 3 rows including front edge border sts. Continue in st st with B working border sts in seed st until armhole measures 1¼", ending with a p row.

Neck Shaping: Next Row (right side): K to last 9

sts, sl these 9 sts on a holder for neck. *Next Row:* P. Dec 1 st at neck edge on next 8 (10, 10, 12) k rows—15 (17, 19, 21) sts. Work even until armhole measures 3¾ (4, 4¼, 4½)".

Shoulder Shaping: At armhole edge bind off 5 (6, 7, 7) sts twice, then 5 (5, 5, 7) sts once.

Right Front: With No. 2 needles and A, cast on 36 (40, 42, 46) sts. *Row 1 (right side):* K 1, p 1, k 1, p 1, k 1 (seed st border); p 1 * k 1, p 1; rpt from * across. *Row 2:* K 1, * p 1, k 1; rpt from * to last 5 sts, k 1, p 1, k 1, p 1, k 1. Rpt last 2 rows until ribbing measures 1", ending on the wrong side. Change to No. 5 needles. *Row 1 (right side):* Work 5 border sts in seed st, k to end of row. *Row 2:* P to last 5 sts, work 5 border sts in seed st. Rpt last 2 rows until 6 rows have been completed. Follow chart for 3 rows keeping border sts in A in seed st. Continue in established pat with A until piece measures same as back to underarm, ending on the right side.

Armhole Shaping: Next Row (wrong side): Bind off first 4 sts, finish row. Continue in established pat until armhole measures 1", ending on the right side. Break off A. Join B. P all sts on next 3 rows including front edge border sts. Continue in st st with B working border sts in seed st until armhole measures 1¼", ending with a k row.

Neck Shaping: Next Row (wrong side): P to last 9 sts, sl these 9 sts on a holder for neck. *Next Row:* K. Dec 1 st at neck edge on next 8 (10, 10, 12) k rows—15 (17, 19, 21) sts. Work even until armhole measures 3¾ (4, 4¼, 4½)".

Shoulder Shaping: At armhole edge bind off 5 (6, 7, 7) sts twice, then 5 (5, 5, 7) sts once.

Sleeves: With No. 2 needles and A, cast on 35 (37, 39, 41) sts. Work in ribbing as on back for 1½". Change to No. 5 needles. Work in st st with A for 6 rows. Follow chart for 3 rows. Continue work in st st with A, inc 1 st each edge every ¾" 6 times—47 (49, 51, 53) sts. Work even until sleeve measures 7 (7½, 8, 8½)" or desired length to underarm, ending with a p row.

Top Shaping: Bind off 4 sts at beg of next 2 rows. Dec 1 st each edge every other row 10 (11, 12, 13) times. Bind off 2 sts at beg of next 4 rows. Bind off rem 11 sts.

Finishing: Sew shoulder, side and sleeve seams. Sew in sleeves.

Seed Stitch Collar: With right side facing you, sl 9 sts from right front neck holder onto No. 2 needles, join B, then pick up and k 67 (69, 71, 73) sts around neck edge to left front holder, k 9 sts from left front neck holder—85 (87, 89, 91) sts. Work border sts in seed st pat as estab-

lished and work across row in seed st pat. Work until 8 rows have been completed. *Next Row (wrong side):* K for turning edge. Starting with a k row work in st st for 7 rows for facing. *Next Row:* Bind off as if to p. Fold on turning edge to wrong side and loosely sew facing in place.

Facing: Cut grosgrain ribbon long enough for border facing and sew to right and left front edge borders. Evenly space buttons and sew to left front. Work vertical machine buttonholes on right front.

Fringe: Cut strands of B yarn 3" long. With 1 strand of B work fringe in each garter st around yoke. *Note:* On a garter st there is a high ridge and a low ridge. Work fringe in the low ridge. Trim evenly.

MAN'S FAIR ISLE PULLOVER

Directions are given for size Small (38-40). Changes for sizes Medium (42-44) and Large (46-48) are in parentheses.

MATERIALS: Coats & Clark's Red Heart Fabulend, (4-ply, 3½ oz. skeins): 2 (3, 3) skeins Eggshell and 1 skein each Black, Lt. Grey and Lt. Natural for each size; knitting needles, 1 pair each of No. 8 and No. 10, *or any size needles which will obtain the stitch gauge below.*

GAUGE: 4 sts = 1"; 5 rows = 1".

MEASUREMENTS SIZES:	SMALL (38-40)	MEDIUM (42-44)	LARGE (46-48)
CHEST:	41"	45"	49"
WIDTH ACROSS BACK OR FRONT AT UNDERARM:	20½"	22½"	24½"
LENGTH FROM SHOULDER TO LOWER EDGE:	24"	25"	26"
LENGTH OF SIDE SEAM *(excluding armhole band):*	15"	15½"	16"

Note: When changing colors always twist the color not in use around the other to prevent making holes. Carry the color not in use loosely on wrong side of work. Pattern is worked in stockinette st (k 1 row, p 1 row). Chart shows one half of pattern. To follow Chart for each row, start at line at right side edge indicating size being made, follow each row across to left side edge, knitting all sts including center stitch; to complete row, do not work center stitch again, but follow same row back from left side to starting line.

DIRECTIONS: *Back:* Starting at lower edge with No. 8 needles and Eggshell, cast on 75 (83, 91) sts. *Row 1 (wrong side):* P 1, * k 1, p 1. Rpt from * across. *Row 2:* K 1, * p 1, k 1. Rpt from * across. Rpt Rows 1 and 2 alternately until ribbing measures 3″ ending with Row 1 and increasing 8 sts evenly spaced across last row—83 (91, 99) sts.

Change to No. 10 needles and work in pattern as follows: *Row 1:* K across. *Row 2:* P across. *Row 3-4:* Rpt Rows 1 and 2. Attach Black. *Row 5:* * With Eggshell k 1, with Black k 1. Rpt from * across, end with Eggshell k 1. *Row 6:* * With Black p 1, with Eggshell p 1. Rpt from * across, end with Black p 1. Starting with Row 7 on Chart, work until Row 40 on Chart has been completed. Rpt last 34 rows (Rows 7 through 40) for pat. Work in pat until total length is 15 (15½, 16)″, end with a p row.

Armhole Shaping: Continuing in pat throughout, bind off 5 (6, 7) sts at beg of next 2 rows. Dec one st at each end every other row 6 (7, 8) times in all—61 (65, 69) sts. Work even in pattern until length from first row of armhole shaping is 9 (9½, 10)″, end with a p row. *Next Row:* With one color, bind off first 16 (17, 18) sts for right shoulder, work across next 29 (31, 33) sts, place these sts on a stitch holder for neckband, bind off rem 16 (17, 18) sts.

Front: Work as for Back until length from first row of armhole shaping is 5½ (6, 6½)″, end with a p row.

Neck Shaping: Row 1: Work in pat across first 24 (25, 26) sts, place rem 37 (40, 43) sts on a stitch holder. *Row 2:* Working over sts on needle only, bind off first 2 sts, complete row. *Row 3:* Work in pat across. *Row 4:* Rpt Row 2. Continue in pat, dec one st at neck edge every other row until 16 (17, 18) sts remain. Work even in pat until length of armhole is same as Back, end

with same Row of pat as on Back. With same color yarn, bind off remaining sts. Leaving center 13 (15, 17) sts on stitch holder, slip rem sts onto a No. 10 needle, attach corresponding color yarn at neck edge and work to correspond with opposite side, reversing shaping. Pin pieces to measurements on a padded surface; cover with a damp cloth and allow to dry; *do not press.* Sew left shoulder seam.

Neckband: With right side facing, using Eggshell and No. 8 needles, k across sts on back stitch holder, pick up and k 15 (17, 17) sts along left side edge of neck, k across sts on front stitch holder, pick up and k 14 (16, 16) sts along right side edge of neck—73 (79, 83) sts. Work ribbing same as on Back for 5 rows. Bind off loosely in ribbing. Sew right shoulder seam, including neckband.

Armhole Bands: With right side facing, using No. 8 needles and Eggshell, pick up and k 89 (93, 97) sts along entire armhole edge. Work ribbing same as on Back for 5 rows. Bind off loosely in ribbing.

Sew side seams, including armhole bands.

FAIR ISLE PULLOVER

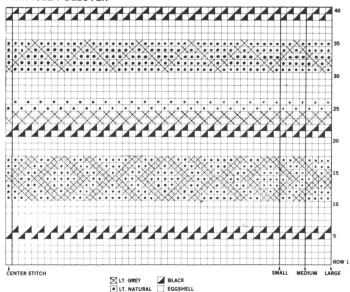

CENTER STITCH

⊠ LT. GREY   ◼ BLACK
⊡ LT. NATURAL   ☐ EGGSHELL

SMALL MEDIUM LARGE

ROW 1

ZIG ZAG PULLOVER

Directions are given for size Small (8-10). Changes for sizes Medium (12-14) and Large (16-18) are in parentheses.

MATERIALS: Spinnerin Wintuk Sport (2 oz. balls): 5 (6, 7) balls Off-White (A); 1 ball each Red (B), and Green (C); knitting needles, 1 pair each No. 4 and No. 5, *or any size needles which will obtain the stitch gauge below;* crochet hook, Size F; 7″ neck opening zipper.

GAUGE: 6 sts = 1″.

MEASUREMENTS:

SIZES:	SMALL (8-10)	MEDIUM (12-14)	LARGE (16-18)
BUST:	33″	36″	40″
WIDTH ACROSS BACK OR FRONT AT UNDERARMS	16½″	18″	20″
WIDTH ACROSS SLEEVE AT UPPER ARM	11″	12″	13″

Note: Sweater is worked entirely with A. The Fair Isle Pattern is embroidered in duplicate st (*see* HOW TO KNIT SECTION, page 232) after knitting has been completed.

DIRECTIONS: *Back:* Start at lower edge with No. 4 needles and A, cast on 98 (108, 120) sts. Work in k 1, p 1 ribbing for 2 rows, inc one st at end of last row — 99 (109, 121) sts. Change to No. 5 needles and working st st (k 1 row, p 1 row), dec one st at each end every 1¼″ 4 times in all — 91 (101, 113) sts. Continuing in st st throughout, work even until length is 6 (6½, 6½)″ from beg. Inc one st at each end of next row and every 1½″ thereafter 4 times in all. Work even over 99 (109, 121) sts until total length is 13 (13, 14)″ from beg, end with a wrong-side row.

Armhole Shaping: Continuing in st st, bind off 5 (6, 7) sts at beg of next 2 rows; then 2 sts at beg of following 2 rows. Dec one st at each end every other row 3 (3, 4) times — 79 (87, 95) sts. Work even for 0 (6, 8) rows, end with a wrong-side row.

Back Opening: Next Row: Work across first 39 (43, 47) sts; place rem 40 (44, 48) sts on a st holder. Work even in st st over sts on needle only until length is 6½ (7½, 8)″ from first row of armhole shaping, end at armhole edge.

Shoulder Shaping: From armhole edge bind off 8, (9, 10) sts at beg of next row and every other row thereafter 3 times in all. Place rem 15 (16, 17) sts on another st holder. Sl sts from first holder onto a No. 5 needle, attach A at base of back opening, bind off one st and work to correspond with opposite side, reversing shaping.

Front: Work same as Back until Armhole Shaping has been completed (do not work back open-

ing). Work even over 79 (87, 95) sts until length is 4½ (5½, 6)″ from first row of armhole shaping, end with wrong-side row.

Neck Shaping: Next Row: Work over first 31 (34, 37) sts; place rem 48 (53, 58) sts on a st holder. Working over sts on needle only, bind off 2 sts at neck edge at beg of next row; then dec one st at same edge every other row 5 times. Work even over rem 24 (27, 30) sts until length of armhole is same as on Back, end at armhole edge.

Shoulder Shaping: From armhole edge, bind off 8 (9, 10) sts at beg of next row and every other row 3 times in all. Leaving center 17 (19, 21) sts on front holder, sl rem 31 (34, 37) sts on a No. 5 needle, attach A at neck edge and work to correspond with opposite side, reversing shaping.

Sleeves: Start at lower edge with No. 4 needles and A, cast on 49 (51, 53) sts. *Row 1:* K 1, * p 1, k 1; rpt from * across. *Row 2:* P 1, * k 1, p 1; rpt from * across. Rpt these 2 rows for ribbing for 2″. Change to No. 5 needles and working in st st, inc one st at each end every 1½ (1¼, 1)″ 9 (11, 13) times — 67 (73, 79) sts. Work even in st st until total length is 17 (17½, 18)″, end with a wrong-side row.

Top Shaping: Continuing in st st, bind off 5 (6, 7) sts at beg of next 2 rows. Dec one st at each end every other row 16 (18, 20) times. Bind off 3 sts at beg of next 4 rows. Bind off rem sts.

Finishing: Pin pieces to measurements on a padded surface, cover with a damp cloth and allow to dry; do not press.

Zig Zag Pattern: Pattern is worked in duplicate st (*see* **HOW TO KNIT SECTION,** page 232). With a basting line, mark center st of each row up center of front. First band of pat is worked over first 17 rows of st st. Chart shows a portion of design. Starting at center st, follow Chart across to right side outer edge; then rpt A to B on Chart across front, ending last rpt at any place of design, according to rem sts on size being made. Omitting center st, work other half of band to correspond. Leaving 14 rows of knitting between bands, starting at center st of next row, work second band of pat same as before. Continue in this manner to work bands throughout front. Work a short band over each shoulder, being careful to keep pat in line with previous long band. Work pat throughout back in same manner. Omit center st on bands worked at each side of back opening. Mark center st on first row of st st on each sleeve; work band of pat over first 17 rows of st st on each sleeve same as for front. Sew shoulder seams.

Neckband: With right side facing, using No. 4 needles and A, k sts from left back holder, pick up and k 18 sts along left side edge of neck, k sts on front holder, pick up and k 18 sts along right side edge, k sts on right back holder — 83 (87, 91) sts. Work in k 1, p 1, ribbing same as sleeve ribbing for 2". Bind off in ribbing. Fold neckband in half to wrong side and stitch in place. With right side facing, using crochet hook and A, work 1 row of sc along edges of back opening, including neckband. Sew side and sleeve seams. Sew in sleeves. Sew in zipper.

ZIG ZAG SWEATER

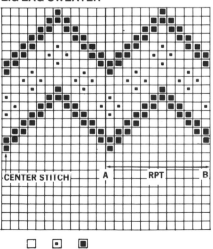

GUATEMALAN VEST

Directions are given for size Small (8-10). Changes for sizes Medium (12-14) and Large (16) are in parentheses.

MATERIALS: Coats & Clark's Red Heart Wintuk (100% Orlon ®) Sock and Sweater Yarn, 3-ply (2 oz. skns): 1 skn each Vibrant Orange (A), Wood Brown (B), Paddy Green (C), Atomic Pink (D), Dk. Turquoise (E), Baby Yellow (F), Red (G), Robin Blue (H), Apple Green (I), White (J), Navy (K); knitting needles, No. 5, *or any size needles which will obtain the stitch gauge below;* crochet hook, Size F.

GAUGE: 11 sts = 2"; 6 rows = 1".

MEASUREMENTS:

	SMALL (8-10)	MEDIUM (12-14)	LARGE (16)
SIZES:			
BUST:	32½"	36"	39"
WIDTH ACROSS BACK AT UNDERARMS:	16"	18"	19½"
WIDTH ACROSS EACH FRONT AT UNDERARM:	8¼"	9"	9¾"

DIRECTIONS: Start at lower edge of entire

vest with H, cast on 180 (200, 214) sts.

Bottom Edging—Row 1 (right side): K 6 for front border, place a marker on needle; k 1 (1, 3), k 3 tog, * k 3, *k in front, back and front of next st—3 sts made in one st;* k 3, k 3 tog; rpt from * across to within last 10 sts, k 3, k in front, back and front of next st, place a marker on needle; k 6 for front border. *Row 2:* K 6, slip marker, p across to within next marker, slip marker, k 6. Slip markers in every row. *Row 3:* K 0 (0, 2), k 3 tog, * k 3, make 3 sts in next st as before, k 3, k 3 tog; rpt from * across to within last 11 sts, k 3, make 3 sts in next st, k 1, slip marker, k 6. *Row 4:* Rpt Row 2, decreasing 0 (1, 0) st at center of row—180 (199, 214) sts. Break off H; attach A and work pat as follows: *Note:* When changing colors, always pick up new color from under dropped color to prevent making holes in work; carry colors not in use loosely along wrong side. Break off and attach colors as needed. Front and armhole borders are worked in garter st (k each row) throughout. Patterns are worked between borders in st st (k 1 row, p 1 row). Border sts are not shown on Charts. To follow Charts for *each right-side row,* start at line on right side edge indicating size being made and follow Chart across to B, rpt A to B across; then work to line indicating size being made. For *each wrong-side row,* start at left side edge and repeating B to A across, follow Chart from left to right between lines indicating size being made. Always follow Charts over sts between front borders. *Rows 1 through 9:* Using A for garter st front borders, follow Chart 1 as directed over sts between borders from Row 1 to end of top row. *Rows 10 through 23:* Making borders with C for first 7 rows and with E for following 7 rows, follow Chart 2. *Row 24:* With G k 6 for border, p across to within next marker, k 6. *Row 25:* With G k 6, * with H k 2, with G k 2; rpt from * across to next marker, end with H k 2, with G k 2 (1, 0); with G k 6. *Row 26:* Working colors as established on last row, k 6, p across to next marker, k 6. *Row 27:* With G, k across. *Rows 28 through 48:* Using I for borders, follow Chart 3. *Rows 49 through 56:* Using D for borders, follow Chart 4.

To Divide Stitches for Armholes: Row 1: From right side, with K, k 38 (42, 45); place these sts just worked on a stitch holder for upper right front; bind off next 13 (15, 17) sts for underarm, k until there are on right-hand needle 78 (85, 90) sts for upper back; place rem sts on another stitch holder.

Upper Back: Row 2: With K, k 6 for armhole border, place a marker on needle, p across to within last 6 sts, place a marker on needle; k 6 for armhole border. *Rows 3 through 17:* Continuing to use K for armhole borders, follow Chart 5. *Rows 18 through 37:* Using G for borders, follow Chart 6. *Rows 38 through 45:* Using D for borders, follow Chart 7. With I only continuing garter st borders, work 1 (3, 6) more rows. Bind off.

Upper Left Front: Row 1: Sl sts from 2nd holder onto a needle; attach K, with right side facing bind off 13 (15, 17) sts for underarm, k until there are 6 sts on right-hand needle, place a marker on needle, k across—38 (42, 45) sts. *Row 2:* K 6, p to next marker, k 6. *Rows 3 through 17:* Using K for borders, work rpt only on Chart 5, 2 (2, 3) times across center 22 (22, 33) sts, working any rem sts between borders in st st with K.

Neck Shaping: Row 18: Using G, k 6 for border, p to last 6 sts, k 6. *Row 19:* K 6 for border, follow rpt only on Row 3 of Chart 6 once over next 18 sts; with G, k to within 2 sts before next marker, *k 2 tog—dec made inside border at neck edge;* k 6 for border. *Rows 20 through 37:* Working borders with G, continue to work rpt on Chart 6 over the 18 sts immediately next to armhole border as established, *at the same time,* dec one st at neck edge inside front border as before every other row until 17 (21, 24) sts rem between borders. *Rows 38 through 45:* Using D for borders, follow rpt on Chart 7, 2 (3, 3) times over sts next to armhole border, using D for all other sts and decreasing one st inside front border 4 more times. With I only continuing decs at neck edge, work 1 (3, 6) rows. Bind off rem 24 (27, 29) sts for shoulder.

Upper Right Front: Sl sts from first holder onto a needle and work to correspond with Upper Left Front, reversing shaping and position of pats.

Finishing: To block, pin vest to measurements on a padded surface, cover with a damp cloth and allow to dry; do not press. Fold fronts over back and sew front shoulders to corresponding sts of back. With right side facing, using crochet hook and H, sc evenly along right front edge, back of neck and left front edges. Break off and fasten. *Ties:* With 1 strand each of H and D held tog, using crochet hook attach yarn to right front edge in line with beg of neck shaping; make a chain desired length. Break off and fasten. Make 3 more ties along right front edge at 3½" intervals. Make ties along left front edge to correspond with opposite edge.

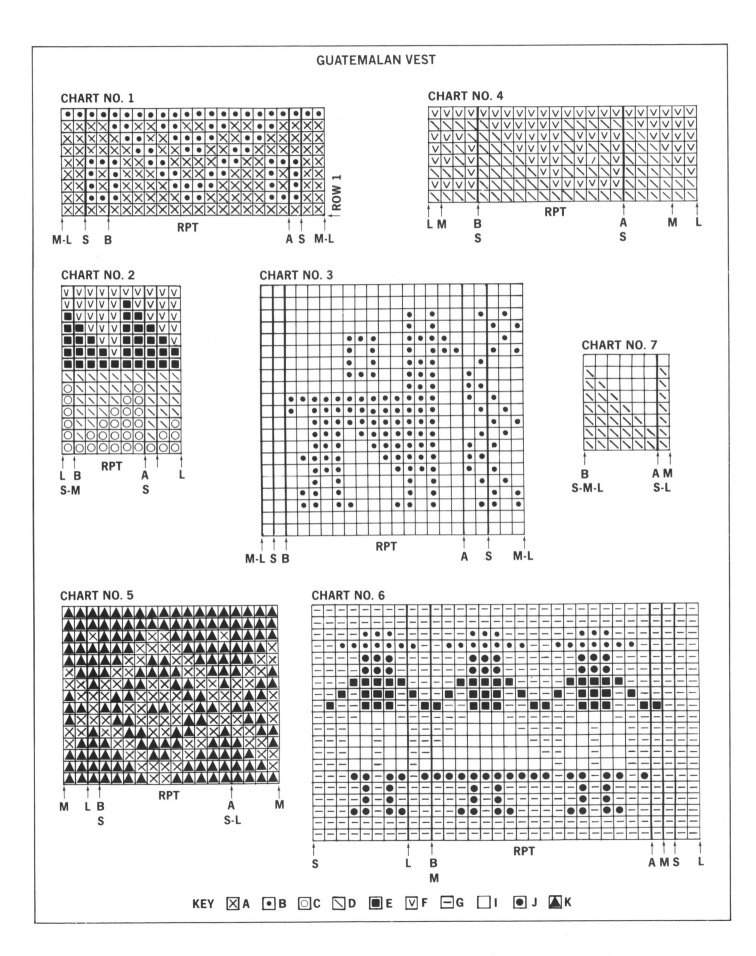

GUATEMALAN VEST

CHART NO. 1

CHART NO. 4

CHART NO. 2

CHART NO. 3

CHART NO. 7

CHART NO. 5

CHART NO. 6

KEY ⊠ A ⊡ B ◎ C ◺ D ▣ E ⋁ F ⊟ G ☐ I ◉ J ▲ K

BABY PULLOVER

Directions are given for 6 Months' size. Changes for sizes 12 Months, 18 Months and 2 Years are in parentheses.

MATERIALS: Spinnerin Frostlon Petite (1 oz. ball): 3 (3, 4, 5) balls Pink or Blue; knitting needles, 1 pair each No. 5 and No. 6, *or any size needles which will obtain the stitch gauge below*; one double-pointed needle, No. 6; crochet hook, Size F; 3 small buttons.

GAUGE: Stockinette St—5 sts = 1"; 7 rows = 1".

MEASUREMENTS:

SIZES:	6 MOS.	12 MOS.	18 MOS.	2 YRS.
CHEST:	20"	21"	22"	24"
WIDTH ACROSS BACK OR FRONT AT UNDERARMS:				
	10"	10½"	11"	12"
WIDTH ACROSS SLEEVE AT UPPER ARM:				
	6¼"	6¾"	7¼"	8"

DIRECTIONS: *Back:* Starting at lower edge with No. 5 needles, cast on 48 (52, 56, 60) sts. Work in k 1, p 1 ribbing for 6 (6, 8, 10) rows. Change to No. 6 needles and work in pattern as follows: *Row 1 (right side):* K 15 (17, 19, 21), yo, k 2 tog through back of sts, k 2 tog through front of sts, yo, p 2, k 6, p 2, yo, k 2 tog through back of sts, k 2 tog through front of sts, yo, k 15 (17, 19, 21). *Row 2:* P 19 (21, 23, 25), k 2, p 6, k 2, p 19 (21, 23, 25). *Row 3:* K 15 (17, 19, 21), yo, k 2 tog through back of sts, k 2 tog through front of sts, yo, p 2, *place next 2 sts on dp needle and hold in back of work, k next st, k the 2 sts from dp needle, place next st on dp needle and hold in front of work, k next 2 sts, k st from dp needle*—SLIPPED CHAIN CABLE STARTED; p 2, yo, k 2 tog through back of sts, k 2 tog through front of sts, yo (last 18 sts made form center panel); k 15 (17, 19, 21). *Row 4:* Rpt Row 2. *Rows 5 and 6:* Rpt Rows 1 and 2. *Row 7:* K 15 (17, 19, 21), yo, k 2 tog through back of sts, k 2 tog through front of sts, yo, p 2, *place next st on dp needle and hold in front, k next 2 sts, k st from dp needle, place next 2 sts on dp needle and hold in back, k next st, k 2 sts from dp needle*—SLIPPED CHAIN CABLE COMPLETED; p 2, yo, k 2 tog through back of sts, k 2 tog through front of sts, yo, k 15 (17, 19, 21). *Row 8:* Rpt Row 2. Rpt last 6 rows (Rows 3 through 8) for pattern. Work in pattern until total length is 6 (6½, 7, 8)" from beg, ending with a wrong-side row.

Armhole Shaping: Keeping continuity of center panel pattern throughout and working all other sts in stockinette st (k 1 row, p 1 row) as before, bind off 2 (2, 2, 3) sts at beg of next 2 rows. Dec one st at each end every other row 2

Color photo on page 140

(3, 3, 3) times. Work even over 40 (42, 46, 48) sts until length from first row of armhole shaping is 3½ (3¾, 4, 4½)".

Shoulder Shaping: Keeping in pattern, bind off 5 (5, 6, 6) sts at beg of next 4 rows. Place rem 20 (22, 22, 24) sts on a st holder for neckband.

Front: Work same as for Back until length of armhole is 2½ (2¾, 3, 3½)" above first row of armhole shaping, ending with a wrong-side row.

Neck Shaping: Row 1: K 12 (12, 14, 14); place rem sts on another st holder. *Row 2:* P 12 (12, 14, 14). Working in stockinette st (k 1 row, p 1 row) over sts on needle only, dec one st at neck edge in each of next 2 rows. Work even over 10 (10, 12, 12) sts until length of armhole is same as on Back, ending at armhole edge.

Shoulder Shaping: Row 1: Bind off 5 (5, 6, 6) sts, complete row. *Row 2:* Work across. *Row 3:* Bind off rem 5 (5, 6, 6) sts. Leaving center 16 (18, 18, 20) sts on front holder, slip rem 12 (12, 14, 14) sts onto No. 6 needle; attach yarn at neck edge; work to correspond with opposite side, reversing shaping.

Sleeves: Starting at lower edge with No. 5 needles, cast on 24 (24, 26, 28) sts. Work in k 1, p 1 ribbing for 6 (6, 8, 10) rows. Change to No. 6 needles and work in pattern as follows: *Row 1 (right side):* K 3 (3, 4, 5), yo, k 2 tog through back of sts, k 2 through front of sts, yo, p 2, k 6, p 2, yo, k 2 tog through back of sts, k 2 tog through front of sts, yo, k 3 (3, 4, 5). *Row 2:* P 7 (7, 8, 9), k 2, p 6, k 2, p 7 (7, 8, 9). *Row 3:* Inc one st in next st, k 2 (2, 3, 4); work in pattern as for Row 3 of Back center panel across center 18 sts, k to within last st, inc in last st. Continuing to work in pattern same as for Back across center 18-st panel and working all other sts in stockinette st, inc one st at each end every 6th row 3

(4, 4, 5) more times—32 (34, 36, 40) sts. Keeping continuity of pattern as established, work even in pat until total length is 6 (6½, 7, 7½)", ending with a wrong-side row.

Cap Shaping: Keeping in pattern, bind off 2 (2, 2, 3) sts at beg of next 2 rows. Dec one st at each end every other row 2 (3, 5, 7) times; then dec one st at each end every row until 10 sts rem. Bind off rem sts.

Finishing: Pin each section to measurements on a padded surface; cover with a damp cloth and allow to dry; do not press. Sew right shoulder seam only.

Neckband: With right side facing and No. 5 needles, pick up and k 50 (54, 56, 58) sts (including sts on holders) along entire neck edge. Work in k 1, p 1 ribbing for 3 (3, 4, 4) rows. Bind off loosely in ribbing. Starting at armhole edge, sew left shoulder seam for ½". Sew side and sleeve seams. Sew in sleeves.

Button Band: Row 1: With right side facing, using crochet hook, work 9 (9, 10, 10) sc evenly placed along back edge of left shoulder opening, including neckband. Ch 1, turn. *Rows 2 and 3:* Sc in each sc across. Ch 1, turn. At end of last row, break off and fasten. *Buttonloop Band— Row 1:* With right side facing, work 9 (9, 10 10) sc along front edge of shoulder opening. Ch 1, turn. *Row 2:* Sc in first sc, * ch 2, sk next sc, sc in each of next 2 sc; rpt from * once; ch 2, sk next sc, sc in end 1 (1, 2, 2) sc. Break off and fasten. Sew buttons opposite buttonloops.

IRISH KNIT BAG

MATERIALS: Bernat Blarney-Spun (2 oz. balls): 8 balls; knitting needles, 1 pair No. 10½ *or any size needles which will obtain the stitch gauge below:* 1 cable stitch needle; 1 pair 12" dowels with knobs for handles; ½ yd. fabric for lining; 1 yd. braid trim.

GAUGE: 5 sts = 2".

DIRECTIONS: *Note:* Yarn is used double throughout. Always sl as if to p.

Panel: Make 2. Using yarn double, cast on 62 sts. P 1 row. Now working in pattern st, work as follows: *Row 1:* P 3, sl 1 as if to p, inc 1 st in next st, psso 2 sts (twist 2), p 2, k 4, p 16, k 8, p 16, k 4, p 2, twist 2, p 3. *Row 2:* K 3, p 2, k 2, p 4, k 2, (k, p, k in next st, p 3 tog) 3 times, k 2, p 8, k 2, (k, p, k in next st, p 3 tog) 3 times, k 2, p 4, k 2, p 2, k 3. *Row 3:* P 3, twist 2, p 2, sl next 2 sts onto cable needle and hold in *front* of work, k 2, k 2 sts from cable needle (Cable 4), p 16, sl next 2 sts onto cable needle and hold in *back* of work, k next 2 sts, k 2 sts from cable needle, sl next 2 sts onto cable needle and hold in *front* of work, k next 2 sts, k 2 sts from cable needle (Cable 8), p 16, cable 4, p 2, twist 2, p 3. *Row 4:* K 3, p 2, k 2, p 4, k 2, (p 3 tog, k, p, k in next st) 3 times, k 2, p 8, k 2, (p 3 tog, k, p, k in next st) 3 times, k 2, p 4, k 2, p 2, k 3. *Row 5:* P 3, twist 2, p 2, k 4, p 16, k 8, p 16, k 4, p 2, twist 2, p 3. *Row 6:* K 3, p 2, k 2, p 4, k 2, (k, p, k in next st, p 3 tog) 3 times, k 2, p 8, k 2, (k, p, k in next st, p 3 tog) 3 times, k 2, p 4, k 2, p 2, k 3. *Row 7:* P 3, twist 2, p 2, k 4, p 16, k 8, p 16, k 4, p 2, twist 2, p 3. *Row 8:* K 3, p 2, k 2, p 4, k 2, (p 3 tog, k, p, k in next st) 3 times, k 2, p 8, k 2, (p 3 tog, k, p, k in next st) 3 times, k 2, p 4, k 2, p 2, k 3. Rpt Rows 3 through 8 of pattern st 5 times more.

Border: Row 1: K 1, p 1 across row. *Row 2:* P 1, k 1 across row. Rpt these 2 rows of seed st for border until piece measures 3", ending with Row 2. Bind off.

Strap: Make 2. Using yarn double, cast on 6 sts. *Row 1:* K 1, p 1 across row. *Row 2:* P 1, k 1 across row. Repeat these 2 rows of seed st until piece measures 25 inches. Bind off.

Finishing: With wrong sides touching and starting 5 inches from seed edge, sew panels tog. Sew lining in place. Fold seed st border in half and leaving ends open, sew in place. Sew straps in place. Sew braid around opening. Insert dowels, after removing knobs, then replace knobs.

GOLF CLUB MITTS

MATERIALS: Columbia Minerva "Great Ideas" rug yarn (1¾ oz. pull skeins): 3 skeins Color (A): medium green; 2 skeins Color (B): yellow; Boye knitting needles. No. 8 and No. 10½, *or any size needles which will obtain the stitch gauge below.*

GAUGE: 7 sts = 2"; 5 rows = 1".

DIRECTIONS: Start at wrist with A and No. 8 needles, cast on 27 sts. *Row 1:* K 1, * p 1, k 1. Rpt from * across. *Row 2: (right side):* P 1, * k 1, p 1. Rpt from * across. Rpt Rows 1 and 2 alternately 3 times; then rpt Row 1 once more. Change to No. 10½ needles and work in pat as follows: *Row 1 (right side):* K 3, * p 1, k 3. Rpt from * across. *Row 2:* K 1, p 1, * k 3, p 1. Rpt from * across ending with k 1. Rpt last 2 rows alternately for pat. *For No. 5 Mitt:* (Work 4 rows A, 2 rows B) 5 times. *For No. 3 Mitt:* Work 10 rows A, (2 rows B, 4 rows A) twice; 2 rows B, 6 rows A. *For No. 1 Mitt:* Work 16 rows A, 2 rows B, 12 rows A. *For All Mitts: Row 1:* With A, k across. *Row 2:* P 1, p 2 tog, * k 1, p 1, p 2 tog. Rpt from * across.—20 sts. *Row 3:* K 2, * p 1, k 2. Rpt from * across. *Row 4:* P 2 tog, * k 1, p 2 tog. Rpt from * across—13 sts. *Row 5:* K 1, * p 1, k 1. Rpt from * across. *Row 6:* (P 2 tog) 6 times; p 1. Break off leaving an 18" end. Thread a needle with this end; sl rem 7 sts onto it, draw tog and fasten; with same yarn, sew side seam.

Pompon (make 3): Wind B 100 times around a 4" square of cardboard. Sl strands off cardboard and tie securely at center. Cut loops at each end and trim. Fasten pompon to mitt tips.

Color photo on page 140

NATURAL TURTLENECK SWEATER

Directions are given for size Small (8-10). Changes for sizes Medium (12-14) and Large (16-18) are in parentheses.

MATERIALS: Coats & Clark's Red Heart "Fabulend" Knitting Worsted 4 Ply (3½ oz. skeins): 5 (6, 7) skeins of desired color; crochet hook; knitting needles, 1 pair No. 8, *or any size needles which will obtain the stitch gauge below.*

GAUGE: 9 sts = 2"; 8 rows (4 ridges) = 1".

MEASUREMENTS:

SIZES:	SMALL (8-10)	MEDIUM (12-14)	LARGE (16-18)
BUST:	33"	36"	40"
WIDTH ACROSS BACK AT UNDERARMS:	16½"	18"	20"
WIDTH ACROSS SLEEVE AT UPPER ARM:	11¼"	12"	13"

DIRECTIONS: *Back:* Starting at lower edge, cast on 74 (80, 90) sts. Work in k 1, p 1 ribbing for 3½". Now work in garter st (k each row) until total length is 17 (17½, 18)" from beg, or desired length to shoulder. Bind off all sts.

Front: Work same as Back.

Sleeves: Starting at lower edge, cast on 48 (50, 52) sts. Work in k 1, p 1 ribbing for 3½". *Next Row:* K across, inc 2 (4, 6) sts evenly spaced across row — 50 (54, 58) sts. Work even in garter st until length is 18 (18½, 19)″ above ribbing, or desired length to shoulder.

Collar: Cast on 78 (80, 82) sts. Work even in garter st until total length is 5 (5½, 6)″. Bind off.

Finishing: Pin each piece to measurements on a padded surface, cover with a damp cloth and allow to dry; do not press. (*Note:* Pieces are crocheted together, using sl sts.) To join, first baste (or pin) sections together as directed; with crochet hook, working through both thicknesses of joining edges, sl st evenly across each seam. Starting at side edges, baste 4 (4½, 5½)″ shoulder seams, leaving center sections of top edges open for neck. Fold sleeves in half lengthwise to find center at top edge, match top end of fold of each sleeve with end of shoulder seam; baste top edges of sleeves along 6 (6½, 7)″ of side edges of back and front, adjusting to fit. Baste side and sleeve seams. With crochet hook, sl st evenly across each seam, keep work flat. Sl st short edges of collar together. With collar seam at center back, sl st one long edge of collar to neck edge, adjusting to fit. Fold collar in half to right side.

HOODED SWEATER

Directions are given for size Small (6–8). Changes for sizes Medium (10–12), Large (14–16) and Extra Large (18–20) are in parentheses. Loosely fitting garment.

MATERIALS: Reynolds Poemes, 20 (22, 25, 28) balls; knitting needles No. 7, No. 8 and No. 9 *or any size needles which will obtain gauge below;* dp or cable needle.

GAUGE: On No. 9 needles, Diamond Pat—16 sts = 4½″; Honeycomb Pat—32 sts = 7″.

MEASUREMENTS:

SIZES:	SMALL (6-8)	MEDIUM (10-12)	LARGE (14-16)	EXTRA LARGE (18-20)
BUST:	34″	38″	40½″	43″
WIDTH ACROSS BACK OR FRONT AT UNDERARMS:	17″	19″	20¼″	21½″
WIDTH ACROSS SLEEVE AT UPPER ARM:	12¾″	13¾″	14¾″	15¾″

PATTERN STS: *Diamond Pat* on 12 (14, 16, 18) sts. *Row 1 (right side):* P 4 (5, 6, 7); *sl next 2 sts to cable needle, hold to front of work, k next 2 sts, k 2 from cable needle—cable left (CL) made;* p 4 (5, 6, 7)). *Row 2 and All Wrong Side Rows:* K or p sts as they face you. *Row 3:* P 3 (4, 5, 6); *sl next st to cable needle, hold to back, k next 2 sts, p st from cable needle—cross 2 right (CR2R) made; sl next 2 sts to cable needle, hold*

to front, p next st, k 2 from cable needle—cross 2 left (CR2L) made;* p 3 (4, 5, 6). *Row 5:* P 2 (3, 4, 5), CR2R, p 2, CR2L, p 2 (3, 4, 5). *Row 7:* P 1 (2, 3, 4), CR2R, p 4, CR2L, p 1 (2, 3, 4). *Row 9:* P 1 (2, 3, 4), CR2L, p 4, CR2R, p 1 (2, 3, 4). *Row 11:* P 2 (3, 4, 5), CR2L, p 2, CR2R, p 2 (3, 4, 5). *Row 13:* P 3 (4, 5, 6), CR2L, CR2R, p 3 (4, 5, 6). *Row 14:* Rpt row 2. Rpt. rows 1 thru 14 for diamond pat.

Honeycomb Pat on 32 sts. *Row 1 (right side):* * Sl 2 sts to cable needle, hold to back, k next 2 sts, k 2 sts from cable needle—cable right (CR) made; sl next 2 sts to cable needle, hold to front of work, k next 2 sts, k 2 from cable needle— cable left (CL) made. Rpt from * 3 times more. Row 2 and All Wrong Side Rows: P. Row 3: K Row 5: * CL, CR. Rpt from * 3 times. Row 7: K. Row 8: Rpt row 2. Rpt rows 1 thru 8 for honeycomb pat.*

Back: With No. 7 needles, cast on 56 (60, 64, 68) sts. Work in k 1, p 1 ribbing for 4″. Change to No. 9 needles. *Inc Row (wrong side):* K 4, p 2; * k 4 (5, 6, 7), p in front and back of each of next 2 sts—2 sts inc'd; k 4 (5, 6, 7) for diamond panel *; p next 24 sts, inc 8 sts evenly spaced for honeycomb pat. Rpt between *'s once, p 2, k 4—68 (72, 76, 80) sts. *Pat: Row 1 (right side):* Cast on

Color photo on page 140

18 sts at beg of row for pocket lining and p these 18 sts and next 4 sts (22 sts); sl 1, k 1 for 2 st rib; * work row 1 of diamond pat across next 12 (14, 16, 18) sts *; work row 1 of honeycomb pat across next 32 sts. Rpt between *'s once; sl 1, k 1 for 2 st rib; p 4, cast on 18 sts at end of row for other pocket lining—104 (108, 112, 116) sts. *Row 2:* K 22, p 2, work pat as established across next 56 (60, 64, 68) sts, p 2, k 22. Working pats as established and side sts in rev st st (p on right side, k on wrong side), work even until 10¾" from beg. Bind off 18 sts of pocket linings at beg of next 2 rows—68 (72, 76, 80) sts. Work even in established pats until 16¾" from beg or desired length to underarm. Mark last row.

Armhole Shaping: Keeping to pat, bind off 3 sts at beg of next 2 rows—62 (66, 70, 74) sts. Having 1 rev st st at each armhole edge, work even until armholes measure 7½ (8, 8½, 9)" above marked row.

Shoulder Shaping: Keeping to pat, bind off 6 sts at beg of next 2 rows then 4 (5, 6, 7) sts at beg of next 4 rows; and at the same time, dec 2 sts over diamond pat sts as you are binding off—34 sts. Bind off rem 34 sts, dec 8 sts evenly spaced over honeycomb pat as you are binding off.

Front: Work same as back until inc row has been completed—68 (72, 76, 80) sts. *Pat Row 1 (right side):* K 4; sl 1, k 1 for 2 st rib; * work row 1 of diamond pat across next 12 (14, 16, 18) sts *; row 1 of honeycomb pat across next 32 sts. Rpt between *'s once; sl 1, k 1 for 2 st rib; k 4—68 (72, 76, 80); *Row 2:* K 4, p 2, work pat as established across next 56 (60, 64, 68) sts, p 2, k 4. Continue in above established pats working 4 sts at each side edge in garter st (k each row) for pocket borders. Work even until 10¾" from beg. Discontinuing garter sts and working these 4 sts on each side in rev st st hereafter, work same as back until ½" above beg of armhole shaping.

Neck Shaping: Next Row: Work to within 1 st of honeycomb pat; join 2nd ball of yarn and bind off next 34 sts, dec 8 sts evenly spaced over honeycomb pat as you are binding off; finish row—14, (16, 18, 20) sts each side. Working each side separately, work even until armholes measure same as back to shoulders.

Shoulder Shaping: Keeping to pat bind off at beg of each armhole edge 6 sts once, then 4 (5, 6, 7) sts twice; and at the same time, dec 2 sts over diamond pat as you are binding off.

Sleeves: With No. 7 needles, cast on 32 (34, 36, 38) sts. Work in k 1, p 1 ribbing for 5½". Change to No. 9 needles. *Next Row (wrong side):* P inc 6 (8, 10, 12) sts evenly spaced across row—38 (42,

46, 50) sts. *Pat Row 1 (right side):* P 11 (12, 13, 14); sl 1, k 1 for 2 st rib; work row 1 of diamond pat across next 12 (14, 16, 18) sts; sl 1, k 1 for 2 st rib; p 11 (12, 13, 14). Work pat as established, inc 1 st each edge every 12th row 5 times working added sts in rev st st—48 (52, 56, 60) sts. Work even until 22 (22½, 23, 23½)" from beg or desired length from wrist to shoulder. Bind off all sts; and at the same time, dec 2 sts over diamond pat as you are binding off.

Hood: With No. 8 needles, cast on 29 sts for lower edge of right front. *Row 1 (right side):* P 1, * k 1, p 1. Rpt from * across. *Row 2:* K 1, * p 1, k 1. Rpt from * across. Rpt these 2 rows for ribbing. Work until 9 (9½, 10, 10½)" from beg in ribbing, end right side. *Next Row:* Cast on 14 sts at beg of row for back neck and work across in established ribbing—43 sts. Work even in ribbing for ¾", end right side. *Next Row:* Inc 6 sts across sts of back neck, as follows: * k in front, back and front of next st—2 sts inc'd, rib 3. Rpt from * twice more, finish row—49 sts. Inc 1 st at back edge every 6th row 4 times—53 sts. Mark last inc row. Work even until 12¾" from back neck cast-on edge, ending at back edge. *Next Row:* Bind off first 9 sts, finish row. Work even for 2". Mark for center of hood. Continue for 2" more, ending at back edge. *Next Row:* Cast on 9 sts, finish row. Work even until second half of hood reaches marker at last inc on first half, ending at back edge. Dec 1 st at back edge on next row, then every 6th row at same edge 3 times more, ending right side—49 sts. *Next Row:* Dec 6 sts across sts of back neck, as follows: * k 3 tog, rib 3. Rpt from * twice more, finish row—43 sts. Work even in established ribbing for ¾", end right side. *Next Row:* Bind off 14 sts at beg of row for back neck, work across rem sts in established ribbing—29 sts. Work in established ribbing for 9 (9½, 10, 10½)". Bind off rem 29 sts for lower edge of left front.

Finishing: Steam lightly. Sew shoulder and side seams, leaving 6½" open above ribbing on side seams for pockets. Sew pocket linings in place to wrong side of front. Sew sleeve seams, weaving seam at cuff and leaving about 1" open at underarm to match bound-off sts at armholes on body. Sew in sleeves, sewing the 1" opening at sleeve underarm to the bound-off sts at armhole on back and front. Fold hood in half at center and sew back edge from top to 14 cast-on sts. Weave seam at top of hood. Sew hood to neck and front edges overlapping right front over left front at center front with seams on wrong side.

CROCHETING

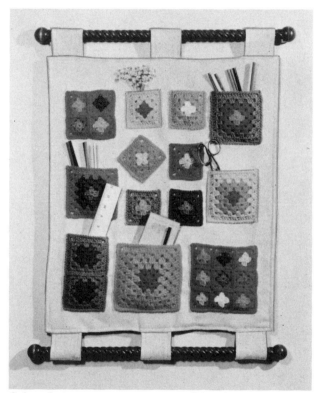

Color photo on page 141   *Directions on page 176*

GRANNY SQUARES

GENERAL DIRECTIONS:

Basic Multi-Color Granny Square Motif

Starting at center with first color, ch 6. Join with sl st to form ring. *Rnd 1:* Ch 3, in ring make 2 dc, ch 3 and (3 dc, ch 3) 3 times. Join with sl st to top of ch-3. Break off and fasten. *Rnd 2:* Attach second color to any ch-3 sp, ch 3, in same sp make 2 dc, ch 3 for corner sp and 3 dc; (ch 1, in next sp make 3 dc, ch 3 for corner sp and 3 dc) 3 times; ch 1. Join as before. Break off and fasten. *Rnd 3:* Attach third color to any corner sp; ch 3, in same sp make 2 dc, ch 3 and 3 dc; (ch 1, 3 dc in next ch-1 sp, ch 1, in next corner sp make 3 dc, ch 3 and 3 dc) 3 times; ch 1, 3 dc in last ch-1 sp, ch 1. Join. Break off and fasten. *Rnd 4:* Attach fourth color to any corner sp, ch 3, in same sp make 2

dc, ch 3 and 3 dc, * ch 1, make 3 dc and ch 1 in each ch-1 sp to next corner sp, in corner sp make 3 dc, ch 3 and 3 dc. Rpt from * 2 more times; ch 1, make 3 dc and ch 1 in each rem ch-1 sp. Join. Break off and fasten. *Rnd 5:* With fifth color, rpt Rnd 4.

Basic Solid-Color Granny Square Motif

Starting at center, ch 6. Join with sl st to form ring. *Rnd 1:* Ch 3, in ring make 2 dc, ch 3 and (3 dc, ch 3) 3 times. Join with sl st to top of ch-3. *Rnd 2:* Sl st in next 2 dc, sl st in sp, ch 3, in same sp make 2 dc, ch 3 for corner sp and 3 dc; (ch 1, in next sp make 3 dc, ch 3 for corner sp and 3 dc) 3 times; ch 1. Join. *Rnd 3:* Sl st in 2 dc and in sp as before, ch 3, in same sp make 2 dc, ch 3 and 3 dc; (ch 1, 3 dc in next ch-1 sp, ch 1, in next corner sp make 3 dc, ch 3 and 3 dc) 3 times; ch 1, 3 dc in last ch-1 sp, ch 1. Join. *Rnd 4:* Sl st across to next sp, ch 3, in same sp make 2 dc, ch 3 and 3 dc; * ch 1, make 3 dc and ch 1 in each ch-1 sp to next corner sp, in corner sp make 3 dc, ch 1 and 3 dc. Rpt from * around joining last ch 1 to top of ch-3. Rpt Rnd 4 as specified.

Finishing: How to Block: On a padded surface, using rust-proof pins, pin each motif out to the measurements given. Cover with a wet cloth and allow to dry before removing pins.

Assembling the Motifs: Motifs are usually sewn tog using a No. 18 tapestry needle and same color as last rnd of motif. Place wrong sides tog, and starting at center st of right-hand corner, sew the 2 center loops (1 loop from each motif) of each st across to center st of next corner *(see Finishing Diagram).*

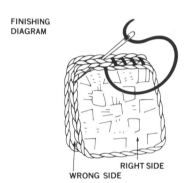

FINISHING
DIAGRAM

RIGHT SIDE
WRONG SIDE

WALL HANGING WITH MULTI-SIZED POCKETS

Directions are given for a wall hanging measuring 22″ × 26″ excluding dowel straps.

MATERIALS: Beige fabric, 29″ × 45″; pink lining fabric, 29″ × 45″; lightweight interfacing, 18″ × 36″; spiral wood dowel, 1″ × 48″; 4 round wood door knobs 1⅜″; epoxy glue; walnut stain; varnish; Coats & Clark Red Heart Wintuk 4-ply (Tangleproof skeins): 2 oz bright red; 1 oz each orange, bright pink, green and blue; yarn oddments of white, yellow, gold and rose; crochet hook, Size F, *or any size hook which will obtain the stitch gauge below.*

GAUGE: 3 dc = ½″.

First Motif (make 13): Note: Excluding red, use all colors for centers. Follow *Basic Multi-Color Granny Square Motif* in **GENERAL DIRECTIONS** using red for all the 2nd rnds. Referring to *Finishing Section* in **GENERAL DIRECTIONS**, sew motifs tog 2 × 2 to form one pocket; sew motifs tog 3 × 3 to form another pocket.

Second Motif (make 6): Follow *Basic Multi-Color Granny Square Motif* in **GENERAL DIRECTIONS**, until Rnd 2 has been completed. *Do*

not break off. Rnd 3: Sl st in next 2 dc, sl st in sp, ch 3, in same sp make 2 dc, ch 3 and 3 dc, * ch 1, 3 dc in next ch-1 sp, ch 1, in corner sp make 3 dc, ch 3 and 3 dc. Rpt from * around. Join, break off and fasten—6 pockets made.

Third Motif (make 3): Work as for *Second Motif* until Rnd 3 has been completed. Break off and fasten. *Rnd 4:* Attach 3rd color to any corner sp, ch 3, in same sp make 2 dc, ch 3 and 3 dc, * ch 1, make 3 dc and ch 1 in each ch-1 sp to next corner sp, in corner sp make 3 dc, ch 1 and 3 dc. Rpt from * around. Join. *Do not break off. Rnd 5:* Sl st in next 2 dc, sl st in sp, ch 3 and work as for last rnd. Join, break off and fasten—3 pockets made.

Fourth Motif (make 2): Follow *Basic Solid-Color Granny Square Motif* in **GENERAL DIRECTIONS** until Rnd 2 has been completed. Break off and fasten. *Rnds 3 and 4:* Attach 2nd color to any corner sp. Ch 3 and work as for Rnds 4 and 5 of *Third Motif.* Join, break off and fasten. Sew motifs tog along one edge—1 pocket made.

Fifth Motif: Work as for *Fourth Motif* until Rnd 4 has been completed. Break off and fasten. *Rnds 5 and 6:* Attach 3rd color to any corner sp and work as for last 2 rnds. Join, break off and fasten—1 pocket made.

Pocket Edging: With right side facing, using same color as last rnd of pocket, work sc in each dc and in each ch-1 sp and 3 sc in each corner sp around. Join, break off and fasten—13 pockets made. Press pockets lightly through damp cloth. Cut interfacing ¼″ smaller all around for each pocket. Sew interfacing to wrong side of each.

Fabric Backing and Dowels:

DIRECTIONS: Cut spiral wood dowel in two 22″-lengths. Epoxy-glue round wood knobs to each end of dowels. When dry, brush with walnut stain; let dry. Finish with 2 light coats of varnish; let dry between coats. Set aside.

Hanging: From each color fabric, cut a piece measuring 23″ × 27″, and 6 strips, each 4″ × 7″, for straps. (Use ½″ seam allowance throughout.) With right sides facing, pin and stitch together long edges of 1 beige and 1 pink strap, (leave top and bottom open). Turn strap inside out, press and topstitch ½″ from sewn edges. Fold strap in half crosswise and stitch raw edges together to make 3½″ loops. Make 5 more loops in same manner. Place 23″ × 27″ beige fabric face up on flat surface. Pin 3 loops evenly spaced apart (with folded edges facing center of fabric) to top and bottom edges. Lay pink fabric face down on top of beige fabric, (loops will be sandwiched between two layers of fabric). Pin together all around but leave a 6″ opening on one of the 27″ sides for turning. Machine stitch ½″ seam all around. Remove pins, trim corners diagonally and turn hanging inside out. Press seams and whipstitch opening together. Topstitch ½″ from edge all around to finish. Using photo as a guide, pin pockets in place through both fabrics, leaving top of each pocket open. With matching thread, machine stitch each pocket in place ³/₁₆″ from edge. Remove pins, slip dowels through top and bottom loops to hang.

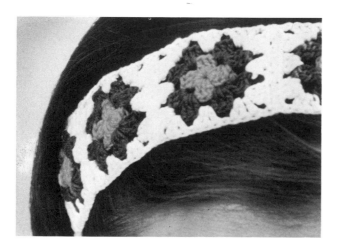

HEADBAND WITH MINI-SIZE GRANNY SQUARES

Directions are given for a headband measuring approximately 23″ long.

MATERIALS: J. & P. Coats Knit-Cro-Sheen, 1 ball each White, Yellow, Flamingo; steel crochet hook, No. 4, *or any size hook which will obtain the stitch gauge below.*

GAUGE: Each 3-rnd motif measures 1½″ × 1½″ square.

Motif (Make 15): Starting at center with Yellow, follow *Basic Multi-Color Granny Square Motif* shown in GENERAL DIRECTIONS, making Rnd 2 in Flamingo and Rnd 3 in White. Referring to *Finishing Section* in GENERAL DIRECTIONS, sew motifs tog in a strip.

MULTI-COLOR SASH

Directions are given for a finished sash measuring approximately 48″ long.

MATERIALS: Coats & Clark's O.N.T. Speed-Cro-Sheen, 1 ball each White, Hunter's Green and Watermelon; steel crochet hook No. 1/0 (zero), *or any size hook which will obtain the*

stitch gauge below.

GAUGE: Each 3-rnd motif measures 2¾″ × 2¾″ square.

Motif (Make 17): Starting at center with Watermelon, follow *Basic Multi-Color Granny Square Motif* in GENERAL DIRECTIONS, making Rnd 2 in Hunter's Green and Rnd 3 in White. Referring to *Finishing Section* in GENERAL DIRECTIONS, sew motifs tog in a strip.

Color photo on page 141

FRINGED TABLECLOTH

Directions are given for a finished tablecloth measuring 36″ × 36″ excluding fringe.

MATERIALS: Bear Brand, Fleisher's or Bucilla Wool and Shetland Wool or Botany Scottie, 2 oz. balls or Bear Brand, Fleisher's or Botany Machine Washable Winsom, 2 oz. skeins: 6 skeins white and 2 skeins color; crochet hook, Size F, *or any size hook which will obtain the stitch gauge below.*

GAUGE: Each 6-rnd motif measures 6″ × 6″.

Motif (Make 36): Starting with color, follow *Basic Solid-Color Granny Square Motif* shown in in GENERAL DIRECTIONS until Rnd 2 has been completed. Break off and fasten. Attach white to any corner sp. *Rnd 3:* Ch 3, in same sp make 2 dc, ch 3 and 3 dc, * ch 1, 3 dc in next ch-1 sp, ch 1, in corner sp make 3 dc, ch 3 and 3 dc. Rpt from * around. Join. *Rnd 4:* Same as Rnd 4 in *Basic Solid-Color Granny Square Motif* in GENERAL DIRECTIONS. *Rnds 5 and 6:* Rpt Rnd 4 twice. Break off and fasten.

Referring to *Finishing Section* in GENERAL DIRECTIONS, join 6 motifs to form a single strip, repeat to make 5 more strips. Join strips to make finished tablecloth.

Fringe: Wind white 50 times around a 5″ square of cardboard. Cut strands at one end, thus making 10″ strands. Cut additional strands as needed. Fold 4 strands to form a loop. Insert hook in a sp on edge and draw loop through. Draw ends through loop and pull up tightly to form a knot. Knot a 4-strand fringe in each sp around entire edge. Trim fringe evenly to 3½″.

POP-OVER TUNIC

Directions are given for one size that will fit children sizes 3–6.

MATERIALS: Caron Dazzle-Aire Knitting Worsted, 4 oz. skeins; 1 each Red, White, Blue; Susan Bates crochet hook, Size G, *or any size hook which will obtain the stitch gauge below.*

GAUGE: 1 square = 2¼″.

Square: Make 18 White and 18 Navy. *Rnd 1:* Ch

5, join with sl st in first ch to form ring; ch 3, 2 dc in ring, * ch 1, 3 dc in ring; rpt from * twice, ch 1, join with sl st in top of ch 3. *Rnd 2:* Sl st to first ch-1 sp, ch 3, -2dc, ch 2, 3 dc—all in same sp, * ch 1, -3 dc, ch 2, 3 dc—all in next ch-1 sp; rpt from * twice, ch 1, join in top of ch 3. Fasten off.

Finishing: Working through back lps only with an overcast st, sew squares tog in strips of 3, alternating White, Navy, White and Navy, White, Navy. Join 6 strips for Front and 6 strips for Back as follows: *Row 1:* With right side facing, working across long edge of strip in back lps only, join red in corner st, 1 sc in same st, sc in each st across; 28 sc. *Row 2:* Ch 1, turn, 1 sc in each sc across. Fasten off. Sew an alternate color strip to row 2 of edging, working with an overcast st through back lps only. Work rows 1 and 2 along free edge of 2nd strip. Continue in this manner until 6 strips are sewn tog.

Shoulder and Neck Facing: Along free edge of first strip, work rows 1 and 2. Rpt row 2, 3 more times. *Row 6:* Ch 1, turn, sl st in each of first 3 sts, working in back lps only for turning ridge, sc in each sc to within last 3 sc. *Row 7:* Ch 1, turn, 2 sc in first sc, sc in each sc to within last sc, 2 sc in last sc. Rpt row 7 twice more. Fasten off. Sew shoulder seams. Fold facing to wrong side and sew in place loosely. Along each side edge, from lower edge to lower edge, work 9 rows sc. Along each lower edge work 3 rows sc. *Ties (make 2):* Ch 125. Fasten off lp.

WRAP

Directions are given for a finished wrap measuring 42″ × 42″ square.

MATERIALS: Coats & Clark's Red Heart Wintuk 4-ply (tangleproof skeins): 4 ozs. White and 2 ozs. each Yellow, Lt. Gold, Pink, Coral, Vermillion, Blue Jewel, Skipper Blue, Dk. Turquoise and Maize; crochet hook, size G, *or any size hook which will obtain the stitch gauge below.*

GAUGE: Two 3-dc groups and 2 sps = 2¼″; 5 rnds = 3″.

Following Basic Multi-Colored Granny Square Motif in GENERAL DIRECTIONS, start with Lt. Gold and work through 2nd rnd. Break off and fasten. Work 3rd rnd in Maize, 4th rnd in White, 5th rnd in Pink, 6th rnd in Coral, 7th rnd in Vermillion, 8th rnd in Dk. Turquoise, 9th rnd in Skipper Blue, 10th rnd in Blue Jewel, 11th rnd in White, 12th rnd in Maize, 13th rnd in Yellow, 14th rnd in Lt. Gold, 15th rnd in Vermillion, 16th rnd in Coral, 17th rnd in Pink, 18th rnd in White, 19th rnd in Blue Jewel, 20th rnd in

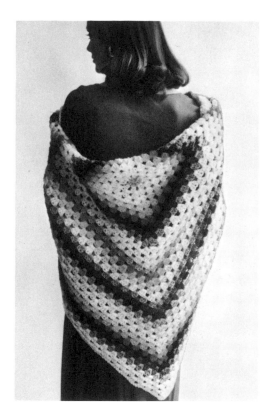

Skipper Blue, 21st rnd in Dk. Turquoise, 22nd rnd in Lt. Gold, 23rd rnd in Yellow, 24th rnd in Maize, 25th rnd in White, 26th rnd in Pink, 27th rnd in Coral, 28th rnd in Vermillion, 29th rnd in Dk. Turquoise, 30th rnd in Skipper Blue, 31st rnd in Blue Jewel. Work 32nd, 33rd, 34th rnds in White; **BUT DO NOT BREAK OFF YARN AT END OF** *32nd and 33rd RNDS*, after joining, work sl st in next 2 dc and in corner sp (ready to start next rnd), continue in same color until 34th rnd is completed.

PLACE MAT AND NAPKIN RING SETS

Directions are given for a finished place mat measuring approximately 11½″ × 18″, with finished Napkin Ring measuring approximately 2¼″ wide and 6¾″ around.

MATERIALS: J.&P. Coats Knit-Cro-Sheen, 8 balls Hunter's Green and 1 ball each White and Watermelon; steel crochet hook, No. 1, *or any size hook which will obtain the stitch gauge below. Note*: Materials are given for two placemats and two napkin rings.

GAUGE: 7 clusters and 7 ch-2 sps = 3″; 5 rows = 2″; each 3-rnd motif measures 2¼″ × 2¼″ square.

PLACE MAT:

Starting at a narrow edge with 2 strands of Hunter's Green held tog, ch 76 to measure 12″.

Row 1: Holding back on hook the last loop of each dc, make 2 dc in 4th ch from hook, thread over and draw through all 3 loops on hook—STARTING CLUSTER MADE; * ch 2, skip next 2 ch, holding back on hook the last loop of each dc, make 3 dc in next ch, thread over and draw through all 4 loops on hook—CLUSTER MADE. Rpt from * across—25 clusters. Ch 3, turn. *Row 2*: Make a starting cluster in tip of first cluster, * ch 2, cluster in tip of next cluster. Rpt from * across. Ch 3, turn. Rpt Row 2 for pattern until 33 rows in all are completed. Break off and fasten. Working as before, make another strip of 7 rows.

Motif for Place mat and Napkin Ring (make 8): Divide White and Watermelon in half and use 2 strands held tog of each color. Starting at center, with Watermelon, follow *Basic Multi-Color Granny Square Motif* in GENERAL DIRECTIONS, making Rnd 2 in Hunter's Green and Rnd 3 in White. Referring to *Finishing Section* in GENERAL DIRECTIONS, sew 5 motifs tog, then sew one long edge of motifs to one narrow edge of large place mat strip. Sew other long edge of motifs to one long edge of small placemat strip.

Edging: Rnd 1: With wrong side facing, using 2 strands of Hunter's Green, work sc evenly along entire outer edge making 3 sc in same place in each corner and being careful to keep work flat. Join with sl st to first sc. Ch 1, turn. *Rnd 2*: Making 3 sc in same place in each corner, work sc in each sc around. Join. Break off and fasten.

NAPKIN RING:

Sew 3 motifs tog to form a ring. With right side facing, using Hunter's Green, work sc evenly along top edge. Join to first sc. Break off and fasten. Finish other edge in same way.

ROLL BRIMMED CAP

MATERIALS: Coats & Clark's Red Heart Knitting Worsted, 4 ply: 2 oz. Eggshell; *for each square:* 3½ yds. of each of 12 different colors; *for Top:* Colorwise from center: 2½ yds., 5 yds., 10 yds., 10 yds.; aluminum crochet hook, Size I, *or any size hook which will obtain the stitch gauge below.*

GAUGE: Each square measures about 3¾" across.

DIRECTIONS: *Square (each rnd on each square is a different color):* Starting at center with first color, ch 4. Join with sl st to form ring. *Rnd 1:* Ch 3, in ring make 2 dc, ch 2 and (3 dc, ch 2) 3 times. Join with sl st to top of ch-3. Fasten off. *Rnd 2:* Attach 2nd color to any ch-2 sp, ch 3, in same sp make dc, ch 1 for corner sp and 2 dc; (sk next dc, dc in next 2 dc, in next ch-2 sp make 2 dc, ch 1 for corner sp and 2 dc) 3 times; sk next dc, dc in last 2 dc. Join, fasten off. *Rnd 3:* Attach Eggshell to any corner sp; ch 3, in same sp make dc, ch 1 and 2 dc; (sk next dc, dc in each of next 5 dc, in next ch-1 sp make 2 dc, ch 1 and 2 dc) 3 times; sk next dc, dc in last 5 dc. Join, fasten off. Make 5 more squares same as this. With wrong sides tog, using Eggshell and starting at center st of right-hand corner, sew the 2 center loops (1 loop from each motif) of sts across to center st of next corner. Sew motifs to form a strip; then sew ends of strip to form a circle.

Top: Use colors as listed in MATERIALS. At center, ch 4. Join with sl st to form ring. *Rnd 1:* Ch 3, in ring make 2 dc, ch 2 and (3 dc, ch 2) 5 times. Join, fasten off. *Rnd 2:* Attach 2nd color to any ch-2 sp, ch 3, in same sp make dc, ch 1 for corner sp and 2 dc; (in next sp make 2 dc, ch 1 for

corner sp and 2 dc) 5 times. Join, fasten off. *Rnd 3:* Attach 3rd color to any corner sp, ch 3, in same sp make dc, ch 1 for corner sp and 2 dc; (sk next dc, dc in next 3 dc, in next ch-1 sp make 2 dc, ch 1 and 2 dc) 5 times; sk next dc, dc in last 3 dc. Join, fasten off. *Rnd 4:* Attach 4th color to any corner sp, ch 5, dc in same sp, (sk next dc, dc in next 6 dc, in corner sp make dc, ch 2 and dc) 5 times; sk next dc, dc in last 6 dc. Join to 3rd ch on ch-5. Fasten off. *Rnd 5:* Attach Eggshell to any corner sp, ch 3, in same sp make dc, ch 1 and 2 dc; (sk next dc, dc in next 7 dc, in corner sp make 2 dc, ch 1 and 2 dc) 5 times; sk next dc, dc in last 7 dc. Join, fasten off. Matching corners, sew top to one edge of joined squares.

With right side facing, attach Eggshell to any dc on lower edge. *Rnd 1:* Ch 1, sc in each st along entire lower edge. Join to first sc. *Rnd 2:* Ch 1, sc in each sc, easing in, if necessary to fit. Join. *Rnd 3:* Ch 1, sc in each sc. Join, fasten off. *Brim:* At narrow edge, ch 8. *Row 1:* Dc in 4th ch from hook, dc in next 4 ch. Ch 3, turn. *Row 2:* Sk first dc, dc in *back* lp of next 4 dc, dc in top of ch-3. Ch 3, turn. Rpt Row 2 for 29 rows or until slightly longer than lower edge of crown. Fasten off. Sew narrow edges tog. With pins, divide one edge of Brim into 6 equal parts. Pin each part evenly to lower edge matching a square. Sew in place.

CLUTCH BAG

MATERIALS: Coats & Clark's Red Heart Wintuk 4-ply (Tangleproof skeins): 1 oz. each White, Paddy Green, Olympic Blue and Claret; crochet hook Size G, *or any size hook which will obtain the stitch gauge below;* ½ yd. of white fabric for lining.

GAUGE: Two 3-dc groups and 2 sps = 2¼"; 5 rnds = 3".

Following *Basic Multi-Colored Granny Square Motif* in GENERAL DIRECTIONS, start with

Claret and work 1st rnd. Break off and fasten. *Rnd 2:* Attach White to joining, ch 3, dc in joining, * ch 1, 2 dc in next dc. Repeat from *. Ch 1, join to top of ch-3—16 dc. Break off and fasten. Attach Paddy Green and work 3rd rnd. *Hereafter, work all even-numbered rnds in White.* Work 5th rnd in Olympic Blue, 7th rnd in Claret, 9th rnd in Paddy Green, 11th rnd in Olympic Blue and 13th rnd in Claret. Work 14th rnd in White.

Lining: Cut a piece of fabric to measure 21½″ × 21½″ square. Turn under all raw edges of fabric ½″ and blindstitch to edges of motif with sewing needle and sewing thread.

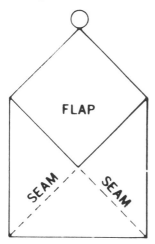

Assembling Bag: Fold in 3 corners of square to meet at center to form an envelope. Referring to *Finishing Section* in GENERAL DIRECTIONS, with white sew adjacent edges of folded corners together. Fourth corner forms flap.

Edging: Starting at top end of seams, with white sc evenly along free edges of motif. Make sc, ch 12 and sc in top corner sp of flap to form loop. Continue along edges and join with sl st to first sc.

Sew button on bag to correspond with loop.

SLIP COVER HAT

MATERIALS: Coats & Clark's O.N.T. Speed-Cro-Sheen Mercerized Cotton (100 yd. balls): 1 ball each Orange, Green, Dark Pink, Dark Turquoise, Brown and Red; aluminum crochet hook, Size E, *or any size hook which will obtain the stitch gauge below.*

GAUGE: 5 dc = 1″, 2 rnds = 1″.

DIRECTIONS: Starting at top of crown, with Brown, ch 4. Join with sl st to form ring. *Rnd 1:* Ch 3, in ring make 2 dc, (ch 3, 3 dc) 3 times; ch 3. Join with sl st to top of ch-3. *Rnd 2:* Ch 3 (to count as one dc, dc in next 2 dc, in next sp make

2 dc, ch 3 and 2 dc; dc in next 3 dc) 3 times; in last sp make 2 dc, ch 3 and 2 dc. Join to top of ch-3—4 corners. Fasten off. *Rnd 3:* Attach Red to a corner sp, ch 3, in same sp make 2 dc, ch 5 and 3 dc, * dc in next 2 dc, *holding back on hook the last lp of each dc, make dc in each of next 3 dc, thread over hook and draw through all 4 lps on hook—2 sts decreased over 3 dc;* dc in next 2 dc, in corner sp make 3 dc, ch 5 and 3 dc. Rpt from * around ending with dc in last 2 dc. Join, fasten off. *Rnd 4:* Attach Green to a corner sp, ch 3 and complete first corner as on last rnd, * dc in each of next 4 dc, dec 2 sts over next 3 dc, dc in next 4 dc, in corner sp make corner as on last rnd. Rpt from * around ending with dc in last 4 dc. Join, fasten off. *Row 5:* Attach Turquoise to a corner sp, ch 3 and complete corner, * dc in next 6 dc, dec 2 sts as before, dc in next 6 dc, make corner over corner as on last rnd. Rpt from * around ending with dc in last 6 dc. Join, fasten off. *Rnd 6:* With Orange, work as for Rnd 5 only have 8 dc (instead of 6 dc) bet decs and corners. Join, fasten off. *Rnd 7:* With Brown, work first corner, * dc next 10 dc, sk next 3 dc, dc in next 10 dc, corner over corner. Rpt from * around ending with dc in last 11 dc. Join, fasten off. *Rnd 8:* With Pink work first corner, * dc in next 11 dc, sk next 4 dc, dc in next 11 dc, corner over corner. Rpt from * around ending with dc in last 11 dc. Join, fasten off. *Rnd 9:* Attach Brown to a corner sp, ch 1, sc in same sp, * ch 17 loosely, sc in next corner sp. Rpt from * around joining last ch 17 to first sc.

Note: The large holes will be filled in later.

Band: Rnd 1: Ch 1, sc in each ch st and in each sc around. Join. Try on for fit. *Rnd 2:* Ch 1, sc in each sc, easing in if necessary, to fit. Join. *Rnds 3 and 4:* Ch 1, sc in each sc around. Join, fasten off.

Fill In Crochet: With last rnd of Band toward you and working along the opposite side of a ch-17 of Rnd 9, attach Green to the 3rd ch to the left of the Brown sc made in the Pink corner sp. *Rnd 1:* Ch 3, dc in next 12 ch, sk first Pink dc, dc in next 11 Pink dc, sk next 4 dc, dc in next 11 dc. Join to top of ch-3. Fasten off. Attach Turquoise to the 3rd dc to the left of joining of last rnd. *Rnd 2:* Ch 3, dc in next 6 dc, sk next 5 dc, dc in next 7 dc, sk next 4 dc, dc in next 7 dc. Join, fasten off. Fill in rem 3 holes varying colors.

Brim: Attach Turquoise to any sc on last rnd of Band. *Rnd 1:* Ch 3, * 2 dc in next dc, dc in next dc. Rpt from * around. Join, fasten off. Attach Red. *Rnd 2:* Ch 3, dc in each dc. Join, fasten off. Attach Green. *Rnd 3:* Rpt Rnd 2. Attach Pink. *Rnd 4:* Ch 3, * dc in 5 dc, 2 dc in next dc. Rpt from * around. Join, fasten off. Attach Brown. *Rnd 5:* Ch 3, dc in next 2 dc * ch 3, dc in next 3 dc. Rpt from * around. Join, fasten off.

MINI SQUARE HATBAND
MATERIALS: J. & P. Coats Knit-Cro-Sheen, 1 ball (175 yd. ball) Black; odds and ends of many colors; steel crochet hook, No. 9, *or any size hook which obtain the stitch gauge below.*
GAUGE: Motif measures 2″ square.
DIRECTIONS: *Motif:* Using a different color for each rnd, work Rnds 1, 2 and 3 as follows: Starting at center with any color, ch 6. Join with sl st to form ring. *Rnd 1:* Ch 3, in ring make 2 dc, ch 3 and (3 dc, ch 3) 3 times. Join with sl st to top of ch-3; fasten off. *Rnd 2:* Attach a different color to any ch-3 sp, ch 3, in same sp make 2 dc, ch 3 for corner sp and 3 dc; (ch 1, in next sp make 3 dc, ch 3 for corner sp and 3 dc) 3

times; ch 1. Join as before; fasten off. *Rnd 3:* Attach a different color to any corner sp; ch 3, in same sp make 2 dc, ch 3 and 3 dc; (ch 1, 3 dc in next ch-1 sp, ch 1, in next corner sp make 3 dc, ch 3 and 3 dc) 3 times; ch 1, 3 dc in last ch-1 sp, ch 1. Join, fasten off. *Rnd 4:* Attach Black to any corner sp, ch 3, in same sp make 2 dc, ch 3 and 3 dc, * (ch 1, 3 dc in next ch-1 sp) twice; ch 1, in corner sp make 3 dc, ch 1 and 3 dc. Rpt from * around ending with ch 1. Join, fasten off. Make as many motifs as necessary to go around crown of hat. Sew motifs tog in a long strip; then sew ends of strip tog to form circle. Slip over crown and tack in place.

TEENY BIKINI
Directions are given for Size Small. Changes for size Medium are in parentheses.
MATERIALS: Phentex yarn, available from Sunyarn Inc., P.O. Box 1120, Plattsburgh, N.Y. 12901., 1 skein each Green and White; aluminum crochet hook, Size I, *or any size hook which will obtain the stitch gauge below.*
GAUGE: 5 sc = 1″; 4 rows = 1″.

FINISHED MEASUREMENTS		
SIZES:	SMALL	MEDIUM
TOP OF PANTS:	29″	33″
LOWER EDGE OF EACH		
BRA CUP:	7″	8″

DIRECTIONS: *Pants: Buck Panel:* Starting at top of center back with Green, ch 2. *Row 1:* 2 sc in 2nd ch from hook. Ch 1, turn.
Note: Hereafter, work in back loops only of each sc. Row 2: 2 sc in each sc across—4 sc. Ch 1, turn. *Row 3:* 2 sc in first sc, sc in each sc across to last sc, 2 sc in last sc—one sc inc at each end of row. Ch 1, turn. Rpt Row 3 until there are 40 (46) sc on row. Work 1 row even. Ch 1, turn. *Next row:* Sk first sc, sc in each sc across to within last 2 sc, sk next sc, sc in last sc—one sc dec at each end of row. Ch 1, turn. Rpt last row until 8 sc rem. Ch 1, turn. For crotch, work even over 8 sc for 8 rows. Ch 1, turn. For center front panel, inc one sc at both ends of every row until there are 24 (28) sc. Ch 1, turn and work 1 row even. Ch 1, turn. Dec one sc at both ends of every row until 2 sc rem. Fasten off.
Back Triangle (Make 2): With Green, ch 5. *Row 1:* In 5th ch from hook make *3 hdc, ch 1 and 3 hdc—shell made;* ch 4, sl st in same place where shell was made. Fasten off. *Row 2:* With right side of shell facing, attach White in ch-4 lp at *beg of last row, ch 4, 3 hdc in same lp, ch 1, in ch-1 sp of next shell make 3 hdc, ch 1 and 3 hdc—*

corner; ch 1, 3 hdc in last ch-4 lp, ch 4, sl st in same place as last hdc. Fasten off. *Row 3:* Attach Green in ch-4 lp at *beg* of last row, ch 4, 3 hdc in same lp, ch 1, 3 hdc in next ch-1 sp, ch 1, *shell in ch-1 of next shell—corner;* ch 1, 3 hdc in next ch-1 sp, ch 1, in last ch-4 lp make 3 hdc, ch 4 and sl st. Fasten off. *Row 4:* Attach White in ch-4 lp at *beg* of last row, ch 4, 3 hdc in same lp, * ch 1, 3 hdc in next ch-1 sp. Rpt from * across to within ch-1 of corner shell, ch 1, shell in ch-1 of corner shell, ** ch 1, 3 hdc in next ch-1 sp. Rpt from ** across, ending with ch 1, 3 hdc in last ch-4 lp, ch 4, sl st in same lp. Fasten off. *Rows 5 through 9 (10):* Alternating colors, rpt Row 4 five (six) more times. Fasten off. With matching yarn sew the last hdc on the last row of one triangle to the first hdc on the last row of other triangle. Pin corner shells of triangles to both ends of last inc row on Back Panel; pin 2 sc at beg of Back Panel to where triangles were joined. Pin rem edges bet pins. With Green sew edges neatly tog, catching the loop *behind* each hdc and keeping work flat.

Front Triangle (Make 2): Work same as Back Triangle until 5 (6) rows have been completed. Fasten off. Pin and sew triangles to Front Panel same as Back Panel. With White work sc evenly along entire outer edge, easing in at leg edges for good fit. Join with sl st to first sc; then work sc in back lp of each sc around. Join, fasten off.

Ties (Make 2): With White make a 23″ chain. Fasten off. Pass a Tie through top ends of front and back triangles and tie.

Bra Triangle (Make 2): Work same as Back Triangle until 7 (8) rows have been completed. With White work 2 rnds of sc, easing in edges slightly to form cups.

Neck Tie (on each triangle): Attach White to point at corner shell, make a 12″ (14″) chain. Fasten off. Knot end of chain.

Center Tie: With White make a 12″ chain. Fasten off. Pass Tie through lower end point of adjoining triangles; tie at center front.

Back Tie (on each triangle): Attach White to rem lower end point of a triangle, make a 16″ chain; then sc in 2nd ch from hook, sc in each ch across, sl st where yarn was attached. Fasten off.

JUTE TOTE BAG

Directions are given for a tote bag measuring approximately 19″ × 22″.

MATERIALS: Lily Jute-tone (75 yd. spools), 3 spools Brown; left-over Craft and Rug yarn in various colors; No. 18 tapestry needle; crochet hook, Size G, *or any size hook which will obtain the stitch gauge below;* 1¼ yds. 1″ grosgrain ribbon.

GAUGE: Each square measures 4½″ × 4½″.

Square (make 15 Brown Jute and 25 of various colors): At center, ch 4. Join with sl st to form ring. *Rnd 1:* Ch 3, in ring make 2 dc, ch 3 and (3 dc, ch 3) 3 times. Join with sl st to top of ch-3.

Rnd 2: Sl st in next 2 dc, sl st in sp, ch 3, in same sp make 2 dc, ch 3 for corner sp and 3 dc; (ch 1, in next sp make 3 dc, ch 3 for corner sp and 3 dc) 3 times; ch 1. Join. *Rnd 3:* Sl st in 2 dc, sl st in sp, ch 3, in same sp make 2 dc, ch 3 and 3 dc; (ch 1, 3 dc in next ch-1 sp, ch 1, in next corner sp make 3 dc, ch 3 and 3 dc) 3 times; ch 1, 3 dc in last ch-1 sp, ch 1. Join and fasten off. Place wrong sides of 2 squares tog and, starting at center sts of right-hand corner, sew the 2 center loops (1 loop from each square) of sts across to center sts of next corner. Assembling colors as desired, sew 4 rows of 8 squares each tog; then sew the 4-square edges tog. Sew rem 3 squares in a strip and sew in place for bottom of bag. Face top edge with grosgrain ribbon.

Handle (make 2): Ch 46. *Row 1:* Sc in 2nd ch from hook, sc in each ch across. Ch 1, turn. *Row 2:* Sc in each sc across. Fold piece in half and sl st each st of last row to corresponding ch on opposite side of starting chain. Sew ends of handles to wrong side, 1″ below center top edge of bag.

HORIZONTAL STRIPED HALTER

Directions are given for halter to fit size Small (8-10). Changes to fit sizes Medium (12-14) and Large (16-18) are in parentheses.

MATERIALS: J. & P. Coats "Knit-Cro-Sheen" (175 yd. balls): 2 balls each Ecru (A), Nu-Purple (B), Spanish Red (C), Mid Rose (D), Crystal Blue (E), Royal Blue (F); steel crochet hook, No. 2 *or any size crochet hook which will obtain the stitch gauge below.*

GAUGE: 6 sc = 1″; 6 rows = 1″

Note: Work with 2 strands of same color held together throughout.

MEASUREMENTS: SIZES	SMALL (8-10)	MEDIUM (12-14)	LARGE (16-18)
WIDTH ACROSS ENTIRE HALTER:	19″	22″	25″
LENGTH UP CENTER:	11¼″	12″	13″

DIRECTIONS: *Square:* Starting at center with 2 strands of A held together, ch 5. Join with sl st to form ring. *Rnd 1:* Ch 1, 8 sc in ring. Join with sl st to first sc. *Rnd 2:* Ch 1, working in back loop only of each sc, make 3 sc in same sc as joining, * sc in next sc, *3 sc in next sc—* CORNER; rpt from * 2 more times, sc in next sc. Join with sl st to first sc. Break off and fasten. *Rnd 3:* Using 2 strands held together, attach B to back loop of center sc of first 3-sc group, ch 1, 3 sc in same st, * working in back loop only of each sc, make sc in each of next 3 sc, 3 sc in next

Color photo on page 141

sc; rpt from * 2 more times, sc in each of next 3 sc. Join to first sc. Break off and fasten. *Note:* Hereafter continue to use 2 strands of same color held together and work in back loop only of each sc throughout. *Rnd 4:* Attach C to center sc of any 3-sc group, ch 1, 3 sc in same sc, * sc in each sc to within center sc of 3-sc group at next corner, 3 sc in center sc; rpt from * around, ending with sc in each rem sc. Join to first sc. Break off and fasten. *Rnd 5:* Attach D to same sc as joining, sc in same sc, making 3 sc in center sc of each 3-sc group, sc in each sc around. Join. Do not break off. *Rnd 6:* Ch 1, sc in same sc as joining, continue same as for Rnd 5. Join. Break off and fasten. Working same as for Rnd 4, work colors as follows: *Rnd 7:* E. *Rnd 8:* F. *Rnd 9:* E. *Rnd 10:* B. *Rnd 11:* A. *Rnd 12:* D. Repeating colors in the same sequence, make 0 (2, 4) more rnds.

Main Section: Starting at top edge with C, ch 107 (132, 150) to measure 18 (22, 25)″. *Row 1:* Sc in 2nd ch from hook, sc in each ch across—106 (131, 149) sc. Break off and fasten. Turn. *Row 2:* Attach A to back loop of first sc on last row, working in back loop only of each sc, sc in same sc, sc in each sc across, ch 1, turn. *Row 3:* Continuing with A, sc in back loop of each sc across. Ch 1, turn. *Row 4:* Rpt Row 3. Break off and fasten. Turn. *Rows 5 and 6:* With E, work same as Rows 2 and 3. Break off and fasten. Turn. *Row 7:* With F, work same as Row 2. Break off and fasten. Turn. Break off and attach colors as needed. Continuing in this manner, work colors as follows: 1 row E, 4 rows D, 2 rows C, 1 row B, 1 row D, 2 rows A, 2 rows F, 1 row E, 3 rows B, 2 rows E, 1 row B, 4 rows A, 2 rows E, 3 rows F, 1 row A, (2 rows C, 3 rows D) 1 (2, 3) times.

Side Edge: Row 1: Working along ends of rows, attach D to end of last row made, sc over same row, * sk next row, sc over end st of next row; rpt from * across to next corner. Ch 1, turn. *Row 2:* Working in back loop only of each sc, sc in each sc across. *Row 3:* Rpt last row. *Row 4 and Ties:* Sc in first sc, make a chain 12 (13, 14)″ long for tie; sc in 2nd ch from hook, sc in each ch, sc in each sc to within center st of last row, make another chain same length as before, sc in 2nd ch from hook and in each ch, sc in each sc on last row to within last sc, make another tie as before, then sc in last sc. Break off and fasten. Work Side Edge and Ties along opposite side edge in same manner.

Finishing: Sew square to center section of starting chain on main section. Block to measurements.

GRANNY SQUARE AND FABRIC SHAWL

(Size: 60″ across top edge and 30″ up center back, plus fringe)

MATERIALS: Black and white hounds-tooth check wool fabric, 58″-wide, ⅓ yd; Bucilla Bear Brand Win-Knit (2 oz. balls): 5 balls Winter White (A), 1 ball Dusty Rose (B) *or any desired color;* crochet hook, Size H, *or any size hook which will obtain the square gauge below;* steel crochet hook, No. 0 (zero).

GAUGE: Each Granny Square = 5″ × 5″.

Granny Square (Make 16)—Rnd 1: Start at center with B and H hook, ch 5. Join with sl st to form ring; ch 3, 2 dc in ring, (ch 3, 3 dc in ring) 3 times; ch 3. Join with sl st to top of ch-3—4 groups of 3 dc each, counting ch-3 as 1 dc. Break off and fasten. *Rnd 2:* Attach A to any ch-3 sp, ch 3, in same sp make 2 dc, ch 3 for corner and 3 dc; * ch 1, sk next 3 dc, in next sp make 3 dc, ch 3 for corner and 3 dc; rpt from * 2 more times; ch 1. Join with sl st to top of ch-3. *Rnd 3:* Sl st in each of next 2 dc, sl st in next ch-3 sp, ch 3, in same sp make 2 dc, ch 3 and 3 dc; * ch 1, sk next 3 dc, 3 dc in next ch-1 sp, ch 1, sk next 3 dc, in next corner sp make 3 dc, ch 3 and 3 dc; rpt from * 2 more times; ch 1, 3 dc in next ch-1 sp, ch 1. Join as before. *Rnd 4:* Sl st in each of next 2 dc, sl st in next sp, ch 3, in same corner sp make 2 dc, ch 3 and 3 dc; * (ch 1, sk next 3 dc, 3 dc in next ch-1 sp) twice; ch 1, sk next 3 dc, in next corner sp make 3 dc, ch 3 and 3 dc; rpt from * 2 more times; (ch 1, sk next 3 dc, make 3 dc in next sp) twice; ch-1. Join as before. Break off and fasten.

Fabric Squares and Triangles: Cut twelve 5″ square pieces from fabric. *If using houndstooth material, when joining pieces be sure pat of fabric is running in the same direction on all squares and triangles.* Cut 4 more 5″ squares, then cut each of these 4 pieces in half diagonally, making 8 triangles. Overcast outer edge of each piece by machine (or by hand). With a blunt needle, make 12 holes evenly spaced along each side of all squares, ¼″ in from outer edge, plus one hole at each corner (52 holes in all). Using No. 0 hook and A, make a lp on hook, with right side facing, insert hook in a corner hole and draw up a lp, pull up this lp to top edge of square and complete sc, make 2 more sc in same way in same corner hole, sc in each hole around, making 3 sc in each corner hole. Join with sl st to first sc. Break off and fasten. Work one rnd of sc along outer edge of each fabric square in same

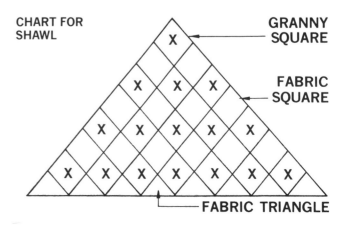

CHART FOR SHAWL

GRANNY SQUARE

FABRIC SQUARE

FABRIC TRIANGLE

way. Make 12 holes evenly spaced along each short edge of the triangles and 17 holes along long edge, ¼″ in from outer edge, plus one hole in each of the 3 corners (44 holes in all). Work 1 rnd of sc along outer edge of triangles same as for square.

Finishing: Pin crocheted squares to measurements on a padded surface, cover with a damp cloth and allow to dry; do not press. Steam fabric pieces lightly from wrong side. Arrange squares and triangles as shown on Shawl Chart.

To Join: From wrong side, with A, working through back lp only of each sc, crochet all pieces tog with 1 row of sc from corner to corner. When 3 or more corners meet, make joining in previous joining.

Edging: From right side, using H hook, attach A to corner st on crocheted square at center back point of shawl, ch 1, working in the back lp only of each st, make 3 sc in same corner st, sc in each sc and in each ch around, making 3 sc in center sc of 3-sc group of each corner of shawl. Join with sl st to first sc. Break off and fasten.

Fringe: Wind A several times around a 6½″ square of cardboard; cut at one edge, making 13″ strands. Continue to cut strands as needed. Hold 3 strands together and fold in half to form a lp. With right side facing insert crochet hook from back to front in corner sc at beg of side edge of shawl and draw lp through, draw lp ends through lp on hook and pull tightly to form a knot. Tie a group of 3 strands in same way in every other sc along the 2 side edges. Trim fringe evenly.

JACKET WITH GRANNY SQUARE SLEEVES

To give new life to an out-of-date loose fitting unlined jacket, remove sleeves and add colorful granny squares sleeves.

MATERIALS: Bucilla Bear Brand Win-Knit (2 oz. balls): 4 (4, 5) balls Black (A), 3 (3, 4) balls Winter White (B), 2 balls each Fireball Red (C), Violite (D), Dusty Rose (E), Yellow (F), Spearmint (G), Bermuda (H); crochet hook Size E (F, G), *or any size hook which will obtain the square gauge below.*

GAUGE: Each Granny Square = 3 (3¼, 3½)″.

Note: Yarn quantities and hook sizes are given for Small size jacket (8-10) followed in parentheses by those for Medium size (12-14) and Large size (16). Sleeves are made with same number of squares for all sizes but, working squares slightly different in size, by using different size crochet hooks.

MEASUREMENTS:			
SIZES:	SMALL (8-10)	MEDIUM (12-14)	LARGE (16)
WIDTH ACROSS SLEEVE AT UPPER ARM:	15″	16¼″	17½″

Note: The color used for center round determines color of square.

First Sleeve: Granny Square (Make 5 each of C and D, 4 each of E, F, G and H): Rnd 1: Starting at center with center color and E (F, G) crochet hook, ch 5. Join with sl st to form ring, ch 3, 2 dc in ring, (ch 3, 3 dc in ring) 3 times; ch 3. Join with sl st to top of ch-3—12 dc, counting ch-3 at beg of rnd as 1 dc. Break off and fasten. *Rnd. 2:* Attach B to any ch-3 sp, ch 3, in same sp make 2 dc, ch 3 for corner and 3 dc; * ch 1, sk next 3 dc, in next ch-3 sp make 3 dc, ch 3 for corner and 3 dc; rpt from * 2 more times; ch 1. Join with sl st in top of ch-3—4 corners. Break off and fasten. *Rnd 3:* Attach A to any corner ch-3 sp, ch 3, in same sp make 2 dc, ch 3 and 3 dc, * ch 1, sk next 3 dc, 3 dc in next ch-1 sp, ch 1, sk next 3 dc, in next ch-3 sp make 3 dc, ch 3 and 3 dc; rpt from * 2 more times; ch 1, 3 dc in last ch-1 sp, ch 1. Join with sl st to top of ch-3. Break off and fasten.

Half Square: Row 1: With E ch 5, 2 dc in 4th ch from hook, ch 3, 3 dc in next ch. Break off and fasten. *Row 2:* Do not turn; attach B to top of starting chain at beg of last row, ch 3, 2 dc in same ch, ch 1, sk next 2 dc, in next ch-3 sp make 3 dc, ch 3 and 3 dc; ch 1, sk next 2 dc, make 3 dc in last dc. Break off and fasten. *Row 3:* Attach A to top of ch-3 at beg of last row, ch 3, 2 dc in same ch, ch 1, sk next 2 dc, 3 dc in next ch-1 sp, ch 1, sk next 3 dc, in ch-3 sp make 3 dc, ch 3 and 3 dc; ch 1, sk next 3 dc, 3 dc in next ch-1 sp, sk next 2 dc, 3 dc in last dc. Break off and fasten. Make another Half Square, using F instead of E for Row 1.

Finishing: Pin each square and half square to measurement on a padded surface; cover with a damp cloth and allow to dry; do not press.

To Join: From wrong side, with A and a darning needle, working through back lp only of each st, sew squares together from corner to corner, matching sts. Following Chart for placement of colors, sew squares in separate strips of 5 squares in each strip; then sew strips together, matching corners. Sew 1 square and the 2 half squares to center top for cap of sleeve.

Top Edging: Working along top edge of sleeve, with right side facing, using E (F, G) hook,

Color photo on page 141.

CHART FOR SLEEVE

	F	C	E		X
G	E	D	H	C	
C	H	F	G	D	
D	G	E	C	F	
F	C	H	D	E	
E	D	G	F	H	

attach A to upper right side corner (*see X on Chart*); working in back lp only of each st (including ch sts), make 1 sc in each of next 4 sts, 1 hdc in each of next 4 sts, 1 dc in each rem st on same corner square; working along next half square make 2 hdc and 1 sc along end of last row, sc evenly along rem edge of half square, across center square and next half square to within end of last row, 1 sc and 2 hdc over end of next row, 1 dc in each st across next square to within last 8 sts before next corner, 1 hdc in each of next 4 sts, 1 sc in each of last 4 sts to corner. Break off and fasten. From wrong side, working through back lp only of each st, sew sleeve seam.

Cuff: Starting at outer edge of cuff with C and size E (F, G) crochet hook, make a chain to fit (without stretching) along lower edge of sleeve; being careful not to twist chain, join with sl st to first ch to form a circle. *Rnd 1:* Ch 1, 1 sc in same ch as joining, 1 sc in each ch around. Join with sl st to first sc. *Rnd 2 and 3:* Ch 1, 1 st in same sc as joining and in each sc around. Join. At end of last rnd, break off and fasten. Attach D to joining. Break off and attach colors as needed. Working same as Rnd 2, work stripes as follows:

3 rnds D, 3 rnds G, 3 rnds E, 3 rnds H, 3 rnds F. Break off and fasten. From wrong side, sew last rnd of cuff to lower edge of sleeve, matching underarm seams with joining of rnds. Turn cuff up.

Second Sleeve: Work to correspond with First Sleeve, reversing color arrangement of squares.

After finishing the granny square sleeves, place them in the armholes with sleeve right side against wrong side of jacket; match underarm seams and center of sleeve cap with shoulder line. Pin in place, either easing in the sleeve cap or stretching it slightly as needed to fit. Slipstitch sleeve edge to jacket, being careful that stitches do not show through on fabric's right side.

STRIPED HAT

Directions are given for hat to fit all sizes.
MATERIALS: Bucilla Bear Brand Win-Knit (2 oz. balls): 1 ball each Yellow (A), Bermuda (B), Dusty Rose (C), Spearmint (D), Violite (E) and Fireball (F); crochet hook, Size H, *or any size hook which will obtain stitch gauge below.*
GAUGE: 4 sc = 1″; 9 rnds = 2″.
DIRECTIONS: *Rnd 1:* Starting at center top with A, ch 5. Join with sl st to form ring; ch 1, 6 sc in ring. Do not join rnds; mark beg of each rnd. *Rnd 2:* 2 sc in each sc around—12 sc. *Rnd 3:* * sc in next sc, 2 sc in next sc; rpt from * around—18 sc. Break off A; attach B. *Rnd 4:* With B, * sc in each of next 2 sc, 2 sc in next sc; rpt from * around—6 sc increased. *Rnd 5:* Sc in next sc, * 2 sc in next sc, sc in each of next 3 sc; rpt from * around, ending with sc in last 2 sc—30 sc. *Rnd 6:* Increasing 6 sc evenly spaced around, sc in each sc around—36 sc. Break off B; attach C. Hereafter, break off and attach colors as needed. *Rnds 7, 8 and 9:* With C, increasing 6 sc evenly spaced on each rnd, sc in each sc around—54 sc on last rnd. Change to D. *Rnd 10:* With D, being careful not to have incs fall directly above previous incs, sc in each sc, increasing 6 sc evenly spaced around—60 sc. *Rnd 11:* Continuing with D, sc in each sc around. *Rnd 12:* Rpt Rnd 10—66 sc. Change to E. *Rnds 13, 14 and 15:* With E, rpt Rnds 11, 10 and 11—78 sc. Change to F. *Rnds 16, 17 and 18:* With F, work sc in each sc around. Change to A. Continuing to work even, same as last 3 rnds, and using colors in the same sequence as before, work 3 rnds of each color once more. At end of last rnd sl st in each of next 3 sc. Break off and fasten.

Color photo on page 142

DAISY RUG

Directions are given for rug to measure approximately 42" × 60".

MATERIALS: Coats & Clark's Craft & Rug Yarn, 3 Ply (4 oz. skeins): 7 skeins Skipper Blue (A), 4 skeins each White (B) and Yellow (C); crochet hook, Size I, *or any size hook which will obtain the stitch gauge below.*

GAUGE: 4 sc = 1½"; 4 rows = 1¼". Each square with border = 18" × 18".

Square (Make 6): Row 1: With A, starting at lower edge, ch 41 to measure 15½", sc in 2nd ch from hook, sc in each ch across—40 sc. Ch 1, turn. *Row 2 (right side):* Sc in each sc across. Ch 1, turn. *Rows 3 through 6:* Rpt Row 2. Ch 1, turn. *Row 7:* Sc in each of first 9 sc, *insert hook in next sc and draw up a loop, drop A to front of work (wrong side), pick up B and draw a loop through the 2 loops on hook—color change made;* with B, work sc in each of next 7 sc, *draw up a loop in next sc, drop B to front of work (wrong side); with a new strand of A, draw a loop through the 2 loops on hook—another color change made;* with A, sc in each sc to end of row. Ch 1, turn. Working 1 sc in each sc throughout and always changing color in last sc of each color group, follow Chart back and forth from Row 8 to end of Row 48.

Note: When working from right side, follow Chart from right to left; when working from wrong side, follow Chart from left to right. Use a separate strand for each section on design; always drop ends of yarn and colors not in use on wrong side of work. When square is completed, cut all strands and darn in ends on wrong side.

Square Border: Rnd 1: With right side facing attach A to first ch on lower edge; working

along opposite side of starting chain, make 3 sc in same ch where yarn was attached, sc in each of next 38 ch, 3 sc in corner ch; working along ends of rows, skip first row, sc in end st of each of next 4 rows, (sk next row, sc in end st of each of next 4 rows) 9 times; 3 sc in first sc on last row, sc in each of next 38 sc, 3 sc in end sc; work along next side edge to correspond with opposite edge. Join with sl st to first sc—164 sc. Cut yarn and fasten. *Rnd 2:* From right side, attach C to first sc after 3-sc group at any corner, ch 1, sc in same sc, sc in each sc around, making 3 sc in center st of each corner group. Join with sl st to first sc. *Rnd 3:* Ch 1, sc in same sc as joining, continue same as for Rnd 2. Join. *Rnd 4:* Ch 1, sc in same sc as joining; making 3 hdc in center st of each corner group, sc in each sc around. Join. Cut yarn and fasten.

To Join Squares: Arrange squares in 2 rows of 3 squares each, being careful to have top row of each square at top edge. With a large-eyed tapestry needle and C, working through back loop only of each sc, from right side, sew squares together using an overcast st from corner to corner, matching corner sts.

Outer Border: Rnd 1: With right side facing (entire border is worked from right side), attach C to center hdc of 3-hdc group at any corner of rug, ch 1, 3 sc in same st, sc in each st across same square to next seam, ending with hdc in first hdc of corner group, hdc in next seam, hdc in corner hdc of next square, sc in

DAISY RUG CHART

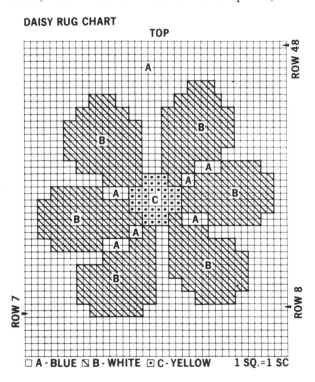

□ A - BLUE ◨ B - WHITE ⊡ C - YELLOW   1 SQ. = 1 SC

next hdc; continue in this manner all around rug, making 3 sc in center st of each rug corner. Join with sl st to first sc. *Rnds 2, 3 and 4:* Ch 1, sc in same sc as joining; making 3 sc in center st of each corner group, sc in each sc around. At end of Rnd 4, cut yarn and fasten. *Rnd 5:* With A, work same as Rnd 2 of Square Border. Cut yarn and fasten.

Scalloped Edging: Rnd 1: Attach A to center sc of upper right corner group; working along long edge of rug, ch 4, in same st make (dc and ch 1) 3 times; ** sk next 2 sc, sc in each of next 3 sc, * ch 1, sk next 2 sc, in *next sc make (dc and ch 1) 3 times*—3 DC SHELL MADE; sk next 2 sc, sc in each of next 3 sts, rpt from single * across to next corner, ending with ch 1; *in center st of corner group make (dc and ch 1) 4 times*—4-DC SHELL MADE FOR CORNER; now rpt from ** around, ending last rpt with ch 1. Join with sl st to 3rd ch of ch-4. *Rnd 2:* Ch 3, dc in next sp, dc in next dc, 3 dc in next corner sp, (dc in next dc, dc in next sp) twice; sk next sc, sc in next sc, * sk next sc, dc in next sp, dc in next dc, dc in next sp, 3 dc in next dc, dc in next sp, dc in next dc, dc in next sp, sk next sc, sc in next sc; rpt from * across to within next corner shell; (dc in next sp, dc in next dc) twice; 3 dc in corner sp, (dc in next dc, dc in next sp) twice; sk next sc, sc in next sc; continue in this manner around, ending with dc in last ch-1 sp. Join with sl st to top of ch-3. Cut yarn and fasten. *To Block:* Place rug on a padded surface wrong side up. Cover with a damp cloth and steam lightly with a warm iron; do not press. Allow to dry completely.

ROUND PLACE MAT

MATERIALS: Coats & Clark's Craft & Rug Yarn: One 4-ounce skein Village Blue; "Boye" plastic crochet hook, Size J, *or any size hook which will obtain the stitch gauge below.*
GAUGE: 3 sc = 1"; 5 rows = 2".
DIRECTIONS: Ch 4, join with sl st. *Rnd 1:* 6 sc in ring. *Rnd 2:* 2 sc in each sc (12 sc). *Rnd 3:* * 1 sc in first st, 2 sc in 2nd st, rpt from * (18 sc). *Rnd 4:* * 1 sc in each of 2 sc, 2 sc in next sc, rpt from * (24 sc). *Rnd 5:* * 1 sc in each of 3 sc, 2 sc in next sc, rpt from * (30 sc.) *Rnds 6 to 8:* Inc 6 sc evenly (48 sc). *Rnd 9:* * ch 3, skip 1 st, sc in next st, rpt from *—24 lps. *Rnd 10:* 3 sc in each lp (72 sc). *Rnd 11:* Sc. *Rnd 12:* Inc 6 sc evenly (78 sc). *Rnd 13 to 18:* Inc 6 sc evenly (114 sc). *Rnd 19:* Ch 3, sk 2 sc, sc in next st, rpt from * (38 lps). *Rnd 20:* 3 sc in each lp. *Rnd 21:* Sl st to center st of 1st lp, * ch 4, sc in center st of next lp, rpt from *. *Rnd 22:* 4 sc in each lp.

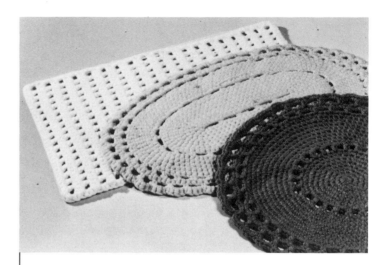

RECTANGULAR PLACE MAT
MATERIALS:
Coats & Clark's Craft & Rug Yarn: one 4-ounce skein Eggshell; "Boye" plastic crochet hook, size J.
DIRECTIONS: Ch 37. *Row 1:* Dc in 5th ch from hook, * ch 1, sk 1 ch, dc in next ch, rpt from *, ch 1, turn. *Row 2:* Sc in first st, * sc in ch sp, sc in dc, rpt from *, 2 sc in last ch sp, ch 4, turn. *Row 3:* Dc in 3rd sc, * ch 1, sk 1 sc, dc in next sc, rpt from *, ch 1, turn. *Repeat Rows 2 and 3 until 19 rows of open pattern are completed.*
Edging: Work Row 2 once, 4 sc in last sp (corner). Continue along long edge, 1 sc in next sc, 2 sc in open sps. Rpt for other 2 corners, short and long sides, join with sl st.

OVAL PLACE MAT
MATERIAL: Coats & Clark's Craft & Rug Yarn: One 4-ounce skein Mid Orange; "Boye" plastic crochet hook, Size J.
DIRECTIONS: Ch 24. *Rnd 1:* Sc in 8th ch from hook, * ch 3, sk 3, ch 1, sc in next sc, rpt from * to end (5 lps). *Rnd 2:* 5 sc in 1st lp, 4 sc in each of next 3 lps, 10 sc in next lp, 4 sc in each of 3 lps, 5 sc in last lp (44 sc). *Rnd 3:* Sc, increasing 2 sc at each end (48 sc). *Rnd 4:* Inc 3 sc at each end (54 sc). *Rnds 5 to 9:* Inc 3 sc at each end (84 sc). *Rnd 10:* * ch 3, sk 2 sc, 1 sc in next st, rpt from * (28 lps). *Rnd 11:* 4 sc in each lp (112 sc). *Rnds 12 and 13:* Sc in each sc. *Rnds 14 and 15:* Inc 3 sc at each end (124 sc). *Rnd 16:* * ch 3, sk 2 sc, 1 sc in next sc, rpt from * around, skipping only 1 sc instead of 2 sc 10 times on each curve—48 lps. *Rnd 17:* 3 sc in each lp. *Rnd 18:* 2 sl sts to center of 1st lp, * ch 3, 1 sc in center st of next lp; rpt from *. *Rnd 19:* 3 sc in each lp. *Rnd 20:* 2 sl sts to center of next lp, *ch 4, 1 sc in center st of next lp. *Rnd 21:* 4 sc in each lp.

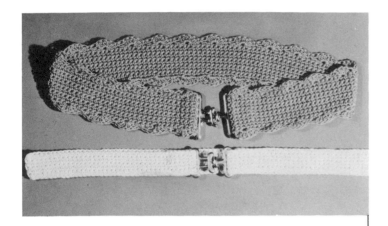

BELTS

MATERIALS: Crochet cotton (Lily Double-Quick 8 Cord Cable Twist), 1 skein (115 yds.) each for man's and woman's belts; crochet hook, size 00; interlocking belt buckle.

GENERAL DIRECTIONS: Ch st to waist length, plus 1″ to turn under. Sc to desired width (man's belt is 6 rows wide; woman's is 10.)

MAN'S BELT

Finish off ends and bottom edge with sl st. To sl st, insert hook from the front through the two top threads of st. Thread over, draw through st and lp on crochet hook.

WOMAN'S BELT

Finish off top and bottom edge with sh st. To sh st, * sc sk next 2 sts, 5 dc in next st, sk next 2 sts. Repeat from * to end of belt.

Note: If belts stretch, simply increase turn under.

HANGER COVERS AND SACHET SACKS

Directions are given for dress hanger, skirt hanger and sachets to match.

MATERIALS: J. & P. Coats "Knit-Cro-Sheen," one ball Robinette (A) and two balls Ecru (B); J. & P. Coats deluxe six-strand embroidery floss, one skein each Treeleaf Green and Dk. Orange; crochet hook, No. 7, *or any size hook which will obtain the stitch gauge below;* wooden dress hanger, 1″ wide; skirt hanger, 1¼″ wide and 9″ long; lining material; sachet filling.

GAUGE: 7 dc = 1″; 3 rows = 1″.

DRESS HANGER

Starting at narrow edge, with A, ch 19. *Row 1:* Dc in 4th ch from hook and in each ch across—17 dc, counting ch-3 as 1 dc. Ch 3, turn. *Row 2:* Dc in each dc across and in top of ch-3. Ch 3, turn. Repeat Row 2 until piece, when tried on hanger

(slightly stretched), reaches from end to end. Break off and fasten. Cover hanger with lining material and sew at upper edge. Fold crocheted cover over lined dress hanger having edges at upper edge. Crochet edges together as follows: Attach A to corner of fold at lower narrow edge, working through both thicknesses of edges throughout, ch 1, sc in same place, then sc evenly along narrow edge to next corner; make 2 sc in corner, ch 3 for picot, sc in same corner; * sc in next 4 end sts, ch 3, sc in last sc used. Rpt from * to next corner, make picot at corner; make 2 sc in same corner; sc evenly along other narrow edge. Break off and fasten.

Sachet: Starting at center, with B ch 4. Join with a sl st to form a ring. *Rnd 1:* Make 7 sc in ring. Join with a sl st to first sc. *Rnd 2:* Ch 1, 2 sc in same sc as joining and in each sc around—14 sc. Join to first sc. *Rnd 3:* Ch 1, *2 sc in same sc as joining—sc increased;* * sc in next sc, 2 sc in next sc. Repeat from * around, end with sc in last sc. Join to first sc. Being careful to keep work flat and increasing 7 sc evenly spaced, sc in each sc around until sachet measures 4″ in diameter. Join. *Next Rnd:* * Ch 2 for picot, sc in next 2 sc, repeat from * around. At end of last rnd, break off and fasten.

Flower (Make 8): Starting at center, with A ch 3. Join with a sl st to form a ring. * Ch 3, sc in ring—1 petal made. Repeat from * until 5 petals are completed. Join with a sl st in base of first ch-3 petal. Break off and fasten, leaving a strand to sew flower on sachet. Sew flowers to sachet as shown in photo.

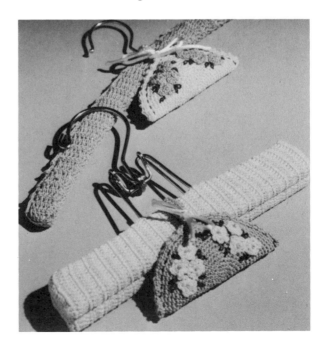

Embroidery: Use four strands throughout. With orange embroider French Knots in center of each flower and with green embroider Lazy Daisy Stitch for leaves (*See* **BASIC EMBROIDERY STITCHES**, page 228). Cut lining piece ½" larger than sachet. Fold in half. Sew edges together, leaving a small opening for sachet filling. Stuff with sachet filling and sew opening together. Fold crocheted sachet over lining. Sew edges together with green running stitches.

Loop: With double strands of B, make a chain to measure 3½". *Row 1:* Sc in 2nd ch from hook and in each ch across. Ch 1, turn. *Rows 2-3:* Sc in each sc across. Break off and fasten. Sew ends of loop to center at top edge of sachet. Loop around hook of dress hanger and tack in place.

SKIRT HANGER

Starting at narrow edge with B, ch 27. *Row 1:* Dc in 4th ch from hook, dc in each remaining ch—25 dc, counting ch-3 as 1 dc. Ch 3, turn. *Row 2:* Dc in each dc across and in top of ch-3. Repeat Row 2 until piece, when tried on one wooden bar of skirt hanger (slightly stretched), reaches from end to end. Break off and fasten. Work another piece for second wooden bar. Cover wooden bars with lining material and sew at upper edge. Fold a crocheted cover over a lined wooden bar, having edges at upper edge; sew seam. Complete other bar in same way.

Sachet: Using A, complete same as Dress Hanger Sachet. Using B, make flowers same as for other sachet. Embroider same as other sachet. Tack in place.

Color photo on page 142

MULTICOLORED PLANT POT COVER

Use leftover 2-ply knitting worsted in a variety of colors (we used ten colors) and stitches,

figuring on a gauge of 9 stitches to measure 2" with a size E crochet hook, *or any size hook which will obtain that gauge.*

DIRECTIONS: Make a row of chain stitches equal to the circumference at the bottom of the flower pot. Add as many rows of single, double and triple crochet as necessary for the height of your pot, changing colors and stitches with every row and increasing 8 to 10 to 12 stitches per row to accommodate the increase in the pot size from bottom to top. In the last row, make a picot every 8 to 10 stitches for a pretty top edge. Sew band short edges together and slip over pot.

SHUTTER INSERT AND LATTICE CURTAIN

MATERIALS: Coats & Clark's O.N.T. "Speed-Cro-Sheen" mercerized cotton (100 yd. balls) Nu Ecru; crochet hook, No. ¹/₀ (zero), *or any size hook which will obtain the stitch gauge below.*

GAUGE: Large Motif measures 2¾" in diameter and requires 6¾ yds.

Fill-In Motif measures 1¼" in diameter and requires 1¾ yds.

DIRECTIONS: *Large Motif:* Starting at center, ch 6. Join with sl st to form ring. *Rnd 1:* Ch 1, 12 sc in ring. Join with sl st to first sc. *Rnd 2:* Ch 3, sk joining, * hdc in next sc, ch 1. Rpt from * around. Join last ch 1 to 2nd ch of ch-3—12 sps. *Rnd 3:* Sl st in next ch, ch 5, dc in same place where sl st was made, * sk next hdc, in next ch, make dc, ch 2 and dc. Rpt from * around. Join to

3rd ch of ch-5—12 sps. *Rnd 4:* Ch 1, make 5 sc in each ch-2 sp around. Join to first sc—60 sc. Break off, leaving a 6″ end.

First Row of Large Motifs: Make as many Large Motifs as required to obtain the desired width measurement. With the 6″ end of each motif at center right and right side facing, place 2 motifs side by side on a flat surface. Using the 6″ end of one motif for sewing, sew the center 3 sc of this 5-sc group to center 3 sc of corresponding 5-sc group of next motif. Join remaining motifs in same way.

Second Row of Large Motifs: Having the same number of Large Motifs as on First Row, work same as for First Row of Large Motifs. Leaving two 5-sc groups free between joinings of motifs on each row, join Second Row of Motifs to First Row of Motifs. Make and join as many Large Motif Rows as required to obtain the desired length measurement, then make and join 1 more motif row (first row will be used for casing).

Fill-In Motif: Starting at center, ch 5. Join with sl st to form ring. *Rnd 1:* Ch 1, 8 sc in ring. Join to first sc. *Rnd 2:* Ch 4, sk joining, * hdc in next sc, ch 2. Rpt from * around. Join last ch 2 to 2nd ch of ch-4. Break off. Now sew Fill-In Motif in open space between 4 Large Motifs as follows: Leaving one 5-sc group on Large Motif free and 2 sps on Fill-In Motif free between joinings, with right side facing, join an hdc of Fill-In Motif to corresponding sc on 4 Large Motifs. Make and join a Fill-In Motif for each space between Large Motifs. For *curtain,* turn top row of Large Motifs to wrong side for Casing; leaving sides open, sew in place. For *shutter insert,* tape or tack in place on back of shutter panel.

EASY-TO-DO EDGINGS

MATERIALS *(for all edgings):* Mercerized Crochet Cotton, Size 20; steel crochet hook, No. 12, *or any size hook which will obtain the measurement given below.*

Width of Edgings: A, C and D are ¾″ wide; B is ⅞″; E is 1¼″; F is 1⅛″. Block each edging to measurement.

Edging A (suitable for straight or curved edges): Row 1: Ch 4, in 4th ch from hook make 2 dc, ch 3 and 3 dc. Ch 5; turn. *Row 2:* Sk first 3 dc, in next ch-3 loop make 3 dc, ch 3 and 3 dc; ch 2, sk 2 dc, dc in top of next chain. Ch 1; turn. *Row 3:* Sc in first dc, 2 sc in next ch-2 sp, sc in next 3 dc, sl st in ch-3 loop, ch 3, in same ch-3 loop make 2 dc, ch 3 and 3 dc. Ch 5; turn. Rpt Rows 2 and 3

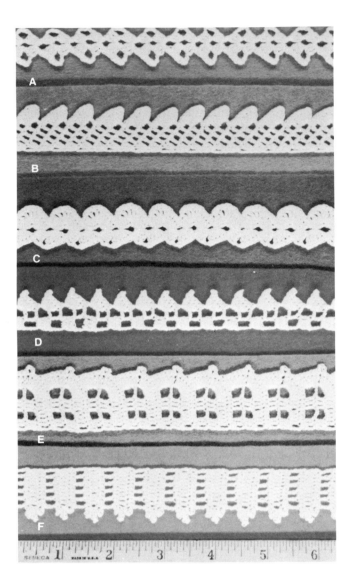

for desired length, ending with last sc of Row 3. Break off and fasten.

Edging B (suitable for straight or curved edges): Row 1: Ch 12, dc in 6th ch from hook, (ch 1, sk next ch, dc in next ch) twice; ch 1, sk 1 ch, 3 dc in last ch. Ch 4; turn. *Row 2:* 2 dc in first dc, ch 1, sk 1 dc, dc in next dc, (ch 1, dc in next dc) 3 times; 5 dc in next chain loop. Ch 1; turn. *Row 3:* Sc in first 6 dc, sc in next ch-1 sp, sl st in next dc, ch 4, dc in next dc, (ch 1, dc in next dc) twice; ch 1, sk next dc, 3 dc in turning ch-4 loop. Ch 4; turn. Rpt Rows 2 and 3 for desired length, ending with the sl st on Row 3. Break off and fasten.

Edging C (suitable for straight or curved edges): Row 1: Ch 6; join with sl st to form ring, ch 3, in ring make 4 dc, ch 3 and 6 dc. Ch 1; turn. *Row 2:* Sk first dc, sc in next 5 dc, ch 3, in ch-3 loop make 4 dc, ch 3 and 4 dc; in next dc make (dc and ch 1) 4 times; sk next 3 dc, sl st in next ch-3 loop. Ch 1; turn. *Row 3:* (Sc in next ch-1 sp, sc in next dc) 4 times; sc in next 4 dc, ch 3, in next ch-3 loop make 4 dc, ch 3 and 4 dc; dc in next dc, sk next 3 dc, dc in top of next ch-3. Ch 1; turn. Rpt Rows 2 and 3 for desired length, ending with Row 2. Ch 1; turn. *Last Row:* (Sc in next ch-1 sp, sc in next dc) 4 times; sc in next 4 dc, 3 sc in next ch-3 loop, sc in next 4 dc, sc next ch-3 loop. Break off and fasten.

Edging D (suitable for straight or curved edges): Row 1: Ch 11, dc in 8th ch from hook, dc in next 3 ch. Ch 5; turn. *Row 2:* Sk first 3 dc, dc in next dc, ch 2, dc in 3rd ch of next chain loop, 4 more dc in same chain loop. Ch 3; turn. *Row 3:* Sl st in first dc to form pc, sc in next 4 dc, ch 5, sk next ch-2 sp, dc in dc, 3 dc in turning ch-5 loop. Ch 5; turn. Rpt Rows 2 and 3 for desired length, ending with last sc of Row 3. Break off; fasten.

Edging E (suitable only for straight edges): Row 1: Ch 13, dc in 4th ch from hook, dc in next ch, ch 2, sk 2 ch, dc in next 3 ch, ch 2, sk 2 ch, dc in last ch. Ch 5; turn. *Row 2:* Sk first ch-2 sp, dc in next 3 dc, ch 2, dc in next 2 dc, dc in top of turning chain. Ch 3; turn. *Row 3:* Sk first dc, dc in next 2 dc, 2 dc in ch-2 sp, dc in next 3 dc, 7 dc in turning chain sp, dc in top of end dc of Row 1, 5 dc along same end dc to complete scallop. Ch 1; turn. *Row 4:* Sc in first 5 dc, in next dc make sc, ch 4 and sc for pc, sc in next 14 dc, sc in top of turning chain. Ch 3; turn. *Row 5:* Sk first sc, working in back loop only of each sc, dc in next 2 sc, ch 2, sk 2 sc, dc in next 3 sc, ch 2, sk 2 sc, dc in next dc. Ch 5; turn. *Row 6:* Sk first ch-2 sp, dc in next 3 dc, ch 2, dc in next 2 dc, dc in top of turning chain. Ch 3; turn. *Row 7:* Sk first dc, dc in next 2 dc, 2 dc in ch-2 sp, dc in next 3 dc, 7 dc in turning chain sp, dc in top of end dc on next row, 5 dc along same end dc, sk next 2 free sc on previous scallop, sl st in back loop of next sc to complete scallop. Ch 1; turn. Rpt Rows 4 through 7 for desired length, ending with Row 4. Break off and fasten.

Edging F (suitable only for straight edges): Row 1: Ch 12, sc in 2nd ch from hook and in each of next 10 ch. Ch 4; turn. *Row 2: Sc in first sc, ch 6, sc in last sc made, ch 4, sc in last sc made— 3-pc loop made; dc in next 10 sc. Ch 1; turn. Row 3:* Sc in 10 dc, sc in top of 3-pc loop. Ch 4; turn. *Row 4:* Sk first 2 sc, dc in next sc, (ch 1, sk next sc, dc in next sc) 4 times. Ch 1; turn. *Row 5:* Sc in first dc, (sc in next ch-1 sp, sc in next dc) 4 times; 2 sc in turning ch-4 loop. Ch 4; turn. Rpt Rows 2 through 5 for desired length, ending with Row 3. Break off and fasten.

COVERS FOR HANGERS

MATERIALS: Bucilla machine-washable Multi-Craft (2 oz. skeins): 1 skein (35 yds. will make one hanger); crochet hook, Size K, *or any size hook which will obtain the stitch gauge below;* wooden clothing hanger; double sticking tape.

GAUGE: 8 sc = 3".

DIRECTIONS: At narrow end, ch 8 to measure 3½". *Row 1:* Sc in 2nd ch from hook, sc in each ch across—7 sc. Ch 1, turn. *Row 2:* WORKING IN THE BACK LOOPS ONLY, sc in each sc across—7 sc. Ch 1, turn. Rpt Row 2 until piece (when slightly stretched) is same length as hanger. Fasten off. Pass hook through exact center of piece. Sew narrow ends; then sew long edges tog. Wind hook with double sticking tape. Starting at end of hook, wind yarn evenly over taped hook; fasten end to crochet at base of hook.

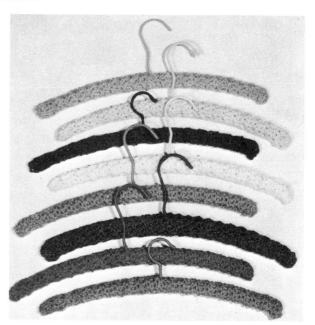

CARTRIDGE BAG

Bag measures 10" across and approximately 18" around.

MATERIALS: Rug Yarn: 8 ozs. of desired color; crochet hook, Size J, *or any size hook which will obtain stitch gauge below;* one matching zipper, 7" long; 2 circles of buckram, each 5½" in diameter.

GAUGE: 5 sts = 2".

End Circle (Make 2): Start at center, ch 4. Join with sl st to form ring. *Rnd 1:* 8 sc in ring. Do not join rnds, but carry a contrasting color strand up between last and first st of each rnd to indicate beg of rnds. *Rnd 2:* 2 sc in each sc around—16 sc. *Rnd 3:* * Sc in next sc, *2 sc in*

next sc—INC MADE; rpt from * around—8 incs made. *Rnd 4:* Sc in each sc around—24 sc. *Rnd 5:* * Sc in each of next 2 sc, 2 sc in next sc; rpt from * around—32 sc. *Rnd 6:* Rpt Rnd 4. *Rnd 7:* Inc 8 sc evenly spaced around, sc in each sc—40 sc. *Rnd 8:* Inc 4 sc evenly spaced around, sc in each sc—44 sc. Sl st in each of next 3 sc. Break off and fasten. Sew a buckram circle to wrong side of each end circle, leaving top edge of crochet free.

Main Section: Start at one side edge, ch 45; this chain should fit around outer edge of end circle. *Row 1 (right side):* Sc in 2nd ch from hook and in each ch across—44 sc. Ch 1, turn. *Row 2:* Sc in first sc, * ch 1, draw up a lp in each of next 2 sc, yarn over hook and draw through all 3 lps on hook; rpt from * across to within last sc, ch 1, sc in last sc. Ch 1, turn. *Row 3:* Sc in first sc, ch 1, draw up a lp in each of next 2 ch-1 sps, yo and draw through all 3 lps on hook, * ch 1, draw up a lp in same sp as last lp of last st, draw up a lp in next ch-1 sp, yo and draw through all 3 lps on hook; rpt from * across, end with ch 1, sc in last sc. Ch 1, turn. Rpt last row until length is 10" from beg or for desired length. Break off and fasten.

To Join End Circles: With wrong sides of a circle and main section together, pin starting chain edge of Main Section along outer edge of circle; with circle toward you and working through back lp only of each st, sl st through both edges, matching sts around. Join. Break off and fasten. Join other circle to opposite edge of main section.

Handle (Make 2): Make a chain the desired length of handle. Sl st in 2nd ch from hook and in each ch across; working along opposite side of starting chain, sl st in each ch st across. Break off and fasten.

Finishing: Line bag, if desired. Starting from end circles, sew 1½" seam at each end of top opening. Sew ends of handles firmly to top seam at each end of bag. Sew zipper in top opening, between ends of handles.

"ARBOUR" PLACE MAT AND NAPKIN RING

Directions are given for a Place Mat measuring 11" × 16" and for a Napkin Ring 2" wide and 6¼" around.

MATERIALS: J.&P. Coats Knit-Cro-Sheen for two Mats and 2 Napkin Rings: 4 balls White (250 yds. each); steel crochet hook, No. 6, *or any size hook which will obtain the stitch gauge below.*

GAUGE: 21 sc = 2"; 7 rows = 1".

Note: Be sure to check your gauge before starting.

PLACE MAT:

Starting at a long edge, ch 170 to measure 16½". *Row 1:* Sc in 2nd ch from hook and in each ch across—169 sc. Ch 1, turn. *Row 2:* Sc in each of first 3 sc, * ch 3, skip next 3 sc, dc in next sc, ch 3, skip next 3 sc, sc in each of next 5 sc. Rpt from * across, ending last rpt with sc in each of last 3 sc, instead of 5 sc. Ch 3 to count as 1 dc, turn. *Row 3:* Skip first sc, dc in next sc, * ch 3, sk next sc, sc in next ch-3 sp, sc in next dc, sc in next ch-3 sp, ch 3, sk next sc, dc in each of next 3 sc. Rpt from * across, ending last rpt with dc in each of last 2 sc instead of 3 sc. Ch 3, turn. *Always count ch-3 as 1 dc.* *Row 4:* Sk first dc, dc in next dc, * ch 3, sc in each of next 3 sc, ch 3, dc in each of next 3 dc. Rpt from * across, ending with ch 3, sc in each of next 3 sc, ch 3, dc in next dc, dc in top of turning chain. Ch 1, turn. *Row 5:* Sc in each of first 2 dc, * sc in next ch-3 sp, ch 3, skip next sc, dc in next sc, ch 3, sk next sc, sc in next ch-3 sp, sc in each of next 3 dc. Rpt from * across, ending last rpt with sc in last dc, sc in top of ch-3. Ch 1, turn. *Row 6:* Sc in each of first 3 sc, * 3 sc in next ch-3 sp, sc in next dc, 3 sc in next ch-3 sp, sc in each of next 5 sc. Rpt from * across, ending with sc in each of last 3 sc—169 sc. Ch 1, turn. *Row 7:* Sc in each sc across—169 sc. Ch 6, turn. *Row 8:* Sk first 4 sc, sc in each of next 5 sc, * ch 3, sk next 3 sc, dc in next sc, ch 3, sk next 3 sc, sc in each of next 5 sc. Rpt from *

Color photo on page 142

across, ending with ch 3, sk next 3 sc, dc in last sc. Ch 1, turn. *Row 9:* Sc in first dc, sc in next ch-3 sp, * ch 3, sk next sc, dc in each of next 3 sc, ch 3, sk next sc, sc in next ch-3 sp, sc in next dc, sc in next ch-3 sp. Rpt from * across to within last 5-sc group, ch 3, sk next sc, dc in each of next 3 sc, ch 3, sc in turning chain loop, sc in 3rd ch of same turning chain. Ch 1, turn. *Row 10:* Sc in each of first 2 sc, * ch 3, dc in each of next 3 dc, ch 3, sc in each of next 3 sc. Rpt from * across, ending with sc in each of last 2 sc. Ch 6, turn. *Row 11:* Sk first 2 sc, * sc in next ch-3 sp, sc in each of next 3 dc, sc in next ch-3 sp, ch 3, sk next sc, dc in next sc, ch 3, sk next sc. Rpt from * across, ending with ch 3, skip next sc, dc in last sc. Ch 1, turn. *Row 12:* Sc in first dc, * 3 sc in next sp, sc in each of next 5 sc, 3 sc in next sp, sc in next dc. Rpt from * across, ending with 3 sc in turning chain sp, sc in 3rd ch of same turning chain—169 sc. Ch 1, turn. *Row 13:* Sc in each sc across—169 sc. Ch 1, turn. Rpt last 12 rows (Rows 2 through 13) for pattern until total length is about 11"; ending with Row 7. Do not break off.

Border: Rnd 1: Working along ends of rows, make 3 sc in corner st, work 96 sc evenly spaced along side edge to next corner, 3 sc in corner st, working along opposite side of starting chain, make sc in each of next 168 ch, 3 sc in corner st, make 96 sc evenly spaced along next side edge, 3 sc in next corner st, sc in each of next 168 sc across last row—540 sc. Join with sl st to first sc. *Rnd 2:* Ch 1, sc in same sc as joining, sc in next sc, * ch 4, sl st in top of last sc made—PICOT MADE; sc in each of next 6 sc. Rpt from * around, ending with picot, sc in each of remaining 4 sc. Join to first sc. Fasten off. *Finishing:* Block to measurements.

NAPKIN RING:
Ch 62 to measure 6¼": Having 61 sc on first row, work same as for Place Mat until 12th row has been completed. Do not break off. *Border:* Making 3 sc in each corner, 12 sc along each side edge and 60 sc along each long edge, work same as for Border of Place Mat.
Finishing: Block to measure 2" × 6½": Overlap side edges for ¼" and sew together.

CROCHETED-WOVEN CAP AND SCARF

Directions for cap are given to fit all sizes. Scarf measures 10"×64"; plus fringe.
MATERIALS: Columbia-Minerva Needlepoint & Crewel Yarn (½ oz. skeins): *For Scarf:* 9 skeins Brown (A), 7 skns Coppertone (B), 5 skeins Springrust (C), 4 skeins Rust (D); *For Cap:* 3 skeins each A, B and C, 2 skeins D. Boye crochet hook, Size I, *or any size hook which will obtain the stitch gauge below.*
GAUGE: 2 sps = 1"; 2 rows = 1".
SCARF

With C, ch 46 to measure 11". *Row 1 (right side):* Dc in 6th ch from hook, * ch 1, sk next ch, dc in next ch—sp made; rpt from * across—21 sps, including sp formed by first dc. Ch 4, turn. *Row 2:* Sk first dc, * dc in next dc, ch 1; rpt from * across, end with sk next ch st on turning chain, dc in next ch—21 sps. Ch 4, turn. *Rows 3–4:* Rpt Row 2. At end of last row, break off and fasten; attach B to end of row, ch 4, turn. Always change color in this manner. *Rows 5 through 8:* With B, work same as for Row 2—each 4-row group forms a horizontal stripe. Change to A. Ch 4, turn. Continuing to work same as for Row 2 throughout, work Stripe pat as follows: *Rows 9 through 12:* 4 rows A. Change to D. Ch 4, turn. *Rows 13 through 16:* 4 rows D. Change to A. Ch 4, turn. *Rows 17 through 20:* 4 rows A. Change to B. Ch 4, turn. *Rows 21 through 24:* 4 rows B. Change to C. Ch 4, turn. *Rows 25 through 28:* 4 rows C. Change to B. Ch 4, turn. Rpt last 24 rows (Rows 5 through 28) for Stripe pat 4 more times. Break off and fasten.

Vertical Stripes: Cut 12 strands C, each 85″ long. Continue to cut strands as needed. Hold 4 C strands together; with right side facing, starting at side edge, bring strands up from back to front in first sp on first row; leaving a 7″ length free for fringe, weave strands down and up lengthwise through line of sps along edge of scarf, being careful to keep work flat; leave 7″ length free at other end for fringe. Hold next 4 C strands together and insert from front to back in next sp on first row; leaving 7″ length at each end, weave these strands up and down through sps up lengthwise along 2nd line of sps. Bring next group of 4 C strands from back to front in next sp on first row and weave down and up along next free line of sps as before (this completes 1st stripe). Continuing in this manner, weave 3 rows B strands, 3 rows A strands, 3 rows D strands—center stripe; 3 rows A strands, 3 rows B strands and 3 rows C strands. Using a darning needle, slip 2 of each 4-strand group at each end through crochet edge and knot the 4 strands of yarn close to edge of scarf to secure fringe. Trim fringe evenly.

CAP

Starting at lower edge with B, ch 76 to measure 19″ without stretching. *Rows 1 through 4:* Having 36 sps in each row, with B work same as for first 4 rows of scarf. Break off and fasten. Attach A to end of row, ch 4, turn. *Rows 5 through 8:* With A, rpt Row 2. Break off and fasten.

Vertical Stripes: Cut 4 strands C each about 24″ long. Cut strands as needed. Starting at side edge, with right side facing, bring strands up from back to front in first sp on first row, leaving a 2″ length on wrong side; weave strands lengthwise through first line of sps up to top edge; pass strands over top edge and weave back through sps of next line of sps from top to bottom edge; then over bottom edge and weave through sps along next line of sps up to top edge again. Darn in end of yarn on wrong side and fasten. Darn in free ends at beg of first

row. Cut 4 strands B, each 24″ long, and starting at top edge, * weave 3 rows B down and up through next 3 lines of sps, as before. Continuing in this manner, weave 3 rows A strands; 3 rows D strands, 3 rows A strands, 3 rows B strands, 3 rows C strands; rpt from * around, ending with 3 rows B. Sew side edges together.

Lower Edge Band: Rnd 1: With right side facing, working along lower edge, attach C to first st of starting chain, sc in same st, sc in each of next 72 sts. Join with sl st to first sc—73 sc. *Next 3 rnds:* Ch 1, sc in same sc as joining, sc in each sc around. Join to first sc. At end of last rnd, break off and fasten.

Top: Rnd 1: Starting at center with D, ch 4. Join with sl st to form ring. Ch 1, 8 sc in ring. Do not join rnds; mark end of each rnd. *Rnd 2:* 2 sc in each sc around—16 sc. *Rnd 3:* * Sc in next sc, 2 sc in next sc; rpt from * around. *Rnd 4:* * Sc in each of next 2 sc in next sc; rpt from * around—32 sc. *Rnd 5:* * Sc in each of next 3 sc, 2 sc in next sc; rpt from * around—8 incs made. Being careful not to have incs fall directly above incs of previous rnd, working in sc's continue to inc 8 sc evenly spaced around each rnd until there are 72 sc. *Next 2 Rnds:* Sc in each sc around. At end of last rnd, sl st in next sc. Break off and fasten. With a darning needle and D, sew top edge of stripe section to outer edge of top.

EVENING BAG

MATERIALS: Jacmore 3-Ply Lamé, 4 Balls; Jacmore Sew-On 7½″ bag frame; crochet hook, Size G; lining material.

GAUGE: 3 groups = 2½″; 4 rows = 2¼″

DIRECTIONS: Use 2 strands of Lamé held tog throughout. Ch 35 to measure 8″. *Row 1:* Yarn over hook, draw up a ¾″ loop in 4th ch from hook, yarn over, draw up a ¾" loop in same ch, yarn over and draw through all 5 loops on hook, ch 1 to fasten—puff st made; ch 1, make a puff st in same ch where last puff st was made, * skip 2 ch, in next ch make puff st, ch 1 and puff st—group made. Rpt from * across ending with dc in last ch—11 groups made. Ch 3, turn. *Row 2:* * Make a group in ch-1 sp of next group below. Rpt from * across ending with dc in top of ch-3. Ch 3, turn. Rpt Row 2 until 24 rows in all have been made (about 13"). End off. Fold piece in half and, starting at fold, sew side seams tog leaving seam partially open at each side for frame sides. Mount on frame. Make and sew in lining.

Color photo on page 142

BAG AND CAP

Directions for cap are given to fit all sizes. Bag measures 8" wide by 6½" deep.
MATERIALS: Columbia-Minerva "Amy II" (1 oz. skeins): 1 skein Bone (A); Nantuk knitting worsted 4-ply (2 oz. skeins): 1 skein each Plum (B), Black (C), Beige (D), Cranberry (E), Dark Red (F); crochet hook, size H, *or any size hook which will obtain the stitch gauge below.*
GAUGE: 13 sts = 4"; 15 rows = 4".
BAG
Start top edge of front with F, ch 26. *Row 1 (right side):* Sc in 2nd ch from hook, sc in each ch across—25 sc. Ch 1, turn. *Note:* Ch 1 and turn at end of each row unless otherwise specified. *Row 2:* Sc in each sc across. *Row 3:* Rpt last row. Break off and fasten; attach E. Ch 1, turn. *Row 4:* With E, rpt Row 2. Break off and fasten; attach F. Hereafter, break off and attach colors as needed. *Rows 5 through 9:* Working same as for Row 2, make 1 row F, 2 rows E and 2 rows B. Break off and fasten. Holding 1 strand each of A

and D tog, attach to end of last row. Ch 1, turn. *Rows 10 through 13:* With double strand work same as Row 2. Break off and fasten; attach B. Ch 1, turn. *Rows 14 and 15:* With B, rpt Row 2. *Rows 16, 17 and 18:* Continuing to work as for Row 2, make 1 row E, 1 row F, 1 row B. Last 18 rows (Rows 1 through 18) form stripe pat. *Row 19:* Work 1 row F. *Rows 20 through 37:* Rpt Rows 2 through 19. *Rows 38 through 51:* Rpt Rows 2 through 15. Break off and fasten. Turn.
Flap: Row 1: Sk first 4 sc on last row, attach E to next sc, ch 1, sc in same st, sc in each of next 16 sc; do not work over rem sts. Keeping in the stripe pat, work 22 more rows over these 17 sc. At end of last row, break off and fasten. *Flap Border:* With right side facing, attach C to end st of first row of flap; working along ends of rows, sc in same end sc, sc in end sc of each of next 21 rows of flap, 3 sc in corner st, sc in each sc across to next corner st, 3 sc in corner st, sc in end sc of each of next 22 rows. Break off and fasten; with 1 strand each of A and D held tog, attach yarn to end of row. Ch 1, turn. *Row 2:* Sc in first sc, (ch 1, sk next sc, sc in next sc) 11 times; ch 1, sc in next corner sc, ch 1, sc in next sc, (ch 1, sk next sc, sc in next sc) 8 times; ch 1, sc in next corner sc, ch 1, sc in next sc (ch 1, sk next sc, sc in next sc) 11 times. Break off and fasten; attach B. Ch 1, turn. *Row 3:* With B, sc in first sc, * working over next ch-1, dc in st directly below, sc in next sc on last row; rpt from * across, making 3 sc in each corner sc and working dc's at each side of corner group in corner sc below—73 sts. Break off and fasten; attach A and D held tog. Ch 1, turn. *Row 4:* Sc in first sc, * ch 1, sk next dc, sc in next sc, ch 1, skipping all dc, work sc and ch 1 in each sc across to within next corner st, sc in corner sc, ch 1, sc in next sc; rpt from * once more; ch 1, work sc and ch 1 in each sc to last sc, sc in last sc. Break off and fasten; attach C. Ch 1, turn. *Row 5:* With C, rpt Row 3—81 sts. Do not break off. Do not turn. With C, sc in end st of each row along main section of bag to starting chain, ch 1 at corner, sl st in each ch across starting chain, ch 1 at corner, sc in end st of each row of bag. Join with sl st to first sc of last row of flap border. Break off and fasten. From wrong side, sew each end of row 3 of flap border to last long row of bag. *Strap:* With C, ch 154 to measure 47". *Row 1:* Sc in 2nd ch from hook, sc in each ch across—153 sc. Break off and fasten; attach A and D held tog. Ch 1, turn. *Row 2:* Sc in first sc, * ch 1, sk next sc, sc in next sc; rpt from * across. Break off and fasten; attach B. Ch 1, turn. *Rows 3, 4*

and 5: Omitting all incs for corners, work same as for Rows 3, 4 and 5 of Flap Border. At end of last row, break off and fasten.

Finishing: Pin pieces to measurements on a padded surface, cover with a damp cloth, allow to dry; do not press. On main section, mark center 5 rows, between starting chain and flap for bottom of bag (first 23 rows form front and last 23 rows [excluding flap] form back of bag). Sew ends of strap to sides of center 5 rows. Fold up front and back sections and pin sides of strap to corresponding edges of back and front, matching number of sts and leaving flap free. With C, start at lower edge of front and working through both thicknesses, sl st side edges of strap and front tog; then continue to sl st in each st along strap only to next side of bag; sl st strap and other side edge of front tog down to bottom portion. Break off and fasten. Join opposite long edge of strap to back section in same manner. Fold flap over front.

CAP

With B, start at center top, ch 7. *Row 1:* 2 sc in 2nd ch from hook, 2 sc in each ch across—12 sc. Ch 1, turn. *Row 2:* Sc in each sc across. Break off and fasten; attach E. Ch 1, turn. *Note:* Ch 1 and turn at end of each row. *Row 3:* With E, 2 sc in each sc across—24 sc. Break off and fasten; attach F. Hereafter, break off and attach colors as needed. *Row 4:* With F, rpt Row 2. *Row 5:* With B, * sc in 1 sc, 2 sc in next sc; rpt from * across—36 sc. *Row 6:* With F, rpt Row 2. *Row 7:* Continuing with F, * sc in each of 2 sc, 2 sc in next sc; rpt from * across—48 sc. *Row 8:* With F, rpt Row 2. *Row 9:* With E, * sc in each of 3 sc, 2 sc in next sc; rpt from * across—60 sc. *Row 10:* With E, rpt Row 2. *Row 11:* With E, * sc in each of 8 sc, 2 sc in next sc; rpt from * across—66 sc. (For a larger than 21½" cap size change last row to: Sc in 4 sc instead of 8 sc, 2 sc in next sc and rpt across.) *Rows 12 through 30:* Working same as for Row 2, work stripe pat as follows: 2 rows B, 4 rows A and D held tog, 2 rows B, 1 row E, 1 row F, 1 row B, 3 rows F, 1 row E, 1 row F, 2 rows E, 1 row B.

Cuff: Row 1: With C, working in the back loop only of each sc, sc in each sc across to last sc, 2 sc in last sc. *Rows 2 through 5:* Work same as for Rows 2 through 5 of Strap.

Finishing: Place cap flat on a padded surface. Cover with a damp cloth and allow to dry; do not press. Sew side edges tog, matching rows and reversing seam on cuff. Turn up cuff.

Tassel: Wind C (or any color) 36 times around a 7" piece of cardboard; tie at one end, cut at opposite end. Wind B tightly several times around tassel, 1" below tied end and tie ends of B tog. With crochet hook attach C to tied end and ch 3; leaving a 6" length for sewing, break off and fasten. Sew tassel to center top of cap.

CIRCLE-ON-CIRCLE RUG

Directions are given for a circular rug approximately 48" in diameter.

MATERIALS: Bucilla Ever-Match Tapestry Wool (100 yd. skein): 12 skeins Brown, 16 skeins Turquoise; crochet hook, Size I, *or any size hook which will obtain the stitch gauge below;* soil retardant spray.

GAUGE: 3 sc = 1"; 3 rnds = 1".

Note: Use 2 strands of a color held tog throughout.

DIRECTIONS: *Center:* With 2 strands of brown held tog, ch 5. Join with sl st to form ring. *Rnd 1:* Ch 1, 9 sc in ring. Join with sl st to first sc. *Rnd 2:* Ch 1, 2 sc in same place where joining sl st was made, 2 sc in each of next 8 sc. Join to first sc—18 sc. *Rnd 3:* Ch 1, sc in same place as joining sl st, *2 sc in next sc*—INC MADE; * sc in next sc, *2 sc in next sc*—ANOTHER INC MADE Rpt from * around. Join—27 sc. *Rnd 4:* Ch 1, sc in joining, sc in next sc, inc in next sc, place a marker in last sc made; * sc in next 2 sc, inc in next sc, place a marker in last sc made. Rpt from * around. Join—36 sc and 9 markers. *Rnd 5:* Ch 1, sc in joining, sc in each sc around. Join—same number of sc as on last rnd. *Rnd 6:* Ch 1, sc in joining, then making an inc in line with each marker, sc in each sc around. Join—9 sc increased. *Rnds 7 and 8:* Rpt Rnd 6—63 sc at end of 8th rnd. *Rnds 9 through 24:* Rpt Rnds 5 through 8 four more times—171 sc at end of Rnd 24. *Rnds 25 and 26:* Rpt Rnds 5 and 6—180 sc. *Rnds 27 and 28:* Rpt Rnd 5 twice—180 sc. Fasten off. Center measures 19″ across.

Large Disk (Make 15): With 2 strands of turquoise held tog, work same as Center until Rnd 7 has been completed—54 sc. Fasten off. Large Disk measures 5″ across. Catching only the 2 center loops of each edge, sew 2 sc of Large Disk securely to any 2 sc of Center. * Sk next 10 sc on Center, sew 2 sc of another Large Disk to next 2 sc on Center. Rpt from * around—15 Large Disks attached with 10 sc bet. Lay out piece so that disks are flat and even around Center. Join all disks by sewing 2 sc of adjoining edges tog.

Small Disk (Make 15): With 2 strands of turquoise ch 5. Join to form ring. *Rnd 1:* Ch 1, 10 sc in ring. Join and fasten off. Small Disk measures 1¼″ across. Place a Small Disk in a triangle formed by 2 Large Disks and edge of Center. Sew in place by sewing 2 sc to Center and 2 sc to each Large Disk. In same way sew a Small Disk in each triangle around Center. Fold each Large Disk in half and mark center sc at outer edge.

Band: Attach 2 strands of brown to back loop on any Large Disk. *Rnd 1:* Ch 1, sc in same place where yarn was attached, working in back loops only, sc in next 2 sc, * ch 16 (to measure 5½″), sc in each of 2 sc before next marked sc, sc in marked sc, sc in next 2 sc. Being sure to keep work flat, rpt from * around ending with ch 16, sc in each of 2 sc preceding first sc. Join—315 sts. *Rnd 2:* Ch 1, sc in joining, sc in each sc and in each ch st around. Join—315 sc. *Rnds 3 and 4:* Ch 1, sc in joining, sc in each sc around. Join—315 sc. *Rnd 5:* Ch 1, sc in joining, sc in next 33 sc, inc in next sc, place a marker in last sc made; * sc in next 34 sc, inc in next sc, place a marker in last sc made. Rpt from * around. Join—324 sc and 9 markers. *Rnds 6, 7 and 8:* Ch 1, sc in joining, then making an inc in line with each marker, sc in each sc around. Join—9 sts increased on each rnd. *Rnd 9:* Ch 1, sc in each sc around. Join—same number of sc as on last rnd. *Rnds 10 through 13:* Rpt Rnds 6 through 9—378 sc on last rnd. Work one rnd even. Fasten off.

Medium Disk (Make 15): With 2 strands of turquoise, ch 5. Join to form ring. *Rnd 1:* Ch 1, 6 sc in ring. Join. *Rnd 2:* Ch 1, 2 sc in each sc. Join—12 sc. Fasten off. Medium Disk measures 1⅞″ across. Place a Medium Disk in a triangle formed by 2 Large Disks and inner edge of Band. Sew in place by sewing 2 sts to Band and

2 sts to each Large Disk. Make 27 Large Disks and sew 2 sc of one disk securely to any sc on outer edge of Band. * Sk next 12 sc on Band, sew 2 sc of another Large Disk to next 2 sc on Band. Rpt from * around—27 Large Disks attached with 12 sc bet. Lay out piece so that disks are flat and even around Band. Join all disks by sewing 2 sc of adjoining edges tog. Make 27 Small Disks. Sew a Small Disk in each triangle formed by 2 Large Disks and outer edge of Band.

Finishing: Press on wrong side through damp cloth. Treat with soil-retardant spray.

Color photo on page 143

RAINBOW RUG

Rug measures approximately 6 feet in diameter.

MATERIALS: Aunt Lydia's Heavy Rug Yarn (70-yard skeins): 1 Navy (A), 2 each Medium Blue (B) and Hemlock (C), 3 Light Avocado (D), 4 each Lavender (E) and Cerise (F), 5 Folly Pink (G), 6 Tangerine (H), 7 Sunset (I), 8 Original Cream (J), Crochet hook Size J, *or any size hook which will obtain stitch gauge below;* large tapestry needle.

GAUGE: 5 joint-sc = 2¾″; 8 rows = 3½″.

Note: To make rug reversible do not crochet over yarn ends after completing each ring of color. Weave ends invisibly thru rows bet ridges.

DIRECTIONS: *First Circle: Rnd 1:* Starting at center with A, ch 2. Work 6 sc in 2nd ch from hook; join with sl st to first sc. *Rnd 2:* Ch 1, 2 sc in each sc; join with sl st to first sc—12 sc. Fasten off.

Note: Start all rem rnds at different place from

previous joining to avoid making seam.
Rnd 3: Turn. With A, 1 sc in any sc, * *(insert hook in last sc worked, yo and draw up a lp, insert hook in next sc, yo and draw up a lp, yo and thru all 3 lps on hook*—JOINT-SC MADE) twice, *1 sc in last sc worked*—1 SC INC MADE; rpt from * 4 times, work 1 joint-sc over last 2 sc, *1 sc in last sc worked*—1 SC INC MADE; join with sl st to first sc—18 sc. Fasten off. *Rnd 4:* Turn. With A, 1 sc in 2nd sc to right of joining-sc, * work 3 joint-sc, *1 sc in last sc worked*—1 SC INC MADE; rpt from * to within 2 sts of start, work 2 joint-sc, *sc in last sc worked*—1 SC INC MADE; join with sl st to first sc—24 sc. Fasten off. *Rnd 5:* Turn. With A, 1 sc in 2nd sc to right of joining-sc, * work 4 joint-sc, *1 sc in last sc worked*—1 SC INC MADE; rpt from * to within 3 sc of start, work 3 joint-sc, 1 sc in last sc worked; join with sl st to first sc—30 sc. Fasten off. *Rnd 6:* Turn. With A, 1 sc in 3rd sc to right of joining-sc, * work 5 joint-sc, *1 sc in last sc worked*—1 SC INC MADE; rpt from * to within 4 sc of start, work 4 joint-sc, 1 sc in last sc worked; join with sl st to first sc—36 sc. Fasten off. *Rnd 7:* Turn. With A, work 1 sc in 3rd sc to right of joining-sc, * work 6 joint-sc, *1 sc in last sc worked*—1 SC INC MADE; rpt from * to within 5 sc of start, work 5 joint-sc, 1 sc in last sc worked; join with sl st to first sc—42 sc. Fasten off. *Rnd 8:* Turn. With B, 1 sc in any sc, work joint-sc around without increasing. Fasten off. Mark for incs on next rnd by placing 6 markers, using safety pins, evenly spaced around circle, making sure you do not place a marker directly over inc of previous rnd. Place markers at base of st, not in the st, to avoid having markers interfere with work. Remove markers after completing rnd. On Rnd 9 place a marker in every 7th st, on Rnd 10 place a marker every 8th st, on Rnd 11 place a marker every 9th st and so on. *Rnd 9:* Turn. With A, 1 sc in first sc after any marked st, * work joint-sc across ending in next marked st, *1 sc in marked st*—1 SC INC MADE; rpt from * around; join with sl st to first sc—48 sc. Fasten off. Place markers for next rnd in every 8th st.
Second Circle: Rnds 1 and 2: With B, rpt Rnd 9 of First Circle twice—60 sc. *Rnd 3:* Rpt Rnd 8 of First Circle—60 sc. *Rnds 4–6:* Rpt Rnd 8 of First Circle 3 times—78 sc. *Rnd 7:* With C rpt Rnd 8 of First Circle—78 sc. *Rnd 8:* With B, rpt Rnd 9 of First Circle—84 sc. Work 7 more circles same as Second Circle in the following sequence: C, D, E, F, G, H, I. Always work Rnd 7 with color of next circle. Work Rnd 8 with color

of previous circle.
Tenth Circle: With color J work same as Second Circle thru Rnd 6. Work Rnds 7 and 8 with color J. Fasten off.
Edging: Turn. With color J sl st in each sc around entire rug; join with sl st to first st. Fasten off.

SWEATER VEST

MATERIALS: Reynolds Lopi Yarn, one package (3.6 ounces) each of colors A, B, C (A—White; B—Dark Gray; C—Medium Gray); crochet hook, Size K *or any size hook which will obtain the stitch gauge below;* tapestry needle.
SIZES: Directions are for size Small. Changes for Medium and Large are in parentheses.
GAUGE: 5 sc = 2″; 2 rows = 1½″.
FINISHED MEASUREMENTS: Shoulder to waist: 16½″ (17½″, 18½″).
DIRECTIONS: *Rectangle:* Make 2. With Color A, ch 78 (82, 86). *Row 1:* One sc in 2nd ch from hook and in each ch across. At end, ch 1; turn. *Rows 2 to 6:* Work only in back lp throughout to make ridge st. 1 sc in each sc across. Ch 1 to turn. Make last lp of last sc in row 6 in Color B. Ch 1, turn. *Rows 7 to 10:* 1 sc in each sc across. Ch 1 to turn. Make last lp of last sc in row 10 in Color C. Ch 1, turn. *Rows 11 to 14:* 1 sc in each sc across. Ch 1, turn. Make last lp of last sc in row 14 in Color B. Ch 1, turn. *Rows 15 and 16:* 1 sc in each sc across. Ch 1 to turn. At end of row 16, break yarn, fasten off. Repeat, to make a second rectangle.
Center Seams: Lay the 2 rectangles side by side

with the right side (row 1) facing you. Thread a yarn needle with Color B and sew the pieces tog with a whip st (see below), matching sts of left side to corresponding sts of right side. Sew 26 (28, 30) sts tog in the back. Sew 19 (21, 23) or desired amount in the front.

Side Seams: Fold garment in half. With Color A and matching sts sew 21 (22, 24) sts tog.

Whip Stitch: Starting on wrong side of left rectangle and working into the first st, sew from back to front. Then, working from front toward back, sew into first st of right rectangle. Working from back towards front, sew into next st of left rectangle. Then working from front towards back, sew into next st of right rectangle.

Color photo on page 143

TUNISIAN PILLOWS

MATERIALS *(for two pillows):* Unger Cozy, 1¾ oz. balls: 3 balls gray, 3 balls bright blue, 1 ball rust; ½ yd. backing fabric; two 16″ pillow forms; iron; blue thread; gray thread; size J afghan hook, *or any size hook which will obtain the stitch gauge below.*

FINISHED SIZE: 16″ × 16″.

GAUGE: 3 sts = 1 inch; 5 rows = 2 inches.

Working color in the tunisian (afghan) stitch: Make a bobbin for each color change on the graph. On first row where color change is shown, draw up a loop of new color, twisting it around old color to avoid holes in work. When working off loops, work old color up to loop of new color, twist yarns and work off loop with matching color. If you have never done color work in crochet, make a sample swatch with color changes to check gauge and tension.

DIRECTIONS: *Pillow 1:* With J afghan hook and gray, ch 48. Work 1 row of tunisian crochet

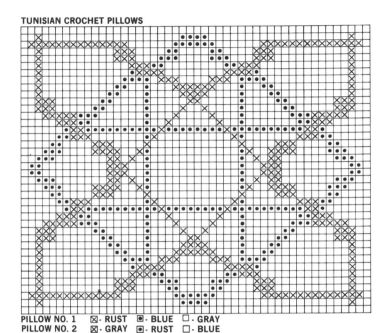

TUNISIAN CROCHET PILLOWS

PILLOW NO. 1 ⊠ - RUST ⊡ - BLUE ☐ - GRAY
PILLOW NO. 2 ⊠ - GRAY ⊡ - RUST ☐ - BLUE

(afghan stitch) in gray (Row 1 in chart), then begin adding colors according to chart. For top row of chart, work single crochets in each loop of previous row instead of working in tunisian stitch.

Pillow 2: Repeat as for Pillow 1, changing colors as noted in chart.

Finishing: Following manufacturer's directions for handling yarn, block pillow top to finished size (16″ × 16″). Cut a 17″ square of backing fabric and iron a ½″ seam allowance under on all edges. With sewing thread to match main color of yarn, blind stitch backing to pillow top, wrong sides together, along 3 edges. Insert pillow form and blind stitch along fourth edge.

BABY'S COAT AND CAP

MATERIALS: Coats & Clark's "Red Heart" Knitting Worsted, 4 Ply (4 oz. "Tangle-Proof" Pull-Out Skns): 12 ozs. White; crochet hook, Size F *or any size hook which will obtain the stitch gauge below;* 3½ yds. white ribbon, ½″ wide.

GAUGE: 9 sts (including ch sts) = 2″; 4 rows = 1¾″.

FINISHED MEASUREMENTS:
BACK WIDTH AT UNDERARM: 12¼″
EACH FRONT WIDTH AT UNDERARM: 6″

COAT

Back: Start at lower edge, ch 70 to measure, without stretching, 17″. *Row 1:* Dc in 6th ch from hook and in each of next 2 ch, * ch 1, sk next ch, *dc in each of next 3 ch*—3-DC GROUP MADE; rpt from * across to within last 2 ch, ch 1, sk next ch, dc in last ch—16 3-dc groups. Mark this row for right side of pat. Ch 3 to count as 1 dc; turn. *Row 2:* 2 dc in first ch-1 sp, * ch 1, sk next 3 dc, 3 dc in next ch-1 sp; rpt from * across to within last 3 dc, ch 1, sk 3 dc, 2 dc in turning chain sp, dc in next ch of same turning chain—17 3-dc groups, counting ch-3 as 1 dc. Ch 4; turn. *Row 3:* Sk first 3 dc, * 3 dc in next ch-1 sp, ch 1; rpt from * across, end with sk last 2 dc, dc in top of turning chain. Last 2 rows form pat. Ch 3; turn. *Rows 4 through 9:* Rpt Rows 2 and 3, 3 times. At end of last row, ch 3; turn. Always count the ch-3 as 1 dc. *Row 10:* Dc in first sp, ch 1, * sk next 3 dc, 3 dc in next ch-1 sp, ch 1; rpt from * across to within turning chain sp, dc in turning chain sp, dc in next ch of same turning chain—1 dc dec at each end. Ch 3; turn. *Row 11:* Sk first 2 dc, * 3 dc in next ch-1 sp, ch 1; rpt from * across; at end of row *do not* ch 1, sk last dc, dc in top of turning chain. Ch 4; turn. *Row 12:* Sk first 4 dc, * 3 dc in next ch-1 sp, ch 1; rpt from * across to within last 3 dc, sk last 3 dc, dc in top of turning chain—15 3-dc groups. Ch 3; turn. *Rows 13 through 21:* Rpt Rows 2 and 3 alternately 3 times, then rpt Rows 10, 11 and 12 once—14 groups on Row 21. *Rows 22 through 25:* Rpt Rows 2 and 3 alternately twice. *Rows 26, 27, and 28:* Rpt Rows 10, 11 and 12—13 groups on last row. Rpt Rows 2 and 3 alternately until total length is about 15″, end with Row 3. At end of last row, ch 21 for sleeve; drop yarn and loop from hook; attach a separate strand to 3rd ch of ch-4 at beg of same row and ch 19 for other sleeve. Break off and fasten this strand. Pick up dropped loop; turn. *Sleeves and Yoke: Row 1:* Dc in 4th ch from hook and in next ch, (ch 1, sk next ch, dc in each of next 3 ch) 4 times; across last row make (ch 1, 3 dc in next sp) 14 times; ch 1, dc in each of first 3 ch on next chain; (ch 1, sk next ch, dc in each of next 3 ch) 4 times—24 dc groups. Ch 4; turn. *Rows 2 through 7:* Rpt Rows 3 and 2 of Back alternately 3 times. There are 23 dc groups on Rows 2, 4 and 6 of sleeves and yoke. Ch 4; turn. *Neck: Row 1:* Work in pat across until the 9th 3-dc group has been completed; ch 3, sl st in next ch-1 sp. Break off and fasten. Sk next 3 ch-1 sps; attach yarn to following ch-1 sp, ch 3, make 3 dc in next ch-1 sp, ch 1 and complete row in pat. Break off and fasten.

Right Front: Start at lower edge, ch 38 to measure about 8½″. *Row 1:* Rpt Row 1 of Back—8 3-dc groups. Mark right side of this row for

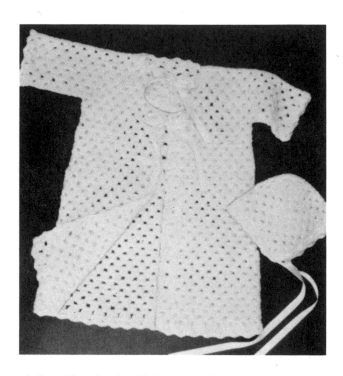

right side of pat. Ch 3; turn. *Rows 2 through 9:* Rpt Rows 2 and 3 of Back alternately 4 times. Ch 3; turn. **THIS IS FRONT EDGE.** *Row 10:* 2 dc in first sp, * ch 1, sk next 3 dc, 3 dc in next ch-1 sp; rpt from * across to within turning chain sp, ch 1, dc in turning chain sp, dc in next ch on same turning chain—1 dc dec at side edge. Ch 3; turn. *Row 11:* Sk first 2 dc, * 3 dc in next ch-1 sp, ch 1; rpt from * across, end with sk last 2 dc, dc in top of turning chain. Ch 3; turn. *Row 12:* 2 dc in first sp, * ch 1, 3 dc in next ch-1 sp; rpt from * across to within last 3 dc, ch 1, sk 3 dc, dc in top of turning chain. Ch 3; turn. *Rows 13 through 18:* 2 dc in first sp, * ch 1, 3 dc in next ch-1 sp; rpt from * across to within last 2 dc, ch 1, sk last 2 dc, dc in top turning chain. Ch 3; turn. End of last row is at side edge. *Row 19:* Dc in first sp, (ch 1, 3 dc in next sp) 7 times; ch 1, sk last 2 dc, dc in top of turning chain. Ch 3; turn. *Row 20:* 2 dc in first sp, (ch 1, 3 dc in next sp) 7 times; do not ch 1, dc in top of turning chain. Ch 4; turn. *Row 21:* Sk first 4 dc, (3 dc in next sp, ch 1) 7 times; sk last 2 dc, dc in top of turning chain. Ch 3; turn. *Rows 22 through 25:* Rpt Rows 2 and 3 twice. Ch 3; turn. *Rows 26, 27, and 28:* Rpt Rows 10, 11 and 12 of Front. Ch 3; turn. Now rpt Row 13 until total length is about 15″, end at side edge. At end of last row, ch 21 for sleeve; turn. *Sleeve and Yoke: Row 1:* Dc in 4th ch from hook and in next ch, (ch 1, sk next ch, dc in next 3 ch) 4 times; ch 1, sk next st, (3 dc in next sp, ch 1) 7 times; sk last 2 dc, dc in top of turning chain. Ch 3; turn. *Rows 2 through 6:* 2 dc in first sp, (ch 1, 3 dc in next ch-1 sp) 11 times; ch 1, dc in top of turning chain. Ch 3; turn. End of last row is at sleeve edge.

Neck: Row 1: 2 dc in first sp, (ch 1, 3 dc in next sp) 9 times; dc in next ch-1 sp. Do not work over rem sts. Ch 3; turn. *Row 2:* Sk first 4 dc, make 3 dc in next sp; complete row in pat. Break off and fasten.

Left Front: Work same as for Right Front until Row 9 has been completed. Ch 3; turn. This is side edge. *Row 10:* Dc in first sp, * ch 1, 3 dc in next sp; rpt from * across to within turning chain, ch 1, 2 dc in turning chain sp, dc in next ch of same turning chain. Ch 4; turn. *Row 11:* Sk first 3 dc, * 3 dc in next ch-1 sp, ch 1; rpt from * across to within last dc, do not ch 1, dc in top of turning chain. Ch 4; turn. *Row 12:* Sk first 4 dc, 3 dc in next sp; complete row in pat. Continue to work to correspond with Right Front, reversing shaping until total length is 15", end last row at front edge; drop yarn and loop from hook; attach a separate strand of yarn to 3rd ch of turning chain at beg of last row; ch 19 for sleeve. Break off and fasten this strand. Pick up dropped loop at end of row; ch 4; turn.

Sleeve and Yoke: Row 1: (3 dc in next sp, ch 1) 7 times; dc in each of first 3 ch on ch-19, (ch 1, sk next ch, dc in each of next 3 ch) 4 times. Ch 4; turn. *Rows 2 through 6:* (3 dc in next ch-1 sp, ch 1) 11 times; 2 dc in turning chain sp, dc in next ch of same turning chain. Ch 4; turn. At end of last row omit the ch-4, turn.

Neck: Row 1: Sl st in each st to within 2nd ch-1 sp, sl st in next sp, ch 3, (3 dc in next ch-1 sp, ch 1) 9 times; 2 dc in turning chain sp, dc in next ch of turning chain. Ch 4; turn. *Row 2:* Work in pat until the 9th 3-dc group has been completed; ch 3, sl st in the ch-3 sp of previous row. Break off and fasten.

Finishing: Block pieces to measurements. Sew side and underarm seams. Sew top of sleeve and shoulder seams. *Border:* Working along opposite side of starting chains at lower edge, with right side facing, attach yarn to lower right front corner. *Rnd 1:* Sc in each ch st across lower edge to next corner, 3 sc in corner st; being careful to keep work flat; sc evenly along entire outer edge of coat, making 3 sc in same st at each corner and having a number of sts divisible by 4. Join with sl st to first sc. Ch 1; turn. *Rnd 2:* Sc in each of next 4 sc; * ch 3, sc in next 4 sc; rpt from * around, end with ch 3. Join to first sc. Ch 1; turn. *Rnd 3:* Make 3 sc in each ch-3 loop and sc in each sc around. Join. Break off and fasten.

Sleeve Borders: With right side facing, attach yarn to end of underarm seam at lower edge of sleeve. *Rnd 1:* Ch 1, being careful to keep work flat, sc evenly along lower edge of sleeve, having a number of sts divisible by 4. Join to first sc. Ch 1; turn. *Rnds 2 and 3:* Rpt Rnds 2 and 3 of Coat Border. Break off and fasten. Press borders. Cut 6 pieces of ribbon, each 14" long. Make half of a bow at one end of each 14-inch piece. Leaving 3 inches free between bows and having first bow at neck, sew the bow-end of 3 ribbons along each front edge.

CAP

Starting at front edge, ch 54 to measure about 11½". Work same as for Back of Coat until Row 8 has been completed, having 12 3-dc groups on first row and on all uneven rows. At end of Row 8, break off and fasten. Turn.

Back Section: Sk first 5 3-dc groups on last row made; attach yarn to next ch-1 sp; ch 3, 2 dc in same sp where yarn was attached, (ch 1, 3 dc in next sp) 3 times. Do not work over rem sts. Ch 4; turn. *Rows 10 through 17:* Rpt Rows 3 and 2 of Back of Coat 3 times; then rpt Row 3 once more. Break off and fasten.

Finishing: Working through back loop only of sts, sew free edges of Row 8 of front section to corresponding side edges of back section, adjusting to fit.

Border: With right side facing, attach yarn to left corner st at lower edge. *Rnd 1:* Working along lower edge of cap, make 3 sc in corner st, sc evenly along left side edge of front section; make 10 sc evenly spaced across last row of back section, continue to sc evenly along outer edge of cap, making 3 sc in same st at corner and having a number of sts divisible by 4. Join with sl st to first sc. Ch 1; turn. *Rnds 2 and 3:* Work same as Rnds 2 and 3 of Coat Border. Break off; fasten.

MOTIF STOLE

Stole measures 10½" × 124".

MATERIALS: Bernat Mohair Plus (1½ oz. balls): 10 balls Natural or desired color; crochet hook, Size I, *or any size hook which will obtain the motif measurement below.*

GAUGE: Each motif measures 7½" wide and 4" deep.

Note: Stole is worked in 2 halves; then halves are sewn together.

First Half: Motif No. 1: Ch 16. *Row 1:* Dc in 11th ch from hook, ch 6, sk next 4 ch, sl st in last ch—2 loops. Ch 3 (to count as 1 dc), turn. *Row 2:*

Make 10 dc in each of the 2 loops of last row—21 dc, counting ch-3 as 1 dc. Ch 5, turn. *Row 3:* Sk first 2 dc, dc in next dc, (ch 2, sk next dc, dc in next dc) 8 times; ch 2, sk next dc, dc in top of ch-3—10 sps. Ch 3, turn. *Row 4:* * 3 dc in each of next 3 sps, dc in next dc; rpt from * 2 more times; 4 dc in last sp—35 dc, including ch 3. Always count ch-3 as 1 dc. Ch 5, turn. *Row 5:* Sk first 2 dc, dc in next dc, * ch 2, sk next dc, dc in next dc; rpt from * across, ending with ch 2, sk next dc, dc in top of ch-3—17 sps. Do not break off. Turn.
Motif No. 2: Sl st in each of first 4 sts on last row of last motif, ch 6, dc in next dc, ch 6, sl st in next dc; ch 2 sl st in next dc—2 ch-6 loops; do not work over rem sts. Turn. *Row 2:* 10 dc in each of the 2 ch-6 loops, sk next 3 sl sts, sl st in next st—21 dc, counting ch-2 and sl st at beg of row as 1 dc. Ch 5, turn. *Row 3:* Sk the sl st and following 2 dc, dc in next dc, (ch 2, sk next dc, dc in next dc) 8 times; ch 2, sk next dc, sl st in next free dc on last motif made; ch 2, sl st in next dc on same motif—10 sps. Turn. *Row 4:* * 3 dc in each of next 3 sps, dc in next dc; rpt from * 2 more times; 4 dc in last sp, sl st in end dc of last row on last motif—35 dc, counting ch-2 and sl st at beg of row as 1 dc. Ch 5, turn. *Row 5:* Sk the sl st and following 2 dc, dc in next dc, (ch 2, sk next dc, dc in next dc) 15 times; ch 2, sk next dc, sl st in next free dc on last motif, ch 2, sl st in next dc on same motif. Do not break off. Turn.
Motif No. 3: Ch 6, sk the 2 sl sts and next sp, dc

in next dc on last motif, ch 6, sl st in next dc on same motif, ch 2, sl st in next dc. Turn. *Row 2:* Make 10 dc in each of 2 ch-6 loops; sl st in next free dc on motif worked before last motif, ch 2, sl st in next dc on same motif. Ch 2, turn. *Row 3:* Sk the ch-2 and following 2 dc, dc in next dc, (ch 2, sk next dc, dc in next dc) 8 times; ch 2, sk next dc, sl st in next free dc on last motif made; ch 2, sl st in next dc on same motif—10 sps. Turn. *Row 4:* * 3 dc in each of next 3 sps, dc in next dc; rpt from * 2 more times; 4 dc in last sp, sl st in next free dc on motif worked before last motif, ch 2, sl st in next dc on same motif. Ch 2, turn. *Row 5:* Sk the ch-2 and following 2 dc, dc in next dc, (ch 2, sk next dc, dc in next dc) 15 times; ch 2, sk next dc, sl st in next free dc on last motif made—17 sps; ch 2, sl st in next dc on same motif. Do not break off. Turn. Rpt *Motif No. 3* for pat until 22 motifs in all have been completed. At the end of 22nd motif, break off and fasten.
Second Half: Work same as *First Half.*
Finishing: Do not block. Sew base of first motif and ends of last 2 rows of second motif of a half to corresponding sts of other half.

BULKY SWEATER
Directions are given for size Small (8-10). Changes for sizes Medium (12-14), Large (16-18) and Extra-Large (40-42) are in parentheses.
MATERIALS: Reynold's "Troll" 100 gr (3.5 oz.) balls; 7 (8, 9, 10) balls Taupe (A), 1 (1, 2, 2) ball Blue (B); Susan Bates crochet hook Size Q, *or any size hook which will obtain the stitch gauge below;* large tapestry needle.
GAUGE: 3 sts = 2"; 2 rows = 2½".

MEASUREMENTS:				
SIZES:	SMALL (8-10)	MEDIUM (12-14)	LRG (16-18)	X-LRG (20-22)
WIDTH ACROSS BACK AT UNDER ARMS:	17"	19"	21"	23"
WIDTH ACROSS EACH FRONT AT UNDER ARMS *(including collar):*	11"	11½"	13"	14½"
WIDTH ACROSS SLEEVE AT UPPER ARM:	14"	15"	16½"	16½"

Back: Starting at lower edge, excluding lower border, with A ch 25 (28, 31, 34) to measure 17 (19, 21, 23)". *Row 1:* Dc in 4th ch from hook, dc in each ch across—23 (26, 29, 32) dc, counting chain at beg of row as 1 dc. Mark Row 1 for wrong side. Ch 3, turn. *Row 2 (right side):* Sk first dc, dc in each dc across, dc in top of chain at end of row—23 (26, 29, 32) dc, counting ch-3 as 1 dc. Hereafter, always count turning ch-3 as 1 dc. Ch 3, turn. Rpt Row 2 for pat until 15 (15, 17, 19) rows in all have been completed—top edge is shoulder and neck edges. At end of last row fasten off.

Edging: With right side facing, attach B with sl st in first st on last row, ch 2 (do not count ch-2 as one st), hdc in same st, hdc in each dc across to last st, 2 hdc in last st; working along ends of rows across next edge, make 2 hdc along side of same row, * hdc over end st of next row, 2 hdc over end st of next row; rpt from * across to next corner, ending with 2 hdc over first row; 2 hdc in corner st; working along opposite side of starting chain, hdc in each ch to next corner, 2 hdc in corner st, work along next side edge to correspond with opposite edge, ending with hdc in same st as first hdc. Join with sl st to top of first hdc. Cut yarn and fasten.

Right Front: With right side of Back facing, attach A with sl st in 2nd hdc of right-hand corner group on top edge of Back. *Row 1:* Ch 3 (to count as 1 dc), dc in each of next 6 (7, 9, 10) sts; do not work over rem sts. Ch 3, turn. *Row 2:* Sk first dc, dc in each dc across, dc in top of ch-3—7 (8, 10, 11) dc. Ch 3, turn. Rpt last row until there are as many dc rows as on Back. Cut yarn and fasten.

Left Front: Sk center 9 (10, 9, 10) sts on top edge of Back for back of neck, attach A with sl st in next st, ch 3, dc in each of next 6 (7, 9, 10) sts. Ch

3, turn. Complete same as for Right Front.

Front Edging: With right side facing, attach B with sl st in side edge at beg of Row 1 of Right Front; working along ends of rows, ch 1, work 2 hdc over end of same row, * hdc over end of next row, 2 hdc over end st of next row; rpt from * across side edge to within next corner, 2 hdc in corner st; working across last row, hdc in each st across to next corner st, 2 hdc in corner st; work along next side edge to correspond with opposite edge; hdc in each skipped st across back of neck. Now continue to work edging along outer edges of Left Front same as for Right Front. Join with sl st to next corner st on Back edging. Cut yarn and fasten. Fold fronts over back, wrong sides together. Leaving upper 10 (11, 12, 12) sts on Back and corresponding sts on Fronts free for armholes, with B and tapestry needle sew side seams matching sts.

Sleeves: Rnd 1: With right side facing, attach A to underarm end of side seam, ch 3, make dc in each st along entire armhole edge. Join with sl st to top of ch-3—21 (23, 25, 25) dc, counting ch-3 as 1 dc. Ch 3, turn. *Rnd 2:* Sk joining, dc in each dc around. Join with sl st to top of ch-3. Ch 3, turn. Rpt last rnd 8 (8, 9, 10) more times. At end of last rnd, ch 2, turn. *Next Rnd:* Sk joining, hdc in each dc around. Join to top of first hdc. Cut yarn and fasten.

Shawl Collar: Row 1: With right side facing, attach A with sl st in first hdc of lower right front corner group, ch 3; make dc in each st along right front edge, across back of neck and down left front edge, ending with dc in each of 2 sts of lower left front corner group; do not work across lower edge. Ch 3, turn. Rpt Row 2 of Back 1 (1, 2, 2) times. Ch 3, turn.

Border: Rnd 1: Make 2 dc in first dc, dc in each dc across last row to within turning chain, 3 dc in top of ch-3; continuing to work across lower edge, make 2 hdc along same ch-3, 2 hdc over end st of next 1 (1, 2, 2) rows of collar, hdc in each st and in each joining across lower edge to within rows of collar, 2 hdc over end st of each row of collar. Join with sl st to top of ch-3. Ch 2, turn. *Rnd 2:* Hdc in each hdc across to next corner group hdc in each of 3 dc of corner group, dc in each dc to within next 3-dc group at next corner, hdc in each of 3 sts of corner group. Join with sl st to top of first hdc. Cut yarn and fasten.

Finishing: Darn in all loose ends on wrong side. Pin sweater to measurements on a padded surface, cover with a damp cloth and allow to dry; do not press. Fold collar in half to right side.

Color photo on page 143

THREE CHURCH LACE PILLOW TOPS
(For Ruffled Pillows)

Directions are given for each *pillow top* measuring 15½" × 17". Materials and directions for the *pillow* follow.

MATERIALS: (for each 15½" × 17" top): J.&P. Coats Knit-Cro-Sheen: 3 balls (250 yds. each) White or Ecru; steel crochet hook, No. 9, *or any size hook which will obtain the stitch gauge below:* one 15½" × 17" ruffled pillow.

GAUGE: 4 sps or 12 dc = 1"; 4 rows = 1".

Be sure to check your gauge before starting pillow top.

Note: Charts for Iris (A) and Pansy (B) Pillow Tops show half of the design. To follow either of these 2 Charts, work first half of each row from right-hand edge across to heavy line indicating center; then work same row back from center line to right-hand edge to complete second half of row. Chart for Columbine (C) Pillow Top shows entire design. To follow this Chart, follow first row and all uneven numbered rows from right to left; follow 2nd row and all even numbered rows from left to right.

DIRECTIONS *(for any one of the Three Designs):* Starting at lower edge, ch 207 to measure 17½": *Row 1 (right side):* Dc in 4th ch from hook, dc in each of remaining 203 ch —205 dc, counting chain at beg of row as 1 dc. Ch 3, turn. *Row 2:* Sk first dc, dc in each of next 6 dc, * *ch 2, sk next 2 dc, dc in next dc* —SP MADE OVER BLOCK; (ch 2, sk next 2 dc, dc in next dc) 18 more times; ch 2, sk next 2 dc, *dc in each of next 7 dc* —2 BLOCKS MADE. Rpt from * 2 more times, making last dc in top of turning chain. Ch 3, turn. *Row 3:* Sk first dc, dc in each of next 6

A — CHART FOR IRIS PILLOW

CENTER   □ = SPACE   ⊠ = BLOCK

B — CHART FOR PANSY PILLOW

CENTER

dc, * *ch 2, dc in next dc* —SP OVER SP MADE; make 6 more sps, *2 dc in next sp, dc in next dc* —BLOCK OVER SP MADE; 4 sps, block over next sp, 6 sps, ch 2, dc in each of next 7 dc. Rpt from * 2 more times, making last dc in top of ch-3. Ch 3, turn.

Note: When 2 or more blocks follow consecutively, work 3 dc for each block plus one extra dc. Ch 3, turn. *Row 4:* Sk first dc, dc in each of next 6 dc, * 6 sps, 2 dc in next sp, dc in each of next 4 dc, 2 dc in next sp, dc in next dc, 2 sps, 2

C—CHART FOR
COLUMBINE
PILLOW

5TH ROW
1st ROW

dc in next sp, dc in each of next 4 dc, 2 dc in next sp, dc in next dc, 5 sps, ch 2, dc in each of next 7 dc. Rpt from * 2 more times, making last dc in top of ch-3. Starting with Row 5 on Chart of design being made, follow chart, as directed, to the top. At end of last row, break off and fasten. *Finishing:* Block piece to measurements. Blindstitch crochet top to ruffled pillow (pillow directions follow).

RUFFLED PILLOWS

MATERIALS: (for each 15½″ × 17″ pillow): Firmly-woven, 40″–44″ fabric, ¾ yds. of Beige and ½ yd. of Dark Brown (or colors of your choice); thread to match fabrics; kapok or other stuffing material; 14″ zipper (optional).

DIRECTIONS: *Cutting:* For pillow top and backing, cut two 16½″ × 18″ pieces from beige fabric. For *bottom* ruffle, from either fabric, cut as many 5″-wide strips as needed to form a 130″-length when stitched together. For *top* ruffle, cut the same number of 4″-wide strips from the other color fabric.

Sewing: Seams are ½″ throughout.

Ruffles: Stitch together the ruffle pieces in each color, to make two strips of the required length. Stitch ends of each strip together. Press seams. Narrowly (¼″) hem one long edge of each. Pin the two strips together along the raw edge, with the wrong side of the top ruffle strip against the right side of the bottom ruffle. Make a double row of gathering stitches ⅜″·

from the pinned edges. Pull up the gathering stitches until the ruffle fits the pillow-top edge. *Assembling:* With right sides together and edges even, pin and stitch the double ruffle to pillow top. Pin pillow backing to top, right sides together. Stitch around three sides and four corners. Turn right side out. Stuff pillow to desired plumpness. Slipstitch open edges together. (*Optional:* Insert zipper in opening.) *Finishing:* Blindstitch blocked crocheted top to pillow top.

SHORT-SLEEVED TOP

Directions are for size Petite (4). Changes for sizes Small (6-8), Medium (10-12) and Large (14-16) are in parentheses.

MATERIALS: Lily Antique Cotton, 2 (2, 3, 3) 600 yard skeins; Crochet hook Size E, *or any size hook which will obtain the stitch gauge below.*

GAUGE: 7 dc = 1″; 6½ pat rows = 2″.

MEASUREMENTS:				
SIZES:	PETITE	SMALL	MEDIUM	LARGE
	(4)	(6-8)	(10-12)	(14-16)
BUST:	29″	32½″	36″	40″
WIDTH OF ONE RECTANGLE FROM CENTER				
FRONT TO CENTER BACK:				
	14½″	16¼″	18″	20″

Note: Top is worked in two rectangles, plus sleeves and joined at center front and back.

First Half: (Left Front, Back and Sleeve): Starting at center front, ch 224 (236, 248, 260) loosely. *Row 1:* Dc in 4th ch from hook, then dc in each rem ch—221 (233, 245, 257) dc. Turn. *Row*

2: Ch 2, dc in each dc across. Turn.

Pattern: Row 1 (Cluster Row): Ch 4 (counts as first 2 sts), sk 1 st, * *work 3 dcs into next dc, leaving the last lp of each dc on hook, yo and thru all 4 lps on hook—1 cl made,* ch 1, sk 1 dc, dc in next dc, ch 1, sk 1 dc; 1 rpt from *, end cl, ch 1, sk 1 dc, dc in next dc, ch 1, sk 1 dc, dc in turning ch. Turn. *Row 2:* Ch 2, dc in ch-1 sp, dc in next dc, dc in ch-1 sp, * dc in cl, dc in ch-1 sp, dc in dc, dc in ch-1 sp; rpt from *, end dc in cl, dc in turning dc—221 (233, 245, 257) dc. Turn. *Row 3:* Ch 2, work dc in each dc across. Turn. Rpt last 3 rows until 23 (26, 29, 32) rows have been completed, ending with 2nd row of dc. *Next Row:* Follow Pat Row 1 (Cluster Row) for 73 (77, 81, 85) sts—18 (19, 20, 21) cls. End off; leave enough to sew seam.

Sleeves: Rnd 1 (Cluster Rnd): Ch 4 at underarm, sk 1 st, * cl in next st, ch 1, sk 1 dc, dc in next dc, ch 1, sk 1 dc; rpt from * 18 (19, 20, 21) times more, end sl st to top of first st—19 (20, 21, 22) cls. Do not turn. *Rnd 2:* Ch 2, dc in first sp, * dc in cl, dc in ch-1 sp, dc in dc, dc in ch-1 sp; rpt from * around, end sl st to top of first st. *Rnd 3:* Ch 2, dc in each dc around, sl st to top of first st. Rpt last 3 rnds 1 (1, 2, 2) times more, then rpt Rnd 1 (Cluster Rnd).

Shell Stitch Edging: Sl st to top of dc, * make 5 dc into top of cl, sl st to top of dc; rpt from * around. Fasten off.

Second Half: (Right Back, Front and Sleeve): Work same as First Half.

Front Borders: Starting at lower edge of right center front on Second Half, work Pat Row 1 (Cluster Row) along entire center edge. Fasten off. Return to beg of previous row, then work 1 row of shell stitch edging. Fasten off. Starting at lower edge of left center back on First Half, work Pat Row 1 (Cluster Row) along entire center edge. Fasten off. Return to beg of previous row, then work 1 row of shell stitch edging joining the shells on this side to the shells on the opposite side by the middle dc, as follows: * Work 3 dcs, sl st to middle dc of corresponding shell on other side, work 2 dc, sl st to top of dc, rpt from * joining 20 (21, 22, 23) back shells, leave 20 (21, 22, 23) shells free for back and front V-neck, then join rem 15 (16, 17, 18) shells on front. *Note:* You can alter the amount of shells joined on the front for desired depth of V-neck.

Hem Edging: Work Pat Row 1 (Cluster Row) along entire lower edge of sweater starting at center front working a tr instead of a dc and make the cl a tr st rather than a dc st. Then work 1 row of shell edging.

Tie: Make a chain 36″ long, turn. *Next Row:* Sl st in 2nd ch from hook, then sl st in each rem ch. Fasten off. Lace the tie thru spaces in the pat at desired length from lower edge for your waist. Have both ends of tie come out at center front and tie into a bow.

U-NECK SWEATER FOR MEN AND WOMEN

Directions are for women small size (8-10). Changes for men small size (38-40) and color are in parentheses.

MATERIALS: Jack Frost Knitting Worsted 4 Ply (3 oz. skns): 4 (4) skns Blue Ombre (Leaf Ombre); crochet hook, size G, *or any size hook which will obtain the stitch gauge below.*

GAUGE: 4 dc = 1″; 5 rows = 2″.

FINISHED MEASUREMENTS:

SIZES:	WOMEN SMALL (8-10)	MEN SMALL (38-40)
BUST OR CHEST	32″	38″
BACK OR FRONT WIDTH AT UNDERARM	16″	19″

Back: Start at lower edge, ch 64 (74). *Row 1:* Dc in 4th ch from hook and in each ch across—62 (72) dc, counting ch at beg of row as 1 dc. Ch 3; turn. *Row 2:* Sk first dc, dc in each dc, dc in top of chain. Ch 3; turn. Hereafter always count

turning ch-3 as 1 dc. *Row 3:* Sk first dc, dc in each dc and in top of ch-3. Ch 3; turn. Rpt Row 3 for pat. Work in pat until length is 15½ (16½)" from beg. At end of last row, omit the ch-3. Turn.

Armholes: Row 1: Sl st in each of first 3 (4) dc, ch 3, dc in each dc to within last 1 (2) dc and turning chain; do not work over rem sts. Ch 3; turn. *Row 2:* Sk first dc, *holding back on hook the last loop of each dc, dc in next 2 sts, yarn over hook and draw through all 3 loops on hook—dec made;* dc in each dc to within last 2 sts and ch-3, dec over last 2 dc, dc in top of ch-3—1 dc decreased at each end. Ch 3; turn. Rpt last row 2 (4) more times—52 (56) dc. Ch 3; turn. Work even until length is 7½ (8½)" from first row of armholes. Turn.

Shoulders: Row 1: Sl st in each of first 4 dc for both sizes, sc in next dc, hdc in next dc, dc in each dc to within last 6 sts, hdc in next dc, sc in next dc. Turn. Rpt last row 2 more times—28 (32) sts. Break off and fasten.

Front: Work same as for Back until length from first row of armholes is about 3½ (4)". Ch 3; turn.

Neck: Row 1: Sk first dc, dc in next 19 (20) dc, hdc in next dc, sc in next dc; do not work over rem sts. Turn. *Row 2:* Sl st in first 3 sts, sc in next dc, hdc in next dc, dc in each rem dc and in ch-3. Ch 3; turn. *Row 3:* Sk first dc, dc in each dc to within last 5 sts (excluding sl sts), hdc in next st, sc in next st; do not work over rem 3 sts. Turn. *Row 4:* Rpt Row 2. Ch 3; turn. *Row 5:* Sk first dc, dc in next 11 sts. Ch 3; turn. Work even in pat over these 12 sts until length of armhole is same as on Back, ending at armhole edge.

Shoulder: Row 1: Sl st in each of first 4 dc, sc in next dc, hdc in next dc, dc in each dc and in ch-3. Ch 3; turn. *Row 2:* Sk first dc, dc in next dc, hdc in next dc, sc in next dc. Break off and fasten. Sk center 8 (10) dc on last row made before neck; attach yarn to next dc, sc in same dc, hdc in next dc, dc in each of rem sts. Ch 3; turn. Complete to correspond with opposite side, reversing shaping.

Finishing: Block pieces to measurements. Sew side and shoulder seams. Starting at a shoulder seam, sc evenly along neck edge, easing in edge slightly. Join with sl st to first sc. Break off and fasten. Starting at top end of side seam, sc evenly along each armhole edge. Join with sl st to first sc. Break off and fasten. With right side facing, starting at lower end of a side seam, sl st loosely in each ch of starting chains along lower edge. Join. Break off and fasten.

Color photo on page 143

STRIPED VEST

Directions are given for size Small (8-10). Changes for sizes Medium (12-14) and Large (16-18) are in parentheses.

MATERIALS: Bernat Blarney Spun (2 oz. balls): 3 (4, 4) balls Hazelmist (A), 3 (4, 4) balls White (B), 1 ball each Copper (C) and Abbey (D); and Bernat Catkin Yarn: 1 (2, 2) ball of Chestnut (E); crochet hook, Size D, *or any size hook which will obtain the stitch gauge below.*

GAUGE: 4 hdc = 1"; 5 rows = 2".

MEASUREMENTS:

	SMALL	MEDIUM	LARGE
SIZES:	(8-10)	(12-14)	(16-18)
BUST (including border):	32"	35"	39"
WIDTH ACROSS BACK AT UNDERARMS:	16½"	18"	20"
WIDTH ACROSS EACH FRONT AT UNDERARM (including border):	7¾"	8½"	9½"

(*Note:* Back and Fronts are worked all in one piece, starting and ending at center front. Pattern is worked entirely from right side. Break off and fasten at end of each row. Always work over loose ends of previous row at beg and end of each row to keep work neat.)

DIRECTIONS: *Left Front:* Starting at Left Front edge with A, ch 72 (74, 76). *Row 1:* Hdc in 3rd ch from hook, hdc in each ch across—70 (72, 74) hdc (do not count chain at beg of row as one st). Cut yarn and fasten. *Row 2:* Do not turn; attach B to top of chain at beg of last row, with B ch 2, leaving top 2 loops of hdc free (this forms a ridge on right side of work) *make 2 hdc in back loop of first hdc*—INC MADE AT LOWER EDGE;

leaving top loops free as before, work 1 hdc in back loop of each hdc across to within last 2 sts, *yarn over hook, draw up a loop in back loop of each of last 2 sts, yarn over hook and draw through all 4 loops on hook*—DEC MADE AT SHOULDER EDGE. Cut yarn and fasten. *Hereafter, leaving top loops free, work in back loop only of each hdc throughout.* Break off and fasten at end of *each* row and do not turn. *Row 3:* Attach A to top of ch-2 at beg of row, working as directed, make 2 hdc in first hdc, hdc in each st across to end of row—71 (73, 75) hdc (do not count ch-2 as one st). Rpt last 2 rows (Rows 2 and 3) 1 (2, 2) more times—72 (75, 77) hdc.

Left Armhole Shaping: Row 1: Attach B to top of ch-2 at beg of last row, ch 2, 2 hdc in first hdc, hdc in each of next 45 hdc, dec over next 2 sts; do not work over rem sts—48 sts on all sizes. *Row 2:* Attach A to top of ch-2, ch 2, hdc in each hdc to within last 2 sts on last row, dec over rem 2 sts. *Row 3:* Using B, work same as last row. *Rows 4 and 5:* Rpt last 2 rows—44 hdc. Continuing to alternate A and B rows for stripe pat, work even (making hdc in each hdc) for 8 (8, 12) rows. There are 13 (13, 17) rows in all on armhole. Keeping continuity of stripe pat, inc one st at end of each of next 4 rows—48 hdc. At end of last row, do not cut yarn; ch 24 (27, 29) for other edge of armhole. Cut yarn and fasten.

Back: Row 1: Attach A to top of ch-2, ch 2, hdc in each hdc and in each ch across—72 (75, 77) hdc. For Left Shoulder, keeping in stripe pat, inc one st at end of every other row 2 (3, 3) times—74 (78, 80) hdc, ending with A row.

Neck Shaping: Row 1: Work in stripe pat to within last 4 sts; do not work over last 4 sts. *Rows 2 and 3:* Keeping in pat, dec one st at end of each row—68 (72, 74) hdc. Work even in pat over these sts for 10 (10, 12) more rows. Inc one st at end of each of next 2 rows. At end of last row, ch 4 . Cut yarn and fasten. *Next Row:* Work hdc in each hdc and in each ch across—74 (78, 80) hdc. For Right Shoulder, (work 1 row even; dec one st at end of next row) 2 (3, 3) times—72 (75, 77) hdc.

Right Armhole Shaping: Work same as for Left Armhole Shaping until the ch 24 (27, 29) at end of last row has been made.

Right Front: Row 1: Keeping in pat, attach next color to top of ch-2, ch 2, hdc in each hdc and in each ch st across—72, (75, 77) hdc. *Row 2:* Attach next color to top of ch-2, ch 2, dec over first 2 hdc, hdc in each hdc to last hdc, 2 hdc in last hdc. *Row 3:* Attach next color, ch 2, dec over first 2 hdc, hdc in each hdc to end of row. Rpt

last 2 rows 1 (2, 2) more times—70 (72, 74) hdc—right front edge.

Underarm Edge: With right side facing, attach matching color to end of B row at beg of underarm edge, place A along underarm edge, * with B, working over A, sc over end of B row, *draw up a loop over end of same row, drop B, pick up A and draw a loop through the 2 loops on hook*—COLOR CHANGE MADE: with A, working over B, make 2 sc over end of next A row, changing to B in last sc; rpt from * across underarm edge. Cut both colors and fasten. Work across other underarm edge in same manner.

Edging: With right side facing, attach E to center of any underarm edge, ch 2, hdc evenly along entire outer edge of vest, making 3 hdc in same st at each corner, and being very careful to keep work flat (dec 2 or 3 sts across underarm edges, if necessary, to keep edges flat).

Finishing: Pin vest to measurements on a padded surface; cover with a damp cloth and allow to dry; do not press. Fold fronts over back and sew shoulder seams.

Border: Rnd 1: With right side facing, attach C to back loop of hdc at center back of neck, ch 2, working in back loop only as before, hdc in each hdc along outer edge of vest, increasing 3 or 4 hdc evenly spaced along lower curved edge of each front (be sure to have a number of hdc divisible by 6). Join with sl st in top of ch-2. Cut yarn and fasten. *Rnd 2:* Attach D to same st used for joining, * sc in back loop of next hdc, sk next 2 sts, 7 dc in back loop of next hdc, sk next 2 sts; rpt from * around. Join with sl st to first sc. Cut yarn and fasten.

Armhole Border: Rnd 1: Starting at center of underarm, attach C to back loop of hdc, ch 2, hdc in each st around, decreasing one st at each inner corner. Join with sl st to top of ch-2. Cut yarn and fasten. *Next Row:* Sk underarm sts, attach D to back loop of first st after inner corner, sc in same st, * sk 2 sts, 7 dc in back loop of next hdc, sk next 2 sts, 1 sc in back loop of next hdc; rpt from * across to within underarm sts. Cut yarn and fasten. Finish other armhole in same manner.

CARTRIDGE-RIBBED COAT

Directions are given for size Small (8-10). Changes for sizes Medium (12-14) and Large (16-18) are in parentheses.

MATERIALS: Brunswick Windrush Yarn, 100% Orlon®: 3 sks each Brick (A), Mocha (B), Oxford (E); 4 sks Denim Blue (C); 2 sks

Color photo on page 144

Heather Blue (D); crochet hook, Size K, *or any size hook which will obtain the stitch gauge below.*
GAUGE: 6 sc = 2½"; 4 rows = 1½".
Note: Use 2 strands of same color held tog throughout. If a different length is desired, make sure to make starting chain 4" shorter than desired length (2" for back and 2" for front) to allow for stretch of fabric after coat is worn.

MEASUREMENTS:

SIZES:	SMALL (8-10)	MEDIUM (12-14)	LARGE (16-18)
BUST *(excluding front folds):*	35"	38"	42"
WIDTH ACROSS BACK AT UNDERARMS:	16½"	19"	21"
WIDTH ACROSS EACH FRONT AT UNDERARM:	9"	9¾"	10½"
WIDTH ACROSS SLEEVE AT UPPER ARM:	15"	16"	17"

Left Side Panel For Front and Back: With 2 strands of A held tog, ch 194 (202, 206) or desired length—half of starting chain is length of coat from shoulder to lower edge, allowing 2" for stretching as mentioned above. *Row 1:* Sc in 2nd ch from hook and in each ch across. Ch 1, turn. At this point check for length, hanging crocheted row over shoulder with center of row at shoulder. If needed, adjust length by adding or subtracting number of sts to obtain desired length. *Row 2:* Working in the back loop only of each sc, sc in each sc across to last sc, *draw up a loop in back loop of last sc, break off A, pick up D and draw a loop through loops on hook—color change made.* Always change color in this manner. With D, ch 1, turn. Entire coat is worked in back loop of each sc to form ridges.
Rows 3 and 4: With D, work same as Row 2, change color to B at end of last row. Ch 1, turn.
Rows 5 through 10: With B, work as Row 2, change to C at end of last row. Ch 1, turn. *Rows 11 and 12:* With C work as before, change to D at end of last row. Ch 1, turn. *Rows 13 and 14:* With D, work as before, change to C at end of last row. Ch 1, turn. With C work 2 (4, 6) rows, change to E at end of last row. Ch 1, turn. Count number of sts and mark center st or 2 sts for shoulder line.
Center Back Panel: Next row: With E, sc in each sc to within 2 sc before marker at shoulder line. Ch 1, turn. Working as before over these sts only, make 7 more rows with E; 2 (4, 6) rows A. At end of last row, break off and fasten.
Right Side Panel For Front and Back: Work same as Left Side Panel. Mark center st or sts as before. Break off and fasten. Turn.
Center Back Panel: Sk 2 sts after shoulder marker, attach E to next sc, sc in same st and in each sc across. Complete to correspond with other back panel. Break off and fasten. Using a large-eyed darning needle and E, sew center back seam, working through back loop only of each st.
Shawl Collar: With wrong side of last row made on front edge facing, attach A to first st at lower edge of front, working in back loop only as before, sc in same sc and in each sc of front edge; sc along neck edge, easing in edge to desired fit, sc in each sc along other front edge. Ch 1, turn.
Rows 2 through 8: With A, sc in each sc across, change to B at end of last row. Ch 1, turn. Continuing as before, make 2 rows B; 4 rows E; (2 rows C and 2 rows E) 3 times. Break off and fasten. Fold crochet in half at shoulder markers to form back and front sections. Starting at lower edge, sew side seams, leaving top 7½ (8, 8½)" open for armholes.
Sleeves: Row 1: With D, starting at top end of side seam, sc in each st along armhole edge. Ch 1, turn. Working in the ridge pat as before, make 1 more Row D; 2 Rows E; 6 Rows C; 2 Rows E; 2 Rows A; 2 Rows D; 12 Rows B or until sleeve measures 1½" shorter than desired length; then with D, work 4 more Rows. Break off and fasten. Sew sleeve seams. Darn in all loose ends on wrong side.
Tie: With 3 strands of C held tog, make a chain the desired length for tie. Sl st in 2nd ch from hook and in each ch across. Break off and fasten. Turn collar to right side.

Color photo on page 144

MULTI-COLOR COAT

Directions are given for size Small (8-10). Changes for sizes Medium (12-14) and Large (16-18) are in parentheses.

MATERIALS: Bear Brand Machine Washable (100% Orlon®) Winsom (2 oz. skeins): 3 sks Red (A); 6 sks each Orange (B), Blue (C) and Green (D); 2 sks each Burgundy (E) and Yellow (F); 4 sks Brick (G); 1 sk each Brass (H) and Violet (I); crochet hook, Size J, *or any size hook which will obtain the stitch gauge below;* quilted material for lining; 6 buttons.

GAUGE: 11 sc = 4"; 11 rows = 4".

Note: Use 2 strands of same color held tog throughout.

MEASUREMENTS:

SIZES:	SMALL (8–10)	MEDIUM (12–14)	LARGE (16–18)
BUST:	38"	40"	44"
WIDTH ACROSS BACK AT UNDERARMS:	19"	20"	22"
WIDTH ACROSS EACH FRONT AT UNDER-ARM *(including border):*	11"	11½"	12½"
WIDTH ACROSS SLEEVE AT UPPER ARMS:	15"	16"	18"

Color Sequence for Pat: * 10 rows B, 8 rows C; 10 rows D, 1 row C, 1 row B, 1 row H, 1 row D, 1 row B, 1 row C, 2 rows D, 1 row C, 2 rows E, 6 rows B, 12 rows G, 1 row E, 4 rows F, 2 rows I, 6 rows C; rpt from * for color rpt. At end of each color stripe, break off and fasten and attach next color.

Body: Row 1 (right side): With B, ch 106 (111, 119). Sc in 2nd ch from hook, sc in each rem ch to end—105 (110, 118) sc. Ch 1, turn. *Row 2:* Sc in each sc across. Ch 1, turn. Rpt Row 2, working color sequence until 86 rows from beg have been completed, end on wrong side. Ch 1, turn.

Upper Right Front: Work first 25 (27, 29) sc. Mark next 2 sc for underarm. Ch 1, turn. Continue in color sequence throughout. *Next Row:* Sk first sc, sc in next 24 (26, 28) sc. Continue to work over these sts until length of upper front is 7 (8, 9)". End at front edge. Break off and fasten.

Neck Shaping: Turn, sk first 4 sts, attach yarn to next sc, work sc in each sc to end—19 (21, 23) sc. Ch 1, turn. *Dec Row:* Sc in each sc to within 2 sc of end, draw up a loop in each of last 2 sc, yo and through all 3 loops on hook—dec made—18 (20, 22) sc. Ch 1, turn. Keeping color sequence, dec 1 sc at neck edge every row 2 (3, 3) times more—16 (18, 19) sc. Ch 1, turn. Work 2 (3, 3) rows even, end at neck edge.

Shoulder Shaping: Sc in first 10 (12, 13) sc. Ch 1, turn, sl st in first 6 sts, sc in each rem 5 (5, 7) sc. Break off and fasten.

Upper Back: From right side, sk 2 marked sts of underarm, attach same color used on first row of upper right front to next sc, sc in same sc and in each of next 50 (51, 55) sc. Mark next 2 sts for underarm. Ch 1, turn. *Next Row:* Sk first sc, sc in each sc to within last 2 sc, dec over last 2 sc—49 (50, 54) sc. Work over these sts until back is same length as right front above underarm marker, end on wrong side. Turn.

Shoulder Shaping: Sl st in first 6 sc, sc in next 37 (38, 42) sc. Turn, sl st in first 6 sc, sc in next 25 (26, 30) sts. Turn, sl st in first 5 (5, 6) sts, sc in next 15 (16, 18) sc. Break off and fasten.

Upper Left Front: From right side, sk 2 marked sts of underarm, attach yarn in next st, sc in same st and in next 24 (26, 28) sts. Work to correspond with upper right front, reversing shaping.

Sleeves: Row 1 (right side): With B, ch 44 (46, 50), work as for Row 1 of body. Mark for lower edge. Working in same color sequence as body, work over 43 (45, 49) sc until 48 rows from beg have been completed. Break off and fasten.

Collar: Row 1 (right side): With C, ch 15. Sc in 2nd ch from hook, sc in each rem ch—14 sc. Ch 1, turn. Working as for body, work 6 rows C, 2 rows I, 4 rows F, 1 row E, 12 rows G, 1 row E, 4 rows F, 2 rows I, 6 rows C. Break off and fasten.

Pocket (Make 2):Row 1 (wrong side): With D, ch 23. Sc in 2nd ch from hook, sc in each rem ch—22 sc. Break off and fasten. Turn. *Row 2:* With B, sc in each sc. Break off and fasten.

Working as for coat, work 1 row C, 2 rows D, 1 row C, 2 rows E, 6 rows B, 12 rows G. Break off and fasten.

Finishing: Pin pieces to measurements flat on a padded surface; cover with a damp cloth and steam lightly.

Lining: Piece lining yardage to make one piece of fabric large enough on which to lay out the *opened* coat. Trace around coat with tailor's chalk. Cut out lining 1″ larger than tracing line all around. Stitch shoulder seams; press open. Sew coat shoulder seams. With wrong sides together, pin lining into coat, turning edges under 1″ and slashing seam allowance at curved edges. Sew in place with invisible stitches.

Coat Border: Row 1: From right side, attach A to corner st at left front neck edge; being careful to keep work flat, sc evenly along left front edge to lower corner, 3 sc in corner st, working along opposite side of starting chain, sc in each ch across to next corner, 3 sc in corner st, sc evenly along right front edge to within neck edge. Ch 1, turn. *Row 2:* Sc in each sc across, making 3 sc in center sc of 3-sc group at each corner. Ch 1, turn. With pins, mark the position of 6 buttonholes evenly spaced along right front edge, having first pin ¼″ below neck edge and last pin about 9″ above lower edge. *Row 3:* Making 3 sc in center sc of each corner group, * sc in each sc to within 1 sc before next pin, ch 2, sk 2 sc, sc in next sc; rpt from * 5 more times; sc in each sc to end. Ch 1, turn. *Row 4:* Making 3 sc in center sc of each corner group, sc in each sc and in each ch across. Ch 1, turn. *Row 5:* Rpt Row 2. Break off and fasten.

Collar Border: Row 1: From right side, with A, leaving one long edge free for neck edge, sc evenly along other 3 sides, making 3 sc in same st at each of the 2 corners. Ch 1, turn. Rpt Row 2 of Coat Border 4 times. Break off and fasten.

Sleeve Border: With A, work 5 rows of sc along lower edge of sleeve. Break off and fasten. Sew sleeve seams. Sew in sleeves. Sew pockets to fronts as shown, matching stripes. Leaving ½ of top edges of coat's border free, sew collar to neck edge, adjusting to fit. Sew on buttons.

BEDSPREAD

Directions are given for bedspread to measure 72″ × 99″, plus fringe.

Note: Bedspread can be made larger or smaller by working more or less squares, allowing 9″ for each square.

MATERIALS: DMC Brilliant Crochet Cotton (218 yd. balls): 30 balls White (A), 25 balls

Beige; stell crochet hook, No. 3, *or any size hook which will obtain the square measurement below.*

GAUGE: Each square measures 9″ x 9″.

Square: (Make 88) *Center Flower:* Starting at center with A, ch 6. Join with sl st to form ring. *Rnd 1:* Ch 3, make 11 dc in ring. Join with sl st to top of ch-3—12 dc, counting ch-3 as 1 dc. *Rnd 2:* Ch 1, sc in same st as joining, * ch 5, sk next dc, sc in next dc; rpt from * around, ending with ch 5, sk last dc. Join with sl st to first sc—6 lps. *Rnd 3:* In each ch-5 lp around make sc, 5 tr and sc. Join with sl st to first sc—6 petals. *Rnd 4:* Ch 1, working in back of last rnd, sc in back lps or first sc on rnd before last, * ch 6, working in back of petals of previous rnd, sc in back lps of next sc between petals on rnd before last; rpt from * around, ending with ch 6. Join to first sc of this rnd—6 lps. *Rnd 5:* In each ch-6 lp around make sc, 7 tr and sc. Join as before. *Rnd 6:* Making ch 7 (instead of ch 6) work a ch lp rnd same as Rnd 4. *Rnd 7:* In each ch-7 lp make sc, 9 tr and sc. Join. *Rnd 8:* Making ch 8 (instead of ch 6), work same as Rnd 4. *Rnd 9:* In each ch-8 lp make sc, 11 tr and sc. Join. *Rnd 10:* Making ch 9 (instead of ch 6), work same as Rnd 4. *Rnd 11:* In each ch-9 lp make sc, 13 tr and sc. Join. Break off and fasten. This completes center flower. *Rnd 12:* Attach B with sl st to back lps of first sc on Rnd 10, sc in same st, * ch 9, working in back of petals along Rnd 10, make sc in back lps of next sc; rpt from * around, ending with ch-9. Join to first sc. *Rnd 13:* Ch 4 (to count as 1 tr), sk joining, tr in each ch and in each sc around. Join to top of ch-4—60 tr. *Rnd 14:* Ch 4, in same st work 1 tr, ch 2 for corner sp and 2 tr, * tr in each of next 14 sts, in next st make *2 tr, ch 2 and 2 tr—corner;* rpt from * 2 more times; tr in each of next 14 sts. Join to top of ch-4—4 corners. *Rnd 15:* Ch 4, sk joining, tr in next tr, * in next corner ch-2 sp make 2 tr, ch 2 and 2 tr; tr in each tr to within next ch-2 sp; rpt from * around, ending with tr in each rem tr. Join to top of ch-4—88 tr, counting ch-4 as 1 tr. *Rnd 16:* Ch 4, tr in each of next 3 tr, * in next corner ch-2 sp make 2 tr, ch 2 and 2 tr; tr in each tr to within next ch-2 sp; rpt from * around, ending with tr in each rem tr. Join as before. *Rnd 17:* Ch 6, sk next 2 sts, tr in next tr, * ch 2, sk next 2 tr, in next corner sp make 3 tr, ch 3 and 3 tr; (ch 2, sk next 2 tr, tr in next tr) 8 times; rpt from * around, ending last rpt with (ch 2, sk next 2 tr, tr in next tr) 6 times; ch 2, sk last 2 tr. Join to 4th ch of ch-6—9 sps between corner groups on each side. *Rnd 18:* Ch 4, 2 tr in next sp, tr in next tr, 2 tr in next sp, tr in each of next 3 tr, * in corner ch-3 sp make 2 tr, ch 3 and 2 tr; work tr in each tr and 2 tr in each sp across to within next corner sp; rpt from * around, ending with tr in each tr and 2 tr in each sp to end of rnd. Join. Break off and fasten. *Rnd 19:* Attach A to any corner ch-3 sp, ch 4 in same sp make tr, ch 3 and 2 tr, * make tr in each tr to within next corner sp, in corner sp make 2 tr ch 3 and 2 tr, rpt from * around, ending with tr in each rem tr. Join. *Rnd 20:* Ch 3, dc in next st, * in next corner sp make 2 dc, ch 3 and 2 dc; dc in each st to within next corner sp; rpt from * around, ending with dc in each rem st. Join to top of ch-3. Break off and fasten.

Finishing: Pin each square to measure 9″ × 9″ on a padded surface; cover with a damp cloth and steam with a warm iron (do not press flower down). Remove when completely dry.

To Assemble: Using a darning needle and A, from wrong side, working through back lp only of each st (front lps remain free on right side), sew squares together from center of corner to center of next corner, matching sts. Sew squares in eight strips of 11 squares in each strip, then sew strips together, matching all corners.

Edging: With right side facing, using A, sc in each dc and in each ch along entire outer edge of joined square. Join with sl st to first sc. Break off and fasten.

Fringe: With right side facing, attach A to center st of corner group at beg of a side (long) edge

of bedspread, sc in same st, ch 40, sk next 3 sc, sc in next sc, * ch 40, turn sc in 2nd sc of 3 sts just skipped, ch 40, turn, sk next 3 free sc (after last 2 sc made), sc in next sc; rpt from * across side (long) edge, across bottom edge and next side (long) edge to upper right corner of bedspread; do not work across top edge. Break off and fasten.

FLOWER PILLOWS
Each pillow measures 12″ in diameter.
MATERIALS: DMC Brilliant Crochet Cotton (218 yd. balls): For each pillow: 2 balls either White or Beige; steel crochet hook, No. 3, *or any size hook which will obtain the stitch gauge below;* 1 round pillow form, 12″ in diameter; 1 yd round elastic.
GAUGE: First 11 rnds = 3¾″ in diameter.
Pillow (Make 1 White and 1 Beige): *Rnds 1 through 11:* Work same as for Rnds 1 through 11 of square for Bedspread. Do not break off at end of last rnd. *Rnd 12:* Having 1 more ch st in each ch lp than on previous ch lp rnd, work a ch lp rnd as before. *Rnd 13:* Having 2 more tr in each petal than on previous petal rnd, work a petal rnd as before. *Rnds 14 through 29:* Continuing to inc number of sts on every rnd as before, work same as for last 2 rnds until there are 31 tr in each petal on last rnd. *Rnd 30:* Ch 1, sc in back lps of first sc on last ch lp rnd, * ch 18, sc in back lps of next sc on last ch lp rnd; rpt from * around, ending with ch 18. Join to first sc. *Rnd 31:* Ch 4 (to count as 1 tr), sk joining, tr in each ch and in each sc around. Join to first sc—114 tr. *Rnd 32:* Ch 4, tr in each of next 4 tr, *2 tr in next tr—inc made;* * tr in each of next 5 tr, 2 tr in next tr; rpt from * around. Join to top of ch-4—133 tr (always count ch-4 as 1 tr). *Rnd 33:* Ch 4, tr in each of next 5 tr, 2 tr in next tr, * tr in each of next 6 tr, 2 tr in next tr; rpt from * around. Join as before—*19 incs made.* *Rnd 34:* Ch 4, being careful not to have incs fall directly above previous incs, tr in each tr, increasing 19 tr evenly spaced around. Join—171 tr. *Rnds 35 and 36:* Rpt last rnd—209 tr. *Rnd 37:* Ch 4, tr in each tr around. Join. *Rnd 38:* Ch 4, tr in each of next 9 tr, * *sk next tr—dec made;* tr in each of next 10 tr; rpt from * around. Join—19 decs made. *Rnds 39, 40 and 41:* Ch 4, making 19 decs evenly spaced around, tr in each tr around. Join. At end of last rnd, break off and fasten.
Finishing: Slip crocheted pillow over pillow form; run round elastic through sts of last rnd; pull tightly. Leaving 3″ length at each end, cut elastic; tie ends together.

More Crocheted Trims: Tack six crocheted flowers (Rows 1 through 11 of Bedspread) to fabric shade, or tack four crocheted flowers to fabric-covered picture frame.

Color photo on page 144

V-NECK SWEATER

Directions are given for size Small (8-10). Changes for sizes Medium (12-14) and Large (16-18) are in parentheses.

MATERIALS: Belding/Lily's Sugar & Cream Yarn (in 100 yd. skeins): 7 (8, 9) skeins Lt. Gold; crochet hook, Size J, *or any size hook which will obtain the stitch gauge below.*

GAUGE: 10 dc = 3″; 2 dc rows = 1″.

MEASUREMENTS:

SIZES:	SMALL (8-10)	MEDIUM (12-14)	LARGE (16-18)
BUST:	33″	36″	40″
WIDTH ACROSS BACK OR FRONT AT UNDERARMS:	16½″	18″	20″
WIDTH ACROSS SLEEVE AT UPPER ARM:	11½″	12½″	14″

DIRECTIONS: *Yoke:* Starting at neck edge (excluding neck border), ch 88 (90, 90).

Row 1 (right side): Dc in 4th ch from hook, dc in each of next 5 ch—*left front;* ch 1 for raglan seam, dc in each of next 24 ch—*sleeve;* ch 1, dc in each of next 24 (26, 26) ch—*back;* ch 1, dc in each of next 24 ch—*sleeve;* ch 1, dc in each of rem 7 ch—*right front*—4 raglan ch-1 sps. Ch 3, turn. Always count ch-3 as 1 dc. *Row 2:* Sk first dc, * dc in each dc to next ch-1 sp, in next ch-1 sp make dc, ch 1 and dc; rpt from * 3 more times; dc in each rem dc, dc in top of ch-3—1 dc inc made at each side of back and sleeves and 1 dc inc at raglan edge of each front. Rpt last row 6 (8, 10)

more times—14 (16, 18) sts on each front, 38 (42, 46) sts on each sleeve and 38 (44, 48) sts on back. Ch 3, turn. *Next Row:* Sk first dc, * dc in each dc to next ch-1 sp, 2 dc in next ch-1 sp, ch 1, dc in each dc across sleeve, ch 1, 2 dc in next sp, rpt from * once more; dc in each rem dc, dc in top of ch-3—2 dc increased at each side of back and at raglan seam edge of each front; no incs made on sleeves. Ch 3, turn. Rpt last row 3 (3, 4) more times—22 (24, 28) sts on each front; 38 (42, 46) sts on each sleeve and 54 (60, 68) dc on back. At end of last row, ch 8 (10, 8) for base of front neck opening. Join with sl st to top of ch-3 at beg of row, being careful not to twist chain. Cut yarn and fasten. Turn. *Hereafter work in rnds.*

To Divide Sections—Body—Rnd 1: Attach yarn in ch-1 sp preceding back sts, ch 2, dc in each dc across back, *holding back on hook last loop of each dc, dc in next ch-1 sp, sk sleeve sts, dc in next ch-1 sp, yarn over hook, draw through all 3 loops on hook*—2-JOINT DC MADE AT UNDERARM: dc in each dc across front sts, including ch sts at center front, make 2-joint dc at underarm as before, sk ch-2. Join with sl st to top of first dc—108 (120,134) sts. Ch 3, turn. *Rnd 2:* Sk joining, dc in each dc around. Join to top of ch-3. Ch 3, turn. *Rnd 3 and 4:* Rpt Rnd 2. Ch 3, turn. *Rnd 5:* Sk joining, *holding back on hook last loop of each dc, make dc in each of next 2 dc, yarn over hook, draw through all 3 loops on hook*—DEC MADE AT SIDE EDGE; dc in each of next 52 (58, 65) dc, dec over next 2 dc, dc in each rem dc. Join to top of ch-3—dec made at each side. Ch 3, turn. *Rnd 6:* Sk joining, dc in each st around. Join to top of ch-3. Ch 3, turn. *Rnd 7:* Work same as last rnd, but dec one st above each of 2 previous decs. Ch 3, turn. *Rnds 8 and 9:* Rpt Rnds 6 and 7—102 (114, 128) sts. Ch 3, turn. Rpt Rnd 6 only 4 (5, 6) times. Cut yarn and fasten. Turn. *Side Slits— First Panel: Row 1:* Sk first 6 sts on last rnd, attach yarn to next dc, ch 3, dc in same st, dc in each of next 38 (44, 50) dc, 2 dc in next dc; do not work over rem sts—42 (48, 54) sts. Ch 3, turn. *Row 2:* Dc in first dc, dc in each dc across, 2 dc in top of ch-3. Ch 3, turn. *Row 3:* Rpt last row. Ch 3, turn. *Row 4:* Sk first dc, dc in each dc across, dc in top of ch-3. Cut yarn and fasten. Turn. *Second Panel: Row 1:* Sk next free 11 (11, 12) sts on last rnd of body, attach yarn to next dc and continue to work same as Row 1 of First Panel. Ch 3, turn. Rpt Rows 2, 3 and 4 of First Panel.

Sleeves: Rnd 1: With wrong side of last rnd on sleeve facing, attach yarn in top of 2-joint dc at underarm, ch 1, sc in same st, dc in each dc around sleeve. Join with sl st to first sc. Ch 2, turn. *Rnd 2:* Sk joining, dc in each dc around, sk ch-2. Join with sl st to top of first dc—38 (42, 46) sts. Ch 3, turn. *Rnd 3:* Sk joining, dc in each dc around. Join to top of ch-3. Ch 3, turn. *Rnd 4:* Rpt last rnd. Ch 3, turn. *Rnd 5:* Sk joining, dec over next 2 dc, dc in each dc around to within last 2 dc, dec over last 2 dc. Join to top of ch-3. Ch 3, turn. Rpt last 3 rnds (Rnds 3, 4 and 5) 2 (3, 4) more times—32 (34, 36) sts. Ch 3, turn. Rpt Rnd 3 only until length from underarm is 11 (12, 12)" ending with a wrong-side row. Ch 1, turn.

Sleeve Border: Rnd 1: Sc in same st as joining, * tr in next st, pushing tr just made to right side, sc in next st; rpt from * around, ending with tr in last st. Join to first sc. Ch 3, turn. *Rnd 2:* Sk joining, * *holding back on hook last loop of each dc, make 5 dc in next tr, yarn over hook, draw through 5 loops on hook, yarn over, draw through rem 2 loops on hook*—CLUSTER MADE; ch 1, sk next sc; rpt from * around, ending with ch 1, sk ch-3. Join with sl st in top of first cluster. Ch 1, turn. *Rnd 3:* Sc in same st as joining, * ch 3, sl st in top of last sc made for picot, sc in next sp, sc in next cluster, sc in next sp, ch 3, complete picot, sc in next cluster, in next sp and in next cluster; rpt from * around, ending last rpt with sc in last sp. Join to first sc. Cut yarn and fasten. Work other sleeve in same way.

Bottom Border: 1st Row: With wrong side facing, attach yarn at side edge of first row on first panel, working along ends of rows, work 2 sc over end of each of 4 rows, make 5 sc in corner st, sc in each st across last row to next corner, 5 sc in corner st, 2 sc over end of each of 4 rows. Ch 1, turn. *Row 2:* Sc in first sc, * tr in next sc, sc in next sc; rpt from * across last row, ending with sc in last 1 (or 2) sc; sk next free dc on last rnd of body, sl st in each of next 3 dc on body. Ch 1, turn. *Rnd 3:* Sk 1 (or 2) sc, * make cluster in next tr, ch 1, sk next sc; rpt from * across last row, ending with ch 1, sk next 4 free dc on last rnd of body, sl st in next dc. Ch 1, turn. *Rnd 4:* Sc in first cluster, starting from * , work same as Rnd 3 of Sleeve Border across, ending with sc in last cluster, sl st in next dc on last rnd of body. Cut yarn and fasten. Work border on second panel in the same way.

Neck Border: Rnd 1: With wrong side facing, attach yarn to first ch at base of front neck opening, work 5 (7, 7) sc evenly spaced across chain, continue to sc evenly along front opening and neck edges, making 3 sc in same st at each

outer corner, and having an even number of sts. Join to first sc. Ch 1, turn. *Rnd 2:* Work same as Rnd 1 of Sleeve Border. Ch 3, turn. *Rnd 3:* Sk next 1 (2, 2) st, make cluster in next st, sk 1 (2, 2) st, dc in next st, ch 1; skipping all sc, make cluster and ch 1 in each tr around. Join to top of ch-3. *Rnd 4:* Sk joining, sc in next sp, sc in cluster; rpt from * on Rnd 3 of Sleeve Border around, ending with sc in sp before dc, sk dc, sc in last cluster. Join to first sc. Cut yarn and fasten.

Finishing: Pin sweater to measurements on a padded surface; cover with a damp cloth and steam lightly with a warm iron. Remove when completely dry.

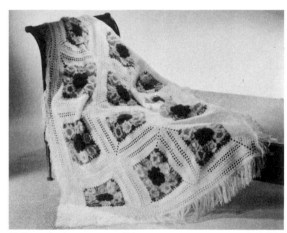

Color photo on page 144

ROSE GARDEN AFGHAN

Directions are given for Afghan to measure 46" × 60", plus fringe.

MATERIALS: "Bucilla Melody" Yarn (1 oz. skeins): 3 skeins each Red (A), Coral (B), Hot Pink (C), Lt. Pink (D), Yellow (E), 2 skeins Olive Green (F) and "Bear Brand" Spectator Sport Yarn (2 oz. skeins): 10 skeins White (G); Bucilla aluminum crochet hook, Size H, *or any size crochet hook which will obtain the motif measurements below.*

GAUGE: Each Nine-Rose Motif = 9" × 9". Each complete Square = 14" × 14".

Square (Make 12): Nine-Rose Motif: Rose #1 (center rose): With A, starting at center, ch 4. Join with sl st to form ring. *Rnd 1:* Ch 1, 8 sc in ring. Join with sl st to first sc. *Rnd 2:* Ch 1, sc in same sc as joining, * ch 1, sc in next sc; rpt from * around, ending with ch 1. Join with sl st to first sc—8 ch-1 lps. *Rnd 3:* Sc in next ch-1 lp, * ch 3, sc in next ch-1 lp; rpt from * around, ending with ch 3. Join to first sc—8 ch-3 lps. *Rnd 4:* * In next ch-3 lp make hdc, 2 dc and hdc; sl st in next

ROSE GARDEN AFGHAN

JOINING DIAGRAM   1 SQ.=1"

CORAL (CC)

HOT PINK (CC)

LT. PINK (CC)

HOT PINK (CC)

- HOT PINK (C) NO. 2
- YELLOW NO. 7
- CORAL (B) NO. 3
- LT. PINK NO. 6
- RED (A) NO. 1
- HOT PINK NO. 8
- YELLOW (E) NO. 5
- CORAL NO. 9
- LT. PINK (D) NO. 4

sc; rpt from * around, making last sl st in joining of last rnd—8 petals. *Rnd 5:* Ch 1, from back of work, make sc around bar of first sc on Rnd 3, * ch 4, working in back of petal, sc around bar of next sc on Rnd 3; rpt from * 6 more times; ch 4. Join with sl st to first sc of this rnd—8 ch-4 lps. *Rnd 6:* * In next ch-4 lp make hdc, 3 dc and hdc; sl st in next sc; rpt from * around, making last sl st in joining of last rnd. *Rnd 7:* Ch 1, from back of work, make sc around bar of first sc on Rnd 5, * ch 4, working in back of petal, sc around bar of next sc on Rnd 5; rpt from * around, ending with ch 4. Join with sl st to first sc. *Rnd 8:* * In next ch-4 lp make 2 hdc, 3 dc and 2 hdc; sl st in next sc; rpt from * around, making last sl st in joining of last rnd—8 petals. Cut yarn and fasten.

Rose #2 (corner rose): Rnds 1 through 5: With C, follow directions for Rose #1 until Rnd 5 has been completed. *Rnd 6 (joining Rnd):* * In next ch-4 lp make hdc, 4 dc and hdc; sl st in next sc; rpt from * 5 more times; in next ch-4 lp make hdc and 2 dc; now join to center Rose as follows: Pick up Rose #1 and hold in back of Rose #2 with wrong side facing, sl st through upper lps of bar of center dc on any petal of Rose #1 (top lps of dc remain free, on right side); in same ch-4 lp on Rose #2 make 2 dc and hdc; sl st in next sc, in next ch-4 lp make hdc and 2 dc; with wrong side of Rose #1 facing, sl st through upper lps of bar of center dc on next petal of Rose #1; in same ch-4 lp on Rose #2 (being made) work 2 dc and hdc, end with sl st in joining of last rnd— corner Rose joined to 2 petals of center Rose. Cut yarn and fasten.

Roses #3, #4, #5 (corner roses): Using colors as indicated on Diagram, follow directions for Rose #2, but joining each Rose to next 2 free petals of center Rose.

Rose #6 (side rose): With D, ch 4. Join with sl st to form ring. *Rnd 1:* Ch 1, 8 sc in ring. Join to first sc. *Rnd 2:* Ch 1, from back of work, sc around bar of first sc, * ch 1, from back of work, sc around bar of next sc; rpt from * around, ending with ch 1. Join to first sc. *Rnd 3:* Rpt Rnd 3 of Rose #1. *Rnd 4:* (In next ch-3 lp make hdc, 2 dc, hdc; sl st in next sc) 3 times; in next ch-3 lp make hdc and dc; pick up joined Roses and hold in back of work with wrong side facing, placing rose being made between Rose #2 and #5; sl st between center 2 dc on next free petal preceding previous joining on Rose #5; in same ch-3 lp on Rose being made work dc and hdc; sl st in next sc, in next ch-3 lp make hdc and dc, sl st through upper lps of next free dc after next joining on Rose #1, in same ch-3 lp on Rose being made work dc and hdc; sl st in next sc; in next ch-3 lp make hdc and dc; sl st in next sl st between petals on Rose #1; in same ch-3 lp on Rose being made make dc and hdc, in next ch-3 lp make hdc and dc, sk next 2 sts on Rose #1, sl st through upper lps of next dc, in same ch-3 lp on Rose being made, make dc and hdc; sl st in next sc, in next ch-3 lp make hdc and dc; sl st between center 2 dc on next free petal on next corner Rose; in same ch-3 lp on Rose being made, make dc and hdc, end with sl st in joining of last rnd. Cut yarn and fasten.

Contrasting Center: Using contrasting colors as indicated in Diagram, attach yarn to top of any sc on Rnd 1 of Rose #6, sc in same st, sc in top of each sc around Rnd 1. Join with sl st to first sc. Cut yarn and fasten.

Roses #7, #8, #9 (side roses): Using colors and placing side Roses as indicated on Diagram, work same as for Rose #6.

Nine-Rose Motif Edging: With right side facing attach F to sl st between 2nd and 3rd free petals on any corner Rose, ch 3 (to count as 1 dc), in same st make dc, ch 3 for corner and 2 dc; * ch 2, sc between center 2 dc on next petal, ch 2, dc in next sl st between petals, ch 2, sc between center 2 dc of next petal, ch 2, in next joining of Roses make tr, ch 2 and tr; ch 2, from back of work, make sc and ch 2 around bar of center dc on each of next 3 free petals on next side Rose; in next joining of Roses make tr, ch 2 and tr; ch 2, sc between center 2 dc of next petal on next corner Rose, ch 2, dc in next sl st between petals, ch 2, sc between center 2 dc on next petal, ch 2, in next sl st between petals make 2 dc, ch 3 for corner and 2 dc; rpt from * around, ending last rpt with ch 2, sc between center 2 dc on next petal, ch 2. Join with sl st to top of ch-3. Cut yarn and fasten.

Square Border: Rnd 1: With right side facing, attach G with sl st in any corner ch-3 sp, ch 3, dc in same sp, * make 2 dc in each of next 6 ch-2 sps, dc in next ch-2 sp, dc in next sc, dc in next sp, 2 dc in each of next 6 ch-2 sps, in next corner sp make 2 dc, ch 3 for corner and 2 dc; rpt from * around, ending last rpt with 2 dc in same corner sp as first dc, ch 1, dc in top of ch-3 at beg or rnd to form last corner sp—124 dc, counting first ch-3 as 1 dc. *Rnd 2:* Ch 3 (to count as 1 dc), dc in corner sp just formed, * dc in each dc to within next corner ch-3 sp, in next corner sp make 2 dc, ch 3 and 2 dc; rpt from * around, ending last rpt with 2 dc in same corner sp as first dc, ch 1, dc in top of ch-3 to form last corner sp. *Rnd 3:* Rpt Rnd 2—156 dc. *Rnd 4:* Ch 3, dc in sp just formed, * ch 1, sk next dc, dc in next dc, ch 1; continue to work dc and ch 1 in every other dc across to within next corner sp, in corner sp make 2 dc, ch 3 and 2 dc; rpt from * around, ending last rpt with ch 1, 2 dc in same corner sp as first dc, ch 1, dc in top of first ch-3. *Rnd 5:* Ch 3, dc in sp just formed, * ch 1, sk next dc, dc and ch 1 in next dc, make dc and ch 1 in each dc to within one dc before next corner sp, sk next dc, in corner sp make 2 dc, ch 3 and 2 dc, rpt from * around, ending same as last rnd. *Rnd 6:* Ch 3, dc in corner sp just formed, * make dc in each dc and in each ch-1 sp across to next corner sp, in corner sp make 2 dc, ch 3 and 2 dc; rpt from * around, ending same as last rnd. Cut yarn and fasten.

Finishing: Pin each square to measurements on a padded surface; cover with a damp cloth; allow to dry; do not press. With a darning needle and G, working through back lp only of each st, from wrong side sew squares together from center of corner to center of next corner, matching stitches. Join squares in 4 rows of 3 squares in each row.

Afghan Border: Rnd 1: With right side facing, attach G with sl st in any corner sp of afghan, ch 3, dc in same sp, * dc in each dc, in each ch and in each joining across to within next corner sp of afghan, in corner sp make 2 dc, ch 3 and 2 dc; rpt from * around joined squares, ending with 2 dc in same sp as first dc, ch 1, dc in top of first ch-3. *Rnd 2:* Rpt Rnd 2 of Square Border. *Rnds 3, 4 and 5:* Rpt Rnds 4, 5 and 6 of Square Border. Cut yarn and fasten.

Fringe: Wind yarn about 50 times around a 5″ square of cardboard; cut at one edge, making 10″ strands. Continue to cut strands as needed. Fold one 10″ strand in half to form a loop; with right side of afghan facing, insert hook from back to front in any st on last rnd of afghan and pull loop through, draw loose ends through loop, pull tightly to form a knot. Tie a 10″ strand in same manner in each st and 3 strands in each corner sp along entire outer edge of afghan. Trim evenly.

BLOUSON TOP

Directions are given for size Small. Changes for sizes Medium and Large are given in parentheses.

MATERIALS: J. & P. Coats "Knit-Cro-Sheen": 14 (15, 16) balls (175 yds. each) Pongee; steel crochet hook, No. 7, *or any size hook which will obtain the stitch gauge below.*

GAUGE: 8 sts = 1″; 4 rows = 1″.

MEASUREMENTS: SIZES:	SMALL (6-8)	MEDIUM (10-12)	LARGE (14-16)
BUST:	34″	36″	38″
WIDTH ACROSS BACK OR FRONT AT UNDERARM:	17″	18″	19″
LENGTH FROM SHOULDER TO LOWER EDGE:	22½″	23½″	24½″
WIDTH ACROSS SLEEVE AT UPPER ARM:	13″	14″	15″

Back: Starting at lower edge, ch 140 (148, 156) to measure 18 (19, 20)″. *Row 1 (right side):* Dc in 6th ch from hook, * ch 1, *skip next ch, dc in next ch—sp made.* Repeat from * across—68 (72, 76) sps, including sp formed by first dc at beg of row. Ch 4, turn. *Row 2:* Dc in next dc, * ch 1, dc in next dc—sp over sp made. Repeat from * across to within last sp, ch 1, skip next ch, dc in next ch. Ch 4, turn. Repeat Row 2 for Space Pattern. Work in Space Pattern until 18 (20, 22) rows in all have been completed. At end of last row, ch 3, turn. Now work Popcorn Stitch Pattern as follows: *Row 1:* Dc in next ch and following dc, * make 5 dc in next ch, drop loop from* hook, *insert hook from front to back in first dc of the 5-dc group and draw dropped loop through, ch 1 to fasten*—FRONT PC ST MADE; (dc in next dc, dc in following ch) 3 times; dc in next dc. Repeat from * across, end last repeat with (dc in next dc, dc in next ch) twice; dc in 3rd ch of turning chain. Ch 3, turn. *Row 2:* Dc in next 4 dc, dc in next pc st, * *make 5 dc in next st, drop loop from hook, insert hook from back to front in first dc of the 5-dc group and draw loop through ch 1 to fasten*—BACK PC ST MADE AND MOVED TO THE LEFT; dc in next 7 sts. Repeat from * across, end last repeat with dc in next dc, dc in top of turning chain. Ch 3, turn. *Row 3:* * Front pc st in next st—*front pc st moved to the right;* dc in next 7 sts. Repeat from * across, end with dc in last 6 dc, dc in top of turning chain. Ch 3, turn. Repeat last 2 rows alternately for pattern, moving each *front pc st to the right and each back pc st to the left,* work to the left, making a new pc st on Rows 5 and 13 of Pc St Pattern. Do not make a pc st in first and last st. Work in Pc St Pat until 18 rows in all have been worked. Ch 4, turn. Now work in Group Stitch Pattern as follows: *Row 1:* Skip next st, dc in next st, (ch 1, skip next st, dc in next st) twice; * *holding back on hook last loop of each dc, make 2 dc in next st, thread over and draw through all 3 loops on hook*—JOINT DC MADE; dc in next st; (ch 1, skip next st, dc in next st) 3 times. Repeat from * across, end last repeat with joint dc in next st, dc in top of turning chain. Ch 4, turn. *Row 2:* Skip next joint dc, dc in next dc, * *joint dc in next sp, dc in next dc*—GROUP ST MOVED TO THE LEFT; (ch 1, dc in next dc) twice; ch 1, skip next joint dc, dc in next dc. Repeat from * across, end last repeat with joint dc in next sp, dc in next dc, ch 1, dc in next dc, ch 1, skip next ch on turning chain, dc in next ch. Ch 4, turn. *Row 3:* Dc in next dc, * *joint dc in next sp, dc in next dc*—GROUP ST MOVED TO THE RIGHT; ch 1, skip next joint dc, dc in next dc, (ch 1, dc in next dc) twice. Repeat from * across, end with ch 1, dc in next dc, ch 1, dc in 3rd ch of turning chain. Ch 4, turn. Continue in pattern as established, moving each group st to the right on each right side row and to the left on each wrong side row, making a new group st on Row 5 and every 4th row thereafter until 18 Group Stitch rows have been completed. At end of last row ch 3, turn. Starting with Row 1 of Pc St Pat, work in Pc St Pat for 18 rows. At end of last row ch 4, turn. Now work Second Space Pat as follows: *Row 1:* * Skip next st, dc in next st, ch 1. Repeat from * across, end with dc in top of

turning chain—68 (72, 76) sps. Ch 4, turn. Starting with Row 2 of Space Pat, work in pat until 18 (20, 22) rows have been worked in Second Space Pat. Turn.

Right Shoulder Shaping: Row 1: Sl st across first 13 (15, 17) sts including ch sts; ch 3, dc in next dc, (ch 1, dc in next dc) 9 times; dc in next dc. Do not work over remaining sts. Ch 3, turn. *Row 2:* Dc in next dc, (ch 1, dc in next dc) 4 times; hdc in following ch, sl st in next dc. Break off and fasten.

Left Shoulder Shaping: With right side facing, skip next 34 (36, 38) sps on last long row worked for neck edge, attach thread to next dc and work as follows: *Row 1:* Ch 3, dc in next dc, (ch 1, dc in next dc) 9 times; dc in next dc. Turn. *Row 2:* Sl st across first 9 sts, sc in next st, ch 2, dc in next dc, (ch 1, dc in next dc) 4 times; dc in last dc. Break off and fasten.

Front: Work as for Back until 14 (16, 18) rows of Second Space Pat have been completed, ending with a wrong-side row. Ch 4, turn.

Neck Shaping: Row 1: Work in pat until 18 (19, 20) sps have been completed, dc in next dc. Ch 4, turn. *Row 2:* Skip next sp, dc in next dc, ch 1, work in pattern across. *Rows 3–4:* Work in pattern across. Turn.

Left Shoulder Shaping: Work as for Right Shoulder Shaping of Back. With right side facing, skip center 30 (32, 34) sps on last long row worked before Neck Shaping, attach thread to next dc, ch 3, dc in next dc. Complete to correspond with opposite side, reversing shaping.

Sleeves: Starting at lower edge, ch 108 (116, 124) to measure 13½ (14½, 15½)". Having 52 (56, 60) sps, work as for Back until 18 Space Pattern rows have been completed. At end of last row ch 3, turn. Now work 18 rows in Pc St Pattern same as on Back. At end of last row ch 4, turn.

Next Row: Work as for Row 1 of Second Space Pat same as on Back. Repeat Row 2 of Space Pat Row until total length is 18 (18, 18½)", end with a wrong-side row. Turn.

Top Shaping: Row 1: Sl st across first 3 (3, 5) sts (including ch sts); ch 3, dc in next dc, work in Space Pattern across to last 3 (3, 4) sps, dc in next dc. *Rows 2–3:* Sl st across first 2 (2, 4) sts, ch 3, dc in next dc, work in pattern across to last 2 (2, 3) sps, dc in next dc. Turn. *Row 4:* Sl st across first 6 sts, ch 3, dc in next dc, work in pattern across to last 3 sps, dc in next dc. Turn. *Rows 5–8:* Repeat Row 4. At end of last row break off and fasten. Sew shoulder seams. Starting at lower edge, sew side seams for 16 (16½, 17)", matching pattern. Sew sleeve seams.

Sew in sleeves, easing in to fit.

Neck Edging: With right side facing, attach thread to any shoulder seam at neck edge, ch 1, sc in place where thread was attached, being careful to keep work flat, work 1 row of sc evenly around. Join with sl st to first sc. Break off and fasten.

Hip Drawstring: With 2 strands of thread held together, make a chain about 60 (64, 66)" long. Working in back loop of each st, sl st in each ch across. Break off and fasten.

Sleeve Drawstring (Make 2): With 2 strands of thread held together make a chain about 25" long. Complete as for Hip Drawstring. Lace Drawstring through sps on first row of garment. Tie a knot at each end. Lace Sleeve Drawstring through sps on first row on sleeve. Knot at each end and tie at the seam.

Color photo on page 144.

POPCORN SWEATER

Directions are given for size Small (8-10). Changes for sizes Medium (12-14) and Large (16-18) are in parentheses.

MATERIALS: Belding/Lily's Sugar & Cream Yarn (100 yd. skeins): 7 (8, 10) skeins Lavender; crochet hook, Size J, *or any size hook which will obtain the stitch gauge below.*

GAUGE: 10 dc = 3"; 2 rnds = 1 ".

MEASUREMENTS:

SIZES:	SMALL (8-10)	MEDIUM (12-14)	LARGE (16-18)
BUST:	33"	36"	40"
WIDTH ACROSS BACK OR FRONT AT UNDERARM:	16½"	18"	20"
WIDTH ACROSS SLEEVE AT UPPER ARM:	11½"	12½"	13¼"

DIRECTIONS: *Yoke:* Starting at neck edge (excluding edging), ch 104 (108, 108). Being careful not to twist chain, join with sl st to first ch to form a circle.

Foundation Rnd: Ch 1, sc in same st as joining, sc in each ch around. Join with sl st to first sc. Ch 3, turn. Always count ch-3 as 1 dc. *Rnd 1 (wrong side):* Sk joining, dc in each of next 25 (27, 27) sc—*back;* ch 1 for raglan seam, dc in each of next 26 sc—*sleeve;* ch 1, dc in next 26 (28, 28) sc—*front;* ch 1, dc in next 26 sc—*sleeve;* ch 1. Join to top of ch 3—4 raglan ch-1 sps. Ch 3, turn.

Rnd 2: In next ch-1 sp make dc, ch 1 and dc; * dc in each dc to next ch-1 sp, in ch-1 sp make dc, ch 1 and dc; rpt from * 2 more times; dc in each rem dc. Join with sl st to top of ch-3—inc made at each side of each section (8 incs in all); there are now 28 (30, 30) dc on back and front and 28 dc on each sleeve. Ch 3, turn. *Rnd 3:* Sk joining, * dc in each dc to within next ch-1 sp, in ch-1 sp make dc, ch 1 and dc; rpt from * 3 more times; dc in next dc. Join to top of ch-3. Ch 3, turn. *Rnd 4:* Sk joining, * dc in each st to next ch-1 sp, in ch-1 sp make dc, ch 1 and dc; rpt from * 3 more times; dc in each rem st. Join as before—32 (34, 34) dc on back and front; 32 dc on each sleeve. Ch 3, turn. Rpt last Rnd (Rnd 4) 2 (4, 5) more times—36 (42, 44) dc on back and front, 36 (40, 42) dc on each sleeve. At end of last rnd, ch 1, turn. *First Popcorn Rnd:* Sc in same st as joining, * tr in next dc, pushing tr just made to right side of work to form popcorn, sc in next dc; * placing one st in each dc, continue to work 1 tr and 1 sc across to next ch-1 sp; ch 1, sk next sp; rpt from * around, ending with tr in last dc. Join to first sc. Ch 3, turn. *Next Rnd:* Work same as Rnd 4. Ch 3, turn. *Next Rnd:* Sk joining, * dc in each st to next ch-1 sp, 2 dc in next sp, ch 1, dc in each dc across sleeve, ch 1, 2 dc in next sp; rpt from * once more; dc in each rem dc. Join to top of ch-3—2 dc increased at each side of back and front only. Ch 3, turn. Rpt last rnd 3 more times—54 (60, 62) dc on back and front; 38 (42, 44) dc on each sleeve. There are 5 rnds from popcorn rnd. *Second Popcorn Rnd:* Rpt First Popcorn Rnd. Ch 3, turn. *For Size 16-18 Only:* Work a dc rnd, increasing 2 sts at each side of back and front only—54 (60, 66) dc on back, front. *For All Sizes:* Cut yarn, fasten. Turn. *To Divide Sections–Body–Rnd 1:* Attach yarn in ch-1 sp preceding back sts, ch 2, dc in each dc across back, *holding back on hook last loop of each dc, make dc in next sp, sk sleeve sts, dc in next sp, yarn over hook, draw through all 3 loops on hook—*2-JOINT DC MADE AT UNDERARM; dc in each dc across front, work a 2-joint dc at underarm as before, sk ch-2. Join with sl st to top of first dc—110 (122, 134) sts. Ch 3, turn. *Rnd 2:* Sk joining, dc in each st around. Join with sl st to top of ch-3. Ch 3, turn. Rpt last rnd 2 (2, 1) more times. Ch 3, turn. There are 4 dc rnds from last popcorn rnd. *Next Rnd:* Sk joining, *holding back on hook last loop of each dc, make dc in each of next 2 sts, yarn over hook draw through all 3 loops on hook*–DEC MADE AT SIDE EDGE; dc in each of next 53 (59, 65) dc, dec over next 2 sts, dc in each rem st. Join to top of ch-3. Ch 1, turn. *Third Popcorn Rnd:* Sc in same st as joining, * tr in next st, sc in next st; rpt from * around, ending with tr in last st. Join to first sc. Ch 3, turn. *Next 5 Rnds:* Working same as Rnd 2 of Body, make a dec directly above each of the 2 previous decs in every other rnd twice; then work 1 rnd even—104 (116, 128) sts. *Fourth Popcorn Rnd:* Rpt Third Popcorn Rnd. *Next 4 Rnds:* Working as Rnd 2, inc 1 dc at each side edge every other row 2 times (to inc, make 2 dc in same st). Now, rpt Rnd 2 until length from underarm is approximately 9 (10, 10)″, ending with a wrong-side row. At end of last rnd, ch 1, turn.

Edging: Rnd 1: Sc in joining, sc in each st around. Join to first sc. Ch 1, turn. *Rnds 2 and 3:* Rpt last rnd. *Rnd 4:* Work same as Third Popcorn Rnd. Ch 1, turn. *Rnd 5:* Sl st in same st as joining, * ch 3, sc in 3 ch from hook for picot, sk next st, sl st in each of next 3 sts; rpt from * around. Join. Cut yarn and fasten.

Sleeves: Rnd 1: With wrong side of last rnd on sleeve facing, attach yarn to top of 2-joint dc at underarm, ch 1, sc in same st, dc in each dc around sleeve. Join with sl st to first sc. Ch 2, turn. *Rnd 2:* Sk joining, dc in each dc around, sk ch-2 at beg of rnd. Join to top of next dc—38 (42, 44) sts. Ch 3, turn. *Rnd 3:* Sk joining, dc in each st around. Join with sl st to top of ch-3. Rpt last rnd 2 (2, 1) more times. Ch 1, turn. *Next 5 Rnds:* Work a popcorn rnd same as Third Popcorn Rnd of Body; ch 3, turn, then work 4 rnds same as Rnd 3 of Sleeve. Ch 1, turn. Rpt last 5 rnds 2 more times. Work 1 (3, 4) more rnds same as Rnd 3 of Sleeve, end with wrong-side row. *Edging:* Work same as Edging for Body. Work other sleeve in same way. *Neck Edging:* With wrong side facing, attach yarn in first ch of starting chain at neck edge. *Rnd 1:* Working along opposite side of starting chain, sc in same st where yarn was attached, sc in each ch around. Join to first sc. Ch 1, turn. *Rnd 2:* Sc in same sc as joining, sc in each sc around. Join. Ch 1, turn. *Rnds 3 and 4:* Work same as Rnd 4 and 5 of Body Edging. Cut yarn and fasten.

Finishing: Pin sweater to measurements on a padded surface; cover with a damp cloth and steam very lightly. Remove when completely dry.

BOUCLÉ CARDIGAN WITH RUFFLES AND DRAWSTRINGS

Directions are for size Petite (4). Changes for sizes Small (6-8), Medium (10-12) and Large (14-16) are in parentheses.
MATERIALS: J. & P. Coats "Knit-Cro-Sheen" 20 (22, 24) 175 yard balls; crochet hook Size G, *or any size hook which will obtain the stitch gauge below*; tapestry needle, crochet hook Size F.
GAUGE: 9 sts = 2″; 3 rows = 1″.

MEASUREMENTS:

SIZES:	PETITE (4)	SMALL (6-8)	MEDIUM (10-12)	LARGE (14-16)
BUST:	32″	34½″	36¾″	39¼″
WIDTH ACROSS BACK AT UNDERARMS:				
	15″	16½″	17¼″	18¾″
WIDTH ACROSS EACH FRONT AT UNDERARM:				
	8½″	9″	9¾″	10¾″
WIDTH OF SLEEVE AT UPPERARM:				
	11¾″	12½″	13¼″	14¼″

Note: Use 2 strands of Knit-Cro-Sheen.
Back: Ch 69 (75, 79, 85). *Row 1 (wrong side):* Hdc in 2nd ch from hook, then hdc in each rem ch—68 (74, 78, 84) hdc. Ch 1, turn. *Row 2:* Hdc in each hdc. Ch 1, turn. Rpt Row 2 until 32 (32, 34, 36) rows from beg or desired length from waist to underarm.
Armhole Shaping: Next Row: Sl st across 3 (4, 5, 6) sts, sc in next st, work hdc across next 60 (64, 66, 70) sts, sc in next st. Ch 1, turn. *Next Row:* Sk sc, hdc across 60 (64, 66, 70) sts. Ch 1, turn. Continue in hdc pat for 18 (18, 20, 22) rows more.

Shoulder Shaping: Next Row: Sl st across 7 (8, 8, 9) sts, sc in next st, hdc across 44 (46, 48, 50) sts, sc in next st. Ch 1, turn. *Next Row:* Sk sc, sl st across 9 (9, 10, 10) sts, hdc across 26 (28, 28, 30) sts for back of neck, sc in next st, sl 1 st. Fasten off.

Left Front: Ch 39 (41, 45, 49). *Row 1 (wrong side):* Hdc in 2nd ch from hook, then hdc in each rem ch—38 (40, 44, 48) hdc. Ch 1, turn. *Row 2:* Hdc in each hdc. Ch 1, turn. Rpt Row 2 until piece measures same as back to underarm, ending at front edge.

Armhole Shaping: Next Row: Hdc across 34 (35, 38, 41) sts, sc in next st. Ch 1, turn. *Next Row:* Sk sc, hdc across 34 (35, 38, 41) sts. Ch 1, turn. Work in hdc across 34 (35, 38, 41) sts for 2 rows.

V-Neck Shaping: Next Row: Draw up a lp in each of first 2 sts, yo and thru 3 lps on hook—1 st dec, work in hdc across row. Ch 1, turn. *Next Row:* Work in hdc across row until 2 sts rem, dec 1 st. Ch 1, turn. Rpt last 2 rows for 15 (15, 17, 19) rows more—17 (18, 19, 20) sts.

Shoulder Shaping: Next Row: Sl st across 7 (8, 8, 9) sts, sc in next st, hdc across 9 (9, 10, 10) sts. Fasten off.

Right Front: Work same as Left Front until piece measures same as back to underarm, ending at side edge.

Armhole Shaping: Next Row: Sl st across 3 (4, 5, 6) sts, sc in next st, hdc across 34 (35, 38, 41) sts. Ch 1, turn. Work hdc across 34 (35, 38, 41) sts for 3 rows.

V-Neck Shaping: Next Row (wrong side): Work in hdc across row until 2 sts rem, dec 1 st. Ch 1, turn. *Next Row:* Dec 1 st, work in hdc across row. Ch 1, turn. Rpt last 2 rows 15 (15, 17, 19) rows more—17 (18, 19, 20) sts.

Shoulder Shaping: Next Row: Hdc across 9 (9, 10, 10) sts, sc in next st, sl 1 st. Fasten off.

Sleeves: Ch 53 (57, 61, 65). *Row 1 (wrong side):* Hdc in 2nd ch from hook, then hdc in each rem ch—52 (56, 60, 64) hdc. Ch 1, turn. *Row 2:* Hdc in each hdc. Ch 1, turn. Rpt Row 2 until 34 (36, 38, 40) rows from beg have been completed.

Top Shaping: Next Row: Sl st across 3 (4, 5, 6) sts, sc in next st, hdc across 44 (46, 48, 50) sts, sc in next st. Ch 1, turn. *Next Row:* Sk sc, *draw up a lp in each of next 2 sts, yo and draw thru 3 lps on hook—1 dec made, hdc across 40 (42, 44, 46) sts, work 1 dec. Ch 1 turn. Dec 1 st at beg and end of every row 13 (14, 15, 16) times—14 sts. Fasten off.

Lace Ruffle on Sleeves: Row 1: From wrong side of lower edge of sleeve, sc in first ch, [ch 1, sk 1 ch, (sc, ch 3, sc) in next ch] 25 (27, 29, 31) times. Turn. *Row 2 (right side):* Sl st into first ch-3 sp, ch 2, 2 dc in first ch-sp, then 3 dc into each of 25 (27, 29, 31) ch-3 sps. Turn. *Row 3:* Ch 6, 1 dc in first 3-dc cl, (ch 1, 1 dc, ch 3, 1 dc) in each sp between 3-dc cls 24 (26, 28, 30) times, end ch 1, 1 dc in last dc st of 3-dc cl. Turn. *Row 4:* Ch 6, 1 dc in first ch-1 sp, [ch 3, 1 sc in ch-3 sp of previous row, ch 3, (1 dc, ch 1, 3 dc) in ch-1 sp of previous row] 24 (26, 28, 30) times, end ch 3, 1 sc in ch-6 sp. Turn. *Row 5:* Ch 1, 1 sc in first sc st, [ch 3, (1 sc, ch 3, 1 sc) in ch-1 sp made on previous row between 2 dcs, ch 3, 1 sc in sc st of previous row] 24 (26, 28, 30) times, end ch 3, (1 sc, ch 3, 1 sc) in ch-6 sp. Fasten off.

Finishing: Lace Edge Around Cardigan: First sew side seam and shoulder seam edges together without seam allowance. *Row 1:* From wrong side beg at lower edge of Left Front and working up Left Front edge work 1 sc in foundation ch, * ch 1, sk 1 row, (1 sc, ch 3, 3 sc) into edge of row *; rpt from * to * to shoulder. Then working along edge of back of neck work ** ch 1, sk 1 st, (1 sc, ch 1, 3 sc) in next st **; rpt from ** to ** to right shoulder. Then rpt from * to * as for Left Front down the Right Front edge to waist. Then rpt from ** to ** as for back of neck along lower edge of cardigan ending (1 sc, ch 3, 1 sc) at Left center front. *Rows 2–5:* Work as for Lace Ruffle on Sleeve, repeating pat about 70 (76, 82, 90) times substituting a ch-1 sp wherever you see a ch-3 sp.

Note: Number of rpts may vary slightly depending on number of sts lost into side seams. Sew sleeve seams. Then sew sleeves into body armholes.

Buttons: Make 8. *Note:* Using Size F hook, ch 4; join with sl st to form ring. *Next Rnd:* Work 2 sc in each ch—8 sc. *Next Rnd:* Work 1 sc in each sc, sl st to first st. Measure about 1 yard of thread; cut and pull end thru the last lp on hook. Wind thread into small ball and stuff into crocheted button. With beg of thread end, sew button tog and attach to cardigan starting at lower edge opposite every 2nd loop in lace edge along Right Front. (Sc, ch 3, sc) lps serve as buttonholes.

Waist Drawstring: Make a chain to measure 2 yards, turn. *Next Row:* Sl st in 2nd ch, then sl st in each rem ch. Fasten off. Thread drawstring thru the first row in Lace Ruffle at waist and tie into bow at center front.

Sleeve Drawstrings: Make 2. Make chains to measure 30″ each and complete as for Waist Drawstring. Thread drawstrings thru first row in Lace Ruffle on each sleeve and tie into bow.

HOW-TO

**HOW TO TAKE
BODY MEASUREMENTS**

It's easy to determine the correct size for any crocheted or knitted garment. First, make sure the person you're measuring is wearing the usual undergarments. For all women's and girls sizes, measure at the fullest part of natural waistline, hips and bust. We've made allowances for ease to insure a proper fit. If you have to make adjustments between the measurements and size differential, do it during the blocking and finishing. Determine men's sizes by loosely holding the tape around the fullest part of the chest.

STANDARD
BODY MEASUREMENTS:

All measurements in inches.

JUNIORS

Size	7	9	11	13	15
Bust	31	32	33½	35	37
Waist	22½	23½	24½	26	28
Hip	33	34	35½	37	39

TEENS

Size	7/8	9/10	11/12	13/14
Bust	29	30½	32	33½
Waist	23	24	25	26
Hip	32	33½	35	36½

MISSES

Size	8	10	12	14	16	18
Bust	31½	32½	34	36	38	40
Waist	23	24	25½	27	29	31
Hip	33½	34½	36	38	40	42

WOMEN

Size	38	40	42	44	46	48
Bust	42	44	46	48	50	52
Waist	34	36	38	40½	43	45½
Hip	44	46	48	50	52	54

MEN

Size	34	36	38	40	42	44
Chest	34	36	38	40	42	44
Waist	30	32	34	36	38	40

HOW TO ENLARGE
AND REDUCE DESIGNS

When you enlarge or reduce a design, it's most important that the proportions remain the same. You can use either of these two simple methods.

METHOD 1

If the design is not already marked off in squares, make a tracing of it. Then mark the tracing off in squares; for a small design, make squares ¼"; for larger designs, use ½", 1" or 2" squares. Decide the size of your reduction or enlargement; on another sheet of tracing paper, mark off the same number of squares that are on the design or original tracing. Remember that to make your design six times larger than the original design, each new square must be six times larger than the original. Carefully copy the outline from your original tracing to the new one, square by square. Use dressmaker's carbon and a tracing wheel to transfer the design to the material you're decorating.

METHOD 2

First, take the original design and make a tracing. Then determine the finished size you want and draw another outline. To accurately proportion the new design, first draw diagonal lines through both outlines. Second, draw one horizontal and one vertical line at the center where the two diagonal lines meet. In each quarter of the original design and outline, complete the other diagonal lines; then divide the quarters with horizontal and vertical lines where the diagonals intersect. Follow Method 1 to copy design from original tracing.

BASIC NEEDLEPOINT STITCHES.

NEEDLES: Always use blunt-tip "tapestry" needles to avoid splitting the mesh threads. The needles come in an array of sizes, so you'll easily find a needle to fit your canvas and threads.

TRANSFERRING A DESIGN: It's easier than you think to transfer a design to canvas. First, cut the canvas about three inches larger on each side than your planned design. Then fold it in half vertically down the center, then horizontally. Unfold canvas and lightly mark the crease lines with a pencil. Fold and mark the design in the same way as you did the canvas. Now tape the design, unfolded, to a window; place and tape canvas over the design, matching centers, and vertical and horizontal lines. Using a *water-proof* marking pen, *starting from the center and working outward*, carefully trace the pattern onto canvas. If you make a mistake, paint over it with white acrylic paint. Remove pattern and canvas from window. Bind canvas edges with masking tape so they will not ravel. Leave canvas as is, or color in design with *waterproof* paints or nylon felt-tip markers.

TO BLOCK NEEDLEPOINT: Cover a table or any other flat board with a piece of brown paper, or old sheet, larger than your canvas; tack it down flat. With a pencil, mark the size of the canvas on the paper or sheet, making sure all corners are square. Soak canvas in cold wa-

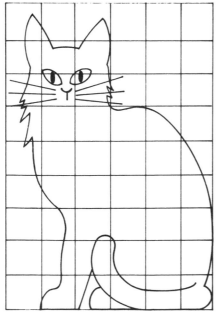

METHOD 1

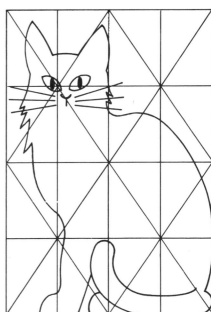

METHOD 2

ter. *Note:* If you wish to wash needlepoint before hanging, use one of the cold water soaps, or a very mild detergent in cool water. Do not wring; rinse thoroughly to remove all soap. Pull or stretch the canvas *worked side up* until it conforms to the penciled outline. *Using rust proof tacks or nails* (if you aren't sure, ask your hardware dealer), tack down the four corners, ½" outside design edge, making sure the corners are at *right angles*, and match the outline you've drawn on the paper or sheet. Then, in the cen-

ter of each side, nail down four more tacks. Continue around all four sides, until tacks are about ¼" apart. *Let dry thoroughly*—approximately 48 hours. Remove canvas from board. If you're not going to immediately mount your canvas, roll it around any cardboard tube, with the worked side out. (This will keep stitches from crushing against each other.)
IMPORTANT: If you're left handed, reverse all the hand directions we give you, or practice stitches in front of a mirror.

BASIC NEEDLEPOINT STITCHES

Algerian Eye

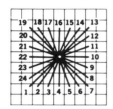

Bargello

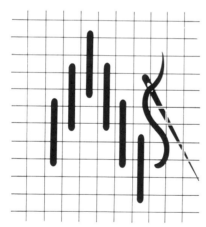

Basket Weave

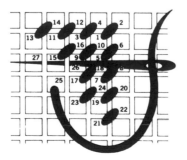

Binding Stitch

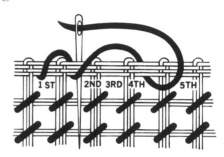

Brick Stitch

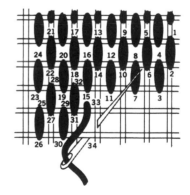

Chevron Stitch

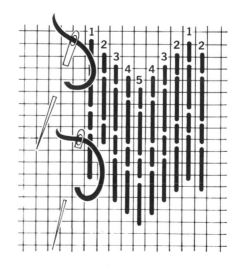

Continental or Tent Stitch

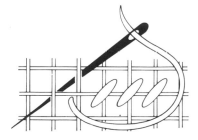

Cross Stitch

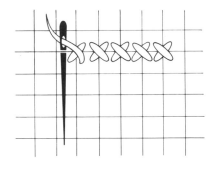

Half Cross Stitch

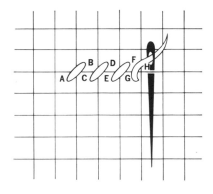

Half Cross Stitch Reversed

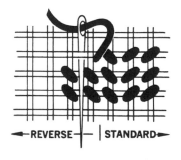

Interlocking Gobelin Stitch

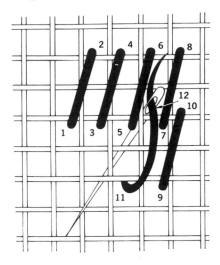

Leaf Stitch

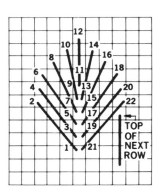

Leviathan Stitch

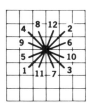

Mosaic Stitch

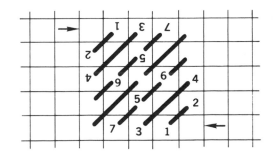

Parisian Stitch

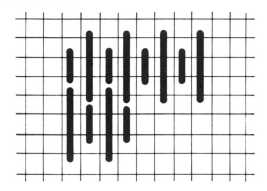

Rice Stitch

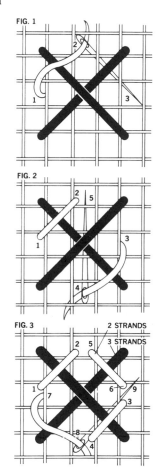

Rya Stitch

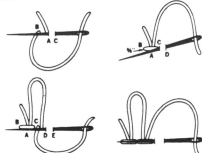

Satin Stitch

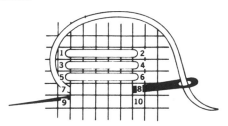

Scotch Stitch

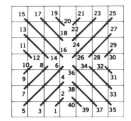

Scotch Stitch Variation

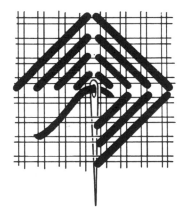

Slanted Gobelin Stitch (worked vertically)

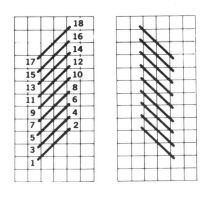

Smyrna Cross Stitch

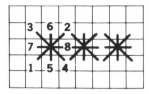

Stem Stitch

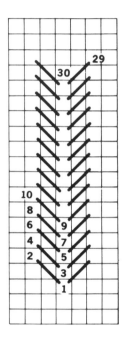

Stem Stitch Variation

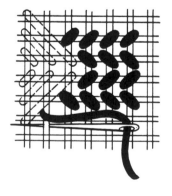

BASIC EMBROIDERY STITCHES

Embroidery has no rigid rules, and it's great fun to invent your own stitches to create a very personal design. The beginner, though, may be confused by what stitch to use where, so we show a selection of basic stitches. Master these stitches, then experiment on your own!

Back Stitch

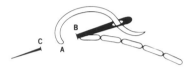

Blanket or Buttonhole Stitch

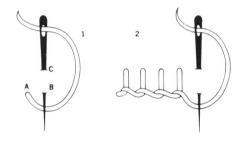

Burden Stitch

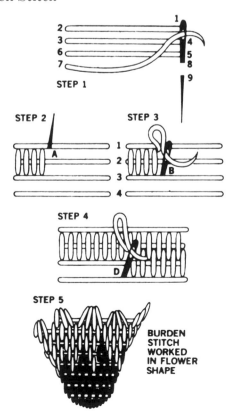

BURDEN STITCH WORKED IN FLOWER SHAPE

Bullion Knot

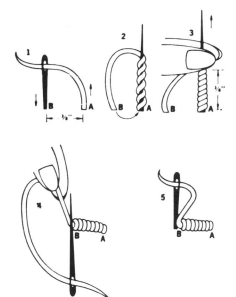

Chain Stitch

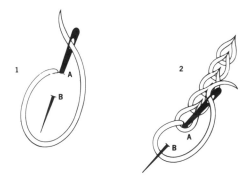

Close Herringbone Stitch

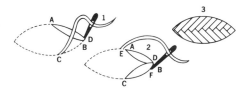

Closed Buttonhole Stitch

Coral Knot

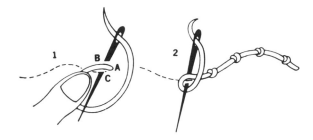

Couching

Cretan Stitch

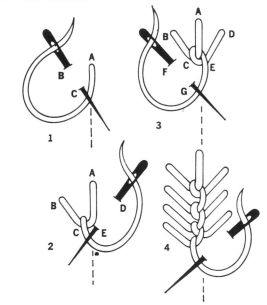

Cross Stitch

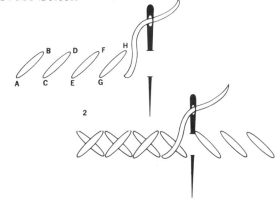

230

Feather Stitch

Fishbone Stitch

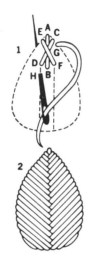

Fly Stitch

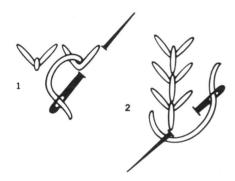

French Knot

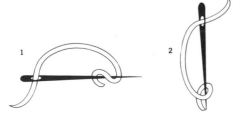

Herringbone Stitch

Lazy Daisy Stitch

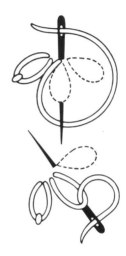

Long And Short Stitch   Straight Stitch

Open Cretan Stitch

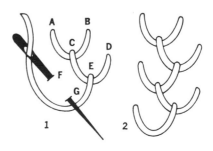

Outline or Stem Stitch

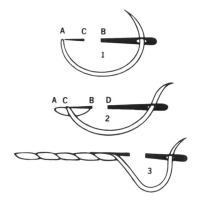

Split Stitch

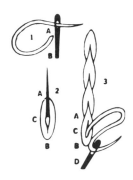

Roumanian Stitch

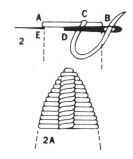

Turkey Work

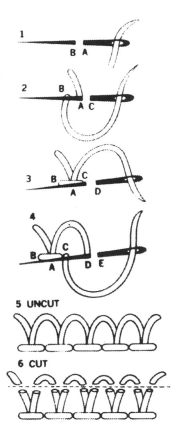

Running Stitch

Satin Stitch

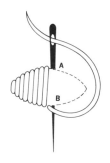

KNITTING ABBREVIATIONS AND SYMBOLS

Knitting directions are always written in standard abbreviations. They look mysterious at first, but you'll soon know them. **beg**—beginning; **bet**—between; **bl**—block; **ch**—chain; **CC**—contrasting color; **dec(s)**—decrease(s); **dp**—double-pointed; ″ **or in(s)**—inch(es); **incl**—inclusive; **inc(s)**—increase(s); **k**—knit; **lp(s)**—loop(s); **MC**—main color; **oz(s)**—ounce(s); **psso**—pass slipped stitch over last stitch worked; **pat(s)**—pattern(s); **p**—purl; **rem**—remaining; **rpt**—repeat; **rnd(s)**—round(s); **sc**—single crochet; **sk**—skip; **sl**—slip; **sl st**—slip stitch; **sp(s)**—space(s); **st(s)**—stitch(es); **st st**—stockinette stitch; **tog**—together; **yo**—yarn over; **pc**—popcorn st.

  * **(asterisk)**—directions immediately following * are to be repeated the specified number of times indicated, in addition to the first time—i.e., "repeat from * 3 times more" means 4 times in all.

  ( ) parentheses—directions should be worked as often as specified—i.e., (k 1, k 2 tog, k 3) 5 times, means to work what is in ( ) 5 times in all.

THE BASIC STITCHES

Get out your needles and yarn and slowly read your way through this special section, practicing the basic stitches illustrated here as you go along. Once you know them you're ready to start knitting.

CASTING ON: This puts the first row of stitches on the needle. Measure off about two yards of yarn, (or about an inch for each stitch you are going to cast on). Make a slip knot at this point by making a medium size loop of yarn; then pull another small loop through it. Place the slip knot on one needle and pull one end gently to tighten (FIG. 1).

Fig. 1

Hold needle in right hand. Hold both strands of yarn in the palm of your left hand securely but not rigidly. Slide your left thumb and forefinger between the two strands and spread these two fingers out so that you have formed a triangle of yarn. Your left thumb should hold the free end

of yarn, your forefinger the yarn from the ball, while the needle in your right hand holds the first stitch (FIG. 2).

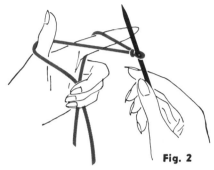

Fig. 2

You are now in position to cast on. See AB-BREVIATIONS for explanation of asterisk (*).
* Bring the needle in your right hand toward you; slip the tip of the needle under the front strand of the loop on left thumb (FIG. 3).

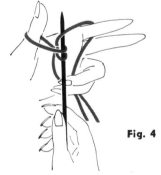

Fig. 3

Now, with the needle, catch the strand of yarn that is on your left forefinger (FIG. 4).

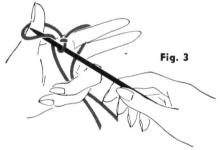

Fig. 4

Draw it through thumb loop to form a stitch on needle (FIG. 5).

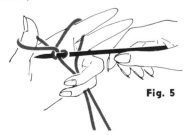

Fig. 5

Holding the stitch on the needle with the right index finger, slip loop off left thumb (FIG. 6).

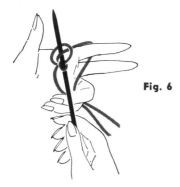

Fig. 6

Tighten up the stitch on the needle by pulling the freed strand back with left thumb, bringing the yarn back into position for casting on more stitches (FIG. 2 again).

Do not cast on too tightly. Stitches should slide easily on the needle. Repeat from * until you have cast on the number of stitches specified in your instructions.

KNIT STITCH: (k): Hold the needle with the cast-on stitches in your left hand (FIG. 7).

Fig. 7

Pick up the other needle in your right hand. With yarn from ball in *back* of the work, insert the tip of right-hand needle from *left to right* through front loop of first stitch on left-hand needle (FIG. 8).

Fig. 8

Holding both needles in this position with left hand, wrap the yarn over your little finger, under your two middle fingers and over the forefingers of your right hand. Hold the yarn firmly, but loosely enough so that it will slide through your fingers as you knit. Return right-hand needle to right hand.

With right forefinger, pass the yarn under (from right to left) and then over (from left to right) the tip of the right-hand needle, forming a loop on needle (FIG. 9).

Fig. 9

Now draw this loop through the stitch on left-hand needle (FIG. 10).

Fig. 10

Slip original stitch off the left-hand needle, leaving new stitch on right-hand needle (FIG. 11).

Fig. 11

Keep stitches loose enough so that you can slide them along the needles, but firm enough so they do not slide when you don't want them to. Continue until you have knitted all the stitches from the left-hand needle onto the right-hand needle.

To start the next row, pass needle with stitches on it to the left hand, reversing it, so that it now becomes the left-hand needle.

PURL STITCH: (p): Purling is the reverse of knitting. Again, keep the stitches loose enough to slide, but firm enough to work with. To purl, hold the needle with the stitches in your left hand, with the yarn in *front* of your work. Insert the tip of the right-hand needle from *right to left* through the front loop of the first stitch on left-hand needle (FIG. 12).

Fig. 12

With your right hand holding the yarn in the same manner as to knit, but in *front* of the needles, pass the yarn over the tip of right-hand needle, then under it, forming loop on needle (FIG. 13).

Fig. 13

Holding the yarn firmly, so that it won't slip off, draw this loop through the stitch on left-hand needle (FIG. 14).

Fig. 14

Slip original stitch off the left-hand needle, leaving new stitch on the right-hand needle (FIG. 15).

Fig. 15

SLIP STITCH (sl st): Insert the tip of the right-hand needle into the next stitch on left-hand needle, as if to purl, unless otherwise directed. Slip this stitch off the left-hand needle onto the right, *without working it* (FIG. 16).

Fig. 16

BINDING OFF: This makes a finished edge and locks the stitches securely in place. Knit (or purl) two stitches. Then, with the tip of the left-hand needle, lift the first of these two stitches over the second stitch and drop it off the tip of the right-hand needle (FIG. 17).

Fig. 17

One stitch remains on the right-hand needle and one stitch has been bound off. * Knit (or purl) the next stitch; lift the first stitch over the last stitch and off the tip of the needle. Again, one stitch remains on the right-hand needle and another stitch has been bound off. Repeat from * until the required number of stitches has been bound off.

Remember that you work *two* stitches to bind off one stitch. If, for example, the directions read, "k 6, bind off the next 4 sts, k 6 . . ." you must knit six stitches, then knit *two more* stitches before starting to bind off. Bind off four times. After the four stitches have been bound off, count the last stitch remaining on the right-hand needle as the first stitch of the next six stitches. When binding off, always knit the knitted stitches and purl the purled stitches.

Be careful not to bind off too tightly or too loosely. The tension should be the same as the rest of the knitting.

To end off the last stitch on the bound-off edge, if you are ending this piece of work here, cut yarn, leaving a six-inch end; pass the cut end through the remaining loop on the right hand needle and pull snugly (FIG. 18).

Fig. 18

SHAPING TECHNIQUES: Now that you know the basics, all that's left to learn are a few techniques which will help shape whatever it is you are making.

INCREASING (inc): This means adding stitches in a given area to shape your work. There are several ways to increase.

1. *To increase by knitting twice into the same stitch:* Knit the stitch in the usual way through the front loop (FIG. 19), but *before* dropping the

Fig. 19

stitch from the left-hand needle, knit *another* stitch on the same loop by placing the needle into the *back* of the stitch (FIG. 20).

Fig. 20

Slip the original stitch off your left-hand needle. You have made two stitches from one stitch.

2. To increase by knitting between stitches: Insert tip of the right-hand needle under the strand of yarn *between* the stitch you've just worked and the following stitch; slip it onto tip of the left-hand needle (FIG. 21).

Fig. 21

Now knit into the back of this new loop (FIG. 22).

Fig. 22

3. To increase by "yarn-over" (yo): Pass the yarn over the right-hand needle after finishing one stitch and before starting the next stitch, *making an extra stitch (arrow in Fig. 23). If you are knitting,* bring the yarn under the needle to the back. *If you are purling,* wind the yarn around the needle once. On the next row, work all yarn-overs as stitches.

Fig. 23

DECREASING: (dec): This means reducing the number of stitches in a given area to shape your work. Two methods for decreasing are:

1. To decrease by knitting (FIG. 24) or *purling* (FIG. 25) *two stitches together:*

Fig. 24

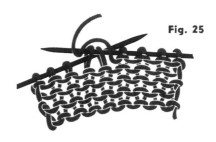

Fig. 25

Insert right-hand needle through the loops of two stitches on left-hand needle at the same time; complete stitch. This is written k 2 tog, or p 2 tog.

If you work through the *front* loops of the stitches in the usual way, your decreasing stitch will slant to the right. If you work through the *back* loops of the stitches, your decreasing stitch will slant to the left.

2. Slip 1 stitch, knit 1 and psso: Insert right-hand needle through the stitch on the left-hand needle, but instead of working it, just slip it off onto the right-hand needle (go back to FIG. 16). Work the next stitch in the usual way. With the tip of the left-hand needle, lift the slipped stitch over the last stitch worked and off the tip of the right-hand needle (FIG. 26).

Fig. 26

Your decreasing stitch will slant to the left. This is written sl 1, k 1, psso.

Pass Slipped Stitch Over (psso): Slip one stitch from the left-hand needle to the right-hand needle and, being careful to keep it in position, work the next stitch. Then, with the tip of the left-hand needle, lift the slipped stitch over the last stitch and off the tip of the needle (FIG. 26 again).

ATTACHING YARN: *When you end one ball of yarn or wish to change colors:* Begin at the start of row and tie new yarn with previous yarn, making a secure joining. Continue to knit or purl.

Making Fringe

Duplicate Stitch Embroidery

CROCHET ABBREVIATIONS

beg—begin, beginning; **ch**—chain; **dc**—double crochet; **dec**—decrease, **dtr**—double treble crochet; **hdc**—half double crochet; **in(s) or "**—inch(es); **inc**—increase; **oz(s)**—ounce(s); **pat**—pattern; **pc**—picot; **rem**—remaining; **rnd**—round; **rpt**—repeat; **sc**—single crochet; **skn(s)**—skein(s); **sk**—skip; **sl st**—slip stitch; **sp**—space; **st(s)**—stitch(es); **tog**—together; **tr**—triple crochet; **work even**—continue without further increase or decrease; **yo**—yarn over; *—repeat whatever follows * as many times as indicated; ( )—do what is in parentheses as many times as indicated.

HOW TO CROCHET

DIRECTIONS FOR RIGHT-HANDED AND LEFT-HANDED CROCHETERS: Most crochet stitches are started from a base of chain stitches. However, our stitches are started from a row of single crochet stitches which gives body to the sample swatches and makes practice work easier to handle. When making a specific item, follow the stitch directions as given.

Holding the crochet hook properly (FIG. 1), start by practicing the slip knot (FIG. 2) and base chain (FIG. 3).

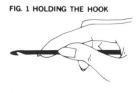

FIG. 1 HOLDING THE HOOK

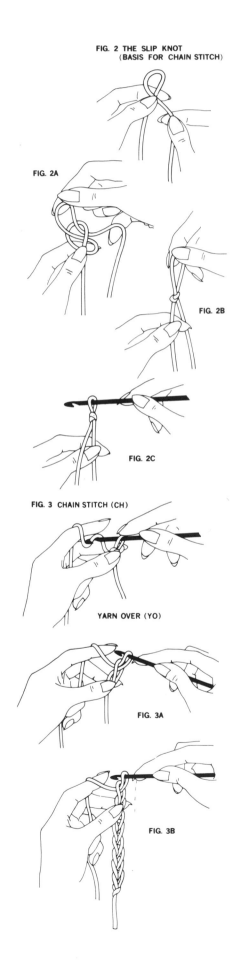

FIG. 2 THE SLIP KNOT
(BASIS FOR CHAIN STITCH)

FIG. 2A

FIG. 2B

FIG. 2C

FIG. 3 CHAIN STITCH (CH)

YARN OVER (YO)

FIG. 3A

FIG. 3B

For Left-handed Crocheters: FIGS. 1 to 3 are for right-handed crocheters and are repeated in FIGS. 1 Left to 3 Left for left-handed crocheters.

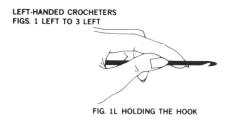

LEFT-HANDED CROCHETERS
FIGS. 1 LEFT TO 3 LEFT

FIG. 1L HOLDING THE HOOK

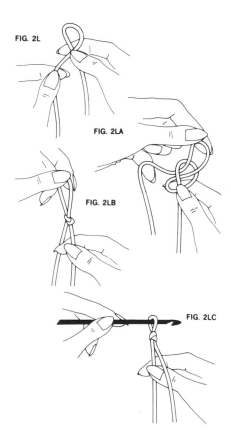

FIG. 2L

FIG. 2LA

FIG. 2LB

FIG. 2LC

FOR LEFT-HANDED CROCHETERS:
From here on we won't be showing hands—just the hook and stitches. Left-handed crocheters can use all the following right-handed illustrations by simply turning the book up-side down and placing a mirror (with backstand) so that it reflects the left-handed version.

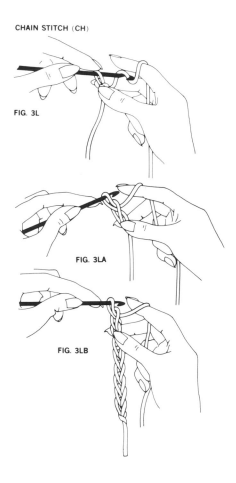

CHAIN STITCH (CH)

FIG. 3L

FIG. 3LA

FIG. 3LB

CHAIN STITCH (ch): Follow the Steps in FIG. 3. As you make the chain stitch loops, the yarn should slide easily between your index and middle fingers. Make about 15 loops. If they are all the same size, you have maintained even tension. if uneven, rip them out by pulling on the long end of the yarn. Practice making chains and ripping out until you have a perfect chain.
SINGLE CROCHET (sc): Follow the Steps in FIG. 4. To practice, make a 20-loop chain (this means 20 loops in addition to the slip knot). Turn the chain, as shown, and insert the hook in the second chain from the hook (see arrow) to make the first sc stitch. Yarn over (yo); for second stitch see next arrow. Repeat to end of chain. Because you started in the second chain from the hook, you end up with only 19 sc. To add the 20th stitch, chain one (called a turning chain) and pull the yarn through. Now turn your work around (the "back" is now facing you) and start the second row of sc in the first stitch of the previous row (at the arrow). Make sure your hook goes under both of the strands at the top of the stitch. Don't forget to make a ch 1 turning chain at the end before turning your work. Keep practicing until your rows are perfect.

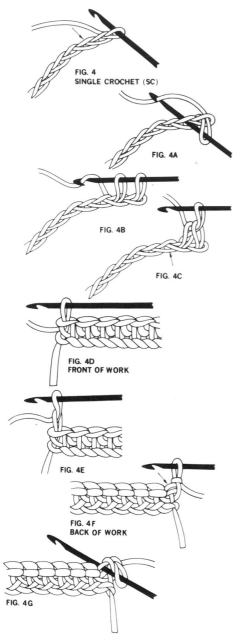

FIG. 4
SINGLE CROCHET (SC)

FIG. 4A

FIG. 4B

FIG. 4C

FIG. 4D
FRONT OF WORK

FIG. 4E

FIG. 4F
BACK OF WORK

FIG. 4G

ENDING OFF: Follow Steps in FIG. 5. To finish off your crochet, cut off all but 6″ of yarn and end off as shown. (To "break off and fasten," follow the same procedure.)

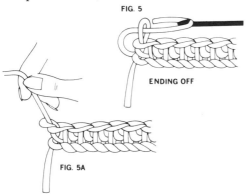

FIG. 5

ENDING OFF

FIG. 5A

DOUBLE CROCHET (dc): Follow the Steps in FIG. 6. To practice, ch 20, then make a row of 20 sc. Now, instead of a ch 1, you will make a ch 3. Turn your work, yo and insert the hook in the second stitch of the previous row (*at the arrow*), going under both strands at the top of the stitch. Pull the yarn through. You now have three loops on the hook. Yo and pull through the first two, then yo and pull through the remaining two—one double crochet (dc) made. Continue across row, making a dc in each stitch (st)

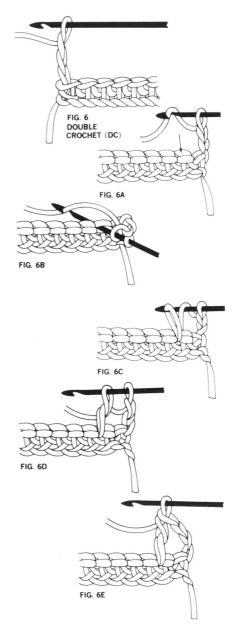

FIG. 6
DOUBLE
CROCHET (DC)

FIG. 6A

FIG. 6B

FIG. 6C

FIG. 6D

FIG. 6E

across. Dc in the top of the turning chain (*see arrow in* FIG. 7). Ch 3. Turn work. Dc in second stitch in the previous row and continue as before.

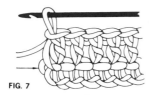

FIG. 7

Note: You may also start a row of dc on a base chain (omitting the sc row). In this case, insert hook in fourth chain from hook, instead of second (FIG. 8).

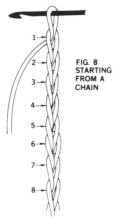

FIG. 8
STARTING
FROM A
CHAIN

SLIP STITCH (sl st): Follow Steps in FIG. 11. This is a utility stitch you will use for joining, shaping and ending off. After you chain and turn, *do not yo.* Just insert the hook into the *first* stitch of the previous row (FIG. 8), and pull the yarn through the stitch then right through the loop on the hook—sl st made.

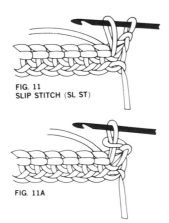

FIG. 11
SLIP STITCH (SL ST)

FIG. 11A

HALF DOUBLE CROCHET (hdc): Follow the Steps in FIG. 12. To practice, make a chain and a row of sc. Ch 2 and turn; yo. Insert hook in second stitch, as shown; yo and pull through to make three loops on hook. Yo and pull the yarn through *all* three loops at the same time—hdc made. This stitch is used primarily as a transitional stitch from an sc to a dc. Try it and see—starting with sc's then an hdc and then dc's.

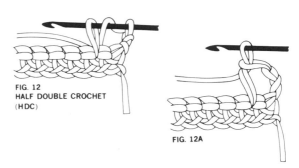

FIG. 12
HALF DOUBLE CROCHET
(HDC)

FIG. 12A

THE TECHNIQUES OF CROCHETING: Now that you have practiced and made sample squares of all the basic stitches, you are ready to learn about adding and subtracting stitches to change the length of a row whenever it's called for. This is achieved by increasing (inc) and decreasing (dec).

TO INCREASE (inc): Just make two stitches in the same stitch in the previous row (*see arrow in* FIG. 13). The technique is the same for any kind of stitch.

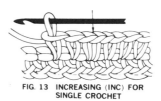

FIG. 13   INCREASING (INC) FOR
SINGLE CROCHET

TO DECREASE (dec) FOR SINGLE CROCHET (sc): Yo and pull the yarn through two stitches to make three loops on hook (*see Steps in* FIG. 14). Pull yarn through all loops at once—dec made. Continue in regular stitches.

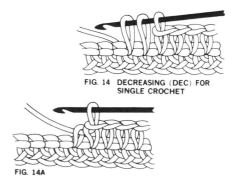

FIG. 14   DECREASING (DEC) FOR
SINGLE CROCHET

FIG. 14A

TO DECREASE FOR DOUBLE CROCHET: In a dc row make the next stitch and stop when you have two loops on the hook. Now yo and make a dc in the next stitch. At the point where you have three loops on the hook, pull yarn through all loops at the same time. Finish the row with regular dc.

Shell Stitch

1

2

3

4

Afghan Stitch

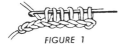
FIGURE 1

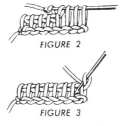
FIGURE 2

FIGURE 3

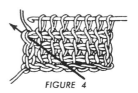
FIGURE 4

HOW TO MAKE AFGHAN STITCH:

Make a foundation ch of desired number of sts called for in your instructions.

Row 1: First half of row: Retaining all loops on hook, draw up a loop in second ch from hook and in each ch across (Fig. 1).

Second half of row: YO and draw through 1 loop, * yo and draw through 2 loops; repeat from * across (Fig 2). The loop which remains always counts as first st of next row (Fig. 3).

Row 2: First half of row: Retaining all loops on hook, draw up a loop in 2nd vertical bar, and in each vertical bar across to within last vertical bar (Fig. 4); insert hook through last vertical bar and the st directly behind it (arrow on Fig. 4) and draw up a loop (this gives a firm edge to this side). There are the same number of loops as on the first row.

Second half of row: YO and draw through 1 loop, * yo and draw through 2 loops; repeat from * across. Repeat 2nd row for specified length called for in your instructions.

HOW TO MAKE SHELL STITCH:

Make a foundation chain of 19 sts (multiple of 6 plus 1).

To begin a row of shell stitch on a foundation chain, thread over and insert hook in the 4th ch from hook (Fig. 1).

Complete a dc and make another dc in this stitch. This makes a half shell, the first step in a shell stitch row (Fig. 2).

The correct order for a shell stitch row is as follows: Beginning of row; half shell (the turning ch and 2 dc in 4th from hook).

Repeat as often as you wish: Skip 2 sts, 1 sc in next st, skip 2 sts, 1 shell (5 dc in next st) (Fig. 3). To turn, ch 3 (Fig. 4).